HERE IS THE MA
modern Germany an
twentieth century w
greatest political dilemmas. The more glamorous Frederick the Great and the more spectacular "Iron Chancellor" have dominated the historical spotlight, but it was Frederick William, the Great Elector, who charted the course which his successors were to travel—first to greatness and then to destruction.

In 1640 Frederick William of Hohenzollern inherited from his father a parcel of lands scattered across northern Europe from Poland to the Rhine. He himself was a refugee. His patrimony was in economic and social ruin, ravaged by war, ringed about and occupied in part by powerful enemies. Its army was little more than a palace guard; it counted for next to nothing in the councils of Europe.

At Frederick William's death forty-eight years later, Brandenburg-Prussia had become the most powerful member of the German confederation and a minor luminary in the newly developed European state system. Its commerce and agriculture were beginning to recover from the ravages of the Thirty Years' War, its bureaucracy was taking shape, and its standing army had won the respect of friend and foe. It had acquired many of the trappings of a modern national state, and this in the face of opposition from such a formidable list of opponents as Bourbon France under Louis XIV, the Hapsburgs of Austria and Spain, and the House of Vasa in Sweden.

After setting the stage on which the Great Elector was to act—an atomized Holy Roman Empire beset by enemies without and religious controversies within—the author unfolds the dramatic career of this man who, more than any other, made possible a unified Germany under Prussia and who called the turn of its early and critical development. Under his regime, the Junker aristocracy made ready to play a leading role by dominating both army and bureaucracy. At the same time, Frederick William vigorously opposed religious intolerance and patronized art and learning to the limit of his resources.

THE GREAT ELECTOR analyzes the forces which made modern Germany and laid the foundations of the power system which has dominated Europe down to the present day. This book forms a distinguished chapter in modern history.

The Great Elector

Engraving by A. Masson of the year 1683 (Bettmann Archive)

THE GREAT ELECTOR

By FERDINAND SCHEVILL

The Great Elector

THE UNIVERSITY OF CHICAGO PRESS . CHICAGO

THE UNIVERSITY OF CHICAGO PRESS, CHICAGO 37
Cambridge University Press, London, N.W. 1, England
W. J. Gage & Co., Limited, Toronto 2B, Canada

 Published 1947. Composed and printed by THE UNIVERSITY OF CHICAGO PRESS, *Chicago, Illinois, U.S.A.*

Foreword

HISTORY in our day is so variously defined and practiced that every historian must feel moved to preface a work put out by him with a statement as to the kind of history to which he is inviting attention. In case his production is addressed in the main to his professional colleagues, he will be disposed fully to state and argumentatively to defend his choice; but if, as in the present instance, he is addressing the general reader, he will feel free to ignore the controversies agitating the academic world and to content himself with setting forth in simple declaratory terms the particular view in regard to history to which his work conforms.

Let it therefore be stated without elaboration or apology that in the present writer's view history is an accredited literary form representing a combination of scholarship and art. The scholarship is concerned with the recapture of past events from the surviving evidence, chiefly in the form of written documents. And here in recent generations a development has taken place which is at the bottom of much of the reigning confusion. By steadily expanding and intensifying its activity not only has scholarship assembled and made available in printed form vast fresh bodies of documents dealing with every aspect of government and society but it has also subjected them to norms of judgment of such severity that historians, elated by these advances, have very generally been encouraged to declare that history is now able to reach conclusions as definite and final as those of the natural sciences. They have therefore not hesitated to proclaim that history as practiced by them has lost its traditional literary character and become "scientific."

The claim is so exaggerated as to invite derision; for, conceding that the latest disciples of Herodotus have at their disposal a vastly enlarged corpus of original material and that they subject it to a far more severely critical method than was formerly the case, the assertion that their conclusions have achieved a precision comparable to those of the natural sciences breaks down on even the most superficial examination. It will therefore serve an always desirable clarity to recognize that history and the natural sciences are two distinct bodies of knowledge and that each follows a particular purpose and employs an appropriate method. The equating of the two purposes and methods is the result of a defective logical analysis. The readiest way of escaping the confusion to which it leads is to abandon the false claim of "science" for the procedure of the historian and to replace it with the ancient and unobjectionable term of "scholarship."

This much agreed, let us next note that the materials assembled and sorted by scholarship are so much dead matter utterly bare of meaning until they have been reanimated by being again set in the stream of life. The stream of life is a continuous stream whose movement began with the infinitely remote first age of man and which will continue on its destined course until the unimaginable day of his extinction. Every segment of the human past, large or small, of which scholarship makes it its business to recover the surviving traces, must, in order to achieve intelligibility and significance, be again returned to the life-stream and be relived by him who undertakes to describe it. Less figuratively and more literally, the historian who by his labors as a scholar has put himself in possession of innumerable, minute, and isolated data must, as his next step, fuse them into a meaningful whole of interrelated parts. This demands his putting into play an entirely different talent from the laborious scholarly faculty. He must call on his imagination and prove himself, as far as in him lies, to be an artist.

There is a product of scholarship pure and simple: the historical monograph. Hundreds of scholars have been and are engaged in preparing these precise and detailed studies, the importance of which for the intimate penetration of the past it is impossible to exaggerate. Historical monographs are in the nature of preparatory sketches which, in spite of their great value, should not be rated as full-bodied histories; for, while performing an important service on the strict scholarship level, they do not create that intelligible whole which is the unfailing mark of the true history and which results from the mass of monographic material being fused and shaped by an individual mind.

If a true history is a work of scholarship and art, it follows that, like all other works of art, it is a communication and seeks a public. Committed to this concept, the author reaffirms his earlier avowal that in writing the present history he has had in mind as audience not his professional colleagues but the broad community of cultivated men and women. While he invites the judgment of his colleagues, which in any case they will not be backward to deliver, his concern lies elsewhere, being directed to the hope that his handiwork will not be found unacceptable by the body of alert readers making up with us, as in every country of the world, the solid core of our continuing civilization. These readers may, of course, reject his offering on the unanswerable ground that it is an inferior product, a professed communication that has nothing to communicate. This would signify the author's defeat and the cancellation of his effort. But as a failure resulting from individual incompetence, it would not, it is only fair to point out, disprove the validity of the theory of history to which his work subscribes.

From the foregoing it will be readily deduced that reference lists and footnotes are not outstanding features of this work. The general reader, to whom it is addressed, is not interested in these features, and, as rattling the dry bones of a scholarship which is not his concern, he is justified in reacting to their clatter, as he invariably does, with sharp annoyance. However, an occasional general reader is endowed with a livelier intellectual curiosity than his fellows and desires to make acquaintance with the authorities from which the author drew his material, provided always that his wish is not overindulged and himself penalized for his daring by being buried under a landslide of ponderous learning. An attempt has been made to satisfy these exceptional readers by a rare and, it is hoped, not too obtrusive footnote. And to facilitate familiarity with the most frequently cited authorities, all of them in the nature of primary sources, they are here enumerated under their full titles together with the abbreviations by which they will be carried in the text.

Urkunden und Aktenstücke zur Geschichte des Kurfürsten Friedrich Wilhelm von Brandenburg. 23 vols. Berlin, 1864–1930. The volumes are assembled under the three subheads of *Politische Verhandlungen* (14 vols.), *Auswärtige Akten* (5 vols.), and *Ständische Verhandlungen* (4 vols.). ABBREVIATION: *UA*.

Protokolle und Relationen des Brandenburgischen Geheimen Rates aus der Zeit des Kurfürsten Friedrich Wilhelm. 7 vols. (reaching to 1666). Berlin, 1889–1919. The volumes are incorporated in the larger source series entitled "Publikationen aus den Preussischen Staatsarchiven." ABBREVIATION: *PR*.

Theodor von Moerner. *Kurbrandenburgs Staatsverträge von 1601 bis 1700.* Berlin, 1867. ABBREVIATION: Moerner.

Forschungen zur Brandenburgischen und Preussischen Geschichte. 1888——. This is a professional journal continuing the older *Märkische Forschungen*, which ran from 1841 to 1887. ABBREVIATION: *FBPG*.

In conclusion, a word on available bibliographies may not prove amiss. More or less serviceable bibliographies carrying both primary and secondary titles will be found in all the more important works dealing with the Great Elector. For the college student a discriminating bibliography will be found in the little volume by S. B. Fay, entitled *The Rise of Brandenburg-Prussia to 1786* (New York, 1937). By far the most complete bibliography covering every conceivable phase of Frederick William's activity is supplied by Dahlmann-Waitz, *Quellenkunde der Deutschen Geschichte* (9th ed.; Leipzig, 1931).

Contents

Introduction

THIS book is about a prince whose claim to distinction is that he founded a state within the European and German framework of the second half of the seventeenth century. It is the story of a statesman. To make his statesmanship intelligible, it will be indispensable to clear the way to it by a fairly detailed introduction. For one thing, it will be necessary to explain the paralysis of the German national state, the so-called "Holy Roman Empire," which, begun hundreds of years before, had by the seventeenth century become settled and incurable. It will be equally necessary to present at least the main facts about the origin and early history of that small territory of the north German plain, called Brandenburg, which was the hereditary possession and operating area of the ruler with whom we are going to be concerned. Finally, no matter how thoroughly we may be informed politically about Germany and Brandenburg, we shall be wandering in a spiritual and intellectual vacuum unless we become acquainted with the ruling aspects of the civilization of that seventeenth century in which our prince lived and which both directed and bounded his personal outlook. That makes a group of three chapters of an introductory character concerned with sketching in the background against which the subject of this biography, conditioned like every other man that ever lived by Time and Place, is projected.

Chapter 1

THE HOLY ROMAN EMPIRE

The Thirty Years' War has impressed itself on the minds of men as one of the most complete disasters ever suffered by a great nation. During the long-drawn-out ordeal, Germany sank to a condition of feebleness and anarchy just short of annihilation. However, devastating as the war proved to be, not only politically but in every area of national existence, it was not a sudden, unpredictable calamity which discharged itself on the country without warning, like a tropical hurricane. It cannot even be said to have represented an appreciable deflection from the line of march followed by German history during the immediately preceding centuries. Much rather, it was the last stage in an amazingly coherent development which leads us, as we inversely retrace its course, further and further back until we arrive at the deep Middle Ages.

Like all the other states which, on the disappearance of the Roman Empire, came gradually into being on the soil of western Europe during the period conventionally called the Middle Ages, the German state was a feudal monarchy of strictly limited authority. In Germany, exactly as in England and France, the supreme power was shared between the king, who was landlord-in-chief, and the other great landlords, lay and spiritual, who held their possessions as fiefs from the king and did homage to him as his vassals.

In the tenth century, when Otto I of the Saxon line was German king and exercised a somewhat fuller authority in his kingdom than his western contemporaries did in theirs, he acquired also, through a combination of circumstances we cannot here examine, the kingship of Italy and through this extension of his power became in a shadowy way identified with the state which had once ruled the world from the city of Rome as its seat—the Roman Empire. Although the famous state bearing the Roman name had perished many centuries before the time when Otto I brought about the union of the feudal crowns of Germany and Italy, it had continued to maintain a ghostly existence in the minds of many people, chiefly of the authoritative clerical class, who longingly looked back to it as the stout pillar of the early church and never ceased to lament its demise. From their passionate nostalgia sprang the attempt to bring the Roman Empire again to life, although, in order to do so, it was necessary to devise and popularize the fiction that the union of the backward, tenth-century territories of Germany and Italy, resting on an unbelievably primitive agrarian level, was tantamount to the re-creation of an empire which at the height of its existence rested on an elaborate urban civilization and embraced the whole Mediterranean world. Rarely has man, prone at all times to feed on illusions, indulged himself in a dream more insubstantial and, as it turned out, more disastrous to both its participants.

From the first day of their unnatural union Germany and Italy gave evidence of an incompatibility that produced an uninterrupted series of internal upheavals. In the thirteenth century they at last reached their only possible resolution by Italy's renouncing her allegiance to her self-imposed Teutonic ruler masquerading in a Roman toga. Theoretically, it is true, the bond between the two countries was not broken, and in a strictly legal sense Italy remained entangled with Germany for several subsequent centuries in what purported to be the imperishable Roman Empire. One more fiction in a situation with a monumental fiction at its core did not fall very heavily into the scale. Let us, however, be absolutely clear in our minds that in every essential respect Italy and Germany parted company in 1250, that is, at the exact middle of the thirteenth century. When in that year occurred the death of Frederick II, the last Rome-crowned emperor of the Hohenstaufen line, the heavy yoke of the conqueror slipped from the back of the liberated peninsula. Thenceforth the pretended Roman Empire, long-since known, owing to its close association with the Christian church, as the Holy Roman Empire, was for all practical purposes reduced to a single member, to Germany.

When on Frederick II's death the fatally enfeebled German state withdrew perforce beyond the Alps, it bore little resemblance to the essentially healthy organism which under Otto I had engaged in the Italian venture, for it had become a body diseased, broken, and dying. The foolhardy attempt, continued through three centuries, to weld Italy and Germany together to the fantastic end of thus bringing back to life the ancient *imperium romanum* had undermined and exhausted the conquering power. Throughout those three hundred years the German sovereigns had been obliged to lead southward over the Alps against their ever contumacious Italian subjects an interminable succession of military expeditions by which they fatally drained themselves of their resources. Not only did they by their stubborn self-infatuation gradually squander the rich lands pertaining to the royal fisc but, in order to obtain the continued military support of their great vassals, they had been forced to make them so many substantial concessions of a political order that they had slowly and disastrously divested themselves of their leading sovereign rights in favor of the dukes, counts, bishops, and abbots constituting the body of the feudal magnates. The death of Frederick II not only, as already said, marked the achievement by Italy of its liberation from German servitude, it was an equally important milestone for Germany and the German people since it led to a complete suspension of the defeated central power during a prolonged, rulerless period called the "interregnum."

During the interregnum the feudal magnates exercised an unchallenged sovereignty in their respective territories which they were loath ever again to surrender. Consequently when, in the year 1273, they at last agreed to meet and choose a new national head, they did not do so without first assuring themselves that his powers had been so vigorously pruned that he would never again be able seriously to threaten their ascendancy. The man they elected king was a small Suabian count, Rudolph of Hapsburg. It was to his very smallness and consequent probable inability to assert himself that Rudolph owed his elevation to the throne. But, against all expectations, his considerable diplomatic and military talents, coupled with the exceptional favors showered on him by Fortune, enabled him to use the right of escheat still inhering in the royal office as a means to acquire a magnificent private domain. This was the duchy of Austria, of which the city of Vienna was the capital; and with his feet thus planted on solid ground the inconspicuous count was raised to a territorial level with the leading German princes. However, despite his unexpected success in creating a Hapsburg house power, he made no headway in regard to the main task he had set himself on mounting the throne. This was to reinvigorate the national kingship by reducing the vassals of the crown to their original dependence. His conspicuous failure was a clear indication that the central office had been irrecoverably drained of its vital energy.

From the time of the first Hapsburg sovereign to the final disappearance of the Holy Roman Empire from the European scene over five hundred years later in the days of Napoleon Bonaparte the German domestic situation presented, in its essential features, very much the same picture that met the eye in Rudolph's reign. The power achieved by the insignificant Suabian count, the ruins of whose original domicile, the castle of Hapsburg, can still be viewed in the present-day Swiss canton of Aargau, was not a flash in the pan. His successors, considered in the mass, so steadily enlarged their Austrian foothold that in the course of the next few generations they completely outdistanced the other princely houses of Germany. From this pre-eminence it followed that, although the German crown continued to be elective, the head of the house of Hapsburg wielded so much influence, both open and concealed, that following a period of fluctuating fortunes and of heated competition with rival candidates, he was regularly promoted to the imperial office. In this manner he acquired something of the aspect and prestige of a ruler by hereditary right. At the same time his position at the gateway to the middle Danube gave him a standing throughout southeastern Europe. It was owing to his throwing a gradually lengthening shadow over this extensive area that, early in the sixteenth century, he acquired, partly by heredity and partly by election, the crowns of the two great kingdoms of Bohemia and Hungary.

The significance, so far as Germany was concerned, of the uninterrupted expansion of the Hapsburg house power lay in the fact that the Emperor Rudolph's successors commanded financial and military resources which enabled them to continue the struggle, wherein he had failed, of strengthening the imperial power and reviving the German national state. And, subject to the ups and downs inseparable from the ceaseless flow of circumstances, they may be said to have done so throughout the five centuries the Holy Roman Empire continued to survive. Nevertheless, it may as well be at once recorded, all their labors came to naught because the decentralizing forces, identified with the temporal and ecclesiastical lords who even before Rudolph's time had undermined the imperial power and attained a substantial sovereignty, proved themselves too deeply intrenched to be again displaced.

The remainder of this chapter will treat the losing struggle of the German emperor against the emancipated princes up to the Thirty Years' War and close by showing in detail to what depth of dissolution the Holy Roman Empire was brought by that catastrophic event. Although throughout this period the conflict never rested, we shall content ourselves with tracing the line along which it developed by lingering over a few of its more crucial incidents. The first event of the post-Rudolphian era of which it is indispensable to take account was in the nature of a forward thrust on the part of the emancipated princes. In an assembly held in the year 1356 they resolved to consolidate the authority they had acquired by embodying it in a formal constitution. The document they drew up came to be known as the Golden Bull from the golden seal (*bulla*) with which the reigning sovereign was obliged to signify his acceptance of it as the fundamental law of the realm. Since it served thenceforward as the solid basis of the German princely power, its main features need to be carefully noted.

Every examination of the Golden Bull, however cursory, must begin with recognizing that, far from introducing a series of innovations into German constitutional procedure, it was essentially nothing more than the enactment into law of the customary practices of the more recent and, in some respects, of even the remoter German past. Its most memorable single feature was the regulation of the imperial election. This, originally the function of all the primary vassals, had been gradually appropriated by a small upper-level group, who then had imposed their decision on their lesser fellows. In the Golden Bull the elective function was unequivocally assigned to the seven greatest German princes who, on the strength of this distinction, were accorded the title of electors or *Kurfürsten.* The seven were the three great Rhenish archbishops of Mainz, Cologne, and Trier, with whom were associated the four secular princes, the duke of Saxony, the count palatine of the Rhine, the margrave of Brandenburg, and the king of Bohemia. The ratio of four to three may be taken as a reasonably accurate reflection of the distribution of power in Germany among its lay and its spiritual rulers. It may also be taken as evidence of the disastrous downward trend of the royal power in Germany compared with its promising upward turn in, for instance, such a country as France. For, in France, as wherever else the central power followed a mounting curve, the great spiritual lords, the bishops and abbots, were in the course of the later Middle Ages deprived of their civil power over their diocesans and confined to the exclusive exercise of their ecclesiastical functions. The absence of a parallel movement in Germany lends point to the political decline which is this chapter's central theme.

From the earliest beginning of the German state or *Reich* the ultimate instrument of authority had been the periodic meeting of the king with his vassals-in-chief, the *Reichstag* or diet. By the terms of the Golden Bull the electors, that is, the seven great vassals with a special function, were authorized to meet apart from the other vassals, thus dividing the Reichstag into two houses, a house of electors and a house of princes. In the following, the fifteenth, century the Reichstag experienced an expansion; for trade, as represented by the free cities *(freie Reichstädte),* had developed so much strength that delegates of the free cities gained admission to the Reichstag as a third, though decidedly inferior, house. The common feature of the free cities was that they were, like the princes, the direct vassals of the emperor and enjoyed the right of self-government under an imperial charter.

Final and conclusive evidence of the weakness of the sovereign under the provisions of the Golden Bull is supplied by his relation and, in effect, his subjection to the Reichstag. Without its consent and, more particularly, without the consent of the two authoritative princely houses he could not undertake any action of national scope. It was the two upper houses alone that counted in making decisions, since the feeble third house, the house of the cities, was not drawn into conference until after the two princely houses had reached an agreement. The most striking evidence of the anti-imperial and obstructive policy dominating the Reichstag was furnished by its unalterable opposition to the maintenance of a national army, navy, administration, or any other central service which, in response to an altered social situation, was elsewhere in Europe coming into existence at this time. Its extreme concession to the king consisted in voting, on the occasion of a pressing national emergency, an insufficient levy for putting in the field an untrained, improvised, patchwork force only too likely to scatter in panic at its first contact with the enemy. Every examination of the Reichstag's debates and enactments will confirm the statement that, more unquesionably even than in Rudolph of Hapsburg's day, the Reich planted on the foundations of the Golden Bull was a congress of princes fixedly hostile to their elected head and selfishly intent on preserving and, if possible, enlarging the extensive powers they had won.

On the eve of the Reformation or, to speak with greater chronological precision, at the turn of the fifteenth century, an opportunity arose which, had the emperor been able to make full use thereof, would have reversed the German political trend of the preceding centuries and have effected at least a partial restoration of the central power. A novel political force made its appearance in the form of a powerful, hitherto nonexistent, national sentiment. It had already manifested itself in the other countries of Europe, owing to the spread of trade and the concomitant rise of busy towns identified with commercial interests that cut sharply across the purely agrarian interests represented by the heretofore dominant feudal classes. In France, Spain, and England the movement acquired such strength that in each instance the monarch was able greatly to enlarge his powers at the expense of the feudality and to provide himself for the first time with a revenue, administration, and armed force under his control. With such success was the monarchical consolidation effected that before the fifteenth century came to a close the three western monarchs exercised a power in their dominions which, compared with that of their predecessors, took on an appearance of absolutism. Thus freed from traditional chains, they began that struggle with each other and their weaker neighbors whereby they inaugurated the lawless international power system which has ruled Europe uninterruptedly from their time to our own.

If the head of the German state could have made himself the spearhead of the rising national sentiment in his country, as his western rivals had succeeded in doing in their areas, he might conceivably have revised the German constitution in his interest. But he failed for a score of reasons, some of them having to do with the stubborn vigor of his princely opponents, others with his lack of personal drive and political acumen. The imperial incumbent at the time this opportunity beckoned was Maximilian I, one of the more colorful figures in the rather drab succession of the Hapsburg rulers of the Reich. He mounted the throne in 1493 and reigned until his death in 1519. Possessed of considerable personal merits, for he had an engaging manner with his subjects and was a patron of art and literature, he was unfortunately captivated by the ideals of chivalry, which, with the advancing commercial age, were rapidly thinning to shadows, and so utterly failed to grasp the social and economic transformation which was going on about him that he blundered at every stage of the ensuing struggle between himself and the Reichstag over the revitalization of the German state. Consequently, the results of the bitter contest proved very meager. While at its close the balked emperor was left as feeble as before, it cannot be denied that the central institutions of the Reich had experienced an ineffective, though not negligible, remodeling.

The remodeling consisted of three legislative enactments. The first was the proclamation of a permanent peace *(ewiger Landfrieden)* within the boundaries of the Reich. Thereby an end was at long last made of the right claimed and exercised by the princes to settle their quarrels by private warfare. The second enactment was a logical consequence of the first, for it set up a national supreme court *(Reichskammergericht)* for the enforcement of the domestic peace. After what has already been said of the general drift of this legislation it will cause no surprise that the court was not located at the residence of the emperor, at Vienna, and that its judges were not appointed by him but by the Reichstag. The same anti-imperial trend manifested itself in the third enactment, which concerned itself with creating a more efficient administration. While it got as far as to divide the Reich into ten districts or *Kreise* planned to serve as the frame for an improved financial and military service, owing to irrepressible jealousies it stalled at that point and remained no better than a blueprint.

Sharp on the heel of this abortive national renovation came the religious revolt known as the Reformation. As everyone knows, its opening gun was fired when on October 31, 1517, Martin Luther posted his "Ninety-five Theses against Indulgences" on the door of the castle church of the Saxon town of Wittenberg. For reasons having to do with the fact that Germany was in effect a country of as many distinct governments as there were members in the Reichstag, the country did not act as a unit in regard to the movement precipitated by Luther. Many princes and free cities, chiefly of northern Germany, took their stand with Luther; many, chiefly of the south and west, clung passionately to Catholicism; and not a few assumed a hesitant, waiting attitude.

The emperor who confronted this movement that shook the nation to the depth of its soul was Charles V, grandson and successor of the incompetent and uniformly unfortunate Maximilian I. A youth of twenty years at his election, Charles was endowed with a political shrewdness completely lacking in his predecessor and with something that counted in his favor even more than shrewdness, a power and an abundance of resources beyond the ever needy Maximilian's wildest dreams. The increased material might of the youthful head of the house of Hapsburg resulted from the successful pursuit through several generations of a marriage policy on the part of his family by virtue of which young Charles became the heir,[1] in addition to Austria, of the Netherlands, the busiest

1. Genealogical table:

MAXIMILIAN I (1493–1519)
m. Mary, heiress of Burgundy and the Netherlands

PHILIP THE HANDSOME (d. 1506)
m. Joan, heiress of Spain

CHARLES V (1519–56)

FERDINAND I (1556–64)
m. Anne, heiress of Hungary and Bohemia

commercial segment of Europe, and of Spain, which, under Ferdinand and Isabella, had ejected the Moors from Spanish soil, expanded across the Mediterranean into southern Italy, and gained a stake of incalculable promise by the discovery and appropriation of America.

With interests, besides Austria and Germany, in the Netherlands, Spain, and Italy, Charles V was not only the most powerful monarch of his age but also the most distracted by reason of the heavy pull on him of innumerable contradictory influences. He was in Spain at the time of his election to the imperial office and did not arrive in Germany until 1521, when he issued a call to the Reichstag to meet him at the city of Worms on the Rhine. With Luther himself present in the role of culprit at the bar, its sessions opened amidst frenzied popular excitement. The pope, Leo X, had recently taken the decisive step of proclaiming Luther a heretic and now demanded, as the next step, that emperor and Reichstag implement his decree by pronouncing sentence of death against the miscreant. It can hardly be doubted that, had Charles felt free to be guided by his private convictions, he would not have hesitated to meet the pope's wishes, for he was a faithful son of the church and filled with lively horror of heresy and schism. But he was not free, since not only the Reichstag but also the German people were divided in their opinion; and he was the more readily disposed to avoid committing himself to violent measures by reason of a strong element of caution in his disposition. It thus came about that, although he succeeded in wringing from the Reichstag a degree of condemnation against Luther, he did nothing to give it effect; and, as immediately after publishing the decree he left Germany for Spain, Luther, protected by his local prince, the elector of Saxony, remained unmolested. In the course of the next few years the movement the onetime friar had set afoot assumed such proportions and acquired so much vigor that it thenceforth defied suppression save by the use of force.

This was the hazardous situation that met the Emperor Charles whenever in the decades following the Reichstag of Worms his absorption in the affairs of his many other dominions permitted him to return to Germany. He still felt a strong personal prompting to draw the sword against the heretical disturbers of the peace, but the obligation he was under of continuous movement over Europe and its surrounding waters paralyzed his arm. Not until toward the close of his reign did he end his long hesitation over the Lutheran schism and resort to the bitter medicine of war. It was too late. While by a swift attack he succeeded in defeating the leagued Lutheran princes and in suppressing their movement, he learned to his sorrow that the enemy would not stay suppressed. A cunningly organized rising took him completely by surprise and obliged him, in 1552, to sign at Passau a humiliating armistice with the Protestant victors.

Three years later, in 1555, the Passau armistice was converted into the definitive Peace of Augsburg. Its outstanding feature was the right granted to each estate of the realm—each prince and free city—to choose between the older Catholic and the newer Lutheran form of Christianity. Constitutionally this signified a further sharp decline of the central power of the Reich, for the vast and crucial field of religion, considered hitherto a concern of the nation as a whole, was by this enactment handed over to the Reich's component members. The transfer of authority took place according to the famous formulation: *cuius regio eius religio* (whoever rules a territory determines its religion).

On now looking more closely at the Augsburg settlement and its aftermath we are struck with the fact that, called a peace, it was not a peace. Almost from the first day it exhibited grave gaps and insufficiencies. For one thing, it gave recognition to none but the Lutheran form of Protestantism; for another, it gave the estates declaring themselves Lutheran legal title to only such Catholic properties (churches, monasteries, houses, lands) as they had seized prior to 1552, the year when the civil war begun by Emperor Charles V was terminated by the armistice of Passau and the negotiations were initiated which, three years later, culminated in the Peace of Augsburg. However, time never stands still, and in the period following Augsburg a second and more militant form of Protestantism, of which the Frenchman, John Calvin, was the father, attracted a considerable body of German adherents, especially in western Germany; and in this same post-Augsburg period the princes, both Lutheran and Calvinist, pursued with undiminished zeal their original policy of appropriating all Catholic properties within their respective jurisdictions. The Catholics were therefore well within their rights when they angrily protested that these two developments clashed with the provisions of the settlement.

Serious as these differences were, an even graver cause of friction between the contentious faiths sprang from an article of the treaty which, called "the Ecclesiastical," might with greater propriety have been named "the Episcopal," Reservation. The article had reference to those bishops of the Catholic church who were also territorial princes and who numbered several score in a country still so predominantly feudal in its organization as we have found backward Germany to be. In regard to these so-called "prince-bishops," the peace declared that, quite like the lay princes, they were free to choose between the two legal Christian versions but that, in case they chose Lutheranism, they would have to resign their episcopal charge. In short, the Ecclesiastical Reservation declared that the prince-bishoprics, in distinction from their rulers, might under no circumstances become Protestant and must remain Catholic in perpetuity. But what actually occurred? Owing to the still unexhausted momentum of the Reformation, it came about that more than a dozen prince-bishoprics were taken over by the Lutherans *after* the treaty date, thereby supplying their Catholic adversaries with welcome additional fuel wherewith to feed the already considerable fires of their indignation.

In view of the religious passions abroad throughout Europe during the Reformation period, we may feel surprise that the abundant controversial matter born of the uncertainties of the Peace of Augsburg did not lead to an early resumption of the German civil war. Our surprise grows when we note that in the generation after the peace the offended Catholics were greatly strengthened by the phenomenal spread of the fighting Jesuit order, by the eager militancy of the Council of Trent, and by numerous other agencies of Catholic recuperation and reform. Wherefrom we may conclude that even angered and inflamed men are inclined to think twice before exchanging a peace, no matter how uneasy, for the incalculable risks of war.

Nonetheless, by the beginning of the seventeenth century the confidence of the greatly revitalized Catholics had reached such a stage that minor acts of aggression against their Protestant fellow-countrymen broke out spontaneously at scattered points throughout the land. At last, in 1618, came the long-expected fatal explosion. It was touched off when the capricious curtailment by the Hapsburg ruler of Bohemia of certain privileges guaranteed by royal charter to his Bohemian subjects of Protestant persuasion led to their rising furiously against him. On the offended ruler's undertaking to suppress the rebels by force in a campaign blessed by the pope and enthusiastically supported by the Catholic princes of Germany, the conflagration spread to the adjoining regions of southern Germany until, with the flames ravenously eating their way in every direction, the country caught fire in all its length and breadth and so continued for thirty interminable years.

THE TREATY OF WESTPHALIA (1648)

When, in 1648, the Treaty of Westphalia ended the unparalleled agony, Germany lay engulfed in material, spiritual, moral, cultural, and every other kind of ruin. But that story, at this point at least, is not our concern, since we have concentrated in this chapter on the successive phases of German political disorganization. And in this tale of an uninterrupted decline the Treaty of Westphalia signifies the nadir, the point lower than which it was impossible to sink; for, apart from the continued pretense of union maintained by a mocking façade of hollow forms, there was, after the Westphalian surgery had been effected, no real union left. In unambiguous language the treaty granted full *Landeshoheit,* that is, "sovereignty," to all the estates of the Reich. While it did not enlarge on the possible deductions to be drawn from the conceded Landeshoheit, it expressly granted to the estates the right to make alliances both with one another and with foreign states. In so doing it endowed them with a privilege than which none more sweepingly sovereign in character can be imagined.

In these circumstances could the empire after 1648 still be correctly designated as a monarchy? Was it not nearer the truth to define it as a federation of sovereign princes? But, in that case, where did the numerous republics of self-governing free cities come in? Or were the actualities best covered by agreeing that the Reich in its calamitous decline had struck bottom in the form of a mixed federation of sovereign princes and republics? Contemporary students of politics cudgeled their brains to find, among the recognized governmental categories deduced by a long line of scholarly predecessors from the inexhaustible casebook of history, the appropriate compartment for the constitutional wreck under their scrutiny. Twist and double as they would, they could not make the sorry patchwork fit into any known variety of political classification. At last the keenest of the brotherhood, a certain Samuel Pufendorf, throwing up his hands in despair, set the Reich apart as a complete novelty, a sport of nature never before seen on land or sea. As he put it in his solemn, iron-shod Latin, it was *irregulare aliquod corpus et monstro simile* (an unclassifiable body comparable to a monster).

During the three hundred years that have elapsed since Pufendorf, no successor of his, no matter how sharp-witted, has been able to improve on his definition. Let us therefore hail his grave pronouncement as the verdict of scholarship through the ages and fortify ourselves in our acceptance of its crushing judgment by a look at the strange assortment of estates which, as constituting the leading federal institution, the Reichstag, were henceforth Germany. Eight of the estates (one more than before 1648) figured as Kurfürsten and sat together in the highest house, the house of electors; sixty-nine ranked as spiritual, and ninety-six as lay, princes with seats in the second house, the house of princes; sixty-one free cities, some of them of barely village size, made up the third house. Although this comes to the alarming total of two hundred and thirty-four sovereign areas, it does not tell the whole story of the dissipation of German authority, as we have not yet taken note of one of the most objectionable of the country's many feudal survivals, the imperial knights *(Reichsritter)*. Several hundred in number and unrepresented in the Reichstag, they nonetheless claimed and actually practiced sovereignty on their landed property, consisting often of nothing more than a dilapidated castle perched on a hill and dominating a small peasant settlement with its adjoining fields. Could the political atomization of what still thought of itself as a great people go further?

To complete the picture of Germany as drawn by the Treaty of Westphalia, at least two other matters must inescapably be set forth. One regards the religious, the other the territorial, settlement decreed by that document. They are both so important that they call for treatment under their respective captions.

The religious settlement.—Among the defects of the original religious settlement of Augsburg of 1555 was, as we have noted, its failure to grant recognition to any other Protestant form than Lutheranism. The Reformed church, identified with Calvinism, was denied legal standing. This petty exclusiveness was in 1648 reluctantly abandoned and the Reformed church put on a level with the Catholic and Lutheran churches. Admitting that this was a step in the direction of religious toleration, it was far removed from the kind of toleration with which the present generation is familiar. It signified no more than that the princes and free cities, constituting the estates of the Reich, might now choose among three, instead of two, forms of Christianity and that, having chosen, they were at liberty, exactly as before, to impose their choice on their subjects according to the narrow, reaffirmed principle of *cuius regio eius religio.* However, generally speaking, it is true that the estates voluntarily surrendered this evil privilege in the course of the succeeding generation. From which we may conclude that a religious attitude more generous than that laid down in the traditional phrasing of the law was slowly gaining ground.

Another provision of the religious settlement dealt with the Ecclesiastical Reservation. Following up their successes of the early period of the war, the Catholics had repossessed themselves of a goodly number of the prince-bishoprics which, contrary to the Treaty of Augsburg, had been appropriated by their adversaries, and naturally they fought hotly at Wesphalia to retain them. In the end they were obliged to accept a compromise and agree to acknowledge January 1, 1624, as a test date. This meant that whatever prince-bishoprics each religious group had in actual possession on that day should be regarded as having been acquired in permanence. The arrangement was, on the whole, favorable to the Protestants, since some fifteen prince-bishoprics thus fell to their share to be distributed as spoils of war among the more powerful princes of the newer faith.

The territorial settlement.—Civil war invariably invites intervention from without, and the German civil war from 1618 to 1648 was no exception to the rule. In the course of the seemingly endless struggle practically every neighbor, great or small, was sucked into the maelstrom, thereby expanding the war to European dimensions. In spite, however, of so many states spilling over into Germany at one time or another, only two of them, France and Sweden, effected a lodgment from which it proved impossible to displace them. Consequently, before they would agree to make peace they had to be placated with cessions of territory. In this manner Sweden received, first, western Pomerania *(Vorpommern)*, together with control of the mouth of the river Oder, and, second, the two former prince-bishoprics of Bremen and Verden along the lower course of the Weser and the Elbe. Through these acquisitions, not insubstantial in area but far more important strategically than territorially, Sweden, the newly risen Scandinavian giant, gained unquestioned control of the German Baltic coast and at the same time a definite foothold on Germany's other, its North Sea, coast. As for France, it received parts of Alsace with certain express exclusions, among them the leading Alsatian city of Strassburg. Such limitations notwithstanding, France was solidly established along the upper Rhine, from where it was henceforth able to thrust forward into southern Germany at its pleasure.

Certain other German territorial losses, practically effective long before the outbreak of the Thirty Years' War, were given legal sanction at Westphalia and, to complete the record, may be enumerated here. Ever since the first German war of religion in Emperor Charles V's time, France had occupied the three bishoprics of Metz, Toul, and Verdun strung along her eastern border. They were in 1648 formally made over to her. In which connection it deserves to be noted that, in distinction from Alsace, a region unquestionably of German speech and culture, the three bishoprics belonged with equal certainty to the French culture area.

Much older than the divorce from the Reich of the above-named bishoprics was that of two regions that had become consolidated under the names, respectively, of Swiss Confederation and the Seven United Provinces (the Dutch Netherlands). As far back as the Middle Ages, they had both undertaken gradually to sever one bond after another tying them to the Holy Roman Empire and had thus long before achieved a substantial independence.

Reasonably, if belatedly, their free and independent status was written into the Treaty of Westphalia and thereby into international law.

Here, with the year 1648, our story of German decline comes for the present to an end. Viewed from the outlook of that year, Germany presented a picture of such unrelieved gloom that no single feature stood out that might be seized upon as giving hope for a better future. The moral and spiritual havoc wrought by the war, alone considered, was so great that to expect other than a very distant recovery was to put the imagination to an impossible strain. But leaving the cultural aspects to one side and concentrating, as we have done from the start, on German political decline, we are forced to admit that no slightest circumstance dotted the landscape anywhere as far as the eye could penetrate that would justify our casting the country a horoscope of national fulfilment, no matter at what remove from the unrelieved dark of the disastrous present.

To leave not so much as a shade of doubt as to whither our story has carried us, let us by way of conclusion and even at the cost of repetition review the German political actualities at the Westphalian milestone. The Reich, a dying organism, still recognized a head called emperor (*Kaiser*), but his authority, like that of the Reich itself, had dwindled to the vanishing point. He could not declare war or make treaties without the consent of the Reichstag, and the Reichstag itself was impotent since, in effect a congress of several hundred sovereign states exercising a jealous watch on one another, it could rarely, and never save after an intolerable delay, reach an agreement on even the simplest course of action. While the sovereignty of the states represented in the Reichstag was not formally asserted until 1648, it would be an error in perspective not to recognize that the Treaty of Westphalia did no more than set the crown on a historical process that had been going on for centuries. The dissolution of the central power went back, as we have explicitly shown, all the way to the Middle Ages, and every effort made since that time to reverse or even halt the movement had proved vain.

Innumerable as are the evidences illustrating the uninterrupted decay of the imperial power, the most convincing single witness of the process was doubtless the crumbling at the German borders that had set in as soon as the emperor's diminished vigor no longer permitted him to make his power felt at the peripheries of his realm. It was in consequence of this loss of strength that the highland Swiss cantons at the headwaters of the Rhine and the Dutch Netherlands at its mouth had gradually disengaged themselves from the diseased and weakened parent-body of the Reich and set up their own governments. By the time of the Thirty Years' War the progressive enfeeblement had become a confirmed dry rot and was apparent to all the world. Without further hesitation the neighboring powers now broke into the empire from every side, and, when the war came to an end, two of them, France and Sweden, were in a position to prefer claims to certain western and northern provinces, respectively, which the shattered Reich was unable to resist. Matters standing thus, not only was it likely that the inroads of France and Sweden would be presently resumed but the probability was great that Germany's other neighbors would be encouraged to follow the example set by France and Sweden and stake out conveniently accessible districts in a country become a mid-European no man's land. To an informed, objective contemporary it could not have looked other than that the appropriation of German territory inaugurated in the recent civil war was a process bound to continue.

And in simple truth, short of a miracle, it was indeed bound to continue. The miracle would have to be a wave of patriotic sentiment so powerful that it would sweep the Holy Roman Empire, become a laughingstock, into oblivion, deprive its princely despoilers of their usurped authority, and call into being a new Reich organized after the manner of the great contemporary states that dominated western Europe. And in the seventeenth century such a miracle was beyond even a poet's dream. The time was not ripe. The meager national sentiment existing in that age in German lands was limited to small scattered groups of intellectuals and was impotent so much as to throw off the dead weight of the decadent Holy Roman Empire, let alone to shake the authority of the princes become undisputed masters in their inherited dominions.

Nor was there any prospect of an early revival of the vanished national feeling, for its feeble heartbeat was an accurate expression of the deadening torpor that had settled on the self-defeated nation. In short, the Germans as a people were in no better case than their paralyzed federal constitution. Whatever sparks of life still glowed within the country's boundaries were to be found exclusively in the few territories large enough to constitute something better than hollow political counterfeits. Such were Austria and Bavaria in the south, Brandenburg and Saxony in the north, with perhaps just one other, the Rhenish Palatinate, in the west.

Since life always and everywhere springs from life and never and nowhere from death, the likeliest forecast regarding a possible national renewal offered from the outlook of the year 1648 would be one that based its calculations on the five above-mentioned territories. In them a manly self-help was still, though no doubt faintly, operative, and an organization had been effected within their boundaries that set a term to the chaos that was devouring the rest of the nation. It was therefore at least conceivable that perhaps one, perhaps all of these states together, might transfuse the red blood that coursed through their veins into the diseased body of the nation and so bring it back to life.

As it happened, it was Brandenburg that played this historical role; it was Brandenburg that, beginning with the generation following the Treaty of Westphalia, became the magnetic center that so compellingly influenced the other German states that very gradually, it is true, and only after the passage of two centuries it was able to bring about a new or second Reich. Reason enough to turn, in our next chapter, to this north German state in order to have a look at its development through the period reaching from its founding in the early Middle Ages to the epoch that closed so disastrously for the German people in 1648.

Chapter 2

BRANDENBURG

Some thirty years after the demise in A.D. 814 of the towering Charles, king of the Franks, who, even before his death, had been transformed into the cloudy, legendary figure known ever since to the world as Charlemagne, the vast empire he had founded came to an inglorious end by division among his puny and incompetent grandsons. By the terms of the agreement signed at Verdun in 834 one of these grandsons, Ludwig, received as his share of the great Frank realm the territory lying in the main between the Rhine and Elbe rivers. In this undistinguished descendant of the great Charles we encounter the first German sovereign and in the narrowly bounded land he ruled the first form of what figures historically as Germany.

A hundred years later under another, a Saxon, line of kings this young and as yet feeble Germany experienced an important increase of strength and under the second king of the new line, Otto I, called the Great (936–73), became the leading state within the bounds of the young occidental culture just beginning to rise into view. We have already learned that Otto's might enabled him to lead an army across the Alps and, with tragic consequences for both countries, to harness Italy and Germany together under the fantastic misconception that he was thus calling from its grave the long-defunct Roman Empire.

But this southward expansion, important as it was for the future of Germany, does not concern us here. Leaving it to one side, we shall take up the eastward expansion which, initiated by the father of this same Otto and energetically sustained by the son, proved in the long run to be as advantageous for his country as the Italian expansion turned out to be disastrous. However, to understand the eastward movement's origin and character, we must first take account of two weighty facts belonging, respectively, to the fields of geography and history. The geographic item is that the whole northern extent of what is now Germany is a level plain with the exception of the single rocky mass of the Harz Mountains. The no-less-important historical fact is that when, during the prolonged *Völkerwanderung* that preceded the downfall of the Roman Empire, the German tribes who had settled on this plain moved off to the south and west, the numerous Slav tribes to their east moved in after them up to and, at many points, even beyond the line of the river Elbe. Consequently, on the earliest emergence in the ninth century of a German state its eastern boundary reached no farther than the Elbe and was exposed to constant incursions from the trans-Elbian Slavs, often in collusion with their numerous outposts within the German limits.

It characterizes Otto's authoritative personality that when, on mounting the throne, he took note of this ceaseless border warfare, he should have determined to put an end to it by bringing the Slav raiders to book. Over a hundred years before, at a time when there was as yet no Germany and the vast Frank empire of Charlemagne included the German area, that energetic sovereign had worked out a plan for protecting his eastern boundary by a chain of fortified border areas along the course of the Elbe called "marches" or "marks." With Charlemagne's death the marks had, like his whole insufficiently cemented state, crumbled slowly to pieces. What Otto, coming over a hundred years later, undertook to do was to set the marks up again on a more effective and ambitious plan. No longer were they to be maintained as mere defensive barriers but to be operated as radiating points from which to carry the war into the land of the enemy and bring him under control and subjection.

One of these Carolingian marks revived by Otto lay along the lower Elbe and bore the name of *Nordmark*. From the Nordmark an important trail led across the Elbe to a powerful Slav fortress and rallying point planted on a hill over a tributary of the Elbe called Havel. By its conquest under Otto this stronghold projected itself for the first time into German history under the Germanized form of its name, under the name of Brandenburg. Its capture, together with the extension of the other marks planted along the Elbe, signified that a first step had been taken in a vigorous co-ordinated movement of eastward expansion.

In the end all the fine labors of Otto along the Elbe came to nothing. Before the end of the tenth century, in the reign of his grandson, Otto III (983–1002), there occurred a concerted movement of revolt among the Elbian Slavs, which in the course of a few decades brought down Otto's too frailly constructed border system and reduced it to ruins. Thereupon, precisely as before Otto had taken hold, an uneasy guerrilla warfare broke out and continued along the German-Slav border until, after a delay of almost a century and a half, a successor of Otto took heart and invited his adventurous and land-hungry vassals to join him in a renewed attempt at Slav subjugation.

By this time the situation in old Germany—the fertile region limited in the west as yet, in the main, to the Rhine and its tributaries—had greatly changed. The forests had been cleared, agricultural production had increased, prosperous towns had sprung up, and the inhabitants had swollen to such numbers that an outlet for the excess population had become a pressing social problem. It was therefore not surprising that the vigorous German feudality, whose attention focused narrowly on the twin interests of fighting and land tenure, should once more have directed their gaze to the thinly populated districts beyond the Elbe. So eager were they to master the no man's land of the border that in some instances they thrust forward against the enemy without first awaiting authorization from their head, the king-emperor. In general, however, the sovereign's might was at this time still sufficiently intact for his vassals not to engage in large-scale enterprise except at his prompting. Accordingly, our particular region of interest, the repeatedly revived and foundered Nordmark, again hove into view when in the year 1134 the Emperor Lothar assigned it to a certain Count Albrecht, known to his contemporaries, enamored of heraldry and the symbolic wild beasts that figured among its most treasured assets, as Albrecht the Bear.

In the circumstances, the imperial diploma was a hollow honor unless Albrecht should succeed in giving it substance by bringing the Nordmark within its former and, possibly, extended limits under his rule. During a long reign (1134–70) he concentrated on this purpose and, in spite of occasional setbacks suffered at the hands of the invaded and resentful Slavs, always returned to the attack. On his death he was able to pass on a doubled and even trebled Nordmark to his heirs. Before long the ruling house, of which he was the founder and which from one of its castles became known as the Ascanians, took rank with the greatest houses of Germany. In evidence of their mounting self-esteem the Ascanian margraves presently gave up calling their expanded realm by the name of its starting-point and nucleus, by the name of Nordmark, and re-baptized it with the more ambitious designation of Brandenburg. It is no longer with the Nordmark but with the mark of Brandenburg that we are dealing after Albrecht's time.

In the light of the very fragmentary accounts which have come down to us, Albrecht the Bear's remarkable successes were due as much and more to his diplomatic conciliation of the native Slavs as to his beating them into submission with the sword. In this respect his procedure was very different from that of many of his highborn fellows engaged in the same work of eastern expansion along other sectors of the river Elbe. By far the most powerful and successful of them all, including Albrecht, was Albrecht's close neighbor (and rival) to his immediate north, Henry the Lion, lord of the great duchy of Saxony. With rare audacity and a much larger feudal following than the relatively inconspicuous Albrecht could summon to his standards, Henry drove across the lower Elbe into the region along the Baltic Sea and giving, at least at first, little quarter, either pushed the particular hostile tribes confronting him from the land or put them to the sword. Thereupon he rewarded his knights with large tracts of the conquered territory, and they and he together dispatched agents to bring in German colonists from the crowded west, chiefly from among his own Saxons and their immediate neighbors, the Hollanders and Flemings.

While Henry's colonizing measures revealed a natural bias in favor of his countrymen, they were in the main inspired much less by national than by material motives. Wanting to make his conquests profitable to his treasury and aware that the advanced agricultural technique of the German peasants would secure a yield unattainable by the more primitive Slavs, he naturally turned to settlers of his own stock. As Adolph of Holstein, to the north of Henry, and Albrecht of Brandenburg, to his south, were no whit less eager for substantial rental returns from the lands they had appropriated, they followed Henry's example and systematically planted Germans in their trans-Elbian conquests. Farther up the Elbe all the way to the borders of Bohemia, other invading lords might be encountered whose seizures were followed up with similar colonizing programs.

The far-ranging, loosely co-ordinated movement of trans-Elbian colonization inaugurated in this manner proved to be the opening stage of a vast eastward migration of the German people which continued uninterruptedly for the next two hundred years. While the first incomers were knights and peasants, that is, swordsmen and plowmen, they were almost at once followed by burgher groups who were settled in the manner of the time in walled towns under a surprisingly broad self-governing charter. In these three sharply differentiated social streams the immigrants drove forward flooding first the lands between the Elbe and the Oder; then, crossing the Oder, they pushed toward the Vistula, which, however, they failed to reach except at its entrance into the Baltic Sea in the region of what is now the city of Danzig. The easiest route from Old Germany to the easternmost Baltic was, of course, the sea route; and, embarking at Bremen and Lübeck, the home-seekers pushed along the northward curving seacoast far beyond Danzig all the way to the Gulf of Finland. The whole amazing development, celebrated by the German historian, Karl Lamprecht, as the greatest deed of the German people in the Middle Ages, almost doubled the area of German speech and culture and gave the country the physical basis without which it would never have been able afterward to play the role of a great European power.

With the colonization of Slavland, its Christianization went hand in hand. This phase of the process of subjection was under the direction of evangelizing bishops assisted by zealous bands of monks and, except for an occasional upflare of fanaticism that took the form of a murderous crusade, was conducted with a laudable absence of force. Leading agents of conversion were the Premontratensian and Cistercian orders which, inspired by the old Benedictine prescription of *ora et labora*, of prayer and work, entered the conquered districts as fearless pioneers often on the very heel of the warriors. Taking possession of uninhabited forests and trackless swamps, they laid out, in connection with the inevitable church and dormitory, an associated group of model farms and helpfully gave both spiritual and economic encouragement to colonists and natives alike. On the whole, it is a fairly justifiable assumption that, after a first period of bloody warfare, the policy of the conquerors toward the Slavs took the form of peaceful cultural assimilation and that, of all the agencies brought into play, it was pre-eminently Christianity which assured the success of the victors. For the heathen, idol-worshiping Slavs the Christ preached by the invading missionaries was the *deus teutonicus,* the German god, and when, after many backslidings and, to the end, reluctantly, they yielded to this apparently invincible deity, they also gave up their national separateness and became merged in a single cultural group with their German masters.

While it is evident from these swift indications that the population of the north German plain, as it took historical shape in the later medieval centuries, is an amalgam of Germans and Slavs, the ratio in which the two stocks are represented in the mixture will always remain a matter of conjecture. Moreover, whatever the ratio may be, it is not uniform throughout the colonized area but fluctuates, and sometimes considerably, from district to district. In certain upper Elbe areas, for instance, lying in what until the revolution of 1918 was the kingdom of Saxony, the Slav figure is very high because no attempt was ever made to displace the original cultivators. In evidence of their continuous undisturbed existence on the lands they had originally occupied, they remained in possession of their Slav speech and customs far into the Modern Period. In fact, a compact body of several hundred thousand persons, mostly peasants, in the region called the Lausitz employ the Slav tongue as the language of the home to this day.

In the case of Brandenburg, on the other hand, there is all but complete consensus in regard to the decisive preponderance within its limits of German over Slav blood. Owing to a thin sandy soil alternating with vast swamps spread among the quiet lakes and sluggish streams that at that time characterized, and to a large extent still characterize, all the area between the Elbe and the

Oder, the Slavs had never held the land in numbers. Their scattered clans led a very meager existence largely in villainously dirty fishing villages, from which the German colonists were at no particular pains to oust them; for the newcomers were not fishermen but farmers with invaluable experience in draining swamps and clearing forests who, besides, carried with them on their hazardous eastward trek the priceless treasure of the iron plow. With it they could, as soon as the necessary drainage and clearance labors had been performed, work the heavier and more productive soils which the Slavs with their wooden plow had not been able to master. It helps us to realize the agricultural transformation wrought by the newcomers to look upon the iron plow as a symbol of the economic and cultural superiority of the invaders over the people they reduced. That Brandenburg, in spite of the stepchild treatment it had received at the hand of Mother Nature, became in due course a far from negligible source of agricultural supplies may without hesitation be attributed to the German colonists, who to achieve this miracle must be assumed to have taken over this unpromising soil in fairly sizable numbers.

Should we next consider the numerous towns that were called into being in complementary endeavor to the peasant villages, we are confronted with another, very important population source. Nor is it possible to question that in their original core the towns were wholly German, since the more primitive Slavs had at their conquest not yet taken to living in urban communities. All things considered, we may regard Brandenburg as perhaps the most German of all the provinces the great eastern migration added to the Reich.

The Ascanian line of Brandenburg margraves founded by Albrecht the Bear held sway in the mark of its creation for almost two hundred years. In all that time the family prospered extraordinarily, with scarcely a break in its ascending fortunes. When in their steady eastward drive the margraves reached the Oder, they did not halt at this river barrier but, boldly overleaping it, conquered and settled the immediately adjoining lands, which, in their sum originally called *marchia transoderana,* became known later as the *Neumark.*

It must not escape us that, in penetrating beyond the Oder,

the Ascanian margraves were no longer dealing with their original adversaries, the unorganized and much-divided east-Elbian Slavs, to whom the early chroniclers assign a great variety of names but whom for convenience' sake we may agree to designate collectively as Wends. The region beyond the Oder was settled by another and distinct Slav people, the Poles. Like still another Slav group, the Czechs, settled along the headwaters of the Elbe in hill-encircled Bohemia, the Poles at an early period of their contact with the Germans had turned Christian of their own volition and, thus fortified against absorption, had gained further power of resistance by organizing themselves as a state. At once, on its creation in the eleventh century, the Polish kingdom had begun to play a considerable role. It continued to make its weight felt well into the second quarter of the twelfth century, when it was greatly weakened by being broken into contentious segments over a disputed succession to the throne. It was precisely at this critical moment of Polish decline that the Germans began their historic eastward push, which but for the timely eclipse of the Polish state might have been much less successful than it was. No ruling German house profited more from the dissipation of Polish energy than the Ascanians. Meeting with only feeble opposition, a Brandenburg margrave was at last encouraged to invade and appropriate, as we have just noted, the distinctly Polish area of the Neumark.

At the beginning of the fourteenth century the Ascanian advance was still proceeding with such momentum that it seemed not improbable that it would reach the next natural north-south barrier, the river Vistula, and therewith penetrate to the very heart of Poland. At this point Chance or Fate stepped into the picture and radically altered its pattern. Always an unusually numerous family, suddenly and, in the absence of documents, inexplicably the Ascanians were reduced to a single uncommonly gifted member, Waldemar by name; and when in the year 1319 the brilliant Waldemar died, still a young man, what we may call the first or heroic chapter of Brandenburg history came to an abrupt close.

The second chapter startlingly reversed the trend hitherto maintained. It covers a period of about a century (1319–1411) under, first, a Bavarian and, second, a Luxemburg dynasty, during whose incumbency the mark suffered serious territorial losses and fell into a distressing state of all but complete internal decay. Among the many circumstances accounting for the decline we may safely assign the chief blame to absentee government. Ludwig of Bavaria, who happened to be emperor when, on the extinction of the Ascanians, the mark reverted to the crown, inaugurated the evil practice by endowing with the vacant province his eight-year-old son, for whom there had, of course, to be substituted a resident administrator. Ludwig's position even in the Reich was so insecure that, after some years, a rival for the throne appeared in the person of Charles of Luxemburg, king of Bohemia. Succeeding Ludwig as Emperor Charles IV, the Luxemburger, a skilful and tenacious diplomat if not a masterful personality, so deftly manipulated the situation that he succeeded in crowding the Bavarian family out of the mark and taking it into his own possession. In the circumstances, it will cause no surprise that, when in the year 1356 he attached his seal to the newly devised constitution for the German Reich—examined in the previous chapter and called the Golden Bull—he should have honored Brandenburg as one of the seven leading principalities, the rulers of which enjoyed the distinction of electing the king-emperor. Henceforth, the mark was commonly designated by the higher title of electorate. During the last years of his life Charles IV, whose normal capital was Bohemian Prague, often resided in his Brandenburg outpost. Taking intelligent interest in its rehabilitation, he stands out as the mark's only constructive and profitable ruler in this second period of its history. But such roots as he succeeded in sinking in the soil were again abruptly cut on his leaving Brandenburg on his death in 1378 to his second son, Sigismund.

For Sigismund, a man of vast ambition and negligible capacity, the reduced and culturally still backward electorate and mark had no attractions and, turning his back on it, he pursued his multicolored dreams. When we consider his vainglorious nature and general lack of substance, we may fairly wonder that he rose as high as he did in the world; for he won the crown of Hungary, just missed adding thereto the crown of Poland, and, following the deposition by the electors of his older brother, the drunken and imbecile Wenzel, was in his middle years elevated to the position of German king and Roman emperor. Requiring money and ever more money for the political machinations in which he was perpetually engaged, he pawned Brandenburg to a usurious relative for this invaluable tool of his ambition. The relative, singly intent on getting his advances back, was pleased to rule the mark through a series of administrators instructed to squeeze the last obtainable penny out of the ruthlessly exploited population. It was the by now habitual absentee government at its worst, inevitably prompting the angered inhabitants to resistance and contempt. With the remote and merely titular margrave no longer endowed with any real authority, the arms-bearing knights, the country's dominant group, looked on themselves in effect as his inheritors. The more lawless elements among them took to plundering the peasants, robbing the merchants on the road, and holding the terrorized towns to cruel and ruinous ransom. The general insecurity signified nothing less than the return to *Faustrecht,* the law of the fist and jungle, and, indefinitely prolonged, threatened to sweep away every remaining trace of a civilized order of society.

And once again Fate interfered, this time, in its often whimsical fashion, to a benign purpose. In 1411 the absentee moneylender and extortionist died, the electorate reverted to Sigismund, its legal lord, and Sigismund, now king of Hungary and emperor, was less than ever disposed to let his attention be diverted to remote and topsy-turvy Brandenburg. He therefore again had recourse to the device of an administrator and sent into the mark as the appeaser of its troubles Frederick, burgrave of Nuernberg. Frederick was a Franconian nobleman of modest territorial possessions but of proved skill both as a soldier and as a statesman. Employing a mixture of caution and firmness, this newest agent of an absentee master succeeded in the course of a few years in wringing the oath of allegiance from the contumacious knights of every section of the mark. It might never have been given but for his making a clamorous example of the most outstanding miscreants. Let us recall that his was the age when iron cannon discharging stone shot were making their appearance as a novel means for battering down objectionable castle walls. To the vast indignation of the leading noble highwaymen of the disordered mark, Sigismund's representative made use of the new invention against their strongholds and with a crash like doomsday brought them down about their owners' ears.

Uncompromising acts like these, accompanied by a spirit of conciliation toward the moderate elements of the ruling class, laid the ground for the recovery of the mark. With the work well advanced, Frederick after some years sought out Emperor Sigismund at the city of Constance, where a General Council of Christendom had just then assembled to put an end to the scandal of two rival popes, each claiming to be head of the indivisible church. Frederick's Brandenburg success signified another and conspicuous service added to a long list of forerunners by which the burgrave had put the emperor in his debt, and Sigismund let himself be persuaded to clear the slate by elevating his faithful servant to the dignity of elector and margrave of the land he had pacified. The document conferring the honor was signed at Constance in 1415, and two years later, in the spacious market place of this same city, where the emperor was still detained by the interminable business of the Council, Sigismund formally enfeoffed Frederick in one of those colorful public spectacles in the staging of which no people has ever excelled our medieval ancestors.

THE HOHENZOLLERN LINE OF MARGRAVES

The family, which in the person of Elector Frederick I entered on the succession in Brandenburg, bore the name of Hohenzollern from its ancestral castle in the ancient duchy of Suabia not far from that very city and lake of Constance which was the scene of Frederick's elevation to a German throne. Over two hundred years before this event an otherwise undistinguished ancestor of Frederick had been promoted by the famous Emperor Barbarossa to the post of burgrave of Nuernberg, a town in the heart of the onetime but long-since-dissolved duchy of Franconia; and although his descendants had been obliged gradually to surrender whatever authority they may originally have exercised over the prosperous and expanding city of Nuernberg, they had used their prestige as imperial agents to acquire title to numerous small parcels of land round about Nuernberg which in their sum made up a sizable dominion and gave its owners a notable standing among the south German princes. On Frederick's winning the electorate of

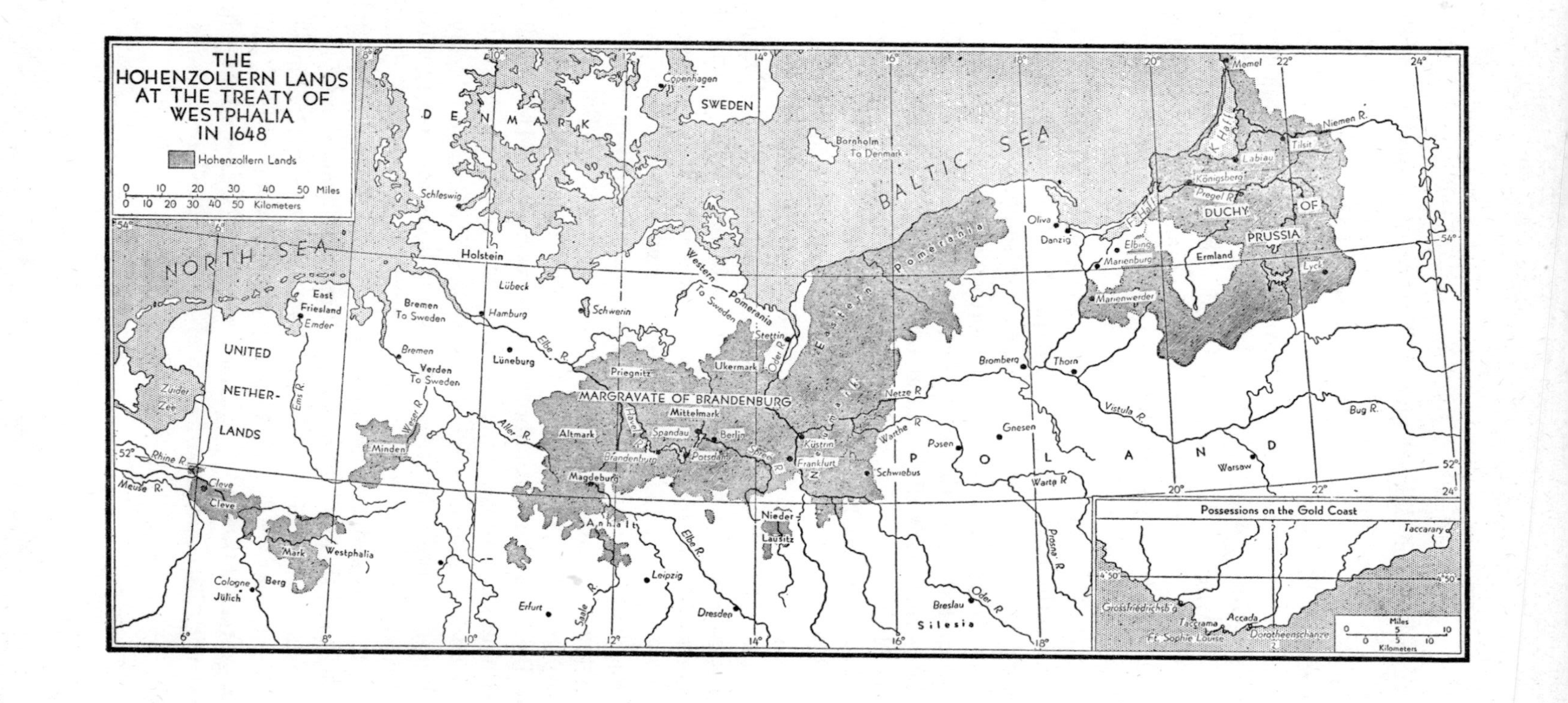
THE HOHENZOLLERN LANDS AT THE TREATY OF WESTPHALIA IN 1648
Hohenzollern Lands
0 10 20 30 40 50 Miles
0 10 20 30 40 50 Kilometers
NORTH SEA
BALTIC SEA
DENMARK
SWEDEN
Copenhagen
Schleswig
Holstein
Lübeck
Hamburg
Bornholm To Denmark
East Friesland
Emder
Bremen To Sweden
Bremen
Verden To Sweden
Lüneburg
Schwerin
Western Pomerania To Sweden
Stettin
Eastern Pomerania
UNITED NETHER-LANDS
Zuider Zee
Ems R.
Weser R.
Minden
Aller R.
Elbe R.
Priegnitz
Ukermark
MARGRAVATE OF BRANDENBURG
Mittelmark
Altmark
Havel R.
Spandau
Berlin
Potsdam
Brandenburg
Spree R.
Magdeburg
Oder R.
Küstrin
Frankfurt
Neumark
Netze R.
Warthe R.
Schwiebus
Anhalt
Nieder Lausitz
Rhine R.
Meuse R.
Cleve
Mark
Westphalia
Berg
Cologne
Jülich
Erfurt
Saale R.
Leipzig
Dresden
Breslau
Silesia
Oder R.
Prosna R.
Warta R.
Posen
Gnesen
Bromberg
Thorn
Vistula R.
POLAND
Warsaw
Bug R.
Oliva
Danzig
Elbing
Marienburg
Marienwerder
Ermland
Frisches Haff
Königsberg
Pregel R.
DUCHY OF PRUSSIA
Labiau
Kurisches Haff
Memel
Tilsit
Niemen R.
Lyck
Possessions on the Gold Coast
Taccarary
Grossfriedrichsburg
Taccrama
Accada
Ft. Sophie Louise
Dorotheenschanze
Miles 0 5 10
0 5 10 Kilometers
54°
52°
4°50'
6° 8° 10° 12° 14° 16° 18° 20° 22° 24°

Brandenburg, he did not give up the ancestral foothold in Franconia, and it was this twofold authority that explains the extensive influence he exercised in all the affairs of the Reich for the remainder of his days.

The considerable authority throughout Germany achieved by the first Hohenzollern elector of Brandenburg was substantially reduced, when on his death in 1440 his inheritance was broken up in accordance with the ancient German practice of division among the sons of legitimate birth. The principle of primogeniture had never been honored in Germany, and its failure to win recognition was at the bottom of the ceaseless subdivisions of territory by which the Reich had been atomized and reduced to a political crazy quilt. By the fortunate decease of some of Frederick's sons without heirs the territories in north and south Germany were again united under the third elector of the house, only, however, to be permanently disjoined at this incumbent's death. Even the unity of the mark of Brandenburg was threatened by the suicidal practice of distributed inheritance which was not definitely superseded by the rule of primogeniture for more than another hundred years. We shall return to this matter when the time is ripe.

Under the Hohenzollerns, the fourth and last dynasty of Brandenburg, the mark began again to prosper as it had done under the Ascanians. Doubtless this was in part due to the more than average capacity of the early rulers who, by and large, proved themselves to be sober, practical men intelligently devoted to the maintenance and strengthening of their territory. But the mark prospered also for so simple a reason as that, in distinction from the Bavarian and Luxemburg predecessors of the Hohenzollerns, the new masters were not absentee but resident rulers who, in spite of a certain nostalgia for their physically more alluring and culturally more attractive Franconian homeland manifested by the earlier margraves, became before long unreservedly identified with the inhospitable north German lowland to which destiny had transferred them. If in the long roll call of German and European dynasties a special merit may be ascribed to the Hohenzollerns, it might most readily be found in their having effected such an integration of themselves with the harsh soil of their adopted home and with its dour, laborious, and square-jawed inhabitants that whatever of loss and gain, of despair and hope, of sorrow and joy, befell one party to the partnership was loyally shared also by the other.

When the Hohenzollerns took over the rule, the general political situation in the broad north European plain was very different from that which the Ascanians had faced. In the time of the first Brandenburg dynasty the kingdom of Poland had fallen into disastrous decay, and no other power arose in its place capable of seriously disputing the eastward colonization movement on which the German people had engaged, not only in the latitude of Brandenburg, but throughout the region beyond the long course of the Elbe. By the time the Hohenzollerns had established themselves in the mark, the Polish kingdom had staged a remarkable recovery. In fact, it rose to an even more towering position than during its first period of authority by its absorption of the vast extent of the realm to its east, the grand duchy of Lithuania. This renewed and territorially doubled Poland at once threatened the famous Teutonic Order, which in the course of the German expansion movement had succeeded in setting up along the coast of the Baltic Sea a flourishing state of a military-monastic character called Prussia. We shall presently return to the ensuing Polish-Prussian conflict which, while not at once affecting Brandenburg, indirectly and, finally, directly assumed such importance for it that it may never again be lost from view.

Our sole purpose for the time being is to make clear that from the moment of its recovery the Polish kingdom stood like a wall across the path of further eastward expansion on the part of the mark. If we now add that at this very time Denmark developed ambitious designs in regard to the duchy of Pomerania along the German Baltic coast and that Saxony and other north German states, having in their turn effected a measure of consolidation, were prepared to dispute with Brandenburg any and every direction in which it might plan to advance, we become aware that the Hohenzollerns had to reckon with a much more powerful and resolute group of neighbors than their Ascanian predecessors had encountered in their day.

In consequence, the territorial expansion of Brandenburg proceeded very deliberately for the next two hundred years. The natural and earliest ambition of the new line of rulers was to recover the lands that had been lopped off from the mark by its rapacious neighbors during the anarchic century following the unfortunate death of Waldemar; and of certain border fragments they managed in one way or another gradually to repossess themselves. Far and away their most important success of this kind was their reacquisition of the Neumark, whereby the boundary of the electorate was again pushed beyond the Oder. The event befell in 1455 and was the work of Frederick, the second elector of the new line and the second of that name. However, the Neumark apart, we may fairly insist that the Hohenzollerns brought no important additional territories under their control until just before the outbreak of the Thirty Years' War. Since this war presents itself to view as the upshot and climax of the Protestant Reformation and the Protestant Reformation shook to its foundations the whole structure of Germany, it is indispensable that we now proceed to take note of the manner in which it affected Brandenburg.

THE REFORMATION, THE ROMAN LAW, AND THE FIRST STAGE OF GOVERNMENTAL REORGANIZATION

When, beginning with his attack on indulgences in the year 1517, Martin Luther loosed a storm against the Roman Catholic church which almost at once drew a majority of the German people and a not inconsiderable percentage of their rulers to his side, the then elector of Brandenburg, Joachim I (1499–1535), did not join the movement. He remained staunchly and even vehemently Catholic, uprooting to the best of his ability the Protestant tares as fast as they raised their objectionable heads in his dominion.

Joachim's son and successor, Joachim II (1535–71), was a man of softer mold. Recognizing that his people leaned strongly toward the new faith and with certain reservations inclining toward it himself, he took in 1539 the decisive step of establishing a local Brandenburg church which, although Lutheran in doctrine, retained the elaborate Catholic usages he personally liked. Profoundly disturbed, like all his fellow-princes, by the contemporary religious turmoil, he aimed to take a middle-of-the-road position and to mediate between the two extremist factions that were tearing Germany asunder. However, having by his action broken with Rome, he inevitably drifted further and further away from Catholicism and gradually dropped one after another of his pretensions to neutrality. Before he died, his Lutheranism hardly lagged in unreflecting passionateness behind that of his Brandenburg subjects, who became so thoroughly imbued not only with the doctrines of the Wittenberg reformer but also with his whole outlook on life, his Weltanschauung, that they came in the course of time to rank among the most stalwart supporters of strict Lutheran orthodoxy in Germany.

Having set up a state church, a *Landeskirche*, Joachim II became its *summus episcopus* or supreme head and provided for it in 1543 a central governing board called the Consistory. Such a board, exercising the administrative functions formerly reserved to the Catholic bishops, represented a considerable extension of the elector's authority. However, it was not the first enlargement which his power had experienced. Ever since, some centuries before, the government of the Reich had fallen into irreparable decay and the territorial lords had assumed the Reich's inheritance, they had been faced with the choice either of implementing their usurped authority or of standing idly by while the social order went to pieces. Under this call to action they had set about providing certain indispensable local services, and the Brandenburg elector had been no exception to the rule. The first, and, after the nature of all beginning things, for a long time rather casual, institution to take shape was the circle of the prince's trusted advisers making up his Council or *Rat*. They met in a room of the palace called the *Ratsstube*. In the earliest days the members were chosen from the nobility, but even before the coming of the Reformation the business submitted to the Rat had expanded so considerably both in the quantity and in the diversity of its matter that the elector's highborn associates proved no longer competent to handle it, and specialists trained in government procedure, and particularly in the technicalities of law and administration, became indispensable.

The more advanced territories of southern and western Germany, such as the Palatinate, Austria, and Bohemia, had been the first to feel the need of specialists in government, and they were the first to meet the need by the establishment of universities to serve as training schools. By the turn of the fifteenth century, backward, colonial Brandenburg experienced an identical need, to satisfy which Joachim I, whom we have just encountered as the contemporary of Luther and his uncompromising opponent, set up in 1506 a university in his town of Frankfurt on the Oder. Of the greatest importance for the subsequent development of juridical relations between both individuals and classes was the fact that at Frankfurt, and at every other German university as well, instruction in the faculty of law came to be based on the Roman code, the famous and immortal *corpus juris civilis.*

Revived in Italy during the Middle Ages—the barbarian invasions had submerged but not destroyed it—the Roman civil law had in the century before the Reformation leaped the Alps and made its way into the German universities as fast as they were founded. This signified a victory, and an astonishingly easy victory, over the ancient customary law, which in a later nationalist age was deeply and generally regretted but the reason for which it is not difficult to grasp. The native law was a vast body of customary practices only rarely and imperfectly committed to writing, dependent on the memory of men, and varying greatly from district to district. The foreign, the invading, system, on the other hand, was written, precise, and uniform and had behind it the sanction of the ancient state which had distinguished itself above all other states that have ever existed in the area of government and administration. Unescapably some evils resulted from the overhasty and too-sweeping reception on the part of Germany of Roman law. But indubitably there were also countervailing benefits which may not be overlooked and among which must emphatically be reckoned the solid training given by the Roman textbooks, not only to the actual followers of the legal profession, but also to prospective civil administrators for whom, in view of the expanding services of government, there was a steadily increasing demand.

Accepting the circle of the prince's friends, the Rat, as the earliest Brandenburg administrative body, we can readily see that whenever a novel and contentious issue was brought to its attention, it would be referred for consideration to a committee of the Rat and that, whenever the life of such a committee was indefinitely prolonged, it would gradually achieve the standing of an independent organ. The process can be observed in the case of a judicial committee started on its way by Joachim I, the very elector who, with a view to improving the system of justice, had in 1506 called the University of Frankfurt into being. Ten years later Joachim resolved to delegate certain, and necessarily specially trained, members of the Rat to hear appeals from the local courts and to sit as a supreme court or *Kammergericht*. It was no more than a tentative first step; but since in the succeeding decades the new institution fully met expectations, it gradually consolidated its authority with the result that by the end of the century that witnessed its inauguration it had been cut loose from its moorings and had become an autonomous unit.

In this manner, in the course of the sixteenth century, the originally undifferentiated Brandenburg administration had been diversified by two special creations, the afore-mentioned Consistory and the Kammergericht. The next development was a consequence of the threatening clouds that were gathering over Germany on the eve of the Thirty Years' War. In the prevailing alarming situation the relations of the elector with his neighbors needed to be subjected to careful daily review with every reasonable provision for secrecy. To this end, in the year 1604, a small and particularly trustworthy group of Rat members was appointed to serve as a *Geheime Rat* or Privy Council. While its chief domain was foreign affairs, it came also to embrace domestic interests and may properly be viewed as an inner cabinet. With no further development of note along administrative lines taking place until after the Thirty Years' War, we may conclude our rapid indications of the governmental changes carried through under the early Hohenzollerns by the summary statement that these princes proved themselves alertly aware that a more complicated society was in their time taking shape throughout Europe and that no state aiming at survival might neglect to adjust itself to the new situation.

Just before the Reformation century came to a close the ever threatening succession issue was at last quieted in the only manner guaranteeing an unbroken development by a declaration in favor of indivisibility and primogeniture. True, over a hundred years before, in 1473, the third Hohenzollern elector, Albert Achilles by name, had taken a first step toward holding his family's possessions together by an enactment called after him *Dispositio Achillea.* However, more honored in the breach than in the observance, it obliged a later elector to revise and fortify its provisions with a more effective instrument. This successor was Joachim Frederick who, on inheriting the electorate in 1598, was outraged by finding on his hands a paternal last will and testament which assigned large slices of the family lands to his younger brothers. Promptly annulling the document, he drew up a law of succession of uncompromising tenor to which every male member of the house was invited to attach his signature. Framed in consultation with the south German, the Franconian, relatives in a council held at Gera in Thuringia, the new house law carries the name of that meeting place. Because of difficulties that could not at once be overcome, it was not until five years later, in 1603, that the measure received its final form. The many eventualities for which it attempted to provide may be dismissed in favor of its unambiguous commitment to territorial indivisibility and primogeniture. Deeply considered, it went beyond the assertion of these two immediately pressing principles; for, by implication if not by direct statement, it discarded the common medieval view that the state was the private property of the ruler and replaced it with the modern view that it is an indivisible living organism and, as such, not subject to the testamentary disposal of a temporary incumbent.

THE HOHENZOLLERNS ACQUIRE PRUSSIA AND A PART OF JÜLICH

The solemn declaration of the indivisibility of the electorate was prompted to some degree by the exciting prospect unfolding at this time of two inheritances which promised to double the area subject to the house of Hohenzollern. Pursuit of this tempting increase involved considerable risks, and only in case the electorate were to benefit permanently from the expected acquisitions could the prospective perils be regarded as justified. It will suffice for our purpose to reduce the relevant facts to their simplest terms. In 1594 the eventual heir of Brandenburg, John Sigismund by name, married the oldest daughter of the duke of Prussia, also a

Hohenzollern, though of the younger, the Franconian, line. As the Prussian duke had no male heir, it had long ago been agreed between him and his Brandenburg relatives that the reigning elector, as his closest male kin, was to succeed him in Prussia on his demise. John Sigismund's claim to Prussia did not therefore derive from his Prussian wife, although it may be admitted to have been fortified through her. However, his Prussian wife, through her mother, was a prospective heiress in her own name, for she had an eventual claim to important territories along the lower Rhine ruled over by the duke of Jülich (Juliers), her mother's father.

The duke of Jülich's territory, consisting of the five separate duchies or counties, Jülich, Berg, Cleve, Mark, and Ravensberg, lay in the extreme west, the duchy of Prussia in the extreme east, of the lands of German speech, while Brandenburg sprawled between them across the north German plain completely out of touch with either. It might have been argued that such remote additions were likely to weaken rather than to strengthen the elector, but that was not a view commanding many supporters in an age when every dynasty, great and small alike, was set on growth and pleased to measure growth by the rudest of all standards, by physical bulk. Therefore, from the day of his marriage to the Prussian princess the waking and sleeping thoughts of John Sigismund turned about Jülich in the west and Prussia in the east, which he was prepared to appropriate as his lawful possessions the moment the news reached him of the demise of the respective reigning dukes.

Perversely, as happens only too frequently in cases of feverish expectation, the dukes—both of them, by the way, hopeless imbeciles vegetating in legal wardship—were an unconscionable time a-dying. When in the year 1608 John Sigismund, the expectant heir of Jülich and Prussia, succeeded to the throne of the electorate, he had not yet been cheered with either of the long awaited messages announcing that his hour had struck. Then, barely six months later, the Jülich half-wit at last expired, and John Sigismund promptly claimed the inheritance in the name of his wife. To his unmeasured indignation it was also claimed by the Rhenish duke of Pfalz-Neuburg on grounds which, in Neuburg's own eyes and those of his legal experts, were unassailable, but with which to clutter up this rapid sketch would be unpardonable pedantry. Is it not enough to recall that never in the history of European ruling houses has it been difficult to make out a plausible case for either of two candidates in a succession squabble?

A heated contest followed which just failed to produce a general European conflict. Rulers as feeble as were the elector of Brandenburg and the duke of Pfalz-Neuburg could not conduct a war by themselves; but the nearness of Jülich to the Netherlands moved the two great powers dominant in that region, Spain and the Dutch republic, to a jealous interference which threatened to revive the war between them only just quieted (1609) by a Twelve Years' Truce. Already for some time the increasingly charged atmosphere over Germany had been releasing flashes of lightning unmistakably heralding the approach of the culminating crisis in the long-drawn-out Catholic-Protestant conflict, the Thirty Years' War. In the sultry air that lay like a suffocating blanket over the land, religion and politics became indistinguishably merged. In witness of this unwholesome condition the duke of Pfalz-Neuburg, a Calvinist Protestant, went over to the Catholic faith in the hope of enlisting the support of Catholic Spain and the Catholic emperor for his claim. Immediately John Sigismund, the Lutheran, joined the Calvinist confession, the proved fighting form of Protestantism, by identification with which he might reckon on the aid of the Protestant activists in Germany and Europe, particularly the Dutch.

Simultaneously with these dramatic shifts of their religious allegiance, the tension between the two claimants approached the breaking-point; but as the great powers, on whose decision alone war hung, were not yet ready for a general showdown, they persuaded their petty clients to relieve the strain, at least for the time being, by accepting an adjustment. Accordingly, at Xanten in the year 1614 the disputed inheritance was divided in such a way that Pfalz-Neuburg received the mainly Catholic lands of Jülich and Berg, and Brandenburg the mainly Protestant lands of Cleve, Mark, and Ravensberg. Incorporated in the Xanten agreement was the declaration that the partition was purely provisional and that each contestant uncompromisingly upheld his claim to the undivided inheritance. Consequently, as we shall have only too abundant opportunity to see, the bad blood between the two claimants, far from being drawn off by the Xanten agreement, settled in the system and led to frequent uncontrollable outbreaks of ill temper in the years ahead.

When, in the year 1618, the idiot duke of Prussia at last expired in his turn, John Sigismund's succession was not disputed as in the case of Jülich. However, the conditions under which he assumed rule in that distant land were so onerous that it might be questioned whether he had much or even at all benefited himself by the Prussian acquisition. Behind these burdensome conditions lies the life-story of the Teutonic Order which in its salient features must needs be recalled at this point.

The territory along the Baltic to the east of the Vistula River was inhabited in the Middle Ages by a Letto-Lithuanian people, called Prussians, who clung stubbornly to their primitive mores and heathen faith. Accordingly, in the thirteenth century a German military-monkish organization, called the Teutonic Order, was intrusted by pope and emperor, the two putative world heads, with the task of bringing them forcibly within the Christian fold. By means of long and bloody crusades the recalcitrant Prussians were either slaughtered or reduced to submission, and a state of wide extent was established subject to the armed knighthood of the Order. It was culturally a German state, first, because the Order itself was composed of Germans and, second, because it took advantage of the eastward migration of the German folk just then proceeding at full tide to settle German arms-bearing gentry and German peasants on the conquered lands and German burghers in the numerous, newly founded towns.

The Prussia of the Teutonic Order was a powerful and prosperous state for well over a hundred years until, early in the fifteenth century, a decline began in connection with, above all, two outstanding events. In the first place, the colonists, especially their two upper groups of landed warriors and burghers, developed a flaming hostility toward the government of the close, exploitatory corporation of oligarchs the knights had become, and, second, there loomed across the border a dangerous enemy in the kingdom of Poland. In the year 1386 this kingdom took a new hold on life by the union it effected between itself and the far-flung grand duchy of Lithuania to its east. Thus invigorated, it at once manifested resentment over the barrier which Prussia formed between itself and the Baltic Sea and undertook to break it down. In prolonged and set pursuit of this aggrandizing policy, renovated Poland at last, in 1410, administered a disastrous blow to the Teutonic Order at the battle of Tannenberg; and, although the Order survived the defeat and continued the struggle, treason in its own camp on the part of the disgruntled landowners and burghers brought it finally so low that in 1466 it was obliged to bend its neck to accept a crushing settlement with Poland in the Treaty of Thorn.

By the Treaty of Thorn the Prussia of the Teutonic Order was divided into an eastern and a western half. The western, more important, half, commanding the basin of the Vistula, was taken over by and incorporated in Poland; the eastern half was returned to the Order in the sadly reduced condition of a fief of the Polish crown. Of course, the diminished grand masters of the Order, pricked to action by the restless, humiliated knights, tirelessly spun plans for the recovery of their vanished grandeur. But as the day for crusading organizations of their kind had definitely passed in Europe, none of their many harebrained schemes ever advanced them so much as an inch.

We thus come to the grand master of Luther's day. This was a member of the house of Hohenzollern of the younger, the Franconian, line, Albrecht by name. Finding himself, like so many of his German contemporaries, gravitating in matters of religion toward Wittenberg, he paid the Protestant leader a visit and in the sequel turned Lutheran himself and secularized the East Prussian remnant of the Order intrusted to his hands. Reluctantly, the Polish king, who naturally had to be consulted about so radical a change, gave his consent (1525) on the understanding that the transformation should not alter the relation of the secularized territory to himself. Consequently, the onetime grand master, now entitled duke of Prussia, journeyed to the Polish capital to do homage on his knees to the king of Poland as his acknowledged overlord. Forty-three years later Albrecht was succeeded by his son; and this son, whose mind died early, vegetated on in the flesh until 1618, when the Elector John Sigismund, his long-designated successor, became the third duke. He did so, let it be carefully noted, on precisely the same humiliating terms as the original ducal incumbent.

That the two acquisitions under John Sigismund brought no immediate advantage to the house of Hohenzollern was made evident when, on John Sigismund's death in 1620, he was succeeded by his son, George William. To him as the father and immediate predecessor of the subject of this book, we shall have to give a somewhat closer consideration than to the rulers who went before him.

ELECTOR GEORGE WILLIAM AND THE THIRTY YEARS' WAR

Elector George William held rule for twenty years, from 1620 to 1640, during which time the Thirty Years' War grew from a local conflagration in Bohemia to a vast blaze leaving no nook or corner of Germany unscorched. The war had hardly begun, when first one and then another neighbor state joined in, thereby expanding the original local crisis to a struggle embracing all Germany and, finally, the whole European Continent. With all the great powers locked in combat for purposes with little or no bearing on the religious differences in which the conflict had originated, the immediate impulse of the innumerable pigmy states of Germany was to withdraw from it behind a sheltering declaration of neutrality. Unfortunately, they could not gain respect for their position for a reason that never fails to operate the moment war breaks out and armies take the field against each other. On this occasion, as invariably before and since, the armies that marched to and fro over Germany were moved by the sole consideration of military necessity and scoffed at the declarations of neutrality displayed along their boundaries by the feeble states that lay across the armies' paths.

In these circumstances neutrality proved to be a will-o'-the-wisp, a delusion, and, unless the small German territories and their princes preferred weakly to let themselves be overrun and plundered, they had no choice but to provide themselves with such forces as by hook or crook they could muster to the end of impressing the ruthless major powers with their possession of a certainly indecisive, but by no means negligible, element of military strength. Only in this way could they hope to be admitted into some kind of partnership with the principals of the struggle and at its close find themselves not only still alive but even, depending on their run of luck, invited to assume a place in the new order of things approximately proportioned to the military effort they had put forth.

It was the misfortune of the Elector George William that, resolving at the outbreak of the Thirty Years' War to remain neutral, he did not grasp, or at least did not grasp with sufficient strength of conviction, that the only kind of neutrality likely to prove of the least help to him was the above-indicated armed neutrality. He was a well-meaning, not unintelligent man, too fatally soft of fiber to summon the resolute temper the tumultuous times required. Ruling under a constitution which left him in each of his three dominions—in Brandenburg, in Cleve-Mark, in Prussia—financially dependent on the estates or diets *(Landstände)* of these realms, he supplied no leadership calculated to make the deputies of the estates relax their grip on the purse strings. Invariably, on his appeal to them for taxes enabling him to assemble a defensive force, they either rejected his request *in toto* or else so thriftily pruned their grant as to deprive it of any positive value. No one knew better than they that their constitutional rights were a sum of class privileges incompatible with the healthy life of the state, and, correctly enough, they nursed the suspicion that their ruler, once provided with an army, would quickly sweep their outmoded usurpations onto the ash heap. While it is therefore undeniable that the chief obstacle to the policy of arming for action imposed by the wild confusion of civil and foreign war was the estates of his three territorial units, the elector himself cannot escape blame since he neither inspired confidence in the quality of his leadership nor did he, on the rejection of his pleas, boldly step out and seize what the emergency required in the very teeth of a selfish parliamentary opposition.

While the lack of co-operation between the elector and his estates suffices of itself to account for the terrible disasters that overtook Brandenburg during the Thirty Years' War, there is still another factor which may not be overlooked. A ruler endowed with so little initiative and self-reliance as George William possessed was sure to look to some nature stronger than his own for guidance; and as the elector did not develop his capital defect in the course of the years but was endowed with it at his birth, we need not be surprised to learn that he had provided himself at the very outset of his career with a political mentor to whom he then clung as long as he lived with a fidelity rare among common men and all but unique among hereditary rulers.

While serving in the days of his youth and before his accession to the electorate as governor of Cleve-Mark, George William had met Count von Schwarzenberg, a Rhenish nobleman, handsome of feature, of assured, distinguished bearing, and endowed with exceptional administrative talents. The young man promptly attached Schwarzenberg to his service, and when, on his accession to the electorate, he returned to Berlin, he carried the capable nobleman along in his baggage and unhesitatingly seated him in the Brandenburg Privy Council. It was not long before the newcomer had become the elector's leading minister, in which capacity he continued with hardly a break throughout George William's stormy reign.

Now, that Schwarzenberg was a man of honor within the seventeenth-century conception of that term and that he consistently advised his friend, the elector, in accordance with his best understanding of the true interests of Brandenburg hardly admits of dispute. If he had the elector endow him, as actually happened, with many remunerative offices and manors, that proves no more than that, like every other wellborn public servant of his age, he loved wealth and the personal magnificence which, without wealth, was an unattainable goal. No document has ever been found which would justify branding Schwarzenberg with the dark stigma of venality. Nor can the upright conduct of his ministry, particularly of the department of foreign affairs, be challenged, although it can readily be found to have been mistaken. Indeed, in the view of some authors, among them the present writer, he championed a policy which, worse than a casual error in judgment, was distinctly and fatally out of line with the interests of Brandenburg as they had taken historical shape during the immediately preceding centuries.

Schwarzenberg was a Catholic who, as was to be expected from his honorable personal code, never wavered in his faith. It was his strange and exceptional lot in life to serve a prince who, although personally of the Reformed and not of the Lutheran confession, was unescapably identified with the German Protestant cause considered as a whole. Always to be remembered too: Politically viewed, this prince of the all-powerful minister was an elector of the Reich and, as such, owed allegiance to the emperor. Contemporary records leave no doubt that the elector himself was conscientiously aware of his double duty and that he had no livelier wish than never to fail in its strict performance.

But now let us suppose that the Hapsburg emperor, who was Ferdinand II and a fanatic Catholic, revolved the plan to destroy Protestantism root and branch—what then? Would George William, obliged in that case to make a choice between two conflicting duties, decide for the emperor or for Protestantism? In point of fact, George William was confronted almost from the start of the war with this precise dilemma and in his feeble, conscientious way sweated blood over it without being able to come to a conclusion. In the end, as might be expected, he unloaded this, the crucial issue of his reign, on Schwarzenberg, and Schwarzenberg, in accordance with his deepest personal conviction, placed the attachment to the emperor above the Protestant cause. But can there be any doubt that this was tantamount to an attempt to check and even reverse the historical German process?

We learned in the preceding chapter that the German empire was by the seventeenth century in hopeless dissolution and that the Protestant schism was the last of a long succession of hammer blows which had battered it into ruin. Out of the ruin itself came the call to life, and it spoke, as it has spoken from the beginning of the world, of a new spring, bringing with it a new hope. While it will not be ascribed as a crime to George William that he did not hear the call, his deafness gives the measure of his political capacity and accounts for the low place he holds in the succession of Brandenburg electors. And precisely because his son and successor heard the whispered message and, obeying its unmistakable intimations, dissociated himself from what was old and dying to align himself with what was young and vital, he succeeded in becoming the founder of a self-sustained state in Germany and, through the distant consequences of his act, the restorer of Germany itself.

The foregoing considerations should serve to make the erratic course followed by Brandenburg during the Thirty Years' War somewhat more intelligible. The neutrality declared by the elector when the civil war first broke out was assailed by both parties to the conflict but not actively interfered with so long as southern Germany remained the theater of action. However, in 1625, when Denmark entered the struggle on the Protestant side, the war was transferred to the north German plain; and the armies of both combatants, of Catholics and Protestants alike, crossed the Brandenburg boundaries at pleasure to harry the countryside and pick up needed supplies. In little more than a year's time the Catholic forces succeeded in establishing an undisputed ascendancy over the Danes and their German allies with the result that the imperial general, Wallenstein, took over neutral Brandenburg as a lucky windfall for the permanent quartering of his troops. In the circumstances there remained no other course than to accept the alliance with the emperor which Schwarzenberg now advocated. Although the tardy decision did not save the electorate from continuing to be ruthlessly stripped by organized robber bands masquerading as soldiers, it offered, or seemed to offer, a measure of assurance against a threatened complete annihilation.

Then, in 1630, came a dramatic turn. King Gustavus Adolphus of Sweden replaced defeated Denmark as the Protestant champion and with a veteran army under inspired generalship completely reversed the course of events. By his very first thrusts he compelled the Catholic armies to give up north Germany and, entering Brandenburg, forced the elector to abandon the emperor and become the ally of Sweden. As Gustavus Adolphus, having George William's sister to wife, was the elector's brother-in-law, the harassed simpleton had hoped to encounter a sympathetic understanding on the part of his relative of his contradictory double obligation to Protestantism and to the emperor. He was disappointed because the clear-thinking Swede was aware that he could not, as was his purpose, make a successful southward drive into Germany without first securing his rear by attaching George William and the other leading north German princes to his cause, at least to the extent to which a sworn treaty might be expected to achieve that result.

The great victory of Breitenfeld in 1631 laid Germany at the feet of the Swedish king. But fate stepped in and nullified his success when in November of the following year he was killed at the indecisive battle of Lützen. In spite of the loss of its inspired leader, the Swedish army kept a firm grip on Germany until two years later, in 1634, it was crushingly defeated at Nördlingen. Thereupon the Catholic and imperial fortunes rose again; and by making at this turning of the road certain religious concessions, to the very idea of which he had hitherto been obstinately opposed, Emperor Ferdinand II was able to negotiate a settlement with the leading German Protestant prince, the elector of Saxony. Drawn up at Prague in 1635, the settlement invited all the other Protestant princes to add their signatures in order to bring the ruinous civil war to a close and turn the strength of the reunited country against the Swedish invader.

The acceptance by George William of the Treaty of Prague marked his return, under Schwarzenberg's auspices, to the imperial connection abandoned under duress five years before. In the meantime a new factor had been injected into the situation which, as probably decisive in bringing about the elector's realignment with the emperor, needs to be carefully noted. Ever since their entering the war, the Swedes had held the Baltic province of Pomerania as an indispensable naval and military base, and, following their startling initial successes, they had gradually fastened on the plan and made it the lodestar of their policy to take over Pomerania as a desirable, permanent foothold on the southern Baltic shore. Now the ducal family of Pomerania had long ago signed with the electoral family of Brandenburg a reciprocal inheritance treaty by which, in the event of the failure of male heirs, each named the other as its successor. As chance would have it, the Pomeranian duke who reigned at the time the Treaty of Prague disclosed to the world the Austro-Saxon plan for ending the grueling war was the last of his line and no longer young. He might die at any moment. But if in that case George William should try to take possession, he would be confronted with the hard fact of the previous Swedish occupation and the openly avowed Swedish counterclaim to Pomerania based on conquest.

Illumined by the persuasive Schwarzenberg, George William convinced himself that the Swedes would have to be dislodged from Pomerania by military might and that the only immediately available might was that of the emperor and his recently acquired Protestant ally, Saxony. He therefore cast his lot with them. Unfortunately, in the very next year, in 1636, the Swedish general, Baner, annihilated the overconfident, Saxon-led German army at Wittstock and, as an aftermath, penetrated into Brandenburg, pushing almost as far as its capital, Berlin. In the face of the new and acute danger, George William made the only serious attempt of his reign to get together an army in order to conduct war in his own name and on an impressive scale. Supported by the emperor, to whom he was now again bound in formal alliance, he hoped not only to drive the Swedes out of Brandenburg but even to wrest Pomerania—his own lost and therefore doubly cherished Pomerania—from their hateful grasp; for, shortly after the defeat at Wittstock, in March, 1637, the aged Pomeranian duke had breathed his last, and the moot question of the Pomeranian succession had passed out of the speculative stage. Nobody, not even the Swedes, disputed the legality of Brandenburg's claim; but every political realist, and no one more stoutly than the victorious Scandinavians, declared that only by a successful war could the claim be enforced.

The campaign against the Swedes, the single recorded warlike deed of the unfortunate and vacillating George William, proved a miserable fiasco. While it is true that the wretched ruler did not get all the support from the emperor that he had been promised, far more responsible for the depressing outcome was his own feeble generalship and the lawlessness and cowardice of his improvised, mercenary troops. After leisurely ravaging the land which they were paid to protect, promptly at the approach of the enemy they scattered in tumultuous flight. Thereupon the Swedes once again entered the electorate to seize and cart away whatever food, cattle, and valuables the bands of successive earlier plunderers had chanced to overlook. By the summer of 1638 the scraping together of even the barest necessities of life in the unhappy province had become so difficult that George William resolved to abandon Brandenburg and take refuge in distant Prussia. His parting act was to appoint Schwarzenberg *Statthalter* or governor in his stead. Then, by now a confirmed invalid because of an ancient injury to his thigh that would not heal, he made the long eastward journey in a litter attended by his fugitive family

With Brandenburg occupied by the Swedes except for a few remaining fortresses and its capital, Berlin; with the Rhenish possession of Cleve-Mark ringed round by the Dutch, Imperialists, and Spaniards and invaded by each in turn; with disaffected Prussia, cut off from the Reich and completely surrounded by Poland, conceding a grudging hospitality, George William lived on at his eastern capital of Königsberg for two more years. Then, exhausted, he laid down his weary load, adding a fairly negligible casualty to the grim, heaped wreckage of destruction which strewed the endless trail of the desolating German war.

Chapter 3

THE SEVENTEENTH-CENTURY PHASE OF WESTERN CIVILIZATION

PURSUING the historical method, which holds to the view that history is a continuous stream and that a later situation cannot be understood except in the light of foregoing developments, we have thus far made acquaintance first with Germany and then with Brandenburg as they moved onward through the years to the middle of the seventeenth century. We paused at this particular century because with it we have reached the period wherein flourished the ruler and statesman with whom this book proposes to deal. However, no whit less important for our purpose than making the acquaintance of the country to which our ruler belonged and of its subdivision which was his immediate field of operation is our familiarizing ourselves with the age in which he lived and which endowed him with his general outlook. This chapter therefore will be given to tracing the leading religious, intellectual, economic, and political trends which characterized our Western civilization in the seventeenth century.

GRADUAL WANING OF THE CATHOLIC-PROTESTANT ANIMOSITY

The most striking feature of seventeenth-century Europe was that it still dwelt under the shadow of the great movement of the Reformation inaugurated in the previous century. Exhibiting at its first appearance an extraordinary vigor and enthusiasm, the Reformation made such rapid headway that it seemed not unlikely to press on until it would take possession of the whole of Europe. Somewhat past the middle of the century, however, its advance was slowed up and finally stopped, owing to the return to life of the enfeebled Catholic church in consequence of a comprehensive program of rejuvenation. Steadied by a reawakened confidence and spurred to feverish effort by the many divisions that had arisen in the enemy ranks, above all, by the bitter feud between Lutherans and Calvinists, the Catholic church, as early as the second half of the sixteenth century, took the offensive in its turn in the hopeful expectation of recovering the lost ground.

In the first half of the following, the seventeenth, century, the Catholic forward movement reached a climax in the devastating Thirty Years' War. Although fought out largely on German soil, the Thirty Years' War was, as we have already learned, an event of European scope and, failing to bring victory to either side, ended in a stalemate. In prolonged negotiations, culminating in 1648 in the Treaty of Westphalia, the exhausted combatants, in effect if not in express words, compromised the religious issue by accepting as fated and incurable the division of what for over a thousand years had been the ecclesiastically unified Occident into a close-knit Roman Catholic church, on the one hand, and into a number of much more loosely knit Protestant churches, on the other.

Nothing would be more mistaken, however, than to conclude that the Westphalian compromise put an end to the blind rage which had ruled the Christian community ever since the advent of Martin Luther. Far from a term being set in 1648 to the hostility with which the opposed Christian groups had for over a hundred years regarded each other, it flourished with almost undiminished violence, unhappily nursed and fed by the theological leaders and zealots in the respective camps. For the rest of the century, therefore, Europe did not cease to resound with the roar and rancor of religious controversy, though it is undeniable that its heat perceptibly abated with the passing of each new decade. While this was to a certain extent due to the growth of a genuine spirit of religious toleration, it may with much greater justice be ascribed to a phenomenon of another order. In the course of the long-drawn-out and cantankerous doctrinal debate between Catholics and Protestants, steadily growing numbers of the intellectual class had uncovered an interest which made a more stirring appeal to them than the abstruse issues of theology which had hitherto monopolized their attention; and when the new interest now began to yield results of an immediate practical value for society, the socially unprofitable study of theology was threatened with the loss of that primacy among the intellectual élite which it had enjoyed without interruption ever since the Christian church had first arisen and driven paganism from the field.

HUMANISM AND THE ADVANCE OF SCIENCE

The new interest sprang from the natural sciences, and a historical account of this interest, however painfully inadequate, is indispensable at this point. While it is not true, as is still frequently alleged, that the Middle Ages paid no attention whatever to science, it may with a fair approximation to accuracy be said that knowledge of the world of nature was valued by the intellectual leaders of that period as no better than an ugly duckling compared with such authentically celestial knowledge as derived from the pursuit of logic, philosophy, and theology. Not until the fourteenth century, when the medieval world was beginning to dissolve, was the dominance of these ecclesiastically approved and passionately pursued studies challenged. From then on, as everybody knows, they encountered in the revived learning of antiquity a vigorous competitor.

Since the revivers of classical learning aimed to discredit the medieval curriculum in order to replace it with studies more immediately concerned with man, their movement has commonly been identified as humanism. Give it what name we will, it originated in Italy and slowly fanned out thence over all the countries of the western cultural bloc. It took over a hundred years from the time of its birth before, in the second half of the fifteenth century, it had gained sufficient strength to penetrate those stubborn strongholds of medieval learning, the universities. Thereupon it spread more rapidly, and its wide dissemination over Europe by the year 1500 is evidenced by the fact that its most authoritative champion at that time was no longer an Italian but a northern scholar and educator, Erasmus of Rotterdam.

Since the learning of antiquity had been overwhelmingly literary and aesthetic, humanism, a conscious return to antiquity, exhibited the same trend. However, as the ancients by no means overlooked science, their humanist imitators could not overlook it either. In this connection it behooves us to remember that the ancients, especially the Greeks, highly distinguished themselves by assembling impressive bodies of scientific data in numerous special fields. Their achievement will be at once admitted if we recall a few famous Greek pioneers together with the areas they respectively explored. Forever memorable, a veritable group of scientific Founding Fathers, were Euclid the geometer, Ptolemy the astronomer, and Galen the physician. But the greatest Founding Father of them all was Aristotle. Refusing, in the spirit of the boundless curiosity that characterized him, to be content with achieving distinction as a scientist in the fields of botany, zoölogy, and biology, he set himself no less a task than that of fusing the vast treasures of his learning into a coherent system of knowledge and so impressed with his achievement his own and a long line of later generations that he actually injured the cause he had at heart by reducing his successors to a state of worshipful subjection.

By appropriating to the best of their ability the scientific matter which the renewers of antiquity found in the recovered Greek and Latin records, they somewhat improved their methods of study and considerably increased the stock of ordered natural phenomena at their command. Mathematics, medicine, and a number of other disciplines fed from Greek sources took on a new vigor. But so overcome were the humanists, practically throughout the period dominated by their outlook, by the achievements and authority of the ancients that they persuaded themselves that their best course would be humbly to con the matter in the classical manuscripts and to decry as idle presumption every attempt to go beyond it. Having with the new cultural dispensation become emancipated from the authority of the medieval theologians, they fell straightway under the no less tyrannical yoke of the long-dead writers of the Greek world, with the result that the stimulus which science had undoubtedly at first received from the revival of learning threatened to exhaust itself in the purely imitative effort to catch up with the past.

Not until the passing of several generations of humanists was science heartened to go beyond the fabulous ancients and increase the corpus of received knowledge by fresh and original contributions. In 1543 Copernicus published his famous *De orbium coelestium revolutionibus,* wherein he argued in favor of replacing the geocentric hypothesis of Ptolemy with his own heliocentric hypothesis; and by a strange coincidence there fell from the press in this same year an equally revolutionary work by Vesalius on the anatomy of the human body which, based on original studies in the dissecting room, ventured to dispute some of the hitherto unchallenged dicta of the idolized Galen.

Thus, toward the middle of the sixteenth century, a first breach may be said to have been made in the authoritative and paralyzing classical tradition. Although too daring an action to meet with immediate general approval, it nevertheless established a precedent which other bold spirits would be sure to follow in the years ahead; and with each fresh breach of the classical walls the prospect before the scientific pioneers was bound to extend and deepen. Two names, Kepler (d. 1630) and Galileo (d. 1642), will serve to indicate the line of advance after Copernicus. In the early seventeenth century Kepler published his three laws of planetary motion by which he put the Copernican system on an irrefutable mathematical foundation, and at about the same date Galileo, more a broad-based physicist than a specialized astronomer, formulated the laws of falling bodies.

However, Galileo has another and, from the point of view of scientific advance, a crowning achievement to his credit. In his time so much new knowledge had already been assembled in so many different fields that science was able to free itself completely from the Greek leading strings. To Galileo and his contemporaries it became indisputable that the formulation of the laws of nature, the accepted goal of science, could not be effected by exhuming the generalizations of dead scholars, no matter how distinguished, but only by untiring direct observation of natural phenomena checked and supplemented by laboratory experiment and the steadily increasing use of such precision instruments as weighing scales, barometer, microscope, and telescope. Galileo's analytic genius enabled him to describe the elements of his and his contemporaries' new procedure in precise terms. It meant the capture for mankind of more than any single law or uniformity yet promulgated, for it put at the service of investigators a method valid for every kind of inquiry involving the world of nature which the devotees of these studies might see fit to undertake.

BIRTH OF MODERN PHILOSOPHY: DESCARTES AND RATIONALISM

Science, made fruitful by a method never attained—never more than faintly adumbrated—by the ancients, may without hesitation be set down as the outstanding novelty in the intellectual landscape of seventeenth-century Europe. Inevitably, so stimulating an agent influenced and ultimately reshaped every other kind of intellectual interest and therefore also philosophy. To understand the contemporary happenings in this field, we are obliged to begin, precisely as was the case with science, with the first discrediting of the solidly established medieval system of thought in consequence of the revival of learning. At once the philosophies that had flourished in the late Greek or Hellenistic world, such as Stoicism, Epicureanism, and Neo-Platonism, achieved the same fashionable vogue as all the other items of the honored classical culture and were reverently passed from hand to hand as finished products incapable of improvement. But when, in the seventeenth century, science had formulated its novel method and by its means had opened avenues to knowledge beyond even the imagination of the Greeks, philosophy was persuaded to give up its classical obsession and, reteating from its blind alley, to undertake the search for interpretations of man and nature that, guided by recent scientific discoveries, would be independent of both the ancient and the medieval thinkers. In this manner, running parallel with modern science and fired by its irrepressible *élan,* a distinctly modern philosophy came to birth.

The first chapter of modern philosophy was written by the Frenchman, Descartes (d. 1650). Reoriented by the procedure and achievements of the scientists, he discarded without exception the several starting-points and postulates of the philosophies inherited from the past. Thus emancipated from traditional trammels, he built his philosophic superstructure on the simple-seeming (but really highly complex) affirmation: I think, therefore I am. From this assumption of his own existence the mathematically precise thinker that Descartes was deduced his whole metaphysical system, that is, he erected it with the sole aid of that proudest boast of the creature, man—his reasoning faculty. Holding reason aloft like a torch, man was able, Descartes averred, to mount from the dark caves of animal ignorance into the clear upper air of truth.

It was natural that the revolutionary procedure of Descartes should arouse the watchdogs of tradition and cause him not only to be furiously attacked but also, in violent reaction to the criticism of the conservatives, to be enthusiastically supported. The net result of a vigorous controversy was that philosophy experienced a notable renewal. Its fresh, its modern, note was to explain the world without the help of the Christian or any other kind of faith, relying for support on nothing beyond man's natural endowment of sense and intelligence. The mere proposal of such an undertaking was denounced as blasphemous by believing Christians who, either as Catholics or Protestants, still exercised an as yet barely challenged domination in the world of thought. Over the new, self-sufficient rationalism they were for once in complete agreement, for, no matter how bitterly they fought each other over shades of Christian doctrine, they were alike convinced that there was no fathoming the mysteries among which our lot is cast, save by divine guidance. While the seventeenth century did not see the issue between Descartes and the Christian theologians brought to a settlement—nor for that matter has any subsequent century done so down to our day—the fact stands out that rationalism and its offspring, philosophic doubt, became firmly established in the world of thought and successfully improved their standing with each new generation.

THE COMMERCIAL REVOLUTION, THE VOYAGES OF DISCOVERY, AND THE COLONIAL MOVEMENT

With the seventeenth-century intellectuals casting off the trammels of theology and relying increasingly in their pursuit of knowledge on man's purely human equipment, we are justified in concluding that their minds had taken on a definitely worldly cast. Incontestably the otherworldliness which had dominated their medieval predecessors had begun to pass into eclipse. But it will not do to take the position that the revised outlook of the later leaders of thought sprang exclusively from an intensified concentration on their professional problems. It sprang also from so simple a circumstance as their being the children of their time, shaped by the same agencies as their contemporaries engaged in the rapidly multiplying commerce, shipping, banking, and industry of the age. Therewith we invite our attention to swing to the vigorous economic forces which, silently operative through many generations, had by the seventeenth century effected a radical transformation of European society. So comprehensive was this socioeconomic development that we would hardly be exaggerating its significance if we represented it as constituting the central ferment from which all the other changes of the period in last analysis stemmed.

No more than in the case of the seventeenth-century developments already treated may consideration of the contemporary socioeconomic situation be confined to its own time. It was in simple fact merely the latest phase of a movement hundreds of yeas old and, to be understood at all, must at the very least be referred to the rise of the towns, around the year A.D. 1000, in the as yet strictly agrarian society of the deep Middle Ages. The towns, at that time springing to life everywhere, owed their existence to a slowly widening neighborhood barter supported by the steadily increasing production of the industrial crafts. The rest of the story cannot be treated here beyond recalling how the crusades quickened the commercial movement by bringing into contact the hitherto separated Christian and Mohammedan worlds; how ships were multiplied in number and enlarged in tonnage to meet the increased demand for cargo; how merchants organized companies for trade both by land and by water and boldly extended their ventures over the known earth; how, helped by improved maps and incited by rumors of undiscovered continents of fabulous wealth, sea captains gradually groped their way beyond the immediate shores of western Europe into the open ocean. The climax of all these intimately connected activities was the daring voyages of the Portuguese and Spanish explorers whereby Africa, Asia, and the Americas were brought within the range of occidental enterprise and invaded by eager bands of adventurers in a furious, competitive rush to appropriate the gold, silver, and other immediately available riches of the new lands.

Then, following the first headlong scramble, came the more carefully planned expeditions under government auspices which aimed to establish oversea trading posts and to secure them against casual trespassers and organized marauders by intrusting them for safekeeping to colonists from the homeland. Already by the middle of the sixteenth century this colonizing movement was in full swing so far as the earliest discoverers, the Portuguese and Spaniards, were concerned; and early in the seventeenth century the Dutch, the English, and the French gained on various coasts around the globe a series of footholds to which they in their turn strove to give a character of permanence. Disunited national groups, like the Germans, the Italians, and the Poles, lacking an effective central government, were unable to join in the movement, with consequences which have put them at a disadvantage compared with their more highly organized neighbors down to our own day. Only a solidly established state was able to seize the uniquely proffered opportunity of reaching beyond its boundaries and staking out claims from which an immediate profit might accrue to the living generation and incalculable advantages of the most diverse kinds to the generations yet unborn.

By the middle of the seventeenth century the colonial situation was already very different from what it had been a hundred years before. Shortly after Columbus' first voyage the Spanish and Portuguese governments had accepted an arbitral decision of the pope which divided the vast, newly discovered world between them. On the theory of its unchallengeable validity they felt encouraged to comport themselves as the legal owners of the transoceanic lands and solemnly warned intruders off the premises. But in the long run they could not enforce their proposed monopoly, since energetic peoples, such as the Dutch, the French, and the English, felt themselves strong enough to treat it as no better than a pretentious fiction. After the catastrophic double failure of the Spaniards to crush the Dutch rebellion and, with the Invincible Armada of the year 1588, to punish the English for their support of the Dutch, the Spaniards—and with them the Portuguese—entered on so uninterrupted a decline that by, let us say, the Treaty of Westphalia, it was already clear to anybody with eyes to see that the commercial and colonial movement would thereafter be shaped not by its first promoters but by the virile and rapacious northern nations planted along the Atlantic seaboard. So long as these groups had been busy wresting advantages from the two Iberian states, their manifest common enemies, they had prudently avoided coming to blows among themselves. But even at that time it was already clear that with their hunger for colonies and commercial profits becoming ever more savage, it would not be long before the truce hitherto observed among them would come to an end and they would as furiously fall on one another as they had once unitedly fallen on the Spaniards and Portuguese.

In the second half of the seventeenth century was inaugurated this new phase of the overseas situation. England, France, and the Dutch republic engaged in not one but a long and complicated series of wars involving their respective commercial and colonial claims. The stubborn contest, into which Spain and Portugal, though now fading powers, were unavoidably drawn, is an event which decisively influenced world history and therefore requires to be scanned closely in an appraisal such as we are here engaged in making of the general atmosphere of seventeenth-century Europe.

Let us not fail to note, however, that when, in the second half of the seventeenth century, the three-cornered commercial rivalry among the Dutch, French, and English became acute, it was the smallest of these national groups, the Dutch, that was fairly in the lead. To begin with, their republic had just triumphantly emerged, with the Treaty of Westphalia of 1648, from another grueling war with Spain. Moreover, in the course of the war the republic had taken possession of the island empire of the East Indies and had steadily intensified the exploitation of its resources. Finally, it dominated with its powerful and victorious fleet the North and Baltic seas and in the wake of this naval mastery was able to find employment for so vast a body of merchant shipping that the bulk of Europe's ocean-borne trade had come to be carried in Dutch bottoms. Countless were the ships flying from their masthead the Dutch flag and laying their course to and from their leading port of origin, the city of Amsterdam, expanded into the leading emporium of the western world.

THE SOCIAL TRANSFORMATION ILLUSTRATED BY THE DUTCH EXAMPLE

The radical economic revolution the Dutch experienced in the course of their rise to colonial and commercial eminence involved a corresponding social revolution. The fact is, social and economic revolutions in this and every other instance are inseparable and yield the greatest measure of enlightenment when considered as two aspects of a single transformation. If, however, attention is here focused on the social rather than on the economic revolution of the Dutch, that is because the writer, obliged by pressure of space to make a choice, considers it less imperative to spread before his readers a heterogeneous body of economic data than to draw a picture, though no better than a thumbnail sketch, of the dynamic new Dutch society. And while it is specifically the Dutch society which we are proposing to take under examination, let it be understood that, owing to the operation of identical influences, the English and French societies, apart from certain inevitable local variations, were being similarly reshaped. Even the much more backward societies of Italy and Germany were brought to a related, though less precisely contoured, mold; for, in spite of their having had no share in the colonial movement, they lay within the frame of Western civilization and could not possibly escape the impact of whatever forces were active within its compass. Since from the beginning of this civilization in the period called the Middle Ages, it has constituted a single cultural unit, its many member-groups have moved forward, if not always at the same pace and on an even front, at least in the same direction.

When the Dutch won their freedom from an attempted Spanish domination, they established themselves as a republic under the name of the Seven United Provinces. However, among the constitutive seven, one province so emphatically overshadowed the rest that practically it alone gave the new state its historical luster. The province was Holland, which fronted the North Sea and embraced all the leading towns of the republic, such as Haarlem, Leyden, Delft, and Rotterdam. More particularly, it embraced Amsterdam, where, as already noted, the intense commercial activity of the young nation rose to a head and climax.

The moment we proceed to a close-up view of the transformed Dutch society of the seventeenth century we are obliged to note a distinction. Since, following the war of independence, the six less important provinces continued to base their existence on agriculture much as they had done before that struggle, their social structure experienced no particular alteration. The peasants, with expanding town markets clamoring for foodstuffs at their doorstep, brought their acres to a high degree of productiveness and at the same time multiplied the returns from their lush lowland meadows by intensified dairy farming. While this notable initiative signified intelligent adjustment to altered economic conditions, it did not involve deep-seated social change. Change was reserved to the towns and that means to the outstanding province of towns, to Holland. But here change was fundamental. Merchants, commission agents, bankers, promoters, shipbuilders, sea captains rose to the top in every trading center. Together they constituted a group of leading citizens called "burghers," who ruled the towns not only economically but politically as well by reserving the suffrage and the town offices exclusively to themselves. While the elastic word "republic" has been commonly used to describe this system, we must be clear in our minds that it was the republic of a privileged middle class intrenched in power and resolved to defend its prerogative against every rival claimant with all the energy at its command.

The rivals of the burghers were two in number, the disfranchised town masses and the house of Orange with its ring of partisans, largely landed proprietors. As political outsiders, the two groups tended to combine. Left to themselves, the exploited masses might not have proved dangerous to the existing regime, had they not been given support and leadership by the famous native family, which, after rendering the national cause invaluable service during the long war of liberation against Spain, on more than one occasion found itself so bedeviled with hampering legislation by a jealous burgherdom that, instead of continuing to direct the nation, it was depressed to the role of an impotent bystander. The general burgher ascendancy notwithstanding, even in the seventeenth century when it was at its peak, the burghers were occasionally obliged to draw in their horns before the combined assault of their opponents. The most famous instance of this kind was the mass movement of 1672 by which the burgher leader, Jan De Witt, was overthrown and killed and young William III of Orange promoted to the headship of the nation. In spite of this and other Orange triumphs the statement may fearlessly be ventured that the Dutch republic, which rose to so great eminence in the seventeenth century, owed its position to a mobile, intelligent bourgeoisie quick and resolute to take advantage of a favorable world situation and exercising an all but complete economic and political control over the society to which it belonged.

So sweeping a supremacy in the areas of wealth and government meant that burgherdom gave to Dutch society also its religious and intellectual imprint. A spirited body of Reformed (or Calvinist) Protestants, the burghers had violently dissociated themselves from the Catholic principle of a directive and hierarchically organized clergy. By this act they became in their own opinion not worse but incomparably better and freer Christians. A veritable liberty virus took possession of them, requiring that they no longer, as in the past, curve their backs under a master, whether bishop or prince, and that thenceforth they govern both church and state by the method of free consultation among themselves alone. And yet these same rock-ribbed Calvinists practiced a religious toleration far beyond that of any contemporary ruling group. Was it owing to their acquaintance as far-ranging merchants and travelers with many countries and conditions of men? Be the explanation what it may, in an age of universal intolerance the Calvinist Dutch republic served as an island of refuge for the religiously persecuted of all lands.

The commercial activities that came to a head at Amsterdam brought about a greater concentration of capital at that point than had ever occurred before in the western world. Assembled in banks, it was borrowed by promoters for the launching of new enterprises, and a stock exchange on a scale unimagined before came into being, intended to serve the general public by facilitating the buying and selling of participations in business undertakings. Nor was the mixed character of the blessings conferred by these developments slow to put in an appearance. Sudden feverish booms were followed by equally sudden crushing collapses in the best manner of capitalist behavior down to our day. There were even examples of aberrations of so monstrous and irrational a kind that they are explicable only on the assumption of an access of temporary insanity. An instance was the historically famous tulip craze. While it lasted, individual rare bulbs were bid up to thousands of guilders until the inevitable abrupt crash made them valueless and their owners paupers.

Summing up, we may say of the whole emerging bourgeosie of the seventeenth century, of the English and French variety as well as of the Dutch, that it constituted a compact social class engaged in ridding itself of the shackles that held trade, government, and religion in the bondage of traditional practice. Though not familiar with the term, the leading townsmen had become what a later generation called "individualists," with each member of the group pursuing the course that seemed most likely to bring him an improved position in the world as measured by the command of wealth and the exercise of political power. And inevitably, on having acquired the outlook of energetic, hardheaded, large-scale traders, they no longer interpreted Christianity as their forebears had done, as voluntary renunciation, no longer distrusted their endowment of sense and intelligence (except under pulpit influence at church on Sunday), no longer followed or had any desire to follow the cramped medieval way of life. In short, they maintained a view of the world substantially identical with that of the two seventeenth-century groups previously considered and classifiable as leaders in the intellectual field, the scientists and the philosophers.

But an essential identity of mental attitude is not the whole story of the seventeenth-century connection between the pioneers of thought, on the one hand, and the men of business, on the other. However distinct in function, socially the two groups were one and the same, since the intellectuals sprang almost without exception from the burghers, with whom they also intermarried and lived in stimulating association. If to the strict intellectuals of science and philosophy, necessarily few in number, we now add their less strict but far more numerous relatives of the professions of law, medicine, and public service and remind ourselves that they, too, were preponderantly drawn from burgherdom, we get some notion of the immense power of this expanding class. By slow accretions during the two or three centuries antedating the Treaty of Westphalia, it had come to embrace the highest economic and intellectual potential of the contemporary world. In final proof of its waxing self-reliance it had broken, though as yet not openly, with the salvation complex of the Middle Ages and, in spite of the occasional twinges of a perturbed conscience, unwaveringly directed its energies to the conquest of the material world.

THE SEVENTEENTH-CENTURY STATE

There is room in this shorthand account of seventeenth-century civilization for only one more of its aspects; and since this book is to be a story of statesmanship, our choice is inescapably reduced to the issue of government. Under no circumstances can we dispense with the knowledge of what form the state assumed in that age and what theory or theories gained currency to account for its latest aspect.

Nothing about the Middle Ages stands out more startlingly than the contrast between the intolerable confusion of civil society and the order and dignity of ecclesiastical society. On the civil side western Europe presented itself to view as an extravagantly subdivided agrarian feudalism of which the component elements were in unceasing conflict with one another; ecclesiastically, on the other hand, this same western Europe was firmly unified under a single authoritative institution called the church.

The first important change in this picture of sharp opposites occurred around the year A.D. 1000 with the revival of commerce and the birth of towns already mentioned in another connection as a transforming agency of central significance. From the very nature of their activities the towns were obliged to interest themselves in a more effective political control, and the result of their efforts through many generations is most strikingly illustrated by the rise of the Italian towns to wealth, power, and, as a final tribute to their energy, to an original and impressive culture. In the course of their rise the Italian towns worked out standards of efficiency in business, finance, and administration hitherto unknown and signifying within the narrow bounds of their authority the replacement of the haphazard and irresponsible governing system called feudalism with republican municipalities, in which we encounter the earliest form of the modern state.

Not, however, until these innovations had been taken over by the great feudal monarchies of France, Spain, and England were they realized on a national scale. The transformation of the three monarchies was a very gradual process since it was stubbornly opposed by the still strong, though steadily weakening, feudal magnates and naturally also by the church, alarmed at the threatening curtailment of its prerogatives. If we may think of the movement of monarchical consolidation as beginning in the fifteenth century, we note that it continued without interruption through the sixteenth century and that in the century of our special interest, the seventeenth, it was still proceeding and had not yet reached its apex. Almost from the beginning certain more acute political observers were aware of what the slow passing of feudalism signified. They spoke of the advancing monarchy first as the "strong" and presently as the "absolute" monarchy and, depending on their class interest and mental orientation, applauded or lamented the removal of the traditional checks on the will of the sovereign.

The three strengthened monarchs were from the beginning of their rise identified with, respectively, the Spanish, French, and English nations. However, they owed their increased power less to the sum of the social groups under their sway than to the single element of the townsmen who lived by commerce and industry. This group gradually added to the narrow town sentiment, which was the earliest expression of its self-esteem, the wider national sentiment and tendered its love and devotion to the king as the embodiment and symbol of the nation. It thus came about that the monarchies, wholly feudal in their origin, were transformed into national monarchies and by the energy of a sentiment which before long became one of the most vigorous group emotions recorded in history gained an enormous increment of power.

It was the newborn nationalism enlisted in behalf of such sixteenth-century monarchs as Francis I and Henry IV of France, Emperor Charles V and Philip II of Spain, Henry VIII and Elizabeth of England, which enabled them considerably to enlarge the royal role played by their predecessors. In fact, they waxed so great that they completely dominated the European stage. It vastly aided their pre-eminence that Germany and Italy had in their time become parceled out among numerous small principalities. While these minor governing units imitated to the best of their ability the improved organization of the great monarchies and became therefore miniature absolutisms, they were so deficient in political and military might that they had to dance as the leading powers piped. Very generally in the hope of gaining a larger measure of security they became the clients of one or the other of their dominant neighbors. In no case was their existence other than precarious, for it was always possible that under some unexpected move on the diplomatic chessboard they might find themselves invaded and conquered.

With the European states, great and small alike, more efficiently organized from the sixteenth century on than their medieval predecessors had been, the Roman Catholic church, far from overshadowing them as had once been the case, dwindled in bulk and power until the strengthened states threateningly overshadowed the church. It is at least an illuminating suggestion that the reversed stature of the rival civil and ecclesiastical institutions affords an approximate measure of the decline of the religious ideal of the Middle Ages before the assault of the secular values brought into existence by an urbanized society passionately given to the increase of material well-being. But that, even if true, would not be the whole story. The church cannot be absolved from the charge of having very substantially contributed to its own decline, primarily through the misdirected and unspiritual policy of the popes. In their conflict back in the Middle Ages with their civil compeers, the emperors, the popes had been carried to the length of claiming supremacy over both church and state and by the attempted exercise of this excessive power had produced the startling collapse of which the Babylonian Captivity, the Great Schism, and the fiasco of the Conciliar Reforms are the distressing successive stages.

In the end the incurably diseased papacy was confronted with the successful revolt against it inaugurated by Martin Luther and called the Protestant Reformation. Tremendous consequences followed. Not only was the religious unity of Europe destroyed once and for all, but the diminished Catholic church and the many nationally circumscribed Protestant churches which replaced it exercised so reduced an authority that they could only in rare instances assert themselves against the civil power. More particularly, the Protestant churches fell into an all but complete subservience to their respective governments. In fact, some of them contributed to their own subjugation by formulating and championing the directly antimedieval doctrine that it was the province and duty of the state to regulate religion.

When, with the Peace of Westphalia, the heat began to go out of the Catholic-Protestant conflict, the medieval situation had been completely reversed. No longer, as in the Middle Ages, was a single ecclesiastical organization lifted high over a multitude of puny civil states. On the contrary, these states had by the discovery and exercise of new social functions acquired a concentrated vigor beside which the diminished Catholic church and its several Protestant replacements were all but lost from view. The towering, self-sufficient, sovereign state—that was the seventeenth-century upshot of the long chain of politicosocial changes which had begun hundreds of years before with the rise of commerce and the towns.

THE EUROPEAN POWER SYSTEM

Wherewith we come to the inseparable companion piece of the unlimited sovereign state, to its twin brother, as it were. As such we must accept the contemporary European interstate system. Even before, but more unquestionably after, the Treaty of Westphalia, it lifted its impressive bulk over the Continent and made itself unconditionally decisive in shaping the general political situation. It will set the significance of these two related growths in the proper light to point out that they have never since their first appearance ceased to dominate the European scene. Even more remarkable perhaps: So few changes have occurred in the manner in which the two agencies operate that whoever has become familiar with their behavior in our day will have no difficulty in following their behavior in the century with which we are concerned.

In that century, and, for that matter, before as well as since that time, there were both large and small states within the European framework. However, it is not a negligible circumstance that there were many more small states in the seventeenth century than at present because the unification of Italy and Germany, brought about in the nineteenth century, has eliminated the two leading areas of petty, independent sovereignties. The point under no circumstances to be overlooked is that, while sovereign states may be and have been of all sizes, their sovereignty is not on the same plane. Even a cursory review of the political developments of the last three or four centuries will reveal that small states enjoy what is at best a precarious sovereignty and that this, their qualified status, results from their being always more or less at the mercy of their larger neighbors. If they are not invaded and overthrown and have, in some instances, maintained an effective independence for centuries, the reason lies in the protection which they are afforded by a principle known as the "balance of power." This works to their advantage because, on the strength of it, an attack on them by a stronger neighbor serves to draw all the other neighbors to the scene with the intent to keep the aggressor from gaining a disproportionate power and thereby disturbing the existing equilibrium. In these circumstances it is an inescapable conclusion that the small states owe their continued independence to the jealous watch that the great states keep on one another.

It follows that the dominating members of the European system have ever since its rise been the great states, designated in recognition of this very domination as the "powers." A state figures as a power by virtue of such factors as the extent of its territory; the size of its population; its wealth as measured by the returns of agriculture, commerce, and industry; the efficiency of its government in respect to administration, taxes, and law courts; and, last and most important of all, by reason of the quality and size of its armed forces. However, while conceding to each and every one of these elements its full weight, it may well be that the most important single factor contributing to the making of a power is the sentiment of nationalism; for, as already indicated, it is nationalism that communicates the emotional energy giving all the other factors their decisive punch. It follows that with Europe, adopting in the sixteenth century the nationalism to which it has ever since increasingly adhered, it was possible even at that time to foresee a future when only nation-states of the type of the three contemporary monarchies of Spain, France, and England would rank as powers. That this was not yet the case in the century of our concern will appear in the course of the story that this book plans to unfold. With nationalism everywhere on the upgrade but not yet universal, such multinational entities as the Holy Roman Empire and the Hapsburg and Ottoman monarchies were still a possibility, though a fading one.

SEVENTEENTH-CENTURY POLITICAL THEORY

In concluding this story of the coming of the absolute, secular state and the European power system resulting therefrom, a word must be conceded to seventeenth-century political theory and to the revisions it underwent under the impact of contemporary political practice. Back in the Middle Ages the political philosophers, like every other kind of philosopher, had been essentially theologians and had developed a theory of both church and state in strict agreement with their theological outlook. God as not only the creator but also the ever watchful, loving guardian of man had provided the two institutions of church and state for the guidance of the respective elements making up man's dual nature, the spirit and the flesh. Both institutions were therefore of divine origin, although the church, as serving a higher purpose than the state, took precedence over it. An occasional rebel, like Marsilius of Padua, who flourished in the first quarter of the fourteenth century, quarreled with this doctrine and ascribed a purely human origin to both institutions, a view which by his frank confession he owed less to his own originality than to the authority of pagan Aristotle. In his and every similar case the prompt excommunication of the rebel coupled with the burning of his books regularly reduced his followers to a vanishing group of frightened dissidents.

With the secularization of society continuing in the century after Marsilius and marked in the intellectual field by such a movement as the revival of classical learning, theorists of the state came to the front whose minds had not received their imprint in the stampmill of the medieval schools. While prudently content to leave the church to the theologians, they undertook to scrutinize the state as a separate and independent phenomenon. However, they were still sufficiently ruled by the inherited Christian ideology to endow the state with a divine origin. As by the sixteenth century it had come about even in small states, and certainly in the outstanding and powerful ones, that rulers of an "absolute" type had succeeded to the government, the accepted divine right of states was converted by an easy thought-transference into the divine right of kings. By the following, the seventeenth, century the doctrine thus reshaped had acquired an immense prestige, in large part because it almost perfectly reflected the actual European situation. It is not to be wondered at, therefore, that it was in this same century that the divine right of kings received its classic formulation at the hands of the Frenchman Bossuet. A bishop of the Catholic church, Bossuet naturally and fervently affirmed the divine character of the institution he immediately served. But also a faithful subject of Louis XIV, the most magnificent embodiment of monarchy that had thus far dazzled Europe, the bishop with the lofty eloquence appropriate to his station hailed the chrism applied to Louis's brow at the coronation ritual as the authentic seal of divinity.

In spite of the steady spread of absolutism and long before Bossuet's day, occasional writers had come forward who, steeped more completely than their fellows in current secular influences, rejected the divine origin of the state and asserted its purely human character. Far from original with them, the idea had been propounded, as already noted, by an occasional medieval heretic who had drunk at the well of Aristotle. Applying the argument of such forerunners to their own time, a number of Renaissance and Reformation theorists projected the view that the state had originated in the dawn of history by an agreement among the free and sovereign individuals, imagined as at that time composing society, to put an end to the uninterrupted warfare which was their unhappy lot by appointing a mediator or prince to rule over them. The agreement was in the nature of a contract, its purpose the greater security and happiness of the contracting parties. So long as the chosen prince or magistrate faithfully served the end for which he was created, he justified himself to his subjects and no fault could be found with him.

Beginning with the Reformation this so-called "contract" theory of the origin of government slowly won an increasing number of adherents among specialists in the political field and not only because its rejection of a divine origin fell in with the secular trend of the age. It won adherents also because in many actual instances the monarchs exercising absolute power proved themselves so vicious and degenerate that they inevitably prompted their subjects to entertain the thought of rising in rebellion against them to effect their overthrow. In case, however, the aroused subjects held fast to the divine-right theory, the sword of insurrection was struck from their hands before they drew it from the scabbard by their fear of offending the Almighty. What more natural, therefore, under the continuing challenge of an evil and oppressive sovereign than for rebelliously inclined men to have recourse to the alternative, the contract, theory and to justify a revolt against the tyrant by asserting his breach of the ancient agreement on which his power rested.

While the contract theory was born and cradled on the Continent, it was brought to maturity in England, where it received the formulation that made it a mighty force in the world of thought for over a century. How it came about that England achieved this distinction is, in the light of what has just been said, not difficult to grasp; for it was in seventeenth-century England that the problem of how to get rid of an undesirable king first reached a stage that would no longer brook postponement. Let us agree at once that when, thereupon, the Stuart king, Charles I, was violently deposed, it was not the doing of a few harmless political philosophers but of a mass of determined subjects led by equally determined politicians and soldiers. But with the grim work accomplished, the political philosopher appeared on the scene and, like an actor who speaks the epilogue that will send the audience home consoled and edified, explained and justified to his troubled countrymen the events of which they had been the startled witnesses.

The first great English statement of the contract theory was made by Thomas Hobbes in 1651 in a work called *The Leviathan;* and it remains an outstanding irony of history that Hobbes, an intransigent royalist, used it not to attack but to defend the absolutist claim. A dialectic trick sufficed for his purpose, for all he had to do, and did, was to declare that the supposititious contract, once made, was irrevocable—and the cause of the king was saved! When some years after Hobbes's time, the English civil wars came to a close with the unequivocal victory of the parliament, that excellent parliamentarian, John Locke, promptly edged his way to the stage in his turn to speak the piece appropriate to the latest aspect of events. In the by-now-prescribed manner he, too, appealed to the contract theory and by a procedure which was the precise, casuistical counterpart of that of his Tory predecessor declared, instead of for the irrevocability, for the revocability of the original but always, let it not be forgotten, purely imaginary contract. Since the victor is always right, it follows that it was in the Lockian and not in the Hobbesian form that the contract theory won a footing in European thought.

It will not have escaped the reader that while the postmedieval political philosophers in the main came down from heaven to earth and accepted the state as a purely human institution, they continued to employ the medieval speculative and not the modern scientific method of inquiry. The speculative (or metaphysical) method had been current since the days of the Greeks and consisted in trying to penetrate by a purely dialectical procedure to the hidden essence of the object or institution under investigation. On abandoning this method, which had proved only moderately fruitful, in favor of observing how a given object behaves, to the end of discovering the principle or law of its behavior, the natural sciences had recently been completely revolutionized. For many years after the new method had gained recognition, it was held to be appropriate only to the natural sciences with which it had originated. But was there anything to hinder a bold spirit from trying it out sooner or later on the studies concerned with man and hence on the study of the state?

Not until the eighteenth century was a beginning made systematically to probe the state by the scientific method, and as we are in this book dealing with the seventeenth century, we are not concerned with what happened at a later time. But by one of those remarkable anticipations of which there are innumerable instances in the history of thought, a Florentine secretary of state, Niccolò Machiavelli by name, as early as the turn of the sixteenth century made a scientifically detached behavior study of the state which remained unique for many generations and which still arouses, as it did when it first appeared, a curious mixture of admiration and loathing. The admiration goes out to Machiavelli's method, the case method as it may be called; the loathing is reserved for his discovery, or purported discovery, that the modern secular state, of which the earliest samples were under his scrutiny, had stripped itself of every moral and religious scruple and become a law unto itself.

Machiavelli's political treatise, called *The Prince* (1513), was widely circulated only to meet with an all but universal rejection. In spite of the liberation brought about by the Renaissance, Europe in Machiavelli's day was still strongly under the influence of medieval thought, and although numerous individuals of the intellectual class had already by that time rejected the purported divine origin of the state, they had not gone the length of tossing out also its purported ethical purpose. Nor did they feel bound to do so on the evidence, since the society in which they lived manifestly accepted a moral law in its private concerns and the state, the collective expression of society, could not be conceived as lying beyond the operation of that law. It was charged by the critics of Machiavelli that he had, in order to establish his thesis, carefully picked extreme examples, chiefly from the vile and execrable story of the petty tyrants of his own Renaissance Italy. Furthermore, these critics pointed out, if it had to be conceded that the Christian church no longer enjoyed the regulatory power it had claimed and in many instances had exercised in the Middle Ages, its place had been taken by interstate agreements constituting an authoritative body of international law. Growing stronger with every decade, international law was asserted to constitute a check, moral as well as legal in its nature, on the exercise of that unrestrained sovereignty which Machiavelli saw everywhere at work and apparently in his unabashed paganism extolled as desirable.

Still, with every allowance made for the strictures of his outraged critics, the Florentine secretary had undoubtedly made an invaluable contribution to our understanding of the state by his adoption of the novel method of the natural sciences. While his thesis of the nonmoral character of the state was and has remained inacceptable to the overwhelming majority of men, he did establish beyond contention that in its modern form the state exercised a far more sweeping and irresponsible power than in the preceding feudal and ecclesiastical age. This should be kept well in mind, for it is essentially in the nonmoral character ascribed to it by Machiavelli that we shall find the European state operating in this book.

Chapter 4

THE NEW ELECTOR SURVEYS HIS INHERITANCE

YOUTH AND EDUCATION OF THE NEW ELECTOR

ON ELECTOR GEORGE WILLIAM'S death on December 1, 1640, he was succeeded by his only son, Frederick William, a young man twenty years of age. Frederick William was born in the castle at Berlin on February 16, 1620,[1] less than two years after the outbreak of the conflict which was destined to win an evil fame as the Thirty Years' War and to fill all his days to his accession with its iron clangor and breath-taking hazards. Following the abandonment by his grandfather, John Sigismund, of the Lutheran for the Reformed faith, which, let us not forget, had at that time no legal standing within the confines of the Reich, the family of the Hohenzollerns was eyed askance by its former associates, the Lutheran princes, and obliged to look for sympathy and support to a small group of rulers who for one reason or another had transferred themselves to the Reformed column.

Far and away the most conspicuous member of the German Reformed body was the count palatine of the Rhine, a prince of the same electoral rank as John Sigismund himself. No wonder, therefore, that when John Sigismund looked around for a suitable wife for his heir, George William, his attention should have been drawn to Elizabeth Charlotte, daughter of his coreligionist and fellow-elector. It was an important additional attraction in his sight that Elizabeth Charlotte was connected through her mother with the

1. According to contemporary accounts, the young prince was born on February 6. In the seventeenth century, Brandenburg and the Protestant world in general were still employing the ancient Julian calendar, which was ten days behind the reformed Gregorian calendar, so called because sponsored by Pope Gregory XIII (1572–85). To avoid the confusion of double dating, this book will date according to the Gregorian calendar.

most vigorous fighting family of the Reformed faith in Europe, for her mother was the daughter of the illustrious William I of Orange-Nassau, called the Silent. If, continuing the inquiry into the next-of-kin of the son born in 1620 to George William and Elizabeth Charlotte, we now recall that it was his mother's brother, the Elector Frederick, who in 1618 accepted the crown of Bohemia offered him by its Protestant rebels only to have it struck from his head at the battle of the White Hill after a brief year, we may agree that the talk around the cradle and in the nursery of the young prince must have been alternately tinged with grief and touched with pride as it rang the changes on the stirring events constituting the household story of the interrelated Reformed families of Brandenburg, Orange, and the Palatinate.

A deep, religious devotion, confirmed rather than shaken by the multiplied anxieties precipitated by the ever expanding war, marked the atmosphere the young prince breathed throughout his early years. Undoubtedly it was to it in large part that he owed the simple, evangelical piety, free alike from Puritan austerity and doctrinal intolerance, that distinguished him all the length of his days on earth. He was not yet six years old when the war, surging for the first time toward Brandenburg and into the vicinity of Berlin, disrupted the close family circle. The troops of both parties to the war paid no regard to George William's declaration of neutrality and roamed the countryside plundering it at will. For the greater security of the young heir his anxious parents sent him under a trusty governor to the Oder fortress of Cüstrin. Here he spent the next five years receiving the education prescriptive for the governing classes of that age and directed as much, and perhaps more, to the development of the body as to that of the mind. The boy learned to ride, hunt, shoot, fence—all indispensable accomplishments of the gentleman and prince—throwing himself into them with so much gusto that it was not always easy to turn him to the less exciting tussle with his books. While he was instructed and made average headway in such routine studies as mathematics and geography, the core of the curriculum mapped out for him was directed to the learning of foreign languages. To this task he gave himself with enough diligence to lay the foundations of a fair command of Latin, Dutch, French, and Polish—languages which, later, owing to his wide European contacts, proved of the greatest advantage. Polish, it may be noted, appeared for the first time in the educational program of a Brandenburg prince. In view of the relation of the recently acquired duchy of Prussia to the Polish king, his wise elders concluded that a knowledge of the tongue of his suzerain might well turn out to be a profitable investment.

A circumstance, the happy consequences of which can hardly be exaggerated, was that the governor under whom the young prince was sent into the isolation of provincial Cüstrin was a high-minded gentleman, Leuchtmar by name, from one of the recently acquired Rhenish dependencies. He was of course a Reformed Protestant, unshakable in his faith; but his fundamental seriousness did not hinder him from associating with his lively charge on a friendly and even intimate and comradely basis. When there were journeys to be made, Leuchtmar accompanied the prince; and at least two such occasions may not be overlooked because of the mark they left on the impressionable spirit of the growing boy.

Frederick William was ten years old when—it was the year 1630—he was sent for by his parents to be introduced to the king and queen of Sweden, who, though lavishly entertained at the capital, could hardly be said to have been present at the urgent invitation of their hosts; for it was clearly not at the behest of Elector George William that King Gustavus Adolphus had recently landed on the Baltic Coast and penetrated into Brandenburg. That the queen of Sweden was Elector George William's sister somewhat lessened the inevitable bitterness of the situation. Nonetheless, it was not his aunt who, on his arrival at Berlin, engrossed the attention of young Frederick William but his aunt's husband, whose warrior reputation, won on Polish battlefields, was already ringing across Europe. It is reported that Gustavus Adolphus expressed delight in his alert and well-grown nephew and, doubtless more in play than in earnest, proposed him as suitor for the hand of his only daughter and heiress, Christina. Two years later the prince and Leuchtmar made a second journey to pay their respects to the great Gustavus. This time they traveled to the Pomeranian town of Wolgast where the magnanimous king, lately killed in action at Lützen, lay in state preparatory to his transfer for burial in his northern realm. We require no recorded evidence of Frederick William's thoughts to realize the awe and admiration with which he gazed on the frozen features of the dead kinsman and warrior, the greatest soldier of his age.

In that period young men were sent to the university much earlier than today. When, on Frederick William's arriving at the age of fourteen, the family circle weighed the question of the institution in which he was to enrol, the decision went against the German universities on account of the wild unheaval prevailing throughout the Reich. It was the influence in all probability of his mother and grandmother that caused the selection of the University of Leyden, owing partly no doubt to the security of persons and property obtaining in the Dutch republic and partly as well to the protective interest that his kin at or near The Hague might be expected to take in the young man; for on this friendly soil he would encounter not only his more distant Orange but also his more immediate Rhenish relatives, since the latter, unable after the Bohemian rout of 1620 to return to their native Rhineland, had found sanctuary under the Dutch flag.

No matter who was responsible for the dispatch of the young prince to Leyden and for what reasons, no wiser or happier decision could have been made. In the first half of the seventeenth century the Dutch republic, overshadowed by and largely summed up in the single province of Holland, marched at the head of European civilization. In commercial enterprise and organization, in bold and, alas, only too often in ruthless exploitation of colonial areas, in the quality and quantity of both its trading and fighting vessels, in the cultivation of the new scientific method and a new expression in the arts, it drew the admiring and envious regard of all its neighbors. When, in the year 1634, Frederick William, still under the faithful Leuchtmar as governor, set out for this favored region, it was engaged, as, with a short intermission, it had been for over sixty years, in its war of liberation from Spain and, in spite of, or rather by very reason of, that tremendous effort it had released the extraordinary cultural energies that still in our day, after the ships and the ships' masters have long since crumbled to dust, constitute the substance of its fame. What a school of the arts of both peace and war for the young prince from lean, ravished, backward Brandenburg! What an enlargement of vision for the cramped inlander exposed to the feverish activity among the wharves of Amsterdam and viewing the interminable lines of carrier vessels moving along the intricate network of Dutch canals!

Duly, as required, Frederick William attended the courses at the University of Leyden and, in spite of a distate for the confinement they imposed, absorbed such elements of their offerings as conformed with his peculiarly direct approach to life and prevailingly practical outlook. Far more important for the executive role for which he was being fitted were the activities encountered in harbor town and military camp which constituted an unofficial, outdoor university and inexhaustibly fed the eyes and ears with living matter. The head of the house of Orange and leading Dutch official, Stadholder Frederick Henry, was just then at the height of his fame as a soldier and on occasion permitted his young grand-nephew to attend him in the field. His Rhenish relatives, the unhappy former royalties of Bohemia, maintained with their many children, all in the heyday of youth, an establishment which, in spite of its poverty and shabbiness, was a center of unquenchable life and merriment. Wherever Frederick William went, he heard talk of the war and always of the war—of its apparent everlastingness, of past mistakes and losses, of future hopes and prospects, and through all the talk ran like a silver thread the determination shared by all these tested and courageous followers of the Reformed faith to stand unwaveringly by their cause and to endure for it to the end.

Frederick William abode in Holland from his fourteenth to his eighteenth year and would have stayed longer, had he been able to invent acceptable excuses for failing to act on the order to return which his father repeatedly dispatched for over a year before it was obeyed. We cannot therefore doubt that he found the Netherlands to be congenial ground. But if, on his departure, we now ask ourselves what he brought away that became incorporated in his being and figured in the later chapters of his life, we are bound, in a matter so recalcitrant to precise measurement, to be content with asking questions. If, in the years ahead, he was ready to make use of Protestants and Catholics indifferently to advance his political plans and yet, despite this conspicuous opportunism, to remain unshaken in his devotion to the faith in which he was baptized, may not this fidelity be attributed not only to the childhood influences already mentioned but also to the resolute example placed before him by his Netherlands kinfolk and all the people of the Netherlands? If, on weighing, after his accession to the electorate, a dozen marriage projects, he finally took to wife a daughter of the house of Orange, may not that choice have been due in last analysis to the stored memories of his Dutch years? If, himself the member of an almost static agrarian society, he came to regard commerce as an indispensable societal stimulant, may not this dynamic attitude have resulted from his having looked so long and with such amazement on the forest of masts in Dutch ports and the bales and boxes piled on Dutch quays? If during a long reign he concentrated with greater intensity on winning an outlet to the sea than on any other of the scores of purposes he at one time or another pursued, and if with as good as no liquid means and without a single usable port he dared project a colonial empire on the coast of Africa, can such vaulting ambition be accounted for save as a dream persisting from his Dutch experience? Coming, finally, to the thoughts occupying the immediate foreground of his consciousness as he at last packed his baggage to obey the parental summons, was not his persistent disinclination to go home ascribable to his profound aversion for the pro-imperial and, therefore, pro-Catholic policy his father had adopted under the inspiration of his Catholic confidant and minister, Count Schwarzenberg? For, with Schwarzenberg in control at Berlin, would he not, with his Reformed sentiments nursed to vigor among his passionately anti-imperial and anti-Catholic relatives at The Hague, find himself in a completely untenable position?

However dark his forebodings may have been regarding what he was about to face in Brandenburg, on his arrival at Berlin in the late spring of 1638 he encountered realities much more desperate than his worst dreams. The campaign against the Swedes inaugurated the year before in alliance with the emperor was already as good as lost, owing to the incapacity of the hireling officers and the lack of discipline of the hireling troops. In measure as they yielded ground, the but-feebly-resisted enemy poured into Brandenburg. Only a few months after the heir apparent's home-coming, his discouraged invalid father felt obliged to abandon the mark entirely and with his family and court to seek the comparative security of distant Prussia. His leaving Schwarzenberg behind as governor was proof that, in spite of the heaped disasters of both the remote and the recent past, he was considering no change of policy.

Nor did the weary elector for even a moment consider a change after he had safely installed himself in his eastern capital of Königsberg. For apparently no other reason than the jealousy with which rulers have habitually regarded their successors, the father, though slowly dying and in sore need of such comfort as only a devoted family can supply, was at pains to exclude his son from any even remote influence on the government. For two dragging years the young prince, active by nature and eager to prove his mettle, hung idly and unhappily about the fringes of the court. At last, on the first day of December of the year 1640, death put an end to the long agony of George William, and, in accordance with immemorial monarchical practice, the sadly reduced and straitened Königsberg court, turning with no more than a moment's hesitation from the dead to the living elector, spontaneously hailed him as the new lord, *der Neue Herr*.

Der Neue Herr!—the grand salute was a bitter mockery; for of what was Frederick William lord on the day he took over the government after the violences and disasters of the last two decades? His Rhinelands, occupied in turn by friend and foe, had passed completely out of his control; Brandenburg, except for Berlin and a few fortresses of the Mittelmark, was a prize of the Swedes; and even in Prussia, his present residence, the authority of a new incumbent rested, that is, was without legal basis, until he had renewed allegiance to the king of Poland by a formal act of homage. In simple truth the new lord was lord, not of territories, but of claims to territories with just sufficient foothold among the few crags to which he clung to measure his risks and to hope, with skiful maneuvering, to avoid plunging into the abyss.

It was the good fortune of the young man who faced this calamitous heritage that nature had endowed him with a sturdy body and a vigorous mind and that, although without any direct experience of affairs, he was at the early age of twenty mature beyond his years. Contemporary accounts are happily sufficiently specific to enable us to picture him as he presented himself to view at this time. Well proportioned and of more than average height, he habitually met the world with a quiet, dignified demeanor. Though of muscular and massive rather than of graceful build, he boasted a more than common bodily agility, due to his love of every kind of exercise, more particularly of the chase, to which he was passionately addicted. A large hooked nose was not out of place in an assortment of vigorous features whose fierce masculinity was softened by a pair of brilliant blue eyes peering from under an abundant brown mane, which, framing his face, fell almost to his shoulders. A portrait done two years after his accession hangs in the gallery at Montbijou[2] (Berlin) and merits an examination, although it is plainly an uninspired confection after a formula taken over by his lesser contemporaries from the leading but none-too-conscientious court painter of the age, Vandyke. The young elector is shown in full figure dressed, after the Dutch fashion, from head to foot in sober black relieved at only wrists and throat with touches of white lace. He stands solidly on two sound legs, looking straight before him with a somewhat haughty air. The rude features are realistically rendered, above all, the hawklike beak, which we are pleased to have the artist confirm as the most striking feature of the facial landscape.

Frederick William lost no time in grappling with the desperate situation confronting him in every section of his scattered dominions. What he undertook to do and what he achieved or failed to achieve from the day of his accession in 1640 through the ensuing forty-eight years of days covering his long reign will henceforth be our single and engrossing theme. However, before broaching it, we must have a closer look than was permitted by the rapid tempo hitherto maintained at the landscape, society, and political constitution of the three separate and distinct territories constituting his inheritance. We may call them—landscape, society, constitution—the permanent factors in the complicated political math-

2. The portrait is by Czwiczek. A reproduction appears as a frontispiece in A. Waddington, *Le Grand Electeur Frédéric Guillaume* (2 vols.; Paris, 1905–8). The artist, apparently of Czech origin, resided at Königsberg with the title and salary of painter to the court.

ematics with which he would henceforth be obliged to wrestle as long as he lived. To refer to them as permanent, with the reservations the historian necessarily attaches to that concept, is justified because they had been in existence before the overshadowing contemporary event, the Thirty Years' War, began and would of a certainty figure in the situation with an identical importance whenever in the near or distant future it should please God to bring the conflict to a close. Always, consciously or unconsciously, the three permanencies would be present in the elector's mind, would indeed have to be present if the policies he might successively adopt were to be rooted in reality and bring him and his country a clear and measurable increment.

In this connection it will suffice to remind ourselves that every head of a state stands on a particular soil among a particular people particularly conditioned and that unless he shapes his program with due regard to these fundamental factors, he may be sure it will crumble to dust in his hands and bring him, a convicted idle dreamer, to merited defeat. We need, therefore, not apologize for putting off the tale of Frederick William's initial attack on the problems crowding in on him at his accession, while we acquaint ourselves with the leading physical, social, and constitutional aspects of the young sovereign's three territories, beginning with the oldest and most important, with Brandenburg.

THE ELECTORATE AND MARK OF BRANDENBURG

The electorate and mark of Brandenburg lay in the north German plain between the Elbe and the Oder rivers, except for a bulge westward of the Elbe and a corresponding bulge eastward of the Oder. The west bulge was substantially identical with the original Nordmark created by Emperor Otto I as a bulwark against the Slavs. After its enlargement by the successive penetrations beyond the Elbe it came, naturally enough, to be designated as the Old or Altmark. By analogy the east bulge, the bulge beyond the Oder, came to be called the New or Neumark. The mass between the Elbe and the Oder figured as the Middle or Mittelmark with a number of subdivisions of which the Priegnitz in the northwest and the Uckermark in the northeast were the most important. Berlin on the Spree River in the heart of the Mittelmark had in the fifteenth century been raised by the second elector of the Hohenzollern dynasty to the honor of chief residence and had since then served as the capital.

At the outbreak of the Thirty Years' War, Berlin (with its sister-city, Cölln, immediately to the west of Berlin between two arms of the Spree) had a population of thirteen thousand which twenty years later, at the time of Frederick William's accession, had been cut to little more than half that figure. The pre-war population of the other towns of the mark, such as Tangermünde on the Elbe, Brandenburg on the Havel, Cüstrin and Frankfurt on the Oder, fell not much below that of Berlin and had been reduced in varying proportion by the same devastating event. The relatively few and sparsely inhabited towns furnished indisputable evidence that, after four hundred years of occupation, commerce and industry pulsed but feebly through the land. Nor, for that matter, was the countryside other than sparsely settled, although it is certain that the bulk of the population, as befitted a community living overwhelmingly by agriculture, resided on the soil. The likeliest estimate—there were of course at that time no official statistics—puts the total population of the mark before it had begun to wither under the fiery breath of war at approximately four hundred thousand.[3] By 1640 it had been reduced to about half that number.

The plain fact is that Brandenburg was economically a backward area, and it is equally plain that its backwardness was referable in the first instance to its shabby treatment at the hands of nature. Throughout its extent the mark was a level, infertile country of alternating sand and swamp overgrown, except where cleared for agriculture, with monotonous pine forests and crisscrossed by free-roving, slow-moving streams frequently coming to an all but complete rest in quiet, variously contoured lakes. The sluggish waterways are explained by the region's mere one to two hundred feet elevation above sea-level. Its later considerable development—much later than the period here considered since it dates only from the nineteenth century—sprang from its becoming

3. See S. B. Fay, *The Hohenzollern Household and Administration in the Sixteenth Century*. On p. 25 Fay treats of the population of the mark. Meinardus in his Introduction to *PR*, Vol. II, upholds, on the basis of cited evidence, the view of a much steeper decline of population in both town and country in consequence of the war.

through its geographical position a land of transit for the products moving from eastern to western Europe and vice versa. But as in the earlier centuries this exchange, in so far as it existed at all, followed the cheaper and safer Baltic Sea route, Brandenburg had, in the period with which we are concerned, drawn as good as no advantage from its transit character.

When, in the twelfth and thirteenth centuries, the meager soil of the mark became available for German settlement, it was necessary in order to persuade prospective colonists to take it over to tempt them not only with larger farmsteads but also with fewer obligations in the way of rent and services than were customary in their western homeland. Under this stimulus the colonization went forward rapidly in its two main streams of peasants, who tilled and reaped the soil, and of knights, who became landlords in return for measured military services owed their landlord-in-chief, the margrave. At the same time, at crossroads or along navigable rivers, small walled towns came into existence, endowed with substantial self-governing privileges. Altogether it was a characteristically medieval society that arose, organized on a primitive subsistence basis and living mainly by barter or exchange in kind. Its greatest peril was the inclination of the knights to hold the profession of arms in such high esteem that they practiced it in and out of season either, with a certain regard for the rules of chivalry, against each other or, without so much as a trace of courtliness and on no higher level than blackmail and murder, against the two unarmed classes, the peasants and the townsfolk. The reader will remember that the numerous noble highwaymen using their turreted strongholds as ports of sally against merchant caravans constituted the great problem with which the first Hohenzollern elector had to wrestle before he could be installed in office. While his success was notable, he so little excised the canker that his successors were obliged to repeat his surgery from time to time throughout the remainder of the fifteenth century.

Then, toward the close of the fifteenth and the beginning of the sixteenth century, the whole medieval setup began to yield to influences which, without destroying, greatly altered it. They sprang from the socioeconomic revolution which, identified with the phase of Western civilization called the Renaissance, swept

Europe, leaving no part of it untouched. Even relatively remote Brandenburg could not escape the revolutionary impact, although it should not be overlooked that here as everywhere else its action, while of a general, was also of a particular kind, in keeping with the particular conditions encountered. Of these determining local conditions we may select two for special consideration: By the beginning of the sixteenth century the elector had waxed strong enough completely to stamp out the lawless elements of the knighthood, thereby securing the peace of the land; and precisely at this time the new money economy, which had already replaced the ancient barter economy in the older parts of Germany, began to make its way into Brandenburg.

As new agencies do not transform a society at a stroke, we shall have to allow several generations for their permeation of the mark. The core of the fermenting process was the dominant order of the knights. We have just heard of the elector's success in at last stamping out their traditional lawlessness. While he thus closed an illegitimate bypath which they had been following in pursuit of a livelihood, they were struck an even more telling blow by a synchronously occurring change in the customs of warfare. Mercenary troops making a steadily increasing use of firearms gradually replaced the ancient feudal levy, and the armored knight mounted on horseback, who for several hundred years had been the mainstay of every European army, saw his importance, and with it his occupation, pass away.

In these circumstances the knights of Brandenburg turned to agriculture as an occupation and were encouraged to persist in their new course by the money economy just coming to the fore. This enabled them to make money profits from the crops grown on their land and to apply them to a wide choice of comforts and luxuries to which they had hitherto been strangers. In short, somewhat belatedly they experienced the impact of the new capitalist society already well established in the regions to the south and west of them and began the reorganization of their lives in accordance with its requirements.

To make that reorganization intelligible, we must once more go back to our starting-point, to the colonization of the east Elbian region. On that occasion the cultivable land was distributed among peasant villagers, each villager receiving a farmstead of varying size to which he was given hereditary title and from which he could not be removed save with his own consent. However, his title was not an absolute title, since he paid annual dues, usually in kind, to a knight settled on an estate of his own close to the village and who, on the strength of the dues paid him by the villagers, was regarded by the law as coproprietor of the peasant holdings. In addition to the annual rental dues, each villager owed his lord a moderate number of days' labor each year to be rendered in the case of the poorer villager with his hands, in the case of the richer villager with cart and horses. This is of course a generalized picture with a wide range of variation in detail.

In this system the immediate land of the knight, the demesne, being relatively small in extent, could be taken care of with the modest labor service provided by the peasants; and the knight himself could live in the frugal medieval fashion on what he himself grew on the demesne supplemented by the rental deliveries of his village dependents. But with the passing of medieval warfare and with the new money economy awakening desires unknown in simpler times the knight was not only pointedly directed to the soil but also to the need of deriving more abundant returns from it, and the only measures calculated to realize this novel ambition were the enlargement of the demesne and the increase of the obligatory labor service of the peasants.

It is agreed by the special students of this development that it set in at scattered points and almost imperceptibly in the second half of the fifteenth century and that by the first half of the following century it had already visibly and generally worked its way through the mark. The main steps have been made reasonably clear by the surviving documents. The usual initial measure of the land-hungry lords was to appropriate and add to the demesne the considerable wastelands that either had never yet been brought under the plow or, having once been cultivated, had by the accidents of chance and time been again abandoned. Not improbably they could prefer some sort of claim to them and might by a liberal interpretation of the law be regarded as acting within their rights in taking them over. Next, still bent on increase, their eyes fastened on such peasant land adjoining the demesne as would conveniently round it off. Let us remember that the knight was coproprietor with the peasant and under circumstances specified by either law or custom was permitted to acquire peasant land by purchase. While the transaction, to be legal, required the peasant's consent, it is more than probable that the consent was usually given under pressure, being obtained by the employment of the kind of extra-legal persuasion that is and always has been at the disposal of a social and political superior in dealing with a neighbor admittedly and traditionally beneath him.

And now let us ask what were all these increases of the knight's immediate holding, his demesne, worth without a parallel increase in the labor supply? Therefore again by extra-legal pressure and by barely noticeable stages the labor traditionally owed the lord was enlarged until it grew from its early extremely modest total per year to a heavy toll of several days per week. The number of days to which the labor requirement was finally expanded varied considerably from district to district. It would seem, on the average, to have grown to three or four days per week; but in certain overwhelmingly landlord-dominated regions, such as the Neu- and Uckermark, all checks were apparently removed and the peasant, owing all his workdays to the lord, lost his holding altogether since he no longer had at his disposal the time necessary for its cultivation. Such a onetime freehold peasant experienced a drop in the social scale until, economically, he had become indistinguishable from a day laborer.

To complete the conquest of the peasant, it remained to deprive him of his legal status, which guaranteed him freedom of movement, and to attach him permanently to the soil. This, too, having by the same policy of stealthy encroachment been effected in the fatal century between 1450 and 1550, the process by which the originally free and proprietary peasant fell into the bondage of a particularly severe form of serfdom was completed. While throughout the rest of Europe, including the western and southern sections of Germany, the commercial revolution, of which the replacement of barter by money was an outstanding feature, was attended by a mitigation of the medieval serfdom of the peasants, over the whole broad expanse of the north German plain, including therefore our territory of Brandenburg, this same revolution had the precisely opposite effect and converted a relatively free body of peasants into serfs deprived of their original property and personal rights and obliged to support an unusually cruel burden of obligatory services.

Long before reaching this point, the reader will have been asking himself in puzzled amazement why the ruler of Brandenburg permitted these violences of one class of his subjects against another class, when, as lord of the land and fountain of justice, his sworn duty was to hinder them. We have insisted that the course followed by the knights developed gradually; in point of fact it did not appear fully in the open until the reign of Joachim II (1535–71). Of this elector we have already taken note in treating of the Reformation, for it was he who established the Lutheran form of worship in Brandenburg. We have now to learn that it was in his time too that the usurpations of the knights, conducted for several generations in a half-concealed and unsystematic manner, were brought into the clear and that, in spite of an occasional twinge of conscience, the ruler ended by formally confirming the degradation of the peasants the gentry had effected. The reason is not far to seek. To begin with, Joachim was a landlord himself, with a natural sympathy for the members of his class; and, a still more decisive factor, by permitting his finances to fall into disorder, he delivered himself, bound hand and foot, over to the local parliament, of which the knights were the major determining element.

At this point we come up against the Brandenburg constitution which, like medieval constitutions in general, was not a written document but a body of customary practices. Also like them, it gave the power of the purse to the estates of the realm in parliament assembled. In the case of Brandenburg the estates had, after the elimination by the Reformation of the Catholic prelates, been effectively reduced to two, the knights and the towns, and their parliament was called *Landtag* or diet. The revenue theory of the diet, again as everywhere else in Europe, was that the elector should live "of his own," that is, he should content himself with the returns from the manors constituting his private domain and from the so-called "regalia," formerly belonging to the emperor and consisting of such items as way tolls and the mint. However, in case of a special and unforeseen event, as for instance the defense of the realm, the elector might summon the estates and request them to authorize a levy of money calculated to meet the exceptional outlay.

Now Joachim II, a display- and pomp-loving gentleman, had no sooner begun to wield the scepter than he contracted debts—huge debts considering the poverty of the mark—and they were in no single instance due to war, the outstanding occasion for which the practice of the past permitted him to approach the Landtag with the request for a subsidy. Throughout his life Joachim scrupulously avoided war and, reasonably enough, made much of his love of peace and the benefits it conferred on the mark whenever he summoned his parliament. On such occasions he pleaded that he deserved to be rewarded for his pacifism by being relieved of the burden of debt that was crushing him. In further argument he would then justify his lapse from good housekeeping by reference to the changed times which had brought new governmental duties and called for an ampler scale of living on the part of the ruler. On concluding his address he had to listen to some rather cutting talk by his parliamentary critics on the subject of his poor management and careless, spendthrift ways. In the end the estates agreed to take over his debts but on very hard terms. They insisted on themselves both collecting the taxes they voted and satisfying the debts they assumed, and in pursuit of this purpose they created a financial administration of their own called the *Creditwerk*. It can be seen at a glance that the Creditwerk was nothing less than an administrative revolution, since it signified the appropriation on the part of the Landtag of the public finances (or the better part of the public finances) from which the elector was henceforth as good as eliminated.

Nor is that the whole story of Joachim's fateful defeat at the hands of the Landtag. While, as we are aware, representatives of the towns sat in the diet together with representatives of the knights, the latter in a prevailingly agrarian community like Brandenburg completely overshadowed their humbler urban colleagues. Consequently, it was chiefly the knights who had to be won over by the elector when, as happened not once but repeatedly, he appealed to his diet to be freed of his debts. Fully aware that they had him at their mercy, the landowners coolly demanded as a return favor that he sanction every violence against the peasants of which they and their predecessors had been cumulatively guilty. Joachim's character figured in his surrender. He was a soft, overfat, easygoing man, who loved lavish expenditures for their own sake and was childishly delighted with the smiling faces which they induced among his courtiers. The consequence was that before he died he had through his weak-kneed dealings with his Landtag brought about two political and social translocations so important that they must, even at the risk of repetition, be distinctly set out: He had permitted the public finances to pass into the all but exclusive control of the diet, and he had put the stamp of his approval on a development of long standing by which the former warrior group of knights had been converted into a money-minded landlord body in unfettered control of the land and its workers. The change in the status of this class, now more dominant than ever, was effectively rendered by a change of title that gained general currency about this time. Known to the ancient law as *Ritter*, that is, as knights, they were henceforth referred to in common parlance as *Junkers,* that is, as gentlemen (literally, young gentlemen) and broadly equivalent to noblemen; and it was in this glamorous social light and no longer in that of rude feudal warriors that their countrymen, and particularly the peasant serfs, viewed them from this time.

In this story of the progressive decline of the social, juridical, and economic status of the peasants, the occasional professional reader, into whose hands this book may come, will miss the presence of such terms as *leibeigen, Leibeingenschaft,* and similar abstractions much tossed about by German scholars in their heated and still continuing debate over the agricultural developments in Brandenburg and the whole German colonial area. They have been intentionally omitted because, subject to varying definitions, they confuse rather than clarify the situation for the general reader, who will be properly curious about the main circumstances that reduced the free peasant to a soil-bound serf but whose understanding of the transformation would be obstructed rather than promoted by the introduction of contentious technicalities.

THE DUCHY OF PRUSSIA

Eastward of Brandenburg, but completely separated from it by a seaward wedge of the kingdom of Poland, lay the duchy of Prussia. Belonging, like Brandenburg, to the north European plain. it closely resembled the mark in its physical aspects, being a level country of pastures, swamps, and lakes and covered, wherever the ancient glacial sands asserted their rule, with somber pine forests. In important distinction from Brandenburg, however, it was not a landlocked province, since by having the Baltic as its northern boundary it commanded a fairly spacious window on that sea. The special feature of the coast were two large, lagoon-like bays, the *Frische Haff* and the *Kurische Haff*, which covered almost its whole length but were shut off from direct contact with the Baltic by long, narrow spits of sand, like protective sea walls, called *Nehrungen.* Communication between the two inclosed bays and the Baltic Sea was by bottleneck openings in the Nehrungen, the opening for the Fische Haff being at Pillau, that for the Kurische Haff at Memel. Accordingly, Pillau and Memel, as the exclusive gates of entry to the duchy from the seaside, were of special importance. For Pillau, but not for Memel, there was a supplementary entrance located farther inland at Köningsberg.

Because Königsberg, while close to Pillau, was also on the navigable Pregel River, it had become the largest town of the duchy and the seat of its government. As might be expected, towns throughout Prussia were small and thinly sown and both economically and socially counted for no more than those of Brandenburg. Apart from the three towns already mentioned, it will suffice to list Marienwerder on the Vistula and Tilsit on the Niemen, especially as naming them brings out the fact that the duchy extended from the Vistula in the west (on which river, it is true, it had but the barest foothold) to and a little beyond the Niemen in the east. Between Vistula and Niemen rolled the great plain which had, as far as feasible, been either broken to the plow or turned to pasture for the raising of cattle and horses. Agriculture and grazing, with forestry added, employed, as they had from the start of the German settlement, the bulk of the population which, after the usual manner of an agricultural group untraversed by animating routes of trade, was a stoutly conservative society disinclined to innovations.

And yet it was not an unchanging society. Indeed, no later than the Reformation period, which on the accession of Frederick William in 1640 was only just coming to a close, it had swung from the Catholic to the Lutheran form of worship, while before and during this period it had gradually effected the identical socioeconomic transformation of which we have taken note in the case of Brandenburg. Since Brandenburg and Prussia, having been colonized at about the same time and on similar terms, greatly resembled each other in social structure, it was, to say the least, highly probable that they would respond in an identical manner to the forces released by the Renaissance phase of Western civilization. We have already set forth in some detail how under influences active just before and after 1500 the ancient relationship between the knights and the peasants of Brandenburg had been profoundly altered. We may therefore spare ourselves useless repetition by declaring summarily that the social upheaval already described in the case of Brandenburg was duplicated in Prussia and that, when it had done its work, the once relatively free Prussian peasantry, exactly like its Brandenburg kin, had been shorn of most of its rights and had been permanently attached to the soil under a peculiarly rigorous form of serfdom.[4]

Having greatly enlarged their estates and provided themselves at the same time with a cheap and steady supply of farm labor, the former warrior class of knights, transformed as in the mark into land-exploiting Junkers, completely dominated the Prussian scene. They had of course always figured importantly in the Landtag, but with their increased economic strength they were encouraged to go further and to encroach on the prerogative of their duke until they had obliged him to share the government with them. Their victory was made possible by a circumstance already related and never, if we are intelligently to follow the Prussian internal

4. For the, after all, not unimportant differences in the agricultural situation of Brandenburg and Prussia see "The Rise of the Junkers in Brandenburg-Prussia (1410–1653)," by Hans Rosenberg, *American Historical Review,* XLIX, Nos. 1 and 2. The author has an impressive command of the sources (cited in the footnotes) and gives a detailed account of currents and countercurrents of which our story is content to record the resulting agricultural revolution.

developments, to be again lost from view. In order to establish the duchy at all, its first duke, installed in office in 1525, had been obliged to become the vassal of the king of Poland. This meant that he was under the constant scrutiny of his powerful close neighbor and overlord and that the diet could bring a highly effective pressure to bear on him by appealing over his head to his suzerain in any issue that might arise. In this manner the king of Poland had repeatedly in the sixteenth century interfered in the quarrels between duke and Landtag to the notable advantage of himself and his parliamentary ally and to the signal discomfiture of their common opponent.

By the time Frederick William succeeded to the duchy, the accumulated agreements between vassal and overlord, which in their sum made up the Prussian constitution, had whittled down the duke's power to such a degree that he was not any longer even remotely a free agent. For one thing, to the original privilege of the diet to vote supplies had been added the acknowledged right to carry any difference of opinion between ruler and estates to the judgment bar of the king of Poland; and, an even graver matter, the duke was enjoined from making any foreign commitments without the previous consent of *both* diet and suzerain. If we add that, before these later servitudes were laid on the ducal office, it had already been fettered by a body of restrictions deriving from an unusually severe definition of vassalage, we are made aware that, on the death of his father, Frederick William came into possession in Prussia of an office largely honorary and that his diet and suzerain between them would strain every nerve to keep him in the dependence to which for their mutual advantage he had been successfully reduced.

THE DUCHY OF CLEVE-MARK

The duchy of Cleve-Mark, composed of the originally distinct territories of the duchy of Cleve and the county of Mark, had in the fourteenth century achieved a working union by means of a common ruler and Landtag. Though not exactly contiguous, they lay within easy hail of each other since they both belonged to the extreme northwest corner of Germany, adjoining the Dutch Netherlands. Cleve, which straddled the Rhine River, was, like the neighboring Netherlands, a level country of rich pastures; while Mark, to the east of Cleve and unwashed by the Rhine, was a picturesque region of hills and valleys covered with dense forests interspersed with waving grainfields and lush meadows.

The river Ruhr flowed through Mark on its way to the Rhine, and with the name there will at once leap to the reader's mind pictures of the industrial might of contemporary Germany. Of this there was in the seventeenth century as yet no trace, since the time was not ripe for exploiting the invaluable treasures of coal buried beneath the sod and timber of the valley. However, both Mark and Cleve possessed, and had possessed for centuries, a considerable number of towns, such as Wesel, Cleve, Duisburg, Soest, which, though small, were lively centers of commerce and industry. In evidence of their vitality they asserted an influence within the borders of the state which, an unusual achievement in the Germany of that day, enabled them to hold their own against the landed nobility. As territories of the older and more fertile Germany, Cleve and Mark were more densely populated, more flourishing, and, economically, more diversified than the two Hohenzollern properties in the poorer colonial east. Nevertheless, their small extent kept them from even approximately reaching the importance for the ruling dynasty of the much larger Brandenburg and Prussia.

On assuming the rule of Cleve-Mark, Frederick William faced difficulties that must have looked to the world in general to be insurmountable. To begin with, his very title was in dispute with the rival duke of Pfalz-Neuburg. We have learned in an earlier chapter that in 1614, by the agreement of Xanten, his grandfather, John Sigismund, got possession of Cleve-Mark (together with tiny Ravensberg), while at the same time reaffirming his claim to the whole undivided dominion of the recently deceased duke of Jülich. Since Neuburg, who by the Xanten treaty was put in occupation of the two duchies of Jülich and Berg, just as stubbornly insisted on his right to the total inheritance undiminished by a jot or tittle, subsequent negotiations between the two contestants did not get beyond periodic renewals of the Xanten partition with at best in each instance a few minor adjustments. The consequence was not only that the ill will between the two ruling families fiercely persisted but also that their subjects in either allotted area became confused in their allegiance. Since Jülich and Berg, in the main Catholic territories, had been acquired by a Catholic prince and Cleve and Mark, in the main Protestant lands (Lutheran and Reformed), by a Protestant prince, the provisional settlement appreciably lessened the probability of tension between the ruler and his subjects. But it in no way lessened the tension between the two claimants, for in the prevailing uncertainty as to who was the lawful incumbent, there was nothing to hinder the Protestant minority of Jülich and Berg from seeking the favor of the Hohenzollern claimant nor the Catholic minority of Cleve and Mark from looking wishfully toward neighboring Neuburg.

The Thirty Years' War enormously deepened the already existing confusion. The disputed properties lay on both sides of the lower Rhine and were of capital importance for every army operating in that critical segment of Europe. To mention only the more outstanding invaders: Imperial (Austrian), Spanish, and Dutch troops had almost from the beginning of the war competed with each other in getting possession of the fortresses, from which, having made themselves at home in them, they levied contributions at will against the miserable inhabitants. When Frederick William succeeded his father, this harrying of his Rhenish lands had been going on for twenty years, and the end was as yet nowhere in sight. In spite of the foreign soldiery, his father had never ceased trying to assert his rule in the territory; but, confronted with hostile armies which took what they wanted and indignant subjects whom he was powerless to protect, he characteristically contented himself in the main with loudly bemoaning his unhappy lot.

In these circumstances it was not surprising that his plundered and offended subjects should have looked about them for a way out of their misery and that the towns, above all, should have persuaded themselves that their best course would be to tie up with the nearby Dutch republic, which, constitutionally viewed, was a loose federation of seven provinces. In the opinion of many desperate townsmen of Cleve-Mark the Dutch republic would not prove averse to adding Cleve-Mark as an eighth province to the fold. Indeed, so well founded was the idea of these malcontents that the Dutch took it up with enthusiasm, and soon their occupation of such fortress as had fallen into their hands presented an alarming appearance of permanence.

Precisely as in Brandenburg, Prussia, and throughout Germany the vigorous self-esteem of the inhabitants had long ago come to expression in a Landtag composed of the two ruling estates, nobles and townsmen. In the course of the sixteenth, or Reformation, century the Cleve-Mark Landtag, like the diets throughout the Reich, had considerably strengthened its position. Then, aided by the chaos of the Thirty Years' War, it had in the course of that struggle usurped much additional power. Consequently, by the time Frederick William became ruler, the estates claimed an extraordinary sum of privileges, of which the most sweeping must be enumerated and carefully pondered. No taxes could be levied or troops maintained without their consent; under the traditional and characteristically medieval *jus indigenatus* they affirmed that only the native-born were eligible to office; they further claimed the right to come together at their pleasure without being summoned by their ruler; and, quite as if they had acquired a share of his executive authority, they felt free to negotiate with foreign states and actually maintained a permanent agent at The Hague.

Wherewith we have completed the round of the Hohenzollern lands and should be in a better position to understand not only the gravity but also the immense range of the problems confronting the young ruler as from his Königsberg lookout he let his gaze sweep over his territories which lay scattered, like seed sown by a careless hand, over the wide north German plain.

Chapter 5

BEGGAR ON HORSEBACK

THE CLASH WITH MINISTER SCHWARZENBERG

No one will want to challenge the statement that on taking up the reins of government the elector was confronted with a desperate situation. But his distressed dominions were not the sum of his perplexities. A youth aged twenty and lacking even a rudimentary experience of government, he did not, as is usual in a succession regulated by heredity, have at his command a body of trusty councilors on whom he might fall back for guidance. For the last two and a half years the government of his main dominion, Brandenburg, had been exercised with virtually independent power by Count Schwarzenberg, who, profiting from the exigencies of the war with Sweden, had in effect elevated himself to the position of a military dictator. It was he who raised the funds for the army, paid the troops, and gave the officers their orders; and, with a view to exercising his authority without interference, he had ceased consulting the supreme governing body of the province, the Privy Council. Consequently, although not abrogated, it was not functioning, and such members as had not resigned in protest against the Statthalter's policy had been scattered over Germany on special missions. In any case they were not available at Königsberg on the young prince's accession.

In this connection it needs to be noted that when Elector George William had effected his retreat to Prussia, he had taken along with him no more than a routine staff of secretaries, not one of them endowed with a vision wider than that of the average myopic bureaucrat. Neither from them nor from anyone else was effective help forthcoming to George William's successor, although a measure of spiritual solace, we may divine, reached him from his immediate family circle, composed of his mother, grandmother, and two young sisters. These devoted women gave to their son, grandson, and brother without stint what they had to give, their love and faith, but since the world of politics lay quite beyond their mental range, they could furnish him no support in his immediate labors. In brief, if ever a prince on taking over his inheritance was left to his own resources of mind and heart, it was Frederick William when, on the day after his father had forever closed his eyes, he seated himself at his father's desk in the ducal cabinet at Königsberg and took cognizance of his position.

If the problems that at once gathered like sheeted ghosts around him caused his heart to fail, he gave no evidence of it in word or action. He promptly (December 2) issued two orders,[1] showing not only that he had already elaborated a program but also that he was aware that with his loose grip on his affairs he would have to employ extreme caution in putting it into effect. The first of the two orders was addressed to Schwarzenberg and was a request couched in cordial terms to continue in his post of Statthalter of Brandenburg. The second was different: It was a secret order. It went to Conrad von Burgsdorf, commandant of the important fortress of Cüstrin on the Oder, and pledged him to see well to the defenses of this stronghold and under no circumstances to admit Imperialists, that is, allied Austrian troops, within its gates. The Statthalter was in charge of the war, and orders to the officers had thus far proceeded exclusively from him. It is therefore clear that while the young elector began his reign with a formal approval of his father's minister, he concurrently issued a command which was a subterranean thrust directed against that minister and which foreshadowed the abandonment of his policy.

Who was this Colonel Conrad von Burgsdorf whom the new ruler chose as his confidant in the execution of a program as yet undisclosed in its details but evidently opposed to that of the all-powerful governor of the mark? A native Brandenburger who in an age of war followed war as his profession, Burgsdorf had some years before taken service with his liege lord and had proved himself one of the few dependable props of the recently formed, loosely organized, and already thoroughly discredited Brandenburg army. He was a bluff soldier with the rude military manners of the

1. *UA*, I, 373 ff.; *PR*, I, 29–30.

time and, like all his kind grown to manhood among the disorders of the Thirty Years' War, rarely visited by moral scruples and ceaselessly on the alert to push his private fortunes. While serving George William, he had established close relations with the heir apparent and, encouraged perhaps by this familiarity, had, alone of all the heads of Brandenburg regiments, consistently shown himself recalcitrant to Schwarzenberg's authority. A further possible reason for his behavior may have been that, as a soldier, he was professionally averse to taking orders from a civilian. But quite the likeliest explanation of the hostility which he rarely troubled to conceal even from Schwarzenberg himself was his objection to the war with Sweden, of which he considered the governor, an impertinent Catholic intruder in Protestant Brandenburg, the moving cause. In Burgsdorf's view the mark, his beloved homeland, was being reduced to utter ruin by the Swedish war, which was now going into its fourth year and which it was imperative to find a means of ending at the earliest possible moment.

As this was also the view held by Frederick William, we have all the explanation needed for the order by which Burgsdorf was made aware that he had been virtually withdrawn from Schwarzenberg's authority to be put under the direct command of his prince. The secrecy of the proceeding shows that an open breach with Schwarzenberg was to be avoided, at least for the time being, owing to his strongly intrenched position coupled with the dark suspicion that he might not hesitate forcibly to resist an attempt to remove him from office. Indeed, so steeped in distrust of this unwelcome *alter ego* was Frederick William that he was convinced that he was himself in danger of being removed by the ambitious count and, what is more, that at least one such attempt had already been made. The event had occurred some two years earlier on the occasion of the return of the young prince from the Netherlands. At a banquet given in his honor in the high style characteristic of the Rhenish-born grandee, Frederick William had been taken violently ill and ever afterward believed he had been the victim of a poison plot.

This and later suspicions of a similar extravagant character may be waived by us as nothing other than the customary emotional by-products of sharp political conflict. It is not these baseless delusions but the political cleavage between Schwarzenberg and his young master, latent as yet but irrepressible in the long run, that alone merits attention. The heir apparent, become sovereign, was set on reversing his predecessor's policy. But he did not dare promptly to come out with his plan, above all to Schwarzenberg himself, because of the great, if imponderable, hazards involved. The plan in general terms may be put thus: While maintaining continued friendly relations with his ally in the Swedish war, his liege, the emperor, he would try to reach an understanding with the Swedes by which Brandenburg would be withdrawn from the war and be given that respite from torment which the reduced and exhausted population demanded with a single voice.

Withholding his project from Schwarzenberg and yet resolved to carry it through, Frederick William was after some ambiguous weeks obliged to put his cards boldly on the table. He thereupon apprised the count of his proposal to negotiate a truce with the Swedes and ordered him in preparation for the event to cease offensive warfare and cut down the intolerable financial burden of the mark by reducing the army to garrison proportions.[2] The cat was out of the bag! And the disconcerted Statthalter recognized that the crisis, of which his sharp intelligence had not failed to forewarn him, had arrived. In an earnest and dignified reply, dated February 10, 1641, he went searchingly over the elector's plan. While he was opposed to every feature of it and frankly said so, he begged and implored, if the elector was set on the Swedish armistice, at least not to inaugurate the negotiations with a reduction of his already slender forces. Such an act, he declared, could have no other effect on the enemy than to cause him to stiffen his terms. From the anxious, the almost shrill tone of the communication, it is clear that Schwarzenberg did not believe he could turn his master from his purpose or avoid a final break with him. The head-on collision provoked a furious inner tumult that refused to be quieted, and, on being seized with a fever,[3] he declined rapidly and died after a few days, on March 14, 1641.

2. *UA*, I, 403 ff.; and Schwarzenberg's reply, *ibid.*, pp. 412 ff.

3. "Horrorem febrilem," says the report of his illness, published *PR*, I, 184.

THE POLICY OF NEUTRALITY RUNS INTO A SNAG

Fate, not his own bold initiative, had removed the stone of stumbling from the elector's path, and he was free to carry out his program without further opposition in his own camp. The dispersed Brandenburg Privy Council was reconstituted with enemies of the deceased former favorite (and, by presumption, friends of the new ruler) and was intrusted with the conduct of affairs until the arrival at Berlin of the margrave Ernst, a young man in the early twenties, whom his still younger cousin, the elector, named as Schwarzenberg's successor. To make sure of the Council's exact adherence to the orders issued from Königsberg, Burgsdorf, the trusted representative of the elector with the army, was promoted to a Council seat.

And now the unobstructed prosecution of the new policy began, greatly aided after his arrival by Statthalter Ernst, who proved to be a tireless and circumspect administrator. The measure offering the greatest difficulty was the reduction of the army, since many of the colonels were Schwarzenberg's partisans and threatened to mutiny if their contracts were not minutely respected. Had it not been for the popularity of Burgsdorf with the common soldiers, the discontented officers might well have gone the length of an assault upon the government. The crisis continued through the summer but ended happily for the new Statthalter with the voluntary departure of some of the troublemakers and the precipitate flight of a number of others too seriously compromised to hope to be let off without trial by military court. The two thousand troops retained in service barely sufficed to garrison Cüstrin, Spandau, and the few other fortresses the Swedes had not yet occupied, but they were a soldier nucleus which, under the energetic leadership of Conrad von Burgsdorf, could be trusted faithfully to stand by its oath and flag.

The armistice negotiations with the Swedes ran parallel to the reduction of the army and on July 14 culminated in the signing of an agreement. Its terms were hard. While the Swedes were to retain the Brandenburg fortresses already in their possession and to be furnished supplies for the army of occupation in liberal amounts, they were not to be bound by these arrangements until after the treaty had been formally ratified. And this ratification the government at Stockholm continually adjourned. The result was that when a new and fiercely determined general, the famous Torstensson, was put in command of the Swedish forces in Germany, he started an offensive against the main or, rather, the only Swedish enemy, the emperor, in pursuit of which he pushed his troops into every section of the mark of Brandenburg that suited his convenience. To the outraged protests of Statthalter Ernst, he was able to answer with a shrug of his shoulders that the armistice was not binding because not ratified. Planned as a first step toward peace, the Brandenburg-Swedish armistice, instead of the hoped-for respite, brought only fresh sufferings on the province and its miserable inhabitants.

Torstensson passed on into Silesia after a while in prosecution of his purpose to deliver a capital blow against the emperor; but the oppressive Swedish exactions continued unabated. An embassy dispatched by Frederick William in the spring of 1642 to Stockholm with the frantic appeal to speed up the ratification brought no result. In the capital of the plundered mark the situation became so desperate that it was no longer possible to count on procuring a supply of the most meager necessities for the governor's private table. Although in the first flush of youth, Margrave Ernst had for years been afflicted with ill health. Incapable of resisting the Swedish exactions and obliged to listen to his countrymen's frantic appeals for relief without being able to help them, he pleaded despairingly with his cousin in distant Prussia to be relieved of an office that kept him perpetually on the rack. Presently his enfeebled constitution gave way, his overwrought nerves snapped, and barely a year after his assumption of office he died in a paroxysm of insanity (October 4, 1642).

By this time it had begun to dawn on the young man at Königsberg that he had made a mistake to disarm prior to effecting a definitive truce with the Swedes. He had been duly warned on this head by the experienced Schwarzenberg, but so sweeping had been his distrust of the minister that he was prompted almost automatically to reject advice of any and every kind emanating from that source. It is not recorded that, following the fiasco of the Swedish armistice, he did his dead opponent belated justice; but it is clear from his conduct of his office from this first capital miscalculation forward to the end of his days that he had learned the lesson Schwarzenberg had tried to impart, to wit, that negotiators, who, themselves unarmed, sit down at the council table with armed men, come off not only stripped of coat and shirt but heaped with ridicule into the bargain.

The unhappy situation continued unchanged until a turn in the affairs of Sweden brought a measure of relief. To no state had the rise of the northern power to European eminence given greater displeasure than to its Scandinavian neighbor, Denmark. After repeated exhibitions of bad temper, King Christian of Denmark now struck a bolder attitude and opened negotiations with the Catholic emperor looking toward an eventual participation in the German war on the emperor's side. As soon as the Swedish government, committed ever since Gustavus Adolphus' death to the capable hands of Chancellor Oxenstierna, got wind of this maneuver, it resolved to anticipate the Danish action by falling on Denmark before that state had completed its preparations for the coming war. This involved the withdrawal of the Swedish army under Torstensson from Silesia and Moravia, where it had been operating against Austria, to dispatch it northward into Jutland. Consequently, it became imperative to render the proposed new Swedish front facing Denmark more secure by a friendlier relationship with Brandenburg. To Frederick William's gratified surprise the Swedes of their own accord reopened the inconclusive conversations touching the armistice and offered a number of alleviations. It is not recorded that they even now ratified the agreement; but the omission of that technicality could be overlooked, since henceforth they not only were at more pains to observe its terms, but in the course of the year 1644 actually eased their hold on their victim by giving him back two of his fortresses they had seized, Frankfurt and Crossen. True, they remained in occupation of a number of others equally important and drew from the country for their support large stipulated amounts of money and provisions; also, not to be forgotten, since no peace had been concluded, they continued officially at war with the occupied country. Unofficially, however, the war may be said to have come to an end for tormented Brandenburg in the summer of 1643 and to have permitted it, five years before the general peace, to set its feet slowly, oh so very slowly, on the road to recovery.

WHY FREDERICK WILLIAM LINGERED ON IN PRUSSIA

By the time the unexpected Swedish amenities sent a first ray of light through the gloom that had so long hung over the country, Frederick William had arrived at Berlin and taken the government into his own hands (March 4, 1643). Wherewith we may at last take account of the question the reader will have impatiently been asking himself this long while: Why, if Brandenburg was the crucial Hohenzollern province, did its sovereign remain as though rooted in distant Prussia and govern the anguished mark *in absentia,* than which there is no form of rule more calculated to stir its victims to bitterness and discontent. The answer is not far to seek. Prussia, uninvolved in the German war, was at peace and, a matter not to be treated lightly, yielded Frederick William and his court what Brandenburg was hardly any longer able to do, a relatively secure subsistence. However, falling far more heavily into the scales was the fact that with his father's death the son was duke of Prussia only in name and, according to the strict letter of the law, was disqualified from exercising rule until he had done homage to his suzerain, the king of Poland. The most immediate, therefore, of the innumerable necessities under which the harassed ruler labored was to secure the investiture of Prussia with the least possible delay. In the most favorable case much time would unavoidably be consumed over the new treaty wherein lord and vassal would be obliged to adjust their claims and counterclaims and to which their respective signatures would have to be set before the decisive act of homage would even be made a topic of discussion.

With his conspicuous good sense Frederick William immediately on his accession broached the issue which the king, in distinction from the duke, had every interest to treat dilatorily in the hope of wearing down the harassed petitioner until he had been induced to accept an increased measure of dependence. However, when the duke put up a stiff front against this policy and refused to let himself be intimidated, the king slowly beat a retreat and finally agreed to enfeoff the prince on substantially the same terms as his predecessors. With these preliminaries disposed of Frederick William set out for Poland and on October 8, 1641, almost a year after his accession, took the oath of fealty to his overlord in a colorful ceremony at Warsaw. In the young prince's own eyes the spectacular event was a crushing humiliation viewed by a gloating crowd of idle onlookers. Its bitterness grew rather than diminished with the passing of time and led in the sequel to tremendous consequences.

An early and revealing, if minor, consequence may be related without delay. It involved the port dues of Pillau and Memel, which constituted one of the most important items of the ducal revenues. In one of his frequent moments of weak submissiveness the elector's father, George William, had agreed to an innovation, which was to share (for a limited period, it is true) the customs collected at these Prussian harbors with his overlord of Poland. Although Frederick William shortly after his accession apprised the Polish king that he planned to terminate this arrangement so injurious to his treasury, he was obliged to reverse himself and confirm its renewal in order to get the indispensable enfeoffment. Accordingly, for the next five years, with an irritation that can be left to the imagination, he diverted half of his port collections to the royal treasury at Warsaw. Then in 1646, by not so much as a preliminary by-your-leave, he arrogated the dues exclusively to himself; and as the king of Poland, handicapped to the point of paralysis by a situation within his country which we shall have to reserve to a later chapter, contented himself with voicing a feeble protest, Frederick William came off victor in the contest. It was an earnest of other and far greater victories over his suzerain in the years ahead.

On his return from Warsaw to Königsberg, the young prince faced a struggle with his Prussian diet no whit less important than the one just concluded with the king of Poland. Both knights and townsmen of the duchy of Prussia nursed a deep-seated grudge against him on account of his adherence to the Reformed faith, which was anathema to their narrowly bounded Lutheranism. Much as it went against the grain of the new ruler he had, before he could make any headway with them at all, solemnly to confirm the exclusion of the Reformed faith from among the legally tolerated forms of Christian worship. Similar tension developed over the oath of fealty due to each duke at his accession. While, following the Warsaw enfeoffment, it could not be legally refused, it could be and was delayed by the estates until they had been sweepingly confirmed in all their traditional rights.

Burningly aware of his impotence, Frederick William recognized that his best course in the precarious situation he faced would be to build up the revenues over which he had the right to dispose without the previous permission of the diet. In distinction from Brandenburg and Cleve-Mark, Prussia was at peace and, as we have seen, had the considerable merit of yielding the returns that enabled him and his court to live. Agriculture and commerce were relatively prosperous, and in each of these activities he had an important personal stake. We have just noted his interest in the customs dues collected at Pillau and Memel. We may now add that, exactly as in Brandenburg and Cleve-Mark, his most sizable single item of income was from the manors constituting the ducal domain. When he found that his purse would profit by leasing these properties to entrepreneurs instead of operating them on his own account, he did not hesitate to do so. In short, he contented himself for the present to play the part of the submissive executive and the thrifty householder, for that was manifestly the only part he could play until the time when a more abundant flow of revenue would enable him to step out more boldly.

THE NEW ELECTOR'S THEORY AND PRACTICE OF GOVERNMENT

On leaving Prussia and establishing himself in the mark, he set up a narrowly restricted bachelor establishment in the long abandoned and sadly dilapidated castle on the Spree. His presence sufficed to communicate a fresh impetus to the whole war-torn Brandenburg administration and particularly to its leading institution, the Privy Council. In so far as he had not already filled the many vacancies in that body ascribable to Schwarzenberg's jealousy of rivals, he did so now, assigning special administrative and diplomatic tasks to the individual members and himself assiduously attending its sessions. Already at Königsberg he had developed habits of work which bored such deep grooves into his mind that they became an essential part of his being. Contemporaries of every station in life have left evidence on this head, sometimes coupled with expressions of naïve surprise that one born to so high a station should subject himself to such exacting drudgery. Desiring the greatest possible measure of instruction from the Council meetings, he invited unhampered discussion of the problem or problems that were the order of the day. However, after listening attentively to every opinion, he would decide the issue in his private cabinet and on his own responsibility.

The procedure deserves to be carefully pondered, as it suggests that he entertained a view of his office not unrelated to the doctrine of divine right as commonly held in his time. If we admit that there was nothing in this doctrine that quarreled with his practice, it is on the whole more probable that, at least in the early years, he still thought of himself rather in the vaguely patriarchal terms of the Christian Middle Ages as the *Landesvater*, the father of his people, under sacred obligation to protect their lives and property and to promote their well-being. However, with accumulating experience his conception of his function became notably less traditional and reflected the influence of the views on government current in his time. Somewhat past the middle of his reign, when *le roi soleil*, the Sun King, was already dazzling Europe, Frederick William came forward with a political declaration which we may accept as the highest insight in this department that he succeeded in attaining. He voiced his judgment in the form of a Latin sentence dictated to his son and heir: "Sic gesturus sum principatum ut sciam rem populi esse, non mean privatam" (I mean to conduct my state in the conviction that it does not belong to me but to the people). A somewhat surprising avowal in the general context of that age! Not only does it breathe an unusual moral fervor, but it falls on the ear almost like a challenge of the divine-right doctrine, pure and simple, that was just then surging everywhere to the front and to which the magnificent Louis XIV presently gave its classical expression in his famous *l'état c'est moi.* Must we not conclude that if Frederick William, a son of the seventeenth century, was in full accord with the absolutism of his age, he was minded to practice it with a difference?

Important as theories of government at all times are as points of reference, they never offer more than an imperfect explanation of the decisions a chief of state is obliged to make from day to day and hour to hour under the most diverse, complicated, and ever shifting pressures. The outstanding factor in this unbroken chain of acts is invariably the individual himself who matches his wits against the forces dominant in his day and triumphs or succumbs in measure as he bends or fails to bend them to his purpose. If Frederick William deserves a place in history, it is because he belongs to the successful and, by implication, creative type of statesman. And this means further that, in distinction from the common run of political mankind, not only did he possess sharp powers of analysis and an anchored, balanced character but he also could on occasion become completely anchorless and unbalanced in consequence of the eruption from his depths of a smoldering volcanic fire. This we may call the irrational or demonic component of his being which defies exact valuation but of which we may unhesitatingly say that it regularly distinguishes the innovator among statesmen and is the true source of the energy which enables him to overcome the obstacles heaped in his path.

Apart, therefore, from his measurable endowment of heart and mind, there was in Frederick William a rare and incalculable central spark. As the free gift of the capricious gods, it must have been planted in him at his birth and have been present when he mounted the throne. But as our story will disclose, it remained dimmed and obscure during his early years, perhaps because, wounded in his self-esteem by the rebuffs he had suffered at the hands of his father, he had become distrustful of his youth and inexperience. True, by at once abandoning his father's policy, he showed that he was not without a will of his own; but he needed to be sustained in the course to which he inclined by the encouragement of an older man endowed with a more self-centered and confident spirit.

This welcome and necessary helper he found in Colonel Burgsdorf, who, in a nation and country that through the terrible attrition of war had gone morally to pieces, had developed the stout self-reliance which in the prevailing flux was the best, in fact, the only, assurance of survival. That Burgsdorf also exhibited the soldier vices of the age, that he was given to drunkenness and gambling, was a regrettable by-product of his mercenary career which in no way diminished his good opinion of himself. While the young elector was neither drunkard, gambler, nor, let us not fail to add, a libertine, was indeed on all these counts a veritable paragon in that disordered age, he was nonetheless magnetically attracted to the solid mass of resolution that was Burgsdorf. We have already seen that he picked the doughty colonel to head the opposition to the all-powerful Schwarzenberg and that, on Schwarzenberg's death, he promoted him, though totally without political experience, to the Privy Council. His favor reached its highest pitch when, in tribute to their close relationship and as a pledge of its continuance, he conferred on Burgsdorf the high court dignity of *Oberkammerherr* or lord chamberlain. For the whole first decade of the elector's reign Burgsdorf appears not only as his prince's leading adviser but also, especially in the early years of the decade, as his bosom companion and crony.

Importantly as the favorite figured in Brandenburg affairs during that decade, it would be a mistake to imagine that he became the dictator of his prince's policy; for Frederick William never permitted any doubt to arise that he was laying his own course. However, perpetually threatened by grave perils regardless of what winds he sailed by, he was cheered by the support of the swaggering buccaneer, who was forthright and outspoken and tempered his braggadocio with more than a pinch of native shrewdness. After a ten-year association Frederick William had got out of the self-assured colonel everything he could use and let him drop; but there can be no doubt that he owed a great deal to the support of Burgsdorf at a time when he had not yet by a successful exercise of authority validated his understanding and courage in his own eyes.

FREDERICK WILLIAM CREATES AN ARMY AND FORMULATES HIS WAR AIMS

From the policy with which he initiated his reign the elector did not again depart. We know what that policy was: He would give Brandenburg peace because it was at the end of its tether and, in the natural extension of that program, he would to the best of his ability promote the peace of the Reich for the same reason. But an immediate hitch had appeared when he disbanded his field army before concluding a binding truce with the Swedes. By continuing for two years to plunder Brandenburg in spite of the truce, the Swedes brought home to him the mistake he had made and convinced him that the measure inexorably called for by the humiliating experience was to rearm. The records of the Privy Council make it perfectly clear that by the winter of 1643–44 he had fixed definitely on this purpose and that the most vigorous support toward its execution came from the faithful Burgsdorf. Faraway Cleve supplied an advocate of equal ardor in General Norprath, a recent addition to the ranks of his advisers whom Frederick William, on discovering in him a man not afraid of facing hazards, had made his representative in the western duchy. While the program of rearmament was the elector's own, it was a bold, a forward-looking, program, and it is not surprising that he leaned, to give it effect, on two hot-blooded officers with an instinctive persuasion of the superiority of arms over words in time of war.

But soldiers, uniforms, muskets, cannon, meant money—chests and barrels of money—and where and how was he to get hold of that indispensable commodity? Well, to begin with, there was Prussia, which, lying beyond the boundaries of the Reich, was at peace and doing rather better with the financial program adopted at his accession than had been expected. In 1644 Frederick William sent Burgsdorf to Prussia with the order to get together all the money he could lay hands on and use it to assemble an armed force dependent solely on the ruler and free from the interference of the estates. Burgsdorf went ahead so energetically that after a twelve-month period he had recruited a number of brigades amounting altogether to about a thousand men.

Why should not what had succeeded in Prussia succeed in Cleve also? So the word was passed along to General Norprath to squeeze every possible penny out of every available source, out of river tolls, leases of manors, sales of timber, and, yes, if possible, out of Landtag grants, and apply the returns to armament. After Prussia and Cleve there remained Brandenburg, where in 1641, on the occasion of the dismissal of the field army, the Landtag had tentatively agreed to provide for a purely garrison force of two thousand infantry and one hundred and twenty-five cavalry. So reluctant, however, was the diet to confirm its verbal agreement that two years passed before it voted the necessary supplies. By small irregularities, which the continuing war encouraged, the elector in addition gradually assembled a bodyguard (*Leibgarde*) of five hundred musketeers which he could at his pleasure keep in attendance on his person in any of his dominions he happened to be visiting and which he never again dissolved.

The indicated formations did not of course spring lightly out of the ground like mushrooms after a rain. Nonetheless, after some two years of tireless effort important results had been achieved, for by that time there were fully equipped under Frederick William's supreme command about one thousand men in Prussia, two thousand in Cleve, and twenty-five hundred in Brandenburg—a grand total of between five thousand and six thousand men ready to take the field at a moment's notice. Admittedly, it was a small army, not remotely large enough to constitute a threat to the two powers, Sweden and Austria, that pressed upon him, but sufficient nonetheless to require them to treat him with a certain respect; and it had the further merit of enabling him to put a measure of authority behind the peace policy with which he had identified himself on his accession and from which he neither wished nor was able again to depart.

Returning to this policy, we repeat that the elector aimed at peace, yes, but he aimed also at the assured return to him of all the regions rightfully his under the ruling laws of inheritance. That meant the ultimate, unqualified delivery into his hands not only of the territories belonging to his dynasty at the outbreak of the Thirty Years' War but also of Pomerania, to which his house had fallen heir at the death (1637) of the last Pomeranian duke. It was the occupation of that province by Sweden that lay at the bottom of the war his father had undertaken in alliance with the emperor. The war had conspicuously failed and in its failure had all but engulfed Brandenburg itself in ruin. The armistice agreement with Sweden was Frederick William's frank admission that he could not hope to drive the Scandinavian power out of Pomerania by force of arms. But did the admission signify that he surrendered his claim? By no means! For even while negotiating the truce that had put him at the mercy of the Swedes, he had been busy with a cunning parallel proposal by which the Swedes were to be persuaded of their own volition to relax their double grip on his territory and his throat. It was a project with a strong dose of drama and even melodrama in it, for it contemplated nothing less than the merging of the opposed claims of Sweden and Brandenburg to Pomerania by the union of their ruling dynasties.

There was nothing harebrained about the idea since the great Gustavus in his meteor-like appearance over Germany had himself fathered it. His only child and heiress was Christina, and on meeting at Berlin his young nephew and her cousin he was so impressed with the alert appearance of the lad that he impulsively proposed the match. Although the matter had been permitted to rest since then, there was nothing extravagant or improper about reviving it the moment the twenty-year-old bachelor had acceded to the Brandenburg electorate. On the contrary, as he was his father's only son, there was a pressing dynastic reason for his early marriage; and since the ruinous war had obliged him to treat with Sweden about ending hostilities, he could without groveling before his adversary inject the marriage issue in an easy, casual way into the negotiations.

Queen Christina was at the time not yet of age, and the government rested with Chancellor Oxenstierna and the military junta. To this group the Pomeranian foothold was an indispensable feature of Swedish control not only of Germany but of the wider area of the Baltic Sea, and in their sober moments these representatives of the governing class were perfectly clear in their minds that their own and Brandenburg's claim to Pomerania were forever irreconcilable. This must be understood and never again forgotten, since it remains the basic factor in the relation of the two states, not only during the years under present consideration but for the whole long stretch of Frederick William's reign. Notwithstanding, there were moments when the calculating mind of the Swedish chancellor discovered a certain attraction in the marriage proposal which, for face-saving purposes, the envoys of Frederick William kept in shy half-concealment and never laid squarely on the table.

While Oxenstierna neither in 1641 on the first emergence of

the marriage proposal nor in any of the following years flatly rejected it, neither on that first occasion nor afterward did he let it move him to relax the hold the war had given him on unlucky Brandenburg. To Oxenstierna, Sweden's interests came first and foremost. Beside them everything else sank completely out of sight. But as it was to the advantage of his country not unnecessarily to offend the suitor, already sufficiently humbled by the occupation of a large part of his territory, the chancellor kept him waiting at the door, so to speak, while he pondered from every conceivable angle the effects of an act of state which would elevate a contemptible (and yet not too contemptible) German prince and neighbor to the Swedish throne. Since in that case Brandenburg was almost certainly bound to disappear within the greater power and the whole cantankerous quarrel to be in this manner magically put to sleep, the chancellor could never quite bring himself to terminate the negotiations with a direct refusal. However, in his more realistic mood—and that is the mood which in the long run regularly prevailed—the wily old diplomat cast far from him the notion that the hunter and his quarry could ever be divested of their fated respective roles.

Owing to the Swedish hesitations, the negotiations on the marriage project were spun out for years. The only reason the baffled and indignant elector did not break them off was that, in view of his conceded political impotence, there seemed to be no other way of getting hold of the passionately coveted Pomerania. But when at length he could no longer blind himself to the fact that the Swedes were making sport of him, he took another line, prompted and abetted by the circumstance that the long-talked-of negotiations for a general peace had at long last been inaugurated by a congress called together in the two neighboring Westphalian towns of Osnabrück and Münster. One town did not suffice for the proposed discussions, since the religious differences still burned so hotly that it was found advisable for Sweden and its Protestant clientage to assemble at Osnabrück, while the other foreign victor, France, foregathered with the Catholic principals and subordinates at Münster. By 1645 the military successes of the two partners, Sweden and France, against Emperor Ferdinand III had reached a point which made it impossible for that ruler any longer obstinately to refuse to consider peace; however, he was still sufficiently strong to reject the political and religious articles which on the opening of the congress the victors presented to him as their minimum demand. Therefore, even while the negotiations at Westphalia continued, the war, the purpose of which on the part of France and Sweden was to beat the emperor into submission to their terms, went on for three more unbearably dreary years.

THE CONGRESS OF WESTPHALIA AND THE POMERANIAN ISSUE

The details of this, the last phase of the Thirty Years' War, are our concern no more than the details of its numerous preceding phases. We linger over the closing phase largely because it is imperative not to overlook the murky, powder-pungent atmosphere enveloped in which all the parties to the war, great and small alike and therefore also Brandenburg, endlessly spun out negotiations with one another at Westphalia with the single purpose of wringing every possible selfish advantage out of the never resting exchanges. We have already taken cognizance of Frederick William's inalterable peace objective as including everything he could rightfully, meaning legally, claim. Prepared to fight for this goal with every diplomatic weapon in his armory, he had himself represented in the two obscure Westphalian towns, suddenly become the twin capitals of Europe, with what, in view of his chronic poverty, was a disproportionately splendid embassy and staff. By this extravagance he identified himself with the period wherein he lived and which with respect to its style and bearing carries the intriguing label of baroque. The baroque is best conceived as the dying phase of the Renaissance and was characterized, among other features, by an unchecked passion for private and public magnificence. Steeped like the other rulers of the age in the atmosphere of the baroque, Frederick William believed that at a reunion of all Europe he could not dispense with a display of fuss and feathers that measured up to his political pretentions.

And now we should be prepared for his revised handling of the Pomeranian question. Too weak to get anything out of the Swedes by direct negotiations—so much the deluded man had learned before his reign was a year old—he had subsequently discovered that they entertained too settled a suspicion of him ever to take seriously his suit for the hand of their queen. He would therefore act on this costly lesson, give up sending embassies to Stockholm, and drop the unsolvable Pomeranian question in the lap of the Westphalian congress. He could do this with fair hope of a not unfavorable solution, first, because Pomerania, while a Brandenburg issue, was also a general German and European one and, second, because among the vast company of Westphalian plenipotentiaries it would have to go hard indeed with him not to find friends and patrons whom the Swedes would not be able to push aside as lightly as they had him.

Nor is that the whole story of his revised policy toward his northern neighbor. With the Swedish marriage proved a will-o'-the-wisp, he would give up its pursuit for a more worth-while, because attainable, prize. And now consider: A stalwart Calvinist with a natural preference for a Calvinist bride, whither would he more readily look than to the leading Calvinist house of Europe, the house of Orange? Moreover, was he not through his mother himself descended from the famous William, founder of the line, and had he not personally renewed the family bond during his long apprentice period in the Netherlands? Finally, there was a political consideration. In marriages of reigning families it invariably ranks first and foremost, and his own case was no exception to the rule. Frederick William needed advocates at Westphalia, and after a close scrutiny of the roster of European states he concluded that no better advocate was available than the Dutch republic, which was issuing from the war as victor and which, besides, was in frequent conflict with his own enemy, with Sweden, over questions of trade in the Baltic.

Enough, in 1646 he abruptly gave up his serenade beneath the chamber of a lady who never condescended even to make a fleeting appearance at her window and applied to his old patron and kinsman, Prince Frederick Henry of Orange, for the hand of his daughter, Louise Henriette. He was so promptly accepted that the marriage could take place at The Hague on December 3 of the same year. His bride was a girl of nineteen, rather small and delicate but of good proportions and pleasing features. Owing to a previous attachment she had formed, it was not without tears and heavy misgivings that she accepted the bridegroom selected by her parents. However, this first difficulty overcome, she put herself in her husband's hands without reserve and became his devoted helpmate, content to remain politically in the background but always making her quiet strength available to him in his hours of crisis. Her evangelical piety and glad acceptance of the earthly task to which God had called her corresponded to an identical strain in her husband and lent to their relationship the fundamental seriousness on which it rested until her death after twenty years of a congenial union. It defines the sound core of her womanhood that, transplanted to the barren sands of Brandenburg, she never forgot the green pastures and colorful, orderly gardens of her Dutch homeland. In her favorite estate near Berlin, rebaptized Oranienburg after her family name, she comforted her nostalgia in a manner profitable to her adopted country by establishing a dairy farm which, stocked with imported Friesian cattle, became an admired object-lesson of efficiency and thrift to the Junker owners of the war-wasted manors of the neighborhood.

While Frederick William never had cause to be other than grateful for his Dutch bride, the political hopes that had led him to her door were not realized. His project for a firm and dependable alliance with the Dutch republic came to nothing. Prince Frederick Henry of Orange, for his part, was fully prepared to accede to his son-in-law's wish and, when Frederick Henry died some six months after his daughter's marriage, his son and successor, William II, was equally willing to be associated closely with his Brandenburg relative. However, the decisive word in Dutch affairs rested not with the house of Orange but with the burghers of the towns, and these solid merchants had an insurmountable objection to unprofitable investments. It was as such that they rated the proposed Brandenburg alliance, and they refused to warm to it even on the young elector's taking the bold step of appearing in person at a meeting of the States-General in order to extol its merits with all the eloquence at his command. Besides, they refused to forget that they had certain financial claims against the elector of which we shall presently hear and which they were extremely loath to forgo under the pressure of reciprocal political obligations. However, though they rejected his alliance offer, they were not averse to giv-

From a painting by Honthorst in the Castle of Berlin (Bettmann Archive)

LOUISE HENRIETTE OF ORANGE
First Wife of the Great Elector

Engraving of the year 1672 (Bettmann Archive)

OTTO VON GUERICKE
Inventor of the Air Pump

ing to him as to one of their own Reformed faith such backing at Westphalia and elsewhere as did not cost them anything and such as they, a victor power, could dispense by way of charity out of the plenitude of their prestige. Before long the disappointed elector gave free and frequent vent to his impatience with their cautiously reserved and ponderous High Mightinesses, but the fact nonetheless remains that he owed a number of not inconsiderable favors to their unsystematic, casual support.

One of these favors was conferred within a few months of his marriage in connection with his territory of Cleve-Mark. We have thus far dealt only scantily with Cleve-Mark in our review of his activities since his accession. That was not because he had not concerned himself with these Rhenish lands of his but rather because he was so removed from them in space and because his authority within their bounds was so feeble that it was beyond his power to make a real impression on the situation. Almost from the start of the war the armies of both Protestants and Catholics had camped on the soil of Cleve and Mark and levied contributions on its towns; and throughout that time the local Landtag had proved itself consistently unfriendly to its ruler by turning a cold shoulder to his request for supplies to enable him to maintain an adequate protective force. In so far as a native authority may be said to have at all survived the disorders of the war, it was exercised not by and for the ruler but by the estates in their own class interest.

Then in the very year of the young prince's accession, the Dutch had done him an evil turn. It is a tale of money-lending and, like all such tales, a distinctly sordid affair. Four years before the outbreak of the Thirty Years' War, that is, as far back as 1614, a Dutch banker by the name of Hofyser had lent Frederick William's grandfather the sum of one hundred thousand talers at 7 per cent. The interest having been paid only rarely in the troubled times that followed, principal and interest, according to Hofyser, had swelled by 1640 to about five times the original debt. At this juncture and at Hofyser's instance the Dutch government took a hand in the game and sternly demanded a settlement. The demand figured not unimportantly in the general crisis that Frederick William faced at his accession. All he could do about it, in view of his empty coffers, was to throw up his hands in a gesture of despair. Thereupon the unperturbed Dutch had marched soldiers into Cleve, not omitting the piously annoying mention usual on such occasions of being animated by none but the friendliest intentions. Before calling a halt the invaders had taken over the tolls of a number of Rhine cities and hypothecated such private estates of the elector as lay conveniently at hand. Since up to the time of Frederick William's marriage with the Orange princess, the Dutch government had not receded from its position, it may well be that the Hofyser usury was one of the matters he hoped to have cleared up between himself and the republic in the wake of his marriage. But if so, he miscalculated, for to the four-square burgher mind money was the foundation of civilized society and a debt computed by the creditor as undebatable as the Tables of the Law.

THE JÜLICH INHERITANCE DISPUTE LEADS TO WAR (1646–47)

In another matter which occupied him at this time he was somewhat more successful in wangling support out of the ponderous Dutch. That matter was the ancient feud with the duke of Neuburg over the Jülich succession. The merely provisional settlement between the two claimants not only perpetuated a distressing state of uncertainty but also encouraged the duke of Neuburg to take advantage of Frederick William's manifest weakness to infringe in a number of important respects on the most recent agreement of the two princely houses bearing the date of 1629. The elector's repeated protests having been coolly ignored, he resolved to utilize his presence on the Rhine in connection with his marriage for a demonstration against his usurping rival. Even if he was at the time only negotiating with the Dutch republic in regard to an alliance and had as yet reached no agreement, he had become closely affiliated with the Dutch ruling family and shrewdly reckoned that this connection would not fail to impress his Neuburg enemy. Accordingly, he transported some elements of the force he had succeeded in raising in his eastern dominions to Cleve and, joining them to the Cleve regiments raised by his local agent, General Norprath, in November, 1646, marched an army of three thousand men into Neuburg's territory of Berg.

It was war! While the contemporary world was unanimously

outraged at the creation of a new difficulty at a moment when all efforts were being directed to a general pacification, it did not fail to take note of a political novelty: a Brandenburg army and a ruler minded to use it. Under heavy diplomatic pressure, Frederick William after a few weeks ordered the army to abandon Berg—and the war was over. But his action had not been altogether in vain, for it extracted a promise from Neuburg amicably to adjudicate his differences with his adversary. As a result, on April 8, 1647, a treaty disposed of most of Frederick William's complaints, for Neuburg agreed to cease persecuting the Protestants in his part of the Jülich inheritance, as in his Catholic zeal he had been doing, and definitely and conclusively to make over the small county of Ravensberg to Frederick William as part of the latter's share of the Jülich partition. Still, as each contestant continued to uphold his claim to the undivided inheritance, the vexatious issue was not buried on this occasion. It will therefore have to be kept in mind, as it will more than once turn up again in the years to come.

The attitude of the Dutch toward this martial episode deserves to be clearly defined, since Frederick William in taking his risky action against Neuburg had counted definitely on their help. Passionately committed by this time to the idea of a general peace, the Dutch refused to back the elector's little war and by their icy attitude forced him to give it up. But as soon as war had been replaced with negotiations, they accorded him diplomatic aid and were partly responsible for the several concessions he succeeded in wresting from his opponent.

In connection with the Neuburg war Frederick William took up his residence in Cleve, with the plan of improving his relationship with the Landtag and of recovering his lost authority in that Rhenish outpost. He stuck to this task for three long years without making any appreciable headway. The estates clung as stubbornly as before to what they conceived to be their constitutional rights, refused him the grants of money he demanded for an army capable of defending the territory, and were at no pains to conceal their opinion that their duke was an unwelcome historical accident and no better than a foreigner and interloper. While his stay did not advance his cause in the duchy by an inch, he wisely made use of his proximity to the great Westphalian center of attraction to expedite the issue which touched him above all others, the issue of Pomerania.

THE GAINS AND LOSSES OF WESTPHALIA

When Frederick William had made up his mind to refer the question of Pomerania to the congress of Westphalia, he had counted on finding champions of his cause among the leading powers and more particularly, as we know, he had counted on the Dutch. On the Dutch failing him, he might have found himself in a ticklish position of complete abandonment if the French plenipotentiaries at the congress, seeing his distress, had not now approached him and with a courteous sweep of their plumed hats offered him their services. Their motives in so doing, while unrevealed, were not hard to divine. The French were just then engaged in gaining a foothold in Germany along the upper Rhine, in Alsace, and needed for the struggle against the emperor, which was bound to continue even after the present war was over, as many clients among the German princes as they could gather into a French bloc. More or less they had already taken Bavaria in southern Germany in tow, and if they could now bring Brandenburg in northern Germany into a similar dependence, the emperor's position would be fatally shaken. Frederick William, by now as confirmed a political realist as could be found anywhere in Europe, was fully aware that he jeopardized his independence and the security of Germany into the bargain by accepting the proffered good offices; but with his heart set on Pomerania and himself unable to make any headway with the Swedes, there was nothing else left for him to do. Fortunately, the French prime minister, the famous Cardinal Mazarin, was too subtle and circumspect to demand an immediate *quid pro quo* for such aid as he might be disposed to give. He would let time do its work; and so the elector could, for the present at least, dismiss whatever qualms assailed him with respect to his optimistic view that he was not incurring a recorded debt collectible by the French at a definite future date.

The chief French ambassador at Westphalia was Count d'Avaux, a man who coupled a keen intelligence with considerable personal charm and a wide diplomatic experience. As soon as the question of his mediation regarding Pomerania was posed, he let Frederick

William know that he would not undertake it save on the basis of a compromise settlement and that on no other terms would he even approach the Swedes. There is no use going into the recriminations and outbursts of rage D'Avaux had to face in getting the two obstinate, bullheaded contestants together. In the end he effected a settlement: By a verdict of Solomonic perspicacity disputed Pomerania was to be halved! For the half surrendered by Brandenburg it was, however, to receive full compensation in other areas of Germany. By early February, 1647, the untiring D'Avaux had brought about an agreement formally articled and signed by both parties, although it took a few more months of patient to-and-fro on his part before all the details had been settled. Even then they were not settled, not quite settled, as we shall be abundantly apprised by the long aftermath of bickering between Berlin and Stockholm.

Since the February adjudication between Sweden and Brandenburg was afterward incorporated in the final peace treaty, we may here take note of its main features, although the epochal treaty ending the Thirty Years' War was not brought into port for another year and a half. Sweden received western Pomerania, called *Vorpommern* by the Germans, together with the Oder River port of Stettin and all the Oder outlets. To Brandenburg went the larger but far less valuable eastern Pomerania known as *Hinterpommern.*

What Frederick William, who had spent the most formative years of his youth in Holland, pre-eminently wanted was access by the river Oder and the port of Stettin to the Baltic and thence to the open ocean. The denial of this window on the free world of the sea spoiled all his pleasure in the peace which on other grounds might well have been deep and gratifying; for, with the Swedes, once assured of their German foothold, actually seconding D'Avaux, the serviceable Frenchman succeeded in getting his client amply compensated for his surrender of western Pomerania by the transfer to him of the four secularized bishoprics of Camin (in Pomerania), Minden, Halberstadt, and Magdeburg. In regard to Magdeburg, it is true, there was to be a delay, since the elector was not to gain its possession until the death of the bishop-administrator who was its present incumbent. A glance at the map will show that each of these four episcopal territories happily rounded out some Hohenzollern area already in hand. While no conceivable recompense could in Frederick William's eyes make up for the enforced surrender of his sea position, the fact stood out, and from this time forward threw its shadow over German history, that the head of the house of Hohenzollern had by the settlement of 1648 become the lord of a larger land mass than any other German prince save the head of the house of Hapsburg.

A second advantage with which the elector emerged from the Thirty Years' War he owed to no foreign intervention in his behalf but exclusively to himself. Although the longer the German civil war had lasted, the more had purely political issues gained the upper hand, the fact could not be blinked that, having started over issues of religion, the war could not be brought to a close without their settlement. Ever since Luther's day the leading Protestant prince had been the elector of Saxony and his leadership among his coreligionists had continued to assert itself throughout the Thirty Years' War. It had, however, developed a weakness that threatened to destroy it by reason of the Saxon elector's identification of himself with a narrowly defined Lutheranism and of his coupling therewith a bitter hostility to the Protestant minority of Calvinist or Reformed persuasion. Of this minority Frederick William of Brandenburg was the foremost representative, and from the moment that the discussion of the religious settlement was inaugurated at Westphalia he made it a main point of his individual peace program to win for his fellow-worshipers the full legal recognition to which they considered themselves entitled and which they had not yet succeeded in obtaining.

Therewith we are obliged to look somewhat more closely into his view of the relationship between the Lutheran and the Reformed faiths. He held them both to be truly and equally evangelical and the doctrinal shades that divided them to be relatively unimportant. He even went so far as to declare that the Confession of Augsburg of 1530, on which the Lutheran church officially rested, contained nothing to which the Reformed church did not subscribe and that therefore every correct interpretation of the religious peace of 1555, which had granted toleration to the Lutherans, automatically included the Reformed believers. While admitting that the Lutherans in their animosity toward their Reformed brethren rejected this interpretation, he made himself its undaunted champion and fought for it with open visor in the Westphalian lists. And, owing to the unshaken resolution with which he defended his cause, he won an unqualified victory by having the toleration of his coreligionists incorporated in the final treaty in the precise form he advocated. By the famous Article VII of the treaty the Reformed faith was given the same legal security as Lutheranism by the simple device of declaring it to be embraced within the Augsburg Confession. Thus in its chastened postwar mood the congress admitted, in substance if not in express terms, that the legality of the Reformed faith should never have been questioned.

When the elector of Saxony, John George by name, registered a dogged, futile protest against Article VII, he may be said to have delivered the finishing blow to his house's declining Protestant prestige by his obstinate bigotry. To maintain themselves at all amid the undiminished hazards of the seventeenth century the Protestants of both faiths would have resolutely to stand shoulder to shoulder. That was the view Frederick William not only upheld by word of mouth at every opportunity but also championed now and ever after with his readiness, if need be, to fight for it with all his strength. He thus proved that he possessed a religious breadth shared as yet by very few persons in either Germany or Europe. Without question his liberal attitude sprang in the first place from deep personal conviction; but it may not be overlooked that it was in a sense also imposed on him by his being the ruler in Prussia and Brandenburg of two rootedly Lutheran populations whom he was bound to conciliate. Regardless of what influences combined to shape his policy, he stood for a united Protestantism and, in measure as in the years to come the evidence accumulated that he held his strong shield over Calvinists and Lutherans alike without distinction, the star of Brandenburg gained luster in the sky of Protestant Germany and the already dimmed star of Saxony dropped slowly to its setting.

When the Treaty of Westphalia was at last signed, eight years had passed since Frederick William had acceded to office, a beggar on horseback. Against every probability he had in those eight years considerably improved his position. But let us make no mistake. He was still a beggar, and if the barriers of the paddock within which he was at liberty to practice his horsemanship had been somewhat extended, they still held him to very narrow ground. Perhaps he had already extended them as far as the difficult circumstances among which he struggled would permit. But such was decidedly not his own view. A still small voice within him which was never hushed told him that he would succeed before he died in greatly enlarging his range and that he would then appear before the world no longer as the mounted pauper of these early years but as the authentic cavalier and prince he felt himself to be.

Chapter 6

THE TREATY OF WESTPHALIA: PEACE COMES TO GERMANY AND BRANDENBURG

THE Treaty of Westphalia that ended the Thirty Years' War was signed on October 24, 1648. As its main features have already been set forth,[1] it will suffice at this point to recall, summarily, that it terminated the Protestant-Catholic conflict on a not inequitable basis; that it all but completed the dissolution of the German national state, misnamed the Holy Roman Empire, by attributing sovereign status to its individual members; and that it made the two foreign victors, France and Sweden, the masters of German destiny by territorial concessions enabling them to continue at their pleasure their intervention in German affairs.

But, greeted throughout the tormented land with songs of thanksgiving in the churches and the joyful discharge of musketry and cannon from city walls, its execution proceeded so haltingly that the war clouds continued to hang over the country in hardly diminished blackness for many months to come. Innumerable thorny issues touching amnesty, restitution of property, and indemnities needed to be cleared away before the armies of the various participants could be persuaded to retire from the territories they had occupied. Above all, the victorious Swedish army would have to receive precise assurances regarding the five million talers allotted to it in the treaty as a sort of general quitclaim.

Consequently, it required a second congress chiefly of military men, which assembled at Nuernberg and did not conclude its labors with a supplementary treaty until June 26, 1650, to give effect to the decisions reached at Westphalia. Included in the Nuernberg settlement were the stages by which the Swedes were to receive their indemnity; and not until they had become assured on this

1. Chap. i, pp. 15–18.

point did they begin the evacuation of the territories by the plunder of which they had maintained themselves without cost to the homeland for almost twenty years. Again, it was not until the Nuernberg agreement had been signed that the vast transfers of property and the innumerable rectifications of boundaries laid down in the treaty were carried out. Real, as distinct from formal, peace did not come to the prostrate country until some two years after the ceremonious signing of the famous instrument of 1648.

GERMAN MATERIAL RUIN

So harrowing had been the fate meted out to Germany during the long conflict and so impoverished had every region of the country and every stratum of the population become that we must, in order to appreciate the problem of recovery which on the attainment of peace loomed as the order of the day, probe somewhat more deeply into the destruction wrought by the unprecedented struggle. To this end the historian has at his disposal abundant primary evidence consisting, on the one hand, of contemporary chronicles, diaries, and private correspondence and, on the other hand, of public records of divers sorts such as sworn inventories of losses, church registers, and tax lists. Neither category is free from drawbacks. Owing to such ever present psychological factors as terror, vanity, and self-interest, the chroniclers and letter-writers were commonly prompted to indulge in misstatements running the gamut all the way from naïve distortion to wilful prevarication, while the documents of an official nature, besides having survived in only fragmentary form, at their very best furnish data for but narrowly defined localities and never for the whole country.

It has therefore in recent times become customary to adopt a somewhat skeptical attitude toward the presentations the earlier historians based on these sources and, on the whole, to favor a less shattering picture of the condition in which Germany was left by the armies traversing its soil. However, with every reasonable deduction made the gloom is hardly lightened when we realize that the destruction caused by the armies themselves was only the prologue to calamity and that behind every body of organized fighters trailed famine and pestilence. These twin reapers levied through the years a far heavier death toll than did the sudden violence of battle. Another circumstance not to be overlooked is that, when a given region was overrun in a succession of campaigns without an intervening breathing spell, it sank into a wilderness marked by fire-blackened farmsteads and abandoned villages. In such much-harried areas, and indeed throughout the land, the towns fared better than the countryside since, protected by their ancient walls, they could at least defy the small marauding bands that were the jackal outcropping of the struggle. In case, however, a well-equipped army descended on the towns the only method whereby they could save themselves from being stormed and ravished was to buy a reprieve with a crushing contribution in cash or food or both together. The money was blood money, and its indefinitely repeated exaction was certain to reduce the townsmen to approximately the same level of exhaustion and nakedness as the wholly unprotected peasants.

While these and every other conceivable kind of violence, disease, and death characterized the period, it should be clearly understood that they were not uninterruptedly operative over the whole land throughout the thirty-year period the war lasted and that they did not fall with an identical intensity on every section of the country. The war is correctly seen not as a single over-all crisis but as a succession of local crises, each of which affected certain areas and passed others by. No area was racked by every crisis. Thuringia and Franconia, for instance, while cruelly ravaged in the middle period of the war, were much less wasted by the earliest and the latest campaigns. Of the Palatinate and Suabia a similar statement can be made, that is, the armies sometimes failed to visit them and sometimes fell upon them with relentless fury. In spite of wide destruction in the above-named and every other province, not one of them came out of the war without a substantial core of survivors.

The soil of Brandenburg, the region of our particular interest, did not resound to the tramp of marching men until the eighth year of the struggle. But when disaster came, it wrought a havoc as bad as and possibly worse than anywhere else. On an earlier occasion[2] we have given a conservative investigator's estimate of

2. Chap. iv, p. 87.

the decline of population in town and country. As the more lugubriously minded scholars should not be refused a hearing, we may note that one of their number, basing his calculations on a census of hearths taken in 1645, when the worst torments were over and Frederick William's truce with the Swedes had brought a measure of pacification, affirms that in some of the towns of the mark one-half, in others two-thirds, of the houses stood abandoned. The countryside, according to this same authority, revealed approximately the same picture of desertion with the usual variation from district to district. We learn, by way of example, that the Neumark and Mittelmark suffered much heavier destruction than the Altmark.

What use to adduce additional figures? We can hardly go far wrong if we agree that Germany from the North and Baltic seas southward to the Danube and the Alps lost half its population, that its fixed capital of houses and farmsteads declined in about the same proportion, and that its movable capital of horses, cattle, pigs, and sheep, particularly imperiled in wartime, had largely disappeared.

GERMAN MORAL AND SPIRITUAL RUIN

If with this tribute paid to our modern passion for measuring events in concrete terms, we now attempt to get some notion of the suffering and hardships that lie behind the statistical estimates, we are faced with a task before which the readiest pen is likely to be awed to silence. A few great artists, such as Manzoni, Tolstoi, Zola, whose pens, far from ready, were wielded with the deliberate firmness of the etcher's burin, have depicted for us in certain of their novels unforgettable scenes of battle, pillage, and pestilence; but no writer of equal power has yet been moved to draw a picture of the horrors of bloodshed, squalor, and blank misery enacted on the soil of Germany during her thirty-year civil agony. Agreeing that the historian's function differs from that of the novelist and that it is not for him to project purely imaginary scenes of the past, nevertheless he would be showing small respect for the generous Muse he serves if, in a case like the present, he did not, after considering the material destruction, at least make the attempt to assess as well the losses suffered in the moral and spiritual realm. Indeed, he would be disclosing a sorry misconception of human values were he not to concede to the latter a higher consideration, not only because they are more difficult to replace than the material kind, but also because they have been rated by all the more honorable peoples of history as a far nobler order of achievement.

The leading representatives of the moral and spiritual values of any civilization are its educated classes, and the afflictions these classes underwent in the Thirty Years' War were harrowing and continuous. When not literally destroyed in the turmoils of the age, they were in many instances obliged to abandon the church, school, college, or law office which no longer afforded them a livelihood and to take to the road. There they encountered others of their kind and vast numbers besides of peasants, craftsmen, and small traders, who, like themselves, had become outcasts from society. Should you have inquired of the improvised leaders of these war-torn and bedraggled bands toward what goal they were pressing over the wretched roads, heaped with loose dust in summer, plowed into frozen furrows in winter, a town might have been named which rumor represented as still uncaptured and impregnable, but, quite as likely, the answer would have been a benumbed shaking of the head. In the long run so confirmed a hopelessness took possession of these wanderers that they accepted vagrancy as their lot on earth, and many of them sank to the ultimate level of degradation by becoming the starved camp followers of the fighting forces. In the last years of the war an army of, say, twenty thousand men was regularly attended by a civilian band of homeless men, women, and children, as large as the army whose sole thought was to hunt on the trail of the lion and to dispute with one another the few ungnawed bones the lion may have overlooked. Inevitably, ways of living such as these bred thieving, drunkenness, and debauchery and ended in such a dissipation of the social virtues that even the memory of the ancient decencies tended to fade out. Let us not forget to note, however, that, widely distributed as the dislocation of the population was, the greater part always remained fixed and sedentary and in this way succeeded in salvaging for the imperiled nation its cultural continuity. Still, this happier section, too, experienced a marked regression of its moral and intellectual standards, whereof convincing evidence was furnished by the appalling increase of superstition, illiteracy, and ignorance.

When peace finally came, many uprooted peasants drifted back to the farms they had abandoned and many shopmen and artisans to their towns of origin. With renewed courage they began to ply their respective trades, and very slowly something like an economic and social recovery was inaugurated. Its conspicuous failure to show drive and gain momentum is commonly adduced as proof of how radically the social order had disintegrated. While the opinion must be allowed its due weight, a more reasonable explanation of the phenomenon is the unhappy political division of Germany, which, although considerably antedating the war, was given an irrevocable effectiveness by that event. The vast economic expansion of seventeenth-century Europe, really nothing less than a revolution, was a movement the benefits of which accrued exclusively to compact states commanding a sizable home market and affording the ocean-borne commerce of their subjects adequate protection. For Germany, whose federal government, the Reich, was without army, navy, or revenues, that is, by every practical standard nonexistent, and whose hundreds of separate political units signified the crisscrossing of the country in every direction with obstructive trade barriers, the contemporary commercial expansion was completely nullified. While it is a fair assumption that it took the country a hundred years to raise itself again to the material level it had enjoyed before the great disaster, the fact should not be blinked that this startling inability to effect a recovery is ascribable in the first instance to a purely political handicap.

Having already voiced the opinion that moral and spiritual or, summarily, cultural losses are harder to make good than material ones, let us now consider the depth and long persistence of the German cultural twilight. And to avoid misunderstanding, let us agree as to what the term "culture" may be considered to embrace. As used here and hereafter in this book, culture is not identical with civilization but is that segment of civilization which deals with the refinements of living as expressed in manners, dress, social relations, the handiwork of craftsmen, and, above all, in the arts of literature, painting, sculpture, architecture, and music. Culture in this sense reached a high development in the post-Westphalian period in such countries as France, England, and the Netherlands. While in every instance it sprang from the abundant vigor of the nation, it was more particularly associated with a ruling group within each nation, in the case of France and England with a court aristocracy, in the case of the Dutch republic with a solid burgherdom. Whatever area of refinement one may choose to examine, in the two former cases it will be found invariably to have an aristocratic, in the latter case a burgher, flavor.

On turning to Germany we discover that the refinements of its three western neighbors were largely missing, and the phenomenon is adequately explained if, in addition to the exhaustion of the national vitality already noted, we observe that there stood out as carrier element neither a self-secure and self-conscious aristocracy nor a prosperous, pushing bourgeoisie. While the German scene fairly proliferated with tiny courts and impoverished bodies of attendant courtiers making themselves a laughingstock with aping the elegance of Versailles, it will not occur to anyone to regard these costumed manikins as a significant aristocracy; and as for the German burgher class, cut off by its economic backwardness from enterprise, material well-being, and breadth of vision, it shared with its Dutch, and in hardly less degree with its French and English, counterparts nothing but the name.

To guard against exaggeration, let us admit that Germany did not so contentedly relapse into barbarism that it was no longer prompted to reach out toward cultural expression. With the resumption of the ways of peace, the practice of the crafts and arts was timidly renewed; and, among the arts, the art of music, which never, even during the blackest years of conflict, had altogether lost its followers, was again taken up with a particularly notable fervor. Johann Sebastian Bach, who saw the light of day fifteen years before the seventeenth century came to a close, is no freak of nature born out of time and place. He stands upon the shoulders of a long line of Protestant organists and cantors, his deserving predecessors, who of themselves suffice to redeem the period of the charge of utter cultural bleakness. In this connection it is fair to adduce also a literary work, unique of its kind and appearing like an oasis in the desert. It is the picaresque tale, *Der Abentheuerliche Simplicius Simplicissimus,* by Hans Jacob Grimmelshausen. A highly entertaining example of its narrative class, it has, besides, the considerable historical merit of presenting an eyewitness account of the violences, sufferings, and disorders of the Thirty Years' War.

Yet taken relatively, as all value judgments must necessarily be, the cultural bleakness is undeniable. In proof thereof let it suffice, in concluding our survey, to consider the single matter of language, not language *and* literature, although they usually go together, but in this case language alone. Whether spoken or written, language is the fundamental cultural adornment of man. It is the feature that more than any other draws a dividing line between him and the lower animals and lends a certain plausibility to his ancient claim of a divine origin. Every people that has ever set itself the high goal of achieving a culture has cherished its language both as a means and as an end; and the French, the English, and the Dutch, who in the century of our interest held the cultural van, were no exception to the rule. It was in this century that their respective languages developed in sensitive response to the multiplied communications, which were the outstanding feature of the age, an improved, flexible prose of equal advantage to the courtier, the diplomat, the administrator, and the merchant. While certain exceptionally endowed individuals practicing letters as a profession showed the way, the whole national intelligentsia closed in behind them, and the resultant chastening of the instrument of language presents itself to view as one of the most decisive achievements of each people.

How different the development of the German language, how deep its fall! In the political chaos prevailing in the Reich there was no capital city with an authoritative ruling group prepared to accept responsibility for the native idiom, and in the sluggish, hopelessly provincial towns no pressure was exerted in behalf of its quickening and clarification. In this connection it is proper to recall that a rather heavy formality and an excessive elaboration continued to characterize French and English prose even after they had achieved the greater fluency which was their boast. This was so because formality of intercourse and an elaborate etiquette were leading elements of that baroque style which characterized the age and set its imprint on every one of its expressions. Consequently, the doubly formal and trebly circumlocutory inflations of contemporary German prose, painful as they are, may not be adduced as clear-cut evidence of German language decline. This was most convincingly demonstrated by the uninterrupted absorption of foreign words and locutions, chiefly Latin and French. Whenever in the history of language borrowing on so massive a scale as in the German instance takes place, it may be accepted as proof that the language, or languages, from which the borrowings are made has achieved a superior status to the native idiom and that the native idiom has begun to wither.

In preparing this book the author has been obliged to read innumerable public and private documents emanating from the courtiers, diplomats, and administrators, that is, from the most highly educated group of the various German states and particularly of Brandenburg. Among the writers are the individuals who have already figured or will hereafter figure as the dramatis personae of this book and, of course, also Frederick William. The practice of all of them without exception was to sow their communications with so many Latin and French words and phrases as to all but bury the native speech from view; and they adopted this practice not because the German equivalents did not exist or were unknown to the writers but solely for the reason that the two foreign languages in question had become so current in the ruling circles that they carried a greater authority than the mother-tongue, fallen at first unconsciously and, finally, frankly and openly into contempt. We shall have frequent occasion to see that these same people, and foremost among them the elector himself, still cherished the memories of their German past and that there was frequent talk among them of the need of blowing the cold embers of German patriotism again to flame. But to not one of them, though standing in the forefront of political life, did it ever occur that their language constituted their most precious bond with the past and that a national recovery to be effective would have to take its start in a renewed devotion to the nation's core and soul, which is its speech.[3]

In support of this contention it will suffice to recall that it was not until the eighteenth century that a genuine German national sentiment again slowly came to life and that the event was intimately associated with a revival of the German language. The revivers were literary men who took up the reform of the national idiom in order to shape it into what it no longer was, a serviceable artistic medium. From that effort of theirs sprang a general literary movement which continued to gather momentum through the succeeding generations and which more than any other of the many contributory agencies prepared the way for the political reunification of Germany which, even so, was not brought about until the second half of the nineteenth century. Does not this briefly indicated line of the dragging German national recovery lend authority to the view that the true palladium of every people is its language and that, in corroboration of this contention, the seventeenth-century barbarization of the German tongue is the most eloquent evidence that could be adduced of the debased contemporary level of German culture?

THE ELECTOR'S UNSETTLED ISSUES WITH SWEDEN AND PFALZ-NEUBURG

Even after the execution of the Peace of Westphalia had been regulated by the supplementary Treaty of Nuernberg of 1650 unsettled odds and ends of conflict continued to produce friction in a score of different places, and nowhere more than within the range of Hohenzollern authority. Instead of drawing a precise boundary between the sections of Pomerania allotted respectively to Sweden and Brandenburg, the treaty referred the issue to negotiations between the immediately interested parties. Promptly on their coming together Sweden proposed a line which Brandenburg indignantly rejected as excessive, with the result that the Swedes, who with

3. In the course of this book occasional specimens of this linguistic degeneration will be brought to the reader's attention. At this point our purpose will be served by an excerpt from a letter by Samuel Pufendorf, the foremost historian of the period: "Weil ich in meiner Schwedischen historia beider Seits conduite und actiones ohne etwas zu deguisiren also vorgestellet, wie die acta archivi regii mir an die Hand gegeben, etc." In a single incomplete sentence five Latin and two French words!

their victorious armies held in their hands all the trump cards for this sort of game, refused to evacuate the eastern or Brandenburg allotment. It did not make matters pleasanter for Frederick William that the Scandinavians were secretly delighted with his intransigence, since it enabled them to continue to levy requisitions and maintain an army on the elector's territory at the elector's expense. Months, years, passed, and, though impotently exploding with indignation, Frederick William refused to give way.

Another Hohenzollern sore spot which the treaty, instead of healing, had inflamed was the Rhenish west. The latest arrangement between Frederick William and Pfalz-Neuburg regarding the territory in dispute between them had been signed in 1647 and had stipulated, among other matters, that the persecution of the Protestant minority in Jülich-Berg was to cease. It had even directed that the dispossessed Protestants should have their property restored and that a return be made to the religious situation which prevailed before the provisional partition between the two claimants had been effected. This was bitter medicine for Wolfgang Wilhelm, the reigning duke of Jülich, for, like most converts, he was an uncompromising partisan of his newly adopted faith; and it was even more bitter for his son and heir, Philip Wilhelm, who to his father's Catholic enthusiasm added the ardor of impulsive youth.

Trickily delaying, therefore, to carry out the agreement of 1647, father and son openly exulted when in the very next year the Treaty of Westphalia seemed to absolve them from their obligations. It will be remembered that, with respect to the settlement of religious strife within the Reich, the year 1624 was laid down as the *annus normalis* and that this signified that Protestants and Catholics were to rest content with whatever property each of them held or whatever rights each exercised on January 1 of that year. Old Wolfgang Wilhelm at once took advantage of this article to renew the persecution of his Protestant subjects and refused to call a halt when Frederick William, aroused by the outcry of the victims, insisted that the "normal year" for the religious settlement within the limits of the total Jülich inheritance was not 1624 but 1612 as laid down in numerous treaties between the rival claimants and expressly reaffirmed in the treaty of 1647. The twelve-year difference was for the Jülich Protestants the difference between life and death, nothing less, and Frederick William, a heated, though not a persecuting, Protestant, was resolved that his coreligionists should not be sponged out, against, as he viewed the situation, both right and law. He therefore never ceased bombarding Wolfgang Wilhelm with notes of protest; and when, after three years, his paper assault had produced no result, he determined to proceed to a more substantial attack conducted with powder and shot. In short, he undertook to reopen the Brandenburg-Neuburg war.

Another element besides religious passion counted in Frederick William's resolution and, although of a subjective order and sunk beneath the threshold of consciousness, may not be overlooked. The overbearing treatment at the hands of the Swedes to which he was obliged to submit produced an exasperation which needed to be discharged, and on whom could it be more agreeably let loose than on his Rhenish neighbor, who was treating him just as highhandedly as the Swedes but who was of visibly smaller stature than himself? What he had to pocket from the towering Swedes he did not have to put up with from puny Wolfgang Wilhelm, and by the year 1651 he had reached such a state of irritation over the lawless excesses of his Rhenish neighbor that he could no longer contain himself.

In the consultative manner he had early adopted toward the members of the Privy Council, he invited an opinion from each of them on the proposed military intervention against Wolfgang Wilhelm and must have received a shock when with practical unanimity they advised against it. Even Burgsdorf, the soldier of fortune with a constitutional preference for bold deeds, considered the risks of an armed attack too great. So overmastering, however, was the elector's rage that he tossed aside every consideration of self-restraint and, on his sole responsibility, made ready to humble the too-presumptuous Neuburg. On June 13, 1651, he published a violent manifesto against him and ordered his army of about four thousand men to invade his opponent's territory.

In his *Geschichte der preussischen Politik,* J. G. Droysen, that untiring apologist of Frederick William, is at enormous pains to point out that the war must be regarded as a statesman-like enterprise on the part of the elector, not only because of the minor matter of the religious redress whereat it aimed, but chiefly because of the opportunity that beckoned at that moment, to possess himself, through co-ordinated action with the Dutch republic, of the hitherto withheld portion of the Jülich inheritance. But since Droysen himself reveals that every caculation his hero may have based on Dutch co-operation was mistaken, it is far from clear how his blind partisanship improves Frederick William's case. A political action that is based on the nonexistent support of a foreign power must be held to be a mirage, and the best course for its subsequent historian and analyst is frankly to say so. Since in this particular case the victim of the mirage, on again getting his bearings, himself passed, if not a direct, an implied, severe judgment on his self-deception, there is so much less reason for concealing the fiasco.

But we are anticipating and must now return to the war or rather to the excited negotiations which sprang to life when the war, negligible in itself, was launched. On entering enemy territory the electoral troops captured a few border posts and advanced as far as Düsseldorf, Wolfgang Wilhelm's residence. There, since Düsseldorf was a fortress and Frederick William's small army was not equipped to conduct a siege, the advance came to an abrupt stop. The elector's unexpected thrust caused a sensation throughout Germany and was condemned by Protestants and Catholics alike as a criminal breach of the only recently achieved blessings of peace. Nobody, least of all the Dutch, on whose warmly solicited but stoutly withheld assistance the action was predicated, lifted a voice in his behalf, and, on surveying the scene in a more sober mood, he had to confess that he was perilously isolated. Not so his adversary. Wolfgang Wilhelm's appeal for help that made the welkin ring brought him not only general sympathy but also active support, more particularly from his immediate German neighbors, who, a political peculiarity of this Rhenish region, were largely bishops and archbishops of the Catholic church. The result was that in the course of a few weeks the aggrieved duke was able to muster an army of some seven thousand men, to face whom Frederick William was obliged to bring his forces to the same strength.

But there was no fighting to speak of; above all, there was no pitched battle between the two armies for the reason that Frederick William, brought swiftly to the recognition that his temperamental outbreak had been a mistake, resolved to withdraw from the war. However, he had put his head in a noose, and his overjoyed adversary was loath to let him withdraw it. To escape humiliation at the hands of a German prince of a lower station than his own, the elector accepted the lesser evil of humiliation at the hands of their common superior, the emperor. Contrary to his lordly impulse in undertaking the war, he welcomed the intervention of Ferdinand III and hastened to agree to have the quarrel with Neuburg submitted to two commissioners dispatched for this purpose to the Rhineland by the Viennese court. The emperor for his part was only too happy to assume the role of judge and pacifier, since it exhibited him before all the world in the exercise of his ancient supremacy over his vassals; Frederick William, on the other hand, by inviting the emperor's arbitral sentence was put in a position calculated to bring home to him, and to the other German princes as well, that the sovereignty conferred by the Treaty of Westphalia was, after all, not quite so unqualified as they pretended to believe. Even so, Frederick William had every reason to be thankful when the accommodation effected by the imperial emissaries permitted him to end hostilities four months after he had begun them without loss of territory or payment of an indemnity (October 11, 1651).

If the elector was not penalized, he did not gain anything either; in fact, a few face-saving clauses apart, he surrendered what he had proclaimed as the object of the war. This was to oblige his adversary to accept not 1624 but 1612 as the normal year for the Catholic-Protestant adjustments within his boundaries. In Frederick William's chastened state of mind he agreed to refer the disputed point to one of those commissions of the senile Reichstag which, in accordance with by now age-old custom, never succeeded in arriving at a conclusion. Consequently, the duke of Jülich immediately resumed the practice of plaguing his Protestant subjects and continued it for almost two more decades. Then at long last, as our story will disclose in due course, the two hotheaded adversaries settled the religious and every other issue that had for over half a century been in fiery dispute between them.

THE DOMESTIC REORGANIZATION OF 1651

An immediate consequence of the failure of the Jülich enterprise was a thorough revision not only of the elector's mistaken foreign policy but also of the domestic administration which in the course of the short war had disclosed innumerable weaknesses. Concentrating first on the latter, on the problem of administrative reform, we shall begin by agreeing that by this date, some ten years after his assumption of power, Frederick William had come to regard the diets of his various dominions and their pretensions to a share in the government as the chief obstacle to the effective rule on which he had set his heart. In the recent conflict the diet of Cleve had done its utmost to put difficulties in his way by vehemently protesting his recruiting and quartering of troops and every other measure inseparable from the conduct of war. The diet of Brandenburg, to which, too, he had turned with the plea for financial assistance, showed no better understanding of his needs. And as for the diet of Prussia, it had long ago gained the evil distinction in his eyes of being the most intractable of all his parliaments.

While he had clashed with all three of these competing organs of government from the day of his accession, it seems clear that he did not, until after the sting of the Jülich failure, arrive at the inalterable decision to prune their liberties until he was relieved, once and for all, of their power to put a curb on his effective executive control. Throughout what we may view as the post-Jülich period of his reign he labored at this program, labored indeed so successfully that long before his death he had reduced his rivals to all but complete impotence. The victory has been rated in some quarters as his most important achievement and so it may well have been. However, instead of treating the taming of the diets in a patchwork manner by letting it emerge at intervals through several chapters—a procedure that would be in accord with a strictly chronological method—we shall set it forth systematically in a later single chapter in the conviction that only in this way can justice be done to its immense significance.

Another administrative embarrassment experienced during the Jülich fracas was lack of money. This was, alas, a chronic evil, for never yet had the elector seen the time when he had not been obliged to struggle with the problem of an empty purse. As a government is never more hampered by the failure of the universally recognized main nerve of war than during a campaign, Frederick William had no sooner determined on the Jülich venture than he attempted to improve his revenue outlook by adding a financial expert to the Privy Council. This specialist, Tornow by name, had promptly made the discovery of heavy leakages through waste and mismanagement. Nor did he hesitate to lay the responsibility on the shoulders of the favorite, endowed these many years with powers like those of a prime minister, on the shoulders of Burgsdorf. Not that the lord chamberlain had dipped his hands into his master's coffers. The charge was rather that, a blustering soldier, he lacked the patience, diligence, and mathematical precision which are the indispensable qualities of a good administrator, and the very reasonable remedy proposed by Tornow was a stricter system of accounting than had hitherto prevailed.

All of which meant that the prince's old friend and mentor had come to the end of his usefulness. In his grim resolve to clean house the elector at once ordered Burgsdorf to leave his presence—the court on the conclusion of the war was still lingering on at Cleve—and to retire to Berlin there to await his master's pleasure. Unquestionably, other causes contributed to Burgsdorf's fall, as for instance the strong distaste for him entertained by the self-effacing but quietly influential electress. Then, promptly on Burgsdorf's departure, the elector elaborated a broad plan of administrative reorganization. From the first decade of the seventeenth century the authority of the ruler of Brandenburg had, as we know, been centered in the Privy Council; and although the Council was in its origin an institution purely of the mark, inevitably some of the business of Prussia and Cleve had gradually gravitated toward it. With the territorial additions recently sanctioned by the Treaty of Westphalia, the necessity now made itself felt to reorganize the Privy Council in such a way as to raise it to the level of a central governing organ for the whole complex of the Hohenzollern territories.

It was with this end in view that Frederick William issued at Cleve a clarifying ordinance dated December 4, 1651. By its articles the Privy Council was henceforth to be, in effect, a general ministry, although not yet a ministry of the kind with which we of today are familiar, with one minister assigned to agriculture, another to finance, another to commerce, and so on through the list of interests that in their sum make up the society of which the state is the political expression. The seventeenth-century Hohenzollern state with which we are dealing was as yet in simple truth no state at all: It was a group of separate and distinct feudal territories which, gradually accumulated by one family, were by their character and history instinctively opposed to consolidation, nay, prepared to resist it with every means at their command. Accordingly, the act under examination accommodated itself to existing conditions and distributed the as yet separate Hohenzollern lands among the councilors in such a manner that Brandenburg was assigned to one councilor, Prussia to another, and onward in this manner through the latest acquisitions such as Pomerania, Halberstadt, and Minden. While each territory retained its familiar local government headed by a Statthalter, it was henceforth to be represented at Berlin by a member of the Privy Council acting as its agent and fitted into a system that took account of all the individual territories as areas subjected to a single ruler. Association continued through unbroken years, it was surmised and hoped, would bring about an increasing interdependence, and currents of influence radiating to and from the elector's leading residence would ease the recalcitrant local seats of government into a gradual acceptance of Berlin as their common capital. While effective political fusion lay as yet far in the future, it may unhesitatingly be said to have received a powerful impetus from the act of 1651, by which the Privy Council of Brandenburg was lifted into view as the central governing body for all the dominions of the dynasty.

THE FOREIGN-POLICY SWITCH OF 1651–52

Back now to the Jülich war and the conviction to which its failure gave rise of the need, besides an improved domestic organization, of a foreign policy better suited to serve the interests of the state than the foreign policy hitherto pursued. The elector, let us recall, had engaged in the war in the hopeful expectation of Dutch support but without definite assurance to that effect, and he had therefore no one but himself to blame for his disappointment. Owing perhaps to his Reformed faith and Orange blood, he was at the time and had been for years the victim of a kind of Dutch obsession, against which he had been vainly cautioned by more than one of his advisers. Outstanding among the more recent warners was Joachim Friedrich von Blumenthal. To him no less than to the elector himself it was axiomatic that a state so feeble as Brandenburg needed the support of a great power; but whereas Frederick William, in spite of repeated rebuffs, could see only the Dutch republic in that role, Blumenthal urged that the elector should, now that the long civil war was over, seek to arrive at an understanding with his liege, the Kaiser.

A capable administrator and a kindly, high-minded gentleman, Blumenthal had, back in the Schwarzenberg era, given good service to the state. Although a Brandenburger by birth and a Protestant by faith, he had sincerely co-operated with Schwarzenberg because he had shared that statesman's view that the best course for the ruler of the as yet feeble mark was to live on good terms with his legal superior and fellow-countryman. His views had cost him his post in the public service when Schwarzenberg fell from grace. True, he had been restored to favor after some years, and not because he had seen fit, in the interest of his career, to abandon his Austrian predilections. He had again been seated in the Privy Council for no other reason than the respect entertained for him by his prince coupled with the desire to profit from Blumenthal's notable administrative talents. Never for a moment since his restoration to office had he left the elector in doubt that in his view Brandenburg was much more likely to derive advantage from an Austrian than from a Dutch connection.

Because Blumenthal's Austrian partisanship was known and appreciated at Vienna, Frederick William had, at the outbreak of the Jülich war, dispatched him thither to plead his master's cause at a court which, owing to its Catholic sympathies, was only too likely to side with the duke of Neuberg. The ambassador had done excellent work, first in mollifying Kaiser Ferdinand and then in preparing the way for the imperial mediation which brought the war to a close with no loss to the elector except in the important, if insubstantial, region of prestige. Frederick William was duly grateful, and when Blumenthal, following up the credit he had gained, called attention to a considerable advantage to be got from tightening the recently established association with the emperor, he naturally won the ear of his master, especially as the issue broached by the privy councilor was the issue dearest to his prince's heart. Its name, as will at once flash to the mind, was Pomerania.

We have learned that, notwithstanding the allotment to Frederick William of eastern Pomerania by the Treaty of Westphalia, the Swedes had kept it in their grasp and continued to exploit it militarily because the elector would accept neither the territorial nor the financial terms they haughtily dictated. Over three years had passed since the deadlock. It would seem almost as though the immovable elector counted on divine intervention in his behalf, since no one knew better than himself that he lacked the armed power needed to bring his adversary to the offer of better conditions. What Blumenthal now proposed was to seek an accommodation with the Swedes by drawing the emperor into the Pomeranian debate and employing as the means of involving him in the situation on Brandenburg's side the forthcoming session of the Reichstag. That once august body had not met since before the outbreak of the Thirty Years' War, and, although its impotence to effect anything of note had been revealed generations ago, it was, after all, the German national parliament and, as the symbol of an unforgotten unity, enjoyed a traditional esteem among both princes and people. Besides, the Treaty of Westphalia had expressly assigned to it the important task of bringing order into the welter to which the institutions of the Reich had been reduced by the violent divisions inaugurated by the Reformation and deepened by the civil war.

The opening of the Reichstag had been delayed on grounds we need not here examine, and it was not until 1652 that Emperor Ferdinand III announced that it should take place early the following year at the town of Regensburg on the Danube. The new Reichstag was sure, like all its predecessors, to develop into a battlefield of the selfish interests of the members; and overshadowing all the other egotisms would be that of the head of the house of Hapsburg, resolved to restore, less for the sake of Germany than for the credit of his dynasty, the shattered power of the imperial office. More particularly, Ferdinand III, who was in poor health and did not look forward to a long life, would come to the meeting with the plan of having his young son chosen as his successor, thereby securing the crown of the Holy Roman Empire to his family for another generation. The election, it will be recalled, pertained to the house of the electors and not to the Reichstag as a whole. Therefore, set on making his first appearance before the nation's representatives in company with his son in the role of his duly elected successor, the emperor put off opening the Reichstag until by private bargaining with the electors he had won them to his plan.

To gain the election, Ferdinand III showed himself disposed to make important concessions, and it was this situation on which Blumenthal fastened in recommending to Frederick William an understanding with his suzerain. On the one hand, the ruler of Brandenburg disposed of a vote in the electoral college; on the other, the emperor, as head of the Reich, could refuse to enfeoff Sweden with its German acquisitions and to admit it to the seat in the Reichstag which it claimed on the strength of these same German holdings. A more obvious basis for a political trade cannot be imagined, and we need not believe that it had escaped Frederick William's sharp intelligence until Blumenthal brought it to his notice. But unhappy memories and accumulated ancient grudges blocked the way between the two courts and, in spite of Blumenthal's good and untiring offices, almost a year passed before the elector could be persuaded to clinch the bargain. Then, in November, 1652, he set out for Prague, where the emperor had temporarily taken up his residence, and amid manifestations of mutual good will Ferdinand III agreed, in return for the elector's vote for his young son to the imperial succession, to bring to bear on the Swedes the pressure which would oblige them to come to terms with their Brandenburg adversary and to evacuate eastern Pomerania.

But before following the new—and brief—era of good feeling between Brandenburg and Austria to its conclusion, we must return to Conrad von Burgsdorf, who had to pay with banishment from his prince's presence for the unsuccessful Neuburg war and the revelation of the gross financial mismanagement that had attended it. Unable to believe that his sun had set, the former favorite, on his arrival at Berlin, continued to attend the sessions of the Privy Council as a member in good standing. His self-assurance so angered Frederick William, still detained by his affairs at Cleve, that he peremptorily ordered the new favorite to take drastic action against the man he had displaced. Sorely distressed by the command, for Blumenthal cherished ideas of chivalry that in the dawning era of absolutism were rapidly becoming obsolete, on January 30, 1652, he ejected his predecessor from his last foothold in the government. This final disgrace was more than the broken man could bear. His extreme mental perturbation aggravated a serious bodily ailment from which he had been suffering for some time and caused him to decline so rapidly that twelve days later he was dead. The circumstances of his fall from grace and of his sudden end present a striking duplication of the exit from the scene of his ancient enemy, Schwarzenberg. Thus sometimes are the ironical gods pleased to amuse themselves with their human puppets.

No sooner had the elector concluded his bargain with the emperor than the Swedes recognized that they could not any longer withhold eastern Pomerania from its designated owner. They nursed the ambition of playing a leading part at the Reichstag which was about to open and were aware that under the reigning feudal customs they could not take the seat in the house of princes, to which they were entitled, unless they had first received the investiture of their German lands from the source and symbol of the law. Reluctantly they resumed with Brandenburg the suspended Pomeranian negotiations. However, even confronted with the imperial threat, they were able, because of the sword they wielded, in almost all respects to impose their will. The boundary between eastern and western Pomerania was drawn in such a way that eastern Pomerania at no point touched the course of the Oder River. Furthermore, half of the returns from the customs dues (*Lizenten*) collected in the east Pomeranian coastal towns had to be allocated to them. The latter arrangement could be, and actually was, cried up by the Swedish negotiators as a concession since they had originally insisted on the total revenue. Nonetheless, for better, for worse, on May 14, 1653, in a treaty drawn up at Stettin, Sweden and Brandenburg came to terms; and a month later the Swedes ratified the transaction by handing over eastern Pomerania to the elector—not quite five years after it had been assigned to him by the Westphalian settlement!

As soon as the Pomeranian agreement was reported to the meeting of the electors of the Reich, they cast the vote that made the Kaiser's son, another Ferdinand, his successor, with the traditional title of Roman king. Shortly after, young Ferdinand was crowned at Regensburg with all the medieval pomp that still clung to this dying office; and with this prize secured the emperor at last opened the long delayed Reichstag to the satisfaction of himself, the Swedes, Brandenburg, and, we may assume, of all the other participants whom the Pomeranian deadlock had kept cooling their heels in ancient overcrowded Regensburg for six tedious months.

In this manner was the trade carried out between Brandenburg and Austria from which both profited. And almost immediately after they again fell sharply apart. It was not only that they were on opposite sides of the religious fence and that the fence, though lower than it had once been, was still a formidable obstacle; it was rather that the religious differences were constantly reawakened and inflamed by differences of a material kind arising from certain claims of the elector on the emperor which the latter refused to allow. For one item, the ever needy Frederick William never ceased to demand the repayment of a loan of several hundred thousand talers made by one of his forebears to a predecessor of Ferdinand III as far back as the previous century; and, for another item, he demanded that he be put with the least possible delay in possession of Jägerndorf, a small Silesian duchy, of which a Hohenzollern relative, whose heir he was, had been deprived on the charge of rebellion against his lawful lord when he joined the Bohemian rebels back in 1618. If we now add that the emperor, for his part, scented a rising German rival in the elector and instinctively recognized the danger of letting him wax stronger than he already was, we shall agree that there was piled up between Frederick William and Ferdinand III such a fog of suspicion and ill will as could never for more than an occasional fleeting moment be dispelled.

The successful termination of the prolonged Pomeranian dispute lent fresh strength to Blumenthal's authority with his master. Proof thereof was supplied by his appointment as Frederick William's ambassador to the Reichstag at Regensburg, which was charged with the task of reanimating the prostrate German Constitution and of which the emperor entertained such high expectations that he undertook to guide its proceedings by his personal attendance. Universally regarded as Burgsdorf's successor in the esteem of the elector, Blumenthal could without self-deception share the world's view. It was, however, a subtle threat to his influence that, obliged to absent himself from Berlin, he was from the spring of 1653 removed from immediate personal contact with his master. In these circumstances the ancient, barely quieted, anti-imperial sentiments of the elector tended to reassert themselves. If now a capable, intriguing member of the inner circles of the court should take it on himself again to blow the reduced, though not extinguished, animosity into flame, Blumenthal's credit might quickly be dissipated and the days of his ascendancy prove to be numbered.

THE RISE OF COUNT WALDECK

The man who maneuvered Blumenthal's fall was no ordinary courtier and privy councilor; he was a German ruler in his own right. His name was Georg Friedrich von Waldeck, and he was prince (*Graf*) of two small territories on the left bank of the Weser, Waldeck and Pyrmont. Born in 1620, the same year as Frederick William, he had succeeded to his petty principalities during the final phase of the Thirty Years' War. "With a mind bent on honorable employment and great actions," as he says of himself in a later backward glance at his rise in the world,[4] he had refused to be satisfied with the gilded misery of a tiny lordship and had taken service and won distinction with the Dutch armies engaged in fighting Spain under Frederick Henry of Orange. With the Peace of Westphalia he had returned to a home so ravaged that only the barest living could be squeezed out of it. It may therefore be left to the imagination with what relief and joy he responded to an invitation extended to him by Frederick William on the eve

4. "Aufzeichnung des Grafen G. F. von Waldeck über seine Anfänge in brandenburgischen Diensten," *UA*, VI, 129.

of the Neuburg war to enter his service. Immediately on his arrival at Cleve, from where the elector was directing the campaign, he greatly impressed his new employer with his manifold abilities. It added doubtless to the cordiality of his reception that he was of the "family," for his wife was, like the electress, a member of the Orange-Nassau clan.

Count Waldeck at once revealed himself as a man of fiery temper, unbounded ambition, and high-flying political projects. He is the close German counterpart of the Scottish nobleman and partisan of Charles I who portrayed himself in the challenging lines:

> He either fears his fate too much,
> Or his deserts are small,
> That dares not put it to the touch,
> To gain or lose it all.

A portrait of Waldeck of a somewhat later period, when he had reached the middle years and the bloom of youth had vanished from face and figure, shows a massive head which, without resembling Frederick William's either in general shape or individual features gives, like the elector's, the impression of having been roughhewn out of stone. A Reformed Protestant—again like the elector—he had so steeped himself in the Orange atmosphere that the only foreign policy he could conceive for his new employer was to bring him into the closest possible association with all the Protestant states of Germany and Europe in order to checkmate the projects, politically even more nefarious than religiously, of his and the elector's lawful suzerain, the Kaiser. His policy was as partisan and violent as his nature and can fairly be summed up in the battle cry: Death to the house of Hapsburg!

When, some weeks after Waldeck first joined the elector, Blumenthal arrived at Cleve enveloped in the luster of his Viennese services, the count had taken an immediate dislike to him.[5] No wonder! Here was the sponsor of a policy diametrically opposed to his own, a sponsor, moreover, who was gaining greater influence with Frederick William every day. Since the leading objective of the elector at the moment was to get the Swedes out of eastern Pomerania and since even Waldeck had to concede that there was no gaining this end save through good relations with the emperor,

5. *UA*, VI, 134–35.

the ascendancy of Blumenthal had for the time being to be put up with as a necessary evil. But as soon as the Pomeranian quarrel had been disposed of and Blumenthal had been accredited to the Reichstag at Regensburg, a new situation developed; and when Waldeck now made it his business constantly to remind his chief —who was also his social equal and relative by marriage—of the many grievances, real and imaginary, he had against the emperor, he gradually won his case. Only a few months after the mutually advantageous collaboration of the spring of 1653 the elector began to reprove his Regensburg ambassador for being too hotly enlisted for the emperor. The reprimands multiplied until by the end of the year Blumenthal's authority had all but vanished. He asked to be recalled, but, recognizing his usefulness at Regensburg, the elector did not grant the request until the close of the Reichstag in the following May. Blumenthal was then permitted to withdraw to Halberstadt as Statthalter and filled this obscure post until his death in 1657.

It would be a mistake to assume even for a moment that the new favorite, any more than his two predecessors, Burgsdorf and Blumenthal, now became the helmsman of the ship of state and set its course according to his idea of where lay its true port and haven. That was not a possible procedure under a captain such as Frederick William. Nonetheless, the new confidant supplied suggestions and impulses which had such weight and plausibility that the elector not infrequently adopted them. In consequence, the ascendancy won by Waldeck was an event of no mean importance, for in the course of the new year, the year 1654, black thunderclouds began to raise their heads over the north and east of Europe which threatened the loosely consolidated Hohenzollern dominions with such a storm that only by the combination of the most daring with the most prudent counsels could it be expected to be met and weathered.

Chapter 7

BETWEEN THE UPPER AND THE NETHER MILLSTONE: THE POLISH-SWEDISH WAR

BY SLOW advances begun in the thirteenth and continued through the fourteenth century the Teutonic Knights, together with a similar German order which at an early period of its history the Teutonic Knights absorbed, brought under their rule the whole Baltic shore from the mouth of the Vistula River to the Gulf of Finland. The most far-reaching effect of the conquest was that this coastal region and its dependent hinterland were now for the first time in their history drawn into the European system of trade and politics, acquiring an increasing importance therein with each passing generation. Then, in the fifteenth century, conquest had been succeeded by disintegration. In the dawning modern world there was no longer room for a military-monkish order like that of the Teutonic Knights, and it became so enfeebled through arbitrary rule and internal dissension that, unable successfully to compete with the secular states that had come to the fore within the area of its influence, it was gradually destroyed at their hands.

THE STRUGGLE FOR THE BALTIC AMONG SWEDEN, POLAND, AND RUSSIA

The encroaching states were Poland, Sweden, and Russia; and no sooner had they begun to assume the inheritance of the dying order than they developed a lively animosity toward one another. While each of the three states started with the modest proposal to appropriate the slice of Teutonic territory lying nearest its border, each ended with the more sweeping plan of excluding its rivals and seizing the whole prize for itself. By the time the seventeenth century dawned the Teutonic Knights had completely disappeared from the territory they had once ruled, and the dispute that had arisen among the three succession states was familiar to the governments of Europe as the struggle for Baltic supremacy or, in the chancellery Latin they still favored, for the *dominium maris baltici.*

The first notable move of the seventeenth century in this struggle for power was made by Sweden. There, in 1611, a gifted young man, Gustavus Adolphus, mounted the throne and with a purpose as steady as the magnetic needle set out to bring the Baltic issue to a Swedish solution. At that time Russia, still an Asiatic state and rendered temporarily impotent by disturbances attending the extinction (1605) of its first dynasty, had only a narrow foothold on the coast. By 1617 Gustavus Adolphus had obliged the first tsar of the new and as yet feeble Romanov dynasty, Michael by name, to withdraw from the Baltic altogether and surrender his coastal holding to Sweden. Next, the Swedish king turned against Poland, which, as most immediately adjoining the central mass of the region once ruled by the Teutonic Knights, had on their decline appropriated the major portion of the booty. In a war with Poland, Gustavus penetrated and occupied the province of Livonia with its great coastal emporium of Riga. The war ended in 1629 with a truce, which, renewed in 1635, gave a long respite from fighting but left an unsettled situation between the two states. The makeshift arrangement signified that each side was resolved to renew the struggle as soon as the occasion was favorable.

The reason why King Gustavus Adolphus broke off his conquests in Poland is already familiar to us. The Thirty Years' War was raging in Germany and had at that very time carried the Catholic side, identified with Emperor Ferdinand II, to its apogee. In 1629 the triumphant Kaiser, having reduced northern Germany to subjection, was on the point of establishing himself on the Pomeranian coast and, were that to happen, Gustavus Adolphus would manifestly be seriously threatened at the heart of his power. Consequently, with the least possible delay he came to terms with Poland and boldly transferred his army to the German scene of action with the astonishing results of which we have heard. True, he himself was killed at Lützen in 1632, but so deeply had he by that time thrust Sweden into the German body politic that it could never again be dislodged and had to be rewarded in the Treaty of Westphalia with western Pomerania and the bishoprics of Bremen and

Verden, territories signifying in their sum the control at their mouths of the rivers Oder, Elbe, and Weser. Noting the step-by-step Swedish advance in the Baltic area beginning with the accession of Gustavus Adolphus, we are forced to the conclusion that by 1648 the northern kingdom was well on its way to the achievement of its openly proclaimed program of converting the Baltic Sea into a Swedish lake.

If we now turn to Poland, we encounter an extraordinary story of missed opportunities, culminating in an all but unique case of total national breakdown. When, back in the year 1386, Poland and Lithuania were united by the marriage of their respective heirs, a state of vast extent was created stretching across the east European plain all the way from the Baltic to the Black Sea. In the first century of its existence this state proved itself strong enough to beat the Teutonic Knights into submission and to acquire a liberal slice of their Baltic territories. With a fixed purpose enforced by energetic executive action the Polish-Lithuanian kingdom would undoubtedly have won the undivided Teutonic inheritance, since it was not until the sixteenth century that Sweden and Russia girt their loins to join in the game.

The Polish sin of omission, which brought untold calamities for Poland in its wake, is attributable to an internal development which, first, enfeebled the royal executive and, finally, reduced it to all but complete paralysis. More and more decisively with each generation the Polish landowners, a feudal baronage dominating a nation of landless serfs, took all power into their hands. They thus brought into being what they proudly called the Polish republic and strove for and finally achieved a political system in which every nobleman became in effect a sovereign in his own right. While the kingship was not abolished, the king, elected by the assembled nobility and subjected to their pleasure, became a purely ornamental appendage of an essentially aristocratic constitution and in the absence of a strong sentiment of patriotism might as readily be a foreigner as a native.

In these topsy-turvy circumstances it came about that in the year 1587 the Polish diet offered the crown to Sigismund of the house of Vasa, oldest son and heir apparent of the king of Sweden. Sigismund had been brought up as a Catholic by his Catholic mother and was therefore acceptable to the Catholic fervor of the Poles. When, however, some years later, his father died and he automatically acquired the crown of Sweden, too, he came into a head-on collision with the Protestantism of his northern subjects and was driven from the throne. He was succeeded at Stockholm by his uncle and in due time by his young cousin, the famous Gustavus Adolphus, with whose career of conquest we have just dealt.

Inevitably, in view of the tenacity that marked dynastic claims in those days, King Sigismund of Poland looked upon his cousin, Gustavus, as a usurper and never even for a moment abandoned his pretensions to the Swedish throne. This dynastic wrangle must never be lost from view in considering the relations between Poland and Sweden in the seventeenth century, for it added a measure of private family venom to a conflict ferocious enough in itself but purely territorial in origin. Far more important, however, for a proper understanding of seventeenth-century Polish developments is the fact that during the reign of the first two kings of the house of Vasa, Sigismund (1587–1632) and his son, Vladislaus (1632–48), the decline of the royal power continued uninterruptedly. If anything, it was even accelerated, since it was in the period of these two monarchs that the nobles succeeded in completing the supremacy already attained by a culminating measure, a measure indeed without parallel in the whole history of European feudalism. That was the attribution of the veto power to every member of the Polish diet. On the strength of this monstrous usurpation a single deputy sufficed to paralyze the national will, since a proposal in order to become law had to win unanimous support. No wonder that by the middle of the seventeenth century the Polish state was so far gone in dissolution that it was doubtful whether it would or could, if attacked, put up a resistance.

Ever since the creation of a Russian state in the course of the sixteenth century the most striking feature in its general situation was its complete separation from Europe by the vast blockading mass of the Polish-Lithuanian state. Efforts made by the tsars to break through the barrier were attended by some slight successes, which, however, were again canceled when a quarrel over the succession (1605–13) plunged Russia into anarchy. With the accession of a new, the Romanov, dynasty, order was gradually restored, whereupon the state with slowly gathering momentum resumed the policy of western penetration.

The immediate object in dispute between Russia and its Polish-Lithuanian neighbor was the extensive border area of the Ukraine inhabited by bands of warlike, freedom-loving peasants called Cossacks. The Cossacks had, while retaining their local independence, accepted the protection of Poland and evidenced no discontent with the arrangement until, in the course of the seventeenth century, the Poles hit on the unfortunate idea of converting their purely nominal rule into an effective dominion enabling the Polish nobility to transform the free peasants into tax-paying dependents and serfs. At once the Cossacks were up in arms and in 1648, aided by the Mohammedan Tartars from the Crimean area, conducted an invasion of Poland on such a vast scale that the very existence of the country hung in the balance. Polish valor, abetted by the lack of cohesion among the loose bands of the invaders, saved the situation. Cossacks and Tartars were defeated and driven back, though the rebellion was not completely stamped out. Six years later, in 1654, it flared up again when the second Romanov tsar, Alexius, accepted the proffer of the protectorate made to him by the Cossacks and followed up this bold act with an attack on Poland.

While the fertile Ukraine was the immediate cause of the war, Alexius made it clear by his actions that even more pressing for Russia than to acquire the Ukraine was to regain its lost foothold on the Baltic Sea, for he directed his main war effort against the northern or Lithuanian border. Owing to the primitive Russian military organization, he made but slow progress. Nonetheless, Poland had every reason for alarm since, having barely survived the terrible Cossack attack of 1648, it was now forced to face another onslaught from the same quarter supported by the fresh vigor of youthful Russia. And as though this were not enough, in the following year, in 1655, and from another point of the compass such a storm discharged itself over the country as not even much-tried Poland had ever before experienced.

CHARLES X OF SWEDEN RESOLVES TO ATTACK POLAND

On June 16, 1654, the city of Uppsala was on tiptoe with excitement over a meeting of the Swedish Riksdag summoned to witness the abdication of one sovereign and to acclaim the successor. It had long been whispered among the population that Queen Christina, daughter of that Gustavus Adolphus enshrined as a national hero in all Swedish hearts, bore with so little patience the burdens of government that she was resolved to discrown herself as soon as circumstances permitted. While she had allowed this much of her state of mind to become common knowledge, she had concealed—and what a bomb the announcement would have exploded among people and parliament on that June day!—that the secret, driving reason for her action was her desire to abandon Protestantism and join the Catholic church. And this step she actually took as soon as, divested of the royal insignia, she had departed from Sweden and reached the safety of the Continent.

With its chief motive undivulged the abdication elicited no more than polite expressions of regret quickly transformed into lusty cheers on her presenting as her successor her cousin, who mounted the throne as Charles X Gustavus. The new king, little more than thirty years old, was anything but royal to look upon, for he was a short, thick, barrel-shaped man with a face that displayed a pair of bulging eyes, thick lips, and other singularly ill-favored features. However, in spite of his repulsive appearance, he was a man of parts; above all, he was a first-rate fighting man, who, when barely out of his teens, had made a name for himself as Swedish generalissimo in the last phase of the German conflict. Bred to war and enamored of it as the only occupation worthy of a king, he immediately on his accession surveyed the European scene with a view to discovering the enemy on whom he might most profitably discharge his martial ardor.

Inescapably, in this survey Charles X fastened on neighboring Poland. To begin with, Sweden was still officially at war with Poland, for, while the truce of 1629 had been indefinitely prolonged in 1635, it had not yet, twenty years after 1635, been transformed into a peace. Further, with Poland under assault at this very moment by Russia, the shaken kingdom was already so heavily engaged on its eastern frontier that it was not likely to offer much resistance in the west. Finally, and most important, there was the question, the eternal question, of the rule of the Baltic. To recently acquired Pomerania, Sweden would now have but to add the two Prussias, Polish and ducal, and the dominium maris baltici would be—might not the king with good reason hope?—forever in his country's grasp.

Such is the view of the origin of the war which has been and still is retailed in the average general history of Europe. It is not wrong, but it is oversimplified. Admitting that the king's love of war and power figured prominently in the event, it is equally true that he was driven on his course by forces inherent in the Swedish situation and quite beyond his personal control. Sweden was a poor and thinly populated country that had been launched on a career of conquest by a recent sovereign gifted in many directions and, particularly, as a military leader. While Gustavus Adolphus had raised Sweden to the status of a first-rate power, he neither did nor could provide it with the resources indispensable to so imposing a position. As long as the Thirty Years' War lasted, the lack of wealth did not greatly matter, since the armies of Sweden stood on foreign soil and satisfied their various needs by plundering their victims.

With the Peace of Westphalia all this had been disastrously changed. The Swedish forces were, reluctantly enough, obliged to withdraw from Germany and, arrived at home, encountered difficulties of pay and provisionment which they had never known while engaged in active fighting. The nobility, above all, had profited from the war not only because as officers they had received comfortable salaries but also because they had brought back home with them an immense plunder with which they had lavishly furnished forth their country castles and townhouses. For these several reasons a public state of mind had been built up in Sweden that clamored for foreign action and which, even had he wanted to do so, Charles X could not afford to ignore. A country with a war-minded nobility and people and a public economy so feeble that it could not support a standing army marked a paradox which no one has stated more succinctly than Adler Salvius, a leading

Swedish statesman of that age: "Other nations make war because they are rich, Sweden because it is poor." In brief, there was no other way for Sweden to sustain the unnatural eminence of a great power than by the method employed to achieve it, the method of war.

While these statements enumerating causes of both a personal and a national order making for war disclose the real reasons for the conflict in which Charles X was about to engage, he was as desirous as sovereigns and governments have ever been to conceal the real reasons animating him behind a plausible pretext. This was foolishly supplied him by King John Casimir who had recently (1648) been elected to the Polish throne in succession to his brother Vladislaus. As if his country were not yet confronted with sufficient difficulties, John Casimir frivolously added to them by seizing the occasion of Charles X's accession to the Swedish throne not only to lodge a heated protest against it but also, once more, to affirm that he, John Casimir, was before God and man the rightful king of Sweden. From that moment Charles X was able to play down the true purpose of his contemplated war, which was to make himself master of the Prussian coast, and to bury it from view by a smoke screen of indignant clamor against John Casimir's presumption. And promptly, as has happened again and again before and since, many featherbrained people took the pretext seriously and chattered noisily in taverns and newssheets about John Casimir's having unleashed the dogs of war by his single-track dynastic mind.

And now the war. However, before plunging into the long and complex story a singularity about the contested domination of the Baltic must first be attended to. It was political, not economic, domination that was in dispute between Sweden and Poland. The statement hardly makes sense for the living generation of men since conditions prevailing in our own time have made it clear that political and economic domination invariably go hand in hand. In the seventeenth century, at least so far as the Baltic area is concerned, this was not yet the case; for neither Sweden nor Poland was itself a trading nation, and all that they got out of the extensive, close-meshed Baltic trade were the tolls they collected at such ports of entry as were subject to their control.

Most of the ships in the Baltic—and their number ran into the thousands—sailed under the Dutch flag, with the ships under the English flag holding second place, though at a respectful distance behind their Dutch competitors. Economically backward Poland and Sweden had neither the ships nor the sailors nor the merchants nor the cargoes to enter the contest; but wherever they ruled the shore they could levy tribute on the Dutch and English traders to their heart's content. These, though voicing their displeasure at such exactions in the coarse language common to seafaring folk, accepted the situation, first, because it was clear that their respective governments, already sufficiently involved elsewhere, were not prepared to rush in and bring the Baltic under their own rule; and, further, since, after the tribute had been reluctantly paid by the merchants, there still remained in their hands an exceedingly handsome profit. We may agree that Sweden and Poland fought over the Baltic in part for the mere glory of possession or, in more modern terms, to flatter their very lively will to power, but we may not overlook that the harbor dues were a strong additional inducement of a material kind and that the more harbors each of them embraced the greater the resulting revenues.

BRANDENBURG IS DRAWN INTO THE WAR

As our concern in the Polish-Swedish War is going to be chiefly directed to Brandenburg's share in it, we begin by noting that Charles X had hardly succeeded Queen Christina when the sharp-scented Frederick William noted a change in the political atmosphere. He was therefore not particularly surprised when in the autumn, three months after the event at Uppsala, a Swedish diplomat appeared at Berlin to take soundings regarding the elector's disposition to enter the contemplated Polish war on the Swedish side. In keeping with Sweden's traditional disregard for its feeble neighbor, the diplomat haughtily indicated that the safest course for the elector would be to join with Sweden without more ado and to speed Charles X on his way by the cession to him of the two Prussian harbors of Pillau and Memel. Frederick William's answer was as prompt as it was vivacious: He would not enter into negotiations with Sweden on such humiliating terms. On the Swedish ambassador's departure the elector sent an agent of his own to Stockholm to keep in touch with developments, and although a good many conferences were held which made it clear that the king of Sweden felt himself magnetically attracted toward Pillau and Memel, the elector's adamantine refusal to consider their surrender prevented the discussions from being brought to any conclusion.

But even more than at Stockholm, the talk in the Privy Council at Berlin, starting with that September visit of the Swedish agent, turned endlessly around the coming war. What was the elector to do about it? For Sweden to invade Poland it would have to march through eastern Pomerania, and this there would be no way of stopping. Simultaneously it would be prompted to appropriate the ports of Pillau and Memel by seizure, and this could be stopped for a time at least, since Sweden was not powerful at sea. Because Frederick William judged that Sweden was immeasurably stronger than anarchic Poland and therefore likely to topple it over by a concerted rush, he was instinctively moved to align himself with the prospective victor; but he would not do so without guaranties, more particularly without an express commitment on the part of the victor not only to respect the elector's present holdings but even to enlarge them in return for such military assistance as he might be persuaded to render.

There was a further circumstance that needed to be carefully weighed: While the king of Poland was weak, still he was stronger than Frederick William and was besides, as Frederick William's suzerain, possessed of certain undeniable rights in the duchy of Prussia. In the event of war with Sweden (or, for that matter, with any state) the suzerain could order his vassal to furnish the military aid stipulated in the feudal contract. It happened to be rather negligible, for it amounted to no more than a cavalry troop of one hundred men. However, and this was decidedly no laughing matter, if the duke of Prussia should side with Sweden in its war with Poland, the Polish king, as the duke's overlord, could brand him a rebel and judge him to have forfeited his fief.

Since throughout the negotiations conducted at Stockholm during the winter of 1654–55 the king of Sweden refused even to consider the terms of alliance which Frederick William offered, the only self-respecting course that remained was to make himself as strong as possible and take an independent stand. This program when submitted to the Privy Council met, apart from an occasional timid remonstrance, with general approval and, on the part of the Council leader, Count Waldeck, with enthusiastic encouragement. Danger was the element in which Waldeck thrived, and it was sufficiently the elector's element for him in the present instance to be heart and soul with the reigning favorite. There was therefore full agreement that the first and most pressing need, in view of the incalculable future, was an enlarged and well-equipped armed force. Not timorous escape from the impending conflict but eventual participation in it on one side or the other became the admitted purpose of the elector and his councilors. With this much settled they could not avoid raising and answering the question as to the goal to be envisaged as soon as the stone had been set to rolling. While the discussion on this head touched on many possibilities, it invariably swung back to one goal as desirable above all others: to pluck from the bramble of this war the jewel of sovereignty in Prussia.

By the late spring of 1655 Charles X had assembled two armies, one in Livonia, the other in Swedish Pomerania with the plan of smothering Poland by a pincers' movement from the east and west. In July he invited Frederick William to a conference at Stettin in a last effort to bring him into alliance with himself before the war got under way. Instead of going in person, the elector dispatched Waldeck to the meeting along with another councilor, the cautious and reliable Schwerin, to act as a check on his too-impulsive partner. Since, under the instructions carried with him, Waldeck signally expanded the list of advantages hitherto demanded of Sweden as the price of co-operation, the discussions did not open auspiciously. It is worth noting, and a startling indication of the elector's sudden territorial appetite, that by this time his terms, based on the supposition of the imminent doom of Poland, were no longer limited to sovereignty in Prussia but included a far from modest share in the prospective Polish booty. As Charles X for his part continued to harp on the cession of Pillau and Memel, the conference never really got started and was abruptly broken off by the suspicious Swedes as soon as they got wind of a parallel negotiation the elector was conducting at The Hague with the Dutch republic.

As we are aware, it was nothing new in the elector's experience to turn to the Dutch in the hope of help. While these cautious traders had thus far consistently disappointed him, on this occasion he had more than his usual success for a reason that is not hard to grasp. Ever since the great Gustavus Adolphus' first triumphs in the Baltic area he and his successors had systematically pursued a policy of legal plunder against Dutch shipping by the imposition of duties which, to the Dutch at least, were unfair and excessive; and if, as the result of a new aggression, the Swedes should now make a sweep of all the Baltic ports and raise the port dues to still higher levels, the Dutch would be subjected to an intolerable exploitation. They therefore considered it of the first importance that some harbors, and among them Pillau and Memel, should be kept out of Swedish hands. Their transfer, if effected, would be a calamity which to prevent they were ready to go into action on Frederick William's behalf with their most impressive political asset, their fleet. Should their warships appear in the Baltic, basing their movements on Frederick William's Baltic towns, the Swedes, having no navy of remotely commensurate size, would be gravely hampered. It must have filled the elector with elation that for the first time since dealing with the purse-proud mynheers he found them more eager to consummate a bargain than he was. When he agreed that, in return for the aid of their fleet against an attack on him by Sweden, he would maintain the existing tariff rates and never voluntarily surrender his Baltic ports to the Scandinavian power, a treaty of mutual defense was signed (July 27, 1655) between him and the Dutch republic.

Since this treaty was undeniably and pointedly aimed at Sweden, we will not feel surprise that Charles X took umbrage at it and brought the Stettin negotiations to a close. He did so, however, in a form so courteous that it was clearly evident that he had not failed to be impressed with Brandenburg's show of independence. He thereupon sped after his army, which had already begun to move forward into Poland, while another and smaller force stationed along the Livonian coast simultaneously invaded Lithuania. Thus was the Polish-Swedish War inaugurated with Frederick William left standing on the side lines. But not in the role of the idle spectator. The contrary was far nearer the truth; for, as Charles X inaugurated his momentous southward drive, the elector gathered together all available Brandenburg troops with the view to moving them eastward into his duchy of Prussia. He was resolved to be as near as possible to the theater of war, prepared for every turn the uncontrollable events might take.

If this were not the story of a state-builder pledged to follow the road he took and forbidden excursions into bypaths, the occasion would now be furnished for the saga of the conquest of Poland by the Swedes. For everyone familiar with Swedish history the event spontaneously links itself to the adventures of the famed viking forebears of the invaders, since, save for such externals as dress and armament, they were the same tall, blond, blue-eyed warriors that in the early medieval period had irresistibly overrun large sections of Europe. To underscore the resemblance, they took their marching orders from a king of viking caliber, for such the successor of Queen Christina was in spirit, even if, physically, he looked more like a lumbering troll out of the bowels of the metal mountains of his home.

The army commanded by this royal grotesque was the institution that had been brought to its present shape by the lessons of the Thirty Years' War. It was made up of the three conventional divisions of infantry, cavalry, and artillery marching separately but maneuvered on the battlefield as a unified force. With the introduction of lighter and more mobile cannon by Gustavus Adolphus the artillery had become a much more decisive factor in combat than had been the case before his time. When the army was drawn up for battle, the artillery was partly massed in front of the infantry and partly planted in the gaps between the infantry brigades. A brigade, in earlier time a solid phalanx of pikemen carrying eighteen-foot-long pikes who strove to overwhelm the enemy by sheer weight of mass, had recently changed character through the replacement of some of the pikemen by musketeers. At the time with which we are dealing the musketeers had come to outnumber the pikemen in the ratio of two to one. However, while the musket had been notably improved over the earlier models, it was still too unwieldy and temperamental a weapon to enable its bearer to play an offensive role. In its most recent reorganization an infantry brigade, constituted as a core of pikemen flanked on either hand by a troop of musketeers, was best suited for the defensive. Consequently, the offensive was intrusted to the cavalry, and a commander like the king of Sweden, whose bold spirit prompted him habitually to attack, so markedly favored cavalry over infantry that in his armies the former usually greatly outnumbered the latter. While the equipment of the individual horseman called for an iron casque and cuirass, these had in large part been replaced by a heavy leather collar, perhaps because it was cheaper and hardly less effective than steel plate against the saber blows it was worn to ward off. On attacking the enemy in headlong career the riders first discharged their pistols or carbines and then, drawing their sabers, strove to complete the rout and carry the field.

Although the Swedish army did not greatly differ in organization and equipment from the type-army of western Europe, it merits attention that the Brandenburg army in process of formation shaped itself closely on the authoritative Swedish model. Not so the Polish army. In harmony with the backward character of the state and society of the Poles their army still had a strictly feudal character. Nonexistent in peacetime even in skeleton form, it came into being only on the declaration of war, was composed of the loose, mounted masses of the small nobles, and was of necessity unevenly armed and insufficiently disciplined. The disaster that presently overtook the Poles is adequately explained if we realize that a medieval feudal army met a modern professional one and that the difference between the two accurately reflected the difference in level of civilization between the opposed states.

Although every informed onlooker expected a Swedish victory, no one even imagined that the Poles would offer so little resistance and permit Charles X in a bare matter of weeks to drive his army of no more than twenty thousand men clear across the broad plains of Poland and capture in the process the leading Polish cities. A calendar of the more decisive events of his march reveals that he crossed the Polish border toward the end of July, entered the capital city of Warsaw on September 9, and that, after the flight of King

John Casimir to his other capital, Cracow, he followed in pursuit and entered Cracow on September 25. Although John Casimir made good his escape from Cracow, he saw so little chance of further resistance that he abandoned his country and took refuge on Austrian soil.

Since during the late summer months of this same year the Russian tsar had advanced into Lithuania, it looked very much as if the dissolution of Poland was at hand and would of a certainty be followed by a clash of the two victors over their respective shares of the booty. However, if unavoidable in the long run, the clash was not imminent, owing to the vast extent of Poland and the great spaces that still separated the two invaders. The immediate event that was on every tongue was Charles X's sensational conquest, and on the strength of it an excited public opinion acclaimed him in the grandiloquent manner of that classically educated age as the Alexander of the North.

Having, in accordance with the dictates of his martial ardor, pursued and scattered the enemy, the Swedish victor retraced his steps in order to occupy Polish Prussia, the original objective of his campaign. Let us remind ourselves that he had not engaged in the war to destroy Poland but for the limited purpose of appropriating the Prussian coast, thereby completing the Swedish ring around the Baltic. Leaving garrisons in the captured Polish cities, early in December he appeared in Polish Prussia and in the easy manner to which he was now accustomed took town after town in rapid order. The greatest town, in fact the greatest and most prosperous town of the whole Baltic coast, was Danzig. Although technically incorporated in the kingdom of Poland, it was a free, that is, a self-governing, commonwealth of German nationality. It lay at the mouth of the Vistula, depended for its living on the Dutch and English trade, and, protected by a formidable wall, could not be captured save by an army provided with adequate fleet support.

While Charles X had an army, he lacked a fleet and for the present prudently resolved to leave Danzig unmolested. But solidly installed in the coastal region, he was determined to utilize the occasion to bring his unsettled relations with Frederick William to a showdown. Not only had the elector recently transferred his Brandenburg army to Prussia and there joined it to his Prussian troops, thus putting himself at the head of a force constituting a potential threat to the Swedes, but he had ventured to depart from his neutral role by an openly hostile measure. In passing on his eastward march through Polish Prussia at a time when Charles was engaged in his wild huntsman's chase of poor John Casimir, he had signed a defensive alliance with the estates of the threatened province. In the eyes of the Swedish ruler this was a challenge which could not be overlooked, and in his habitually impetuous manner he invaded the duchy of Prussia resolved to have an accounting with its shifty ruler.

It was war. And yet it was not war, since the never ceasing negotiations showed that each side would much prefer a last-minute accommodation. The Swedes might be thought to have small ground for avoiding a clash, since, in high feather over their recent triumph, they could not have felt great respect for the elector's untried army. But other considerations made their influence felt. For one thing there was Russia. Driving boldly through Lithuania to the Livonian coast, the tsar could not be regarded other than as an enemy already in the field. Then there were Sweden's two ancient and implacable foes, Denmark and Austria. Gravely agitated by the invasion of Poland, they had begun negotiations with each other that foreboded action against Sweden in the near future. Finally, Charles had right along wanted the alliance, on his own terms of course, and not the enmity of Frederick William. Precisely this was still his preference as, late in December, 1655, he led an army into Frederick William's territory.

Undeniably the elector had put himself in a tight place. Having assembled an army and tied himself by treaty to the estates of Polish Prussia, he could not without loss of face avoid resisting the Swedish invasion. But, stunned apparently by the prestige of Swedish arms, he did avoid it. In measure as Charles advanced Frederick William backed away from him until his forces were crowded together around the capital city of Königsberg. All the members of his Council, with the single exception of the tempestuous Waldeck, were timorously averse to putting the issue to the test of battle. The recently appointed commander of the field army,

General Sparr, shared the councilor's alarm. Were the men around the elector the victims of a military panic? It is not improbable, and, everything considered, their nervousness was understandable; for, should the decision be taken to attempt to halt the invaders, the Brandenburg army would have to meet an army without a rival at the moment in the world and commanded by a king with a genius that prompted his contemporaries to rank him with the greatest soldiers of history. The trepidation of his leading officials communicated itself to Frederick William, and with chagrin in his heart he decided to avoid battle and meet his opponent's terms.

THE TREATIES WITH SWEDEN OF KÖNIGSBERG, MARIENBURG, AND LABIAU

On January 17, 1656, there was signed between Sweden and Brandenburg the Treaty of Königsberg. While it undoubtedly registered a Swedish success, it was so little an unmitigated triumph that it conceded favors to the smaller state which, in view of its recent exhibition of weakness, are fairly surprising. Outstanding among them was the permission to Frederick William to continue his neutral role. The grant obliges us to conclude that Charles was persuaded that he could bring the Polish war to a satisfactory termination without the help of Brandenburg or, for that matter, without help from any quarter whatever. What the king pre-eminently desired in regard to his neighbor was to reduce him to a regulated dependence on himself, and this was achieved by obliging him to acknowledge Charles as his suzerain, in place of John Casimir, and to receive the duchy of Prussia at his, Charles's, hands as a Swedish fief. To make Frederick William's dependence more effective than it had been under Poland, the humiliated duke of Prussia was obliged to grant to the king of Sweden the use of the harbors of Pillau and Memel for both military and commercial purposes and the right to half of their customs dues. By way of salve to his wounded self-esteem the newly acquired vassal was awarded the prince-bishopric of Ermland, which, a Polish dependency, lay within the embrace of ducal Prussia. By no stretch of the imagination could the Ermland bishopric be regarded as a full equivalent for what was surrendered; and our final judgment on the treaty cannot but be that, in spite of a few, not unimportant, benefits which it conferred on Frederick William, it added up to a grave discomfiture. In its sum it signified an exchange of masters, and who could deny that the outlook for the duke of Prussia under the suzerainty of his new Swedish overlord was decidedly less attractive than under the feeble Pole. If a greatly dejected Frederick William could discover any reason for congratulation on the day the treaty was signed, it might have been found in the circumstance that, if his army had not fought, it was at least intact and ready for action whenever a more propitious occasion should present itself than had hitherto been the case.

And hardly was the ink of the Königsberg document dry when an unexpected movement in Poland created the very chance Frederick William was looking for. Poland ever was and long continued to be a country of surprises. In the recent campaign its feudal warriors had failed to respond in anything like adequate numbers to the call of their king. In many shameless instances they had even welcomed the foreign invader and voluntarily taken the oath of allegiance to him. But the very completeness of the fall of the country produced a revulsion. After all, the Poles were a people with a vigorous national pride; besides, they were a passionately Catholic people whom a numerous and fanatic clergy needed only to remind of their attachment to Rome to fill them with the utmost resentment against a plundering band of foreigners and heretics. A kind of human earthquake rocked the country which, beginning in the south, traveled northward until the whole Polish folk from one end of the land to the other was in commotion. An enthusiastic volunteer army, much larger than any that had ever assembled on orders from the diet, recalled John Casimir from his Austrian exile and then proceeded to pick off the isolated little garrisons King Charles had left behind on his hurried northward retreat into Prussia.

The royal Swede was not the man to be dismayed by this dramatic turn. Although it was deep winter—and winter blasts the open Polish plain with boreal snows and arctic temperatures—he determined to quash the insurrection while it was still young and, without giving the difficulties presented by the hostile climate and the pathless communications a second thought, as soon as the Königsberg negotiations had been concluded led his stalwart Swedes into Poland to conquer it a second time within a brief six months' period. At the head of no more than ten thousand troops he crossed frozen rivers, drove through enveloping swarms of enemy horse, and got almost to distant Lemberg, from where John Casimir was directing the national revolt. Then, able to disperse but not to destroy the foe, he had, in order not to be cut off from his base, to beat a precipitate retreat. By the middle of April, 1656, he was back in Warsaw with a bare four thousand men. The rest of his troops, when they had not perished in battle, had died from exposure, hunger, and disease. At Warsaw, too, there was no possibility of a successful stand, and, leaving a small garrison behind, he made his escape, amid fantastic feats of valor, to the Baltic coast.

If Charles had not had too exclusively a soldier's outlook, he might have been persuaded after two attempts that so large and disorganized a country as Poland could be penetrated almost at pleasure but could not be kept under control by the small forces which in those days made up the field armies of the leading states of Europe. Even if he glimpsed this truth in one of his none-too-frequent rational moments, he refused in his fanatic addiction to heroic exploits to admit it; and he effected his retreat for no other purpose than to assemble necessary Swedish reinforcements, fortify them by the addition of Frederick William's army, and with the least possible delay set out for the third time to crush the many-headed Polish hydra.

The revised program obliged him to modify his political style and, instead of issuing stern commands to Frederick William as he had done in January, some four months later to approach him, hat in hand, as a suitor. Or if that statement gives a wrong impression, since Charles X was not the man ever to exhibit humility and abandon his natural strut, we may fairly say that, caught in the web of circumstance and needing Frederick William as an ally, he was prepared to win him with concessions. Accordingly, he opened negotiations; and hardly had they been inaugurated when Frederick William's original suzerain, John Casimir, appeared upon the scene with a counterproposal not to be rejected without due consideration. He offered full forgiveness for his vassal's late treasonable defection. Instead of showering threats of vengeance on him, both adversaries now besought his favor. While that was an agreeable change, it did not in any essential respect improve his position; for, owing to the Polish rising and the Swedish setback, both warring powers, now more nearly on a par, had closed in on him like a beleaguering host. They camped along the Prussian border and, declaring that his ambiguous neutrality would no longer be tolerated, insisted that he declare unequivocally and without more ado precisely where he stood.

On the new issue being referred to the Privy Council, the cleavage already noted on earlier occasions reappeared. Save Count Waldeck, every member rejected the proffered Swedish alliance as involving too grave a risk. For this very reason, however, the sanguine Waldeck was in favor of it, since, if the risk was great, so also was the prospective profit. He judged that the hard-pressed Charles would offer a slice of the Polish spoils and, depending on the favorable progress of the conflict, might even be moved to increase it, whereas John Casimir, having no spoils to distribute, would merely propose to sponge the slate and let bygones be bygones.

It was in the end Waldeck's arguments that carried the day with his chief. How could it have been otherwise? The elector had provided himself with an army at ruinous cost, for defense, yes, but even more for aggrandizement; and aggrandizement was possible only at the side of Sweden and at the expense of Poland. Add that he suffered keenly from his recent ignominious discomfiture and burned to take the field to win the military distinction which he had never ceased to crave. In the month of May, Waldeck was dispatched to the town of Marienburg, where Charles had established his headquarters for the siege of nearby Danzig which, in spite of the insurmountable difficulties it presented, he felt could no longer be adjourned. Waldeck's instructions called for an interminable list of advantages to be wrested from the Swedes. Diplomacy being the game of bluff it is, that was the usual start of all negotiations. And to keep the competing party of the Poles in a disposing humor as long as the issue hung fire, the Poles were fed with hopes of a successful accommodation in parallel negotiations. That, too, was the established diplomatic procedure.

The king of Sweden and Count Waldeck were men of related mettle and felt for each other an instinctive respect. That did not, however, keep them from being sharp bargainers, and Waldeck, doubtless without the least surprise, soon learned that Charles was far from considering his affairs so desperate that he was willing to pay whatever price was asked for the Brandenburg alliance. In sign of his unbroken belief in his lucky star he refused even to consider the relinquishment of Frederick William from the bonds of vassalage. In lieu thereof he made a lavish offer of Polish territory immediately adjoining the Neumark and to be taken over in full sovereignty as soon as the final victory should be won. In return for this single—and exceedingly doubtful—benefit, the elector was asked to aid Charles with his whole army in the coming campaign. Although the Swedish monarch was to exercise supreme command, the Brandenburg supporting troops were permitted to retain their character of an independent fighting unit.

On these terms a new Brandenburg-Swedish treaty, supplementary to the Treaty of Königsberg of January, 1656, was signed at Marienburg on June 25 of the same year. Its conclusion sufficed to send Charles off like a bolt on his third Polish invasion. He hoped to be in time to relieve the small Swedish garrison that was holding out at Warsaw and that for two months had been subjected to siege by a vast horde of wild-riding horsemen from every province of the broad Polish steppe. His disappointment was keen on learning on his way thither that on July 1 the Warsaw Swedes, shrunk to a pitiful handful by war and disease, had been obliged to capitulate. When, a week later, he pitched camp a little north of Warsaw he was at the head of twelve thousand troops.

It would have conformed with the king's headlong temper to throw himself without delay on the superior enemy forces, but any such plan was prevented by the sudden inundation by the river Bug which flowed between them and him. He had to content himself to wait for Frederick William, who, moving at his own pace, joined him with eighty-five hundred men toward the end of July. Thereupon, leaving some twenty-five hundred Swedes behind to defend the fortified camp, he directed an army of eighteen

Engraving after a painting by De Baan (Bettmann Archive)

GEORGE FREDERICK COUNT WALDECK

Engraving of the year 1690 after an earlier painting (Bettmann Archive)

FIELD MARSHAL GEORGE DERFLINGER

thousand, wherein the Swedes slightly outnumbered the Brandenburgers, against the Poles massed on the right bank of the Vistula opposite their capital. It is worth noting and indicative of Charles's fighting style that, among his Swedes, cavalry and infantry stood to each other in the ratio of seven to two, while, among the Brandenburgers, the two arms about balanced each other. The combined artillery of the allies consisted of fifty-three pieces. As for the fifty thousand Poles posted to meet the attack, they were, except for a few negligible units, mounted troops with some cannon but substantially fewer than those of the enemy. If numbers alone decided the issue of battle, the Poles would have blown the invaders off the field; but being, as already said, a brave but undisciplined feudal host, they could not stand up against the steady, unswerving drive of their expertly maneuvered opponents.

The battle of Warsaw, which lasted three days (July 28–30), ended in the complete rout of the Poles and the recapture by Charles of their capital. While it reverberated deafeningly across Europe for a few days, it was as little a decisive event as any of the earlier victories Charles had harvested in Poland. If the king had had his way, he would now as before have driven deeper into Poland; but he had at the present juncture an ally to consider and was no longer sole master of the situation. And not a step beyond Warsaw would Frederick William move. He had long ago convinced himself that the conquest of Poland was a delusion and that the desirable course for Sweden, and certainly for himself, would be to bring the war to the earliest possible termination. Unable to persuade his headstrong ally, he could at least refuse to sacrifice his own interest in order to share his partner's folly. Accordingly, when the elector learned that the Lithuanians were making destructive forays into Prussia, ignoring the remonstrances of Charles, he backtracked for home to draw, as far as lay in him, a protective barrier around his Prussians and their farms.

In the circumstances there was nothing better for the frustrated king of Sweden to do than to return to Polish Prussia and reopen the abandoned siege of Danzig. By every cool calculation no feat he might perform in Poland could compare in importance with success at this point, for the possession of Danzig was absolutely crucial for the realization of his Baltic ambitions. And now his troubles multiplied until they crowded in on him like a marching jungle. The Dutch sent a fleet under Admiral Opdam into Danzig waters resolved that this pivot of their Baltic trade should not fall into Swedish hands. The fleet made the siege impracticable, and Charles, beaten, not only had to give it up but also to promise (September 11) the Dutch not to increase the levies on their goods in Swedish ports. Then there were the Russians. Charles had intrusted the defense of the Swedish coast south of the Gulf of Finland to one of his generals; but as he had not been able to furnish him with sufficient troops, the general, though a highly competent soldier, had been forced to yield large sections of Ingria and Livonia to the enemy.

Even more alarming was a change in the policy of Austria. Than this ancient enemy Sweden had no more implacable ill-wisher in the world. Nonetheless, still engaged in nursing the wounds inflicted by the Thirty Years' War, Austria was long disinclined to lend an ear to the frenzied cries raised by Poland for assistance. At length, however, heartened by the recent evidences of Polish recovery, the Viennese court roused itself from its lethargy and agreed to put a small auxiliary troop at the disposal of its neighbor. Finally, there was Poland itself, whose recent impressive revival invited a revaluation of its strength. Following his rout at Warsaw, John Casimir, instead of dropping out of sight, had busied himself in reassembling the scattered elements of his army. Thereupon in the autumn, boldly assuming the offensive, he led his troops down the course of the Vistula. He could not have proclaimed his resurgence more resoundingly than he did when, in mid-November, 1656, he entered liberated Danzig amid the jubilation of its citizens.

Meanwhile Frederick William had his hands full defending Prussia from the incursions of the swift-riding Lithuanian raiders. Every consideration of good sense and, more especially, the intolerable financial burden of the war urged him to seek peace, and he never ceased prodding his ally to initiate negotiations to that end. Nonetheless, no matter how anxiously he longed for peace, he was not minded to accept it unless it brought him the coveted sovereignty in Prussia. Gone, or at least dropped into the background, were the schemes of territorial increase at Poland's expense which he had at one time or another turned over with his councilors; he would willingly sacrifice them for the one substantial prize making him a free man in the old land of the Teutonic Order.

Emperor Ferdinand III had recently been persuaded to dispatch an ambassador, Franz von Lisola by name, into the Baltic area to keep him informed on the rapidly shifting situation. Lisola was the keenest diplomat in the imperial service, and his penetrating analyses, now available in print, throw a flood of light on the tangle of national rivalries and personal motives involved in the Swedish-Polish quarrel.[1] Lisola took it on himself to urge the Kaiser to enter the war on the side of Poland and late in the year 1656 achieved at last the success just noted of a small force dispatched to Poland's succor. It was also Lisola's strongly held opinion that Brandenburg would have to be detached from Sweden and reconciled with Poland; and although he regarded the Brandenburg demand of sovereignty in Prussia as rather stiff, he was prepared to recommend it to his master's ally, John Casimir, in the conviction that it was an indispensable preliminary to the ultimate defeat of Charles X. In the autumn and winter of 1656–57 Lisola failed to carry his point with the Poles. The current was at that time running too distinctly in their favor for them to consider buying off an enemy whom they were persuaded they already had at their mercy and who moreover was no better in their eyes than a rebel and traitor.

When Frederick William convinced himself that John Casimir was implacable, there was no other course open to him than to hold fast to the alliance with Charles X. He had, however, by this time become so necessary to the isolated and bedeviled king that he could ask for an improvement of the recent treaty, could ask, nay, demand, that the sovereignty in Prussia he had so long been clamoring for be no longer withheld. Not for a moment was the elector in doubt that the grant, in order to be valid, would have to be made by his legal overlord, John Casimir; but since John Casimir refused to entertain even the thought of such a surrender, Frederick William was moved to do the next best thing and wring it from his immediate master, Charles X. Charles was fundamentally as unwilling to make the desired concession as the king of

1. "Die Berichte des kaiserlichen Gesandten F. von Lisola aus den Jahren 1655–60," *Archiv für Oesterreichische Geschichte*, Band LXX.

Poland; but necessity is stronger than even a viking's resolution, and on November 20, 1656, the belated viking on the Swedish throne put his signature to a treaty (the Treaty of Labiau) wherein he released the duke of Prussia from his feudal bondage. He must at the moment have been exceptionally downhearted, for he also gave up his share in the customs of the Prussian ports of entry. At least so far as Sweden was concerned Frederick William had at Labiau become master in his own house!

THE TREATIES WITH POLAND OF WEHLAU AND BROMBERG

A few weeks later Charles was again riding the crest of the waves. His massive energy directed by a sanguine temperament gave him an unquenchable assurance, and when he now managed to secure the alliance of George Rakoczy, prince of Transylvania, who promised to invade Poland from the south, he felt certain that he need but advance against John Casimir from the north to catch the slippery king in a pincers' hold from which there would be no escape. We may dispense with going into this fourth attempt to win a kingdom at the point of a lance in the manner of a medieval tale of knighthood. Most reluctantly the sober-minded Frederick William ordered a small troop of Brandenburgers under Count Waldeck to help his ally indulge his latest whim. The campaign lasted from March to June of 1657 and, following a prosperous beginning, ended, like all its predecessors, in a calamitous retreat.

If it now came about that the curtain was rung down on the king of Sweden's marchings to and fro and up and down in Poland, it was not because he experienced a change of heart and renounced the idea of crushing John Casimir but rather because of so sweeping a transformation of the general political scene that he was inescapably obliged to let his attention swing away from the distraught Slav kingdom. That the transformation had been in preparation for some time we had occasion to see when we noted Austria's hesitant approach to the brink of war by putting an auxiliary corps at the service of the Polish monarch. Six months later, in May, 1657, the Viennese court went further and deliberately plunged into the maelstrom. On the strength of a new agreement with Poland it entered the war directly as a principal. In the very same month Denmark, too, joined the fray and made ready to attack Sweden in Germany.

Three enemies therefore where there had been one before! Thus threatened on his return in June from inner Poland, Charles decided to wash his hands of the whole disgusting Polish mess and throw himself on Sweden's oldest and dearest enemy, on Denmark. War between these two Scandinavian states had become an all but sacred matter of tradition and was not likely to be brought to a conclusion so long as Denmark was sole mistress of the entrance to the Baltic at the Sound and held besides the southern tip of the Swedish peninsula, which Sweden had never ceased to claim on grounds of geography and nationality. Characteristically, Charles did not ask the allied Frederick William's leave to depart from Poland and march against the Danes. He went for the to him entirely sufficient reason that imperative interests called him away; and he would have been afflicted with a simplicity calculated to bring a blush of shame to the cheek of the veriest political tyro of that age if he had believed that Frederick William, on being thus abandoned, would not give ear to the call of his own interest.

The elector's first step on the road of disincumbered selfishness opened to him through Charles's abandonment of the Polish theater of war was to register his desire for peace with Poland by an order to his troops to refrain from attack. He followed up this move with a gracious communication to the queen of Poland, who, according to the opinion of an observant contemporary, governed her sluggish husband as deftly "as a little Ethiopian does his elephant." These friendly gestures might not have got him anywhere had it not been for that Austrian ambassador, Lisola, whose mission it was to flit about the war-torn area and guide the decisions of his court. Convinced that it was to the vital interest of Austria for Sweden to be defeated and that the defeat was impossible without detaching Brandenburg from Sweden, Lisola had been consistently at work in the soft-treading manner of his kind to inoculate the Polish court with his view. Repeated conferences with Frederick William had persuaded him that for nothing short of sovereignty in Prussia would this ruler renounce the Swedish connection. This concession, therefore, the Austrian diplomat set himself by hook or crook to wrest from John Casimir and, even though the king was a man of feeble resolution, Lisola would never have succeeded had it not been for the recent alliance by which Austria, in effect, had taken over battered Poland as a client. Only on the assumption of this guardian-ward relationship between them can we understand how it came about that the cowed John Casimir finally authorized Lisola to treat with Frederick William in his name and to make the demanded concession as a last resort, if nothing less should prove acceptable.

It cannot therefore be disputed that the Treaty of Wehlau, which was signed by representatives of Poland and Brandenburg on September 19, 1657, was primarily the Austrian mediator's work. In it Frederick William renounced, together with the bishopric of Ermland, such Polish lands as he had occupied in the course of the war and received in exchange the passionately desired Prussian sovereignty. The treaty did not permit him to drop back into his original neutral role. Very probably he would himself have rejected neutrality, even had it been offered, for he was acutely aware that by coming to terms with Poland he had made Swedish Charles his deadly enemy and that his only hope of escaping punishment at the irate monarch's hands was to associate himself with Poland, Austria, Denmark, and every other state that could be induced to join the alliance to the end of assaulting and wearing down the infatuated swashbuckler until he was broken. On certain matters left undecided by the Treaty of Wehlau, agreement was reached in a supplementary treaty signed at Bromberg in the following November. While both treaties taken together define the details of the pacification effected between Brandenburg and Poland, the birthday of Frederick William's sovereignty in Prussia, generally and properly regarded as his greatest achievement in the foreign field, is September 19, 1657, the date of the Wehlau document.

THE WAR'S LAST PHASE: THE FOUR ALLIES AGAINST SWEDEN

When Charles X turned away from Poland in order to fall on Denmark, the war, which had begun as a duel between Sweden and Poland, became a general Baltic struggle in which Frederick William's share was relatively unimportant. Allied with Poland,

Austria, and Denmark, he was every whit as anxious as they to smother the menace that the Swedish king had become. In his first campaign of the enlarged war, the campaign of 1658, he successfully came to the aid of the hard-pressed Danes by driving the Swedes out of the peninsula of Jutland, which they had occupied. Then, in the campaign of the following year he laid siege to Stettin, the Swedish key position on the Oder, in the hope by its capture of driving the Swedes out of what by his never wavering faith was his own Pomerania. This from a purely Brandenburg angle was the main event of the last phase of the war, but it brought no advantage to the elector, for Stettin successfully withstood the assault of his army.

In spite of even mightier deeds of daring on the part of Charles X than he had performed in Poland, his headlong conduct of the war ended in a far more sweeping catastrophe than on the earlier occasion. To the savage end of crushing the Danes beyond the possibility of recovery, he had his fleet transfer him and his army to the island of Zealand on which lies Copenhagen, the Danish capital. Thereupon, when the Dutch fleet, dispatched to keep the Baltic open to Dutch trade, completely destroyed the Swedish naval forces, Charles became a prisoner on the island at the mercy of his enemies. All that now remained was for the hunters to close in on the wounded lion and dispatch him. But that event never took place for the single reason that France interposed with its veto. Under its great minister, Cardinal Mazarin, the Bourbon kingdom had just triumphantly ended its war with Spain and by the Peace of the Pyrenees (1659) had become the leading power of Europe. To Mazarin the elimination of Sweden from its Baltic primacy was intolerable, because in the Westphalian system, which he had mainly originated, Sweden to the north of Germany was the necessary counterpart of France planted on the Rhine for keeping the Reich under permanent threat and in permanent helplessness.

When Mazarin first presented himself to the allied courts of Denmark, Poland, Austria, and Brandenburg with the polite suggestion that he be permitted to arrange a peace between them and their Swedish enemy, they met the plan with a unanimous indignant rejection. But on Mazarin's persisting in his proposal, they successively yielded with the result that a French agent of the cardinal was able, toward the close of 1659, to open a peace congress at the ancient monastery of Oliva, not far from the city of Danzig. Mazarin had from the first made it clear that the negotiations between Sweden and its Danish enemy were not to be conducted at Oliva. Wily diplomat that he was, he opined that he could shape them more to his taste by conducting them separately at Copenhagen.

The Oliva conferees had not been long in session when there fell on them like a clap of thunder the news of the death of their Swedish adversary. Charles X died on February 22, 1660, at the early age of thirty-eight, worn out by his superhuman labors. His successor was his four-year-old son, in whose name a council of regency took over the government. The disappearance from the scene of the madcap monarch hastened the conclusion of peace, for, great as were the advantages France was set on securing for him, he would almost certainly have asked for more and might in his irresponsible manner not even have hesitated to flout his intercessor. With Charles out of the way, the negotiations proceeded with unusual smoothness, and on May 3, 1660, the Peace of Oliva was signed between Sweden and its three allied adversaries of Poland, Austria, and Brandenburg.

By the Oliva terms the Swedes acquired the Baltic province of Livonia which had been in dispute between them and Poland ever since the days of Gustavus Adolphus and, in exchange for Livonia, surrendered their unfounded claims to Polish Prussia. Swedish Pomerania, hotly coveted and partly occupied by Frederick William, was granted him neither in whole nor in part. Had he succeeded in capturing Stettin in the campaign of 1659 the verdict might have been different. But having failed in that attempt, he had to bow to the Olympian decision of all-powerful Mazarin, who refused to entertain the thought of diminishing Sweden's foothold in Germany. What the baffled elector got out of Oliva reduced itself to the acknowledgment of his sovereignty in Prussia by all the treaty's signatories. While this meant no gain in territory, it represented a rise in status, the importance of which can hardly be exaggerated. From now on he was, at least so far as the duchy of Prussia was concerned, on a par with every independent ruler of Europe; and he owed this elevation, as the whole world had witnessed, to a tremendous five-year struggle in which he had proved himself both a master of diplomatic chess and a bold and circumspect leader in war.[2]

There can be no doubt that amid the incalculable hazards of a war waged across his territory by two larger and stronger states Frederick William had found himself, had matured to a vigorous, self-reliant manhood. With the Oliva milestone he had completed a twenty-year period of schooling in government. Looking backward to his accession to the throne as an inexperienced youth of twenty, we recall that he had signalized himself at once as the possessor of an excellent understanding and by an exceptional devotion to his unfamiliar duties. But everything was still to learn both at home and abroad, and while he was not afraid to make the necessary day-to-day decisions according to his lights, he recognized the advisability of giving ear to the opinions of his ministers and even of yielding to the guidance of the particular associate of his labors who seemed at the moment most worthy of his trust.

In this frame of mind the young ruler had continued through the better part of the first two decades of his reign, accepting in succession, as we are aware, Conrad von Burgsdorf, Joachim Friedrich von Blumenthal, and Count Waldeck as his leading advisers. But never even in the hour of their greatest influence could it have occurred to any of them that they had become the effective masters of the state, for Frederick William always bore himself with the dignity proper to his station and permitted no doubt to arise that the final decision in every issue that arose rested with himself. In the course of the recent war even the qualified dependence to which he had hitherto submitted came to an end. It terminated in 1657 on the departure from his service of Count Waldeck, owing to his bitter opposition to the elector's exchange of the Swedish for the Polish alliance. The temperamental count figured as the last minister of whom it can be said with assurance that he had had a conspicuous hand in shaping his master's policy.

Even before Waldeck's withdrawal from office there had come

2. A convenient digest of the Treaty of Oliva as well as of its predecessors, the Treaties of Königsberg, Marienburg, Labiau, and Wehlau, will be found in Moerner. The specifically Brandenburg angle of the war and its attendant negotiations are illuminated by *UA*, Vols. VII, VIII, and *PR*, Vol. V.

to the front a man who without fear of successful refutation may be declared to have been the most valuable and trustworthy, if not the most authoritative, adviser Frederick William succeeded in the course of his whole lifetime in attaching to his service. His name was Otto von Schwerin, by birth a Pomeranian nobleman. There are historians who would have it that he was Waldeck's successor and who speak of an Era Schwerin as following on the heel of eras named, respectively, for Burgsdorf, Blumenthal, and Waldeck. But this is surely a misapprehension of Schwerin's role and personality, due in part no doubt to the high regard in which he was held by the elector. Shortly after Blumenthal's fall from grace Schwerin had been appointed to the headship of the Privy Council with the title *Oberpräsident,* and until his death, over twenty years later, he retained the leading post in the administration and was, besides, dispatched on every political mission requiring a combination of professional skill, sound judgment, and courteous manners. A special trait, which recommended him to the elector and even more to the electress, was his deeply religious nature. Louise Henriette glowed with the same ardor as the president of the Privy Council for the Reformed faith, and when the time came for her sons to be intrusted for their education to a masculine governor, it was the capable and faithful Pomeranian Calvinist whom, with of course her husband's approval, she chose for the office.

In short, Otto von Schwerin acquired a position of such solid structure that he retained it to the end of his days, figuring not only as the leading official of the state after the elector but through his intimacy with the electoral couple as a close and privileged housemate. And yet so lacking was he in the usual egotism of the courtier that with all his many kinds of influence he was never prompted to dominate his master nor to desert his self-elected role of willing and devoted servant.

On the conclusion of the Polish-Swedish War, Brandenburg had become a power to be reckoned with, at least within the Baltic range. The phenomenon did not escape the attention of trained observers verywhere, nor did they hesitate to ascribe it to the alert and indefatigable ruler of the state. Against every probability not only had he not fallen victim to the wrath of the northern conqueror but had besides contributed signally to that conqueror's discomfiture. At the same time he had gained a clear victory over the other neighbor that pressed upon him, the king of Poland, whom he had obliged to release him from the bonds of vassalage. Ever since the accession in 1640 of young Frederick William the name Brandenburg had made itself heard throughout the German lands with increasing frequency. Twenty years later it elicited so much respect that its mention was often coupled with the prophecy that, should the present incumbent live out his normal span, it would leap beyond the boundaries of the Reich and become familiar to all the nations of Europe.

Chapter 8

THE DOMESTIC REVOLUTION

THE IRREPRESSIBLE CONFLICT BETWEEN FREDERICK WILLIAM AND HIS DIETS

We have now attended Frederick William through the first twenty years of his reign. Because he began his rule as the impotent victim of a war that had been raging through the German lands ever since two years before his birth, we have seen that he was obliged to inaugurate his government by concentrating all but exclusively on the bare issue of self-preservation. When, eight years after his accession, the Treaty of Westphalia brought peace to Germany, he was indeed relieved of the immediate pressure of war by this happy event but found himself in a hardly less perilous situation than before. Immediately to the north, in the lost western section of Pomerania, towered the solidly founded might of Sweden, casting its long shadow southward all the way to his very seat and capital. To his east spread the vast, chaotic mass of Poland, perpetually giving off ominous, deep-toned rumbles like a volcano on the point of eruption. To his west lay his Westphalian territory of Cleve-Mark, of which, in spite of unremitting efforts, he had up to the peace settlement been unable to obtain clear and unchallenged possession. And chiefly to his south, but clockwise all around him, stirred futilely but feverishly the innumerable Lilliputian states into which the Holy Roman Empire had been broken as by a shattering interior explosion.

Confronted by these uncertainties threatening from every side, the young prince, apart from a momentary indecision on first assuming office, had proceeded on a plan which he never afterward abandoned. He provided himself with an army, at first a very small army, since that was all that the exhausted mark could support. This force he then proceeded, in measure as his several territories regained their strength, to swell to a larger figure. His centrally motivating thought was that, in view of the permanent perils by which he was encircled, he would see to it that his army, too, his necessary sword and buckler, should be permanent, that is, that it should be not a temporary or emergency army dependent on the capricious favor of his diets but a standing army dependent solely on himself.

To make his plan effective, it would have to be supported by taxes, and taxes could not be had constitutionally except with the consent of the Landtag which in each of his provinces shared the rule with him. Whenever they were approached on this head, these bodies, without exception, manifested a stubborn disinclination to vote the desired supplies, in part no doubt because they were unwilling to load themselves with the proposed new burdens, but overwhelmingly because of their distaste for the very institution the tax money was intended to create and which in the discussions that raged unchecked in these assemblies was held up to infamy in the shape of that bogeyman of seventeenth-century parliaments throughout Europe, the *miles perpetuus.* The result was a hotly contested and long-drawn-out constitutional struggle between the prince and his various diets, which we propose to review in the present chapter.

In the later Middle Ages there had everywhere in Europe come into existence a representative political body which constituted a variously effective check on the authority of the ruler. It was called parliament in England, estates-general in France, Reichstag in Germany, and Landtag or Landstände (estates) in the all but independent principalities into which Germany had gradually dissolved. When, in 1640, Frederick William succeeded his father, he came into possession of three of these principalities with which we have by now become measurably familiar: the electorate and mark of Brandenburg, the duchy of Prussia, and the duchy of Cleve-Mark. In each of them, as we also know, existed a Landtag endowed with a varying body of rights but embracing in each instance control of taxation as the undisputed minimum of its extensive prerogative.

In the three diets sat, organized usually in two houses, the feudal landowners or knights and the delegates of the self-governing towns. That the incumbents represented relatively small, privileged bodies of the population will appear the moment we reflect that, although the knights stood for the interests of agriculture, the great mass of the agricultural laborers, the peasants, were unrepresented; and, further, that the town delegates, who represented commerce and industry, were the agents of a well-to-do, propertied minority, the so-called "burghers," but that the common people, constituting the overwhelming majority of the urban population, boasted no spokesmen of their own. In short, the Landtag was an assembly of property owners, and the theory on which its right of taxation rested was that taxes were paid by property and must be duly authorized by the owners thereof before they might be collected.

On the occasion of Frederick William's accession we looked into the authority exercised by the diets of the territories constituting his inheritance and have taken occasional note of the friction that arose between the two parties to the government. When, at the Peace of Westphalia, the elector received as his share of the German lands available for distribution eastern Pomerania, Minden, Halberstadt, and the expectancy to Magdeburg, he took over with them a political organization closely resembling that prevailing in his older territories. In other words, in the new territories, too, the ruler was obliged to govern in agreement with the diets composed of the two privileged groups of the knights and burghers. However, as each of the new acquisitions was relatively unimportant in terms of size and population and as, furthermore, Frederick William inaugurated his rule in them by confirming to their respective diets their traditional rights, no conflict demanding our attention was precipitated between them and him. An entirely different situation developed in regard to the diets of Brandenburg, Cleve-Mark, and Prussia, all three not only endowed with an ample body of rights but habituated also to their unchecked exercise. In them the elector, on beginning his encroachments, encountered so determined an opposition that the issue was kept in suspense for years and even decades before it was decided in his favor.

As the three conflicts are separate and distinct stories, they will now be taken up in turn, with precedence accorded, properly enough, to the original Hohenzollern dominion, to Brandenburg.

THE CONFLICT WITH THE DIET OF BRANDENBURG

It was in the course of the sixteenth century, in the reign of Joachim II, that the Brandenburg Landstände, taking advantage of the disordered finances of their ruler, reached the highest level of their power. Before they would agree to take over his debts, they forced him to accept a financial administration of their own, called the Creditwerk, which received authority to collect and administer the taxes voted for the extinction of his obligations.[1] It is plain that by means of the Creditwerk they seriously encroached on the authority of their prince. However, as soon as the Thirty Years' War began to spill over the Brandenburg boundaries, their power quickly and startlingly diminished. The successive armies of occupation, Imperialists and Swedes alike, collected by force of arms whatever they required for their sustenance and mocked at the indignant remonstrances of the diet in case they ever condescended so far as even to listen to them. Then, when in the last years of the reign of George William an effort was made, under the all-powerful Schwarzenberg, to create a Brandenburg army, the method of the invader was followed by the home government, and the necessary supplies were brought in by military execution. Schwarzenberg defended his procedure as entirely lawful by reference to what we may call a loophole in the constitution, on the strength of which defense measures might be taken by the prince without consulting the diet in the event of a sudden threat to the safety of the realm. His position was, of course, disputed by the Landtag, the members of which never ceased to denounce the exactions of the Statthalter as the blackest tyranny.

It happened that in order to iron out his mounting difficulties with the diet Schwarzenberg had summoned it to Berlin just before the demise of the elector, George William, and that it was therefore in session when young Frederick William mounted the throne. The diet immediately dispatched a committee to their new ruler in distant Königsberg not only to lodge the most violent complaints against the high-handed Statthalter but also to demand the

1. See chap. iv, p. 93.

immediate reduction of the unbearable burdens under which the country was groaning by coming to terms with the Swedes and disbanding the army. As Frederick William fully shared their aversion to Schwarzenberg, he followed a course which we may call his own but which nonetheless was to a certain extent imposed on him by the exhortations of the visiting committee. He made a truce with the Swedes and, while he did not disperse the army altogether, he reduced it to garrison proportions. So unreasonable did the Landtag prove to be on the army question that it was not until 1643 that it was persuaded to accept the ruler's compromise proposal and to appropriate one hundred and fifty thousand talers for the maintenance of some two thousand men, a body barely sufficient to hold the few fortresses of the electorate not yet seized by the invading Swedes. The one hundred and fifty thousand talers were, after obstinate wrangling, so apportioned between the two estates of knights and towns that the former paid a little less, the latter a little more than half (five-twelfths and seven-twelfths, respectively). Even their smaller share, it must be understood, the knights themselves did not pay since, following established custom, they passed it on to their peasants.

Having reached this accommodation with his Landtag, Frederick William began to regret his helplessness in the face of his enemies and, reversing himself, undertook to augment his military establishment at least to the extent of getting in hand for his better protection a small field force. We are aware that he applied the lever to this end first in Prussia, then in Cleve-Mark, and only in last resort in Brandenburg. Imagine therefore how great was his indignation when the diet of his central and largest territory not only sealed its ears to his plea for increased supplies but even hesitated to renew the credit allowed for the year 1643. In point of fact it was not again voted, and if the elector had not collected it arbitrarily, he would have been obliged to dismiss the small, purely defensive troop which he was maintaining and which represented the utmost concession to his diet that he was prepared to make.

As soon as the year 1648 put an end to the German war, the diet returned with refreshed assurance to the attack and demanded that the disbandment of the army so long refused on the score of the continuing war be now undertaken without further delay. When the sovereign pointed to the new and unforeseen risks he was facing in eastern Pomerania which, in spite of its cession to him at Westphalia, the Swedes continued under various pretexts to occupy, the estates answered that they were Brandenburgers and that Pomerania was no affair of theirs. With this contention they typically displayed their strictly provincial character. The diets of Prussia and Cleve-Mark were inspired by the same narrow provincialism, and it was this limitation of outlook which in last analysis accounted for the gulf that had opened between them and their ruler. By a succession of historical accidents that ruler had become the head of three separate German territories which by every instinct of statesmanship he was prompted to consolidate. The estates, on the other hand, born Brandenburgers, Prussians, and Cleveans, insisted on preserving their separateness and viewed with aversion every move of their ruler in the direction of fusion. In these circumstances the army acquired for both sides the added significance of a symbol. Frederick William regarded it as a Brandenburg-Prussian-Cleve, that is, a united, army and was resolved to put it in play as a unit when and wherever his dynastic interest might be at stake. Opposed even to a local army as a potential threat to their authority, the diets felt nothing less than horror for the strong central instrument their ruler was engaged in shaping. They regarded it as a constitutional monster and held it to be their duty to resist its creation with all the energy at their command.

When on reaching the Westphalian milestone the elector made no move to reduce the army, the Brandenburg Landtag grew more and more vigorous in its remonstrances against his headstrong conduct. In a last effort to solve the crisis amicably Frederick William in 1652 summoned an extraordinary, that is, a full, Landtag to Berlin. A full Landtag had been but rarely called in Brandenburg history, in all probability because it was too large and unwieldy a body for the orderly transaction of business. In a Landtag of this kind every knight had the right to attend in person and might cause the assembly to swell to a multitude of fifteen hundred heads. The usual Landtag, officially called a *Deputationstag*, was a representative body made up of two knights from each of the fifteen districts (*Kreise*), into which the electorate was for administrative purposes divided, and of one or two delegates from each of the towns. It would seem that the elector was moved to call together the unusual or full Landtag by the hope that the whole body of knights would show a better understanding of his military necessities than their chosen delegates.

What therefore, when the Landtag met, he was encouraged to demand was the startling innovation of a perpetual tax sufficient to support an army, small indeed but as perpetual as the tax for its support. True, it was not quite a perpetual tax which he requested, since he knew that the word alone would suffice to set the jaws of the estates like flint against him. His actual proposal was for a contribution of five hundred thousand talers distributed over the next six years. As ever since 1643 he had been collecting one hundred and fifty thousand talers per annum, he was in fact making a not inconsiderable concession to the estates on the material side, and he counted heavily on its effect. But against the easement in money stood the stretch of years, and not even the dullest cabbage-patch Junker failed to seize the implication: An army sanctioned for six years would be an army sanctioned for eternity! At the very least it would signify the surrender by the Landstände of their most cherished right, their dearly treasured "liberty," coupled with the triumph of that abomination of an encroaching absolutism, the perpetual soldier.

Since the full Landtag turned out to be as opposed to Frederick William's army plans as the usual representative Landtag had been, he made no headway with it. It was presently prorogued by him in the forlorn hope that reflection would make the members more amenable to his proposal. In the course of the next fifteen months he prorogued it seven times and then, persuaded that he would, after all, fare better with a restricted Landtag, in the summer of 1653 returned to the smaller and more business-like Deputationstag. From this he succeeded in wringing the substance of what he was after. The representatives at last submitted to the masterful prince, in part because he had worn them down by his stubborn dilatory tactics, but overwhelmingly because the knights, the dominant element of the assembly, gained the conviction that they could secure highly important class concessions in exchange for their vote. On August 5, 1653, the elector, in return for the inexorably demanded subsidy, gave his assent to an ordinance (more properly a sweeping constitutional enactment) which, although not containing anything startlingly new, so fortified the existing politicosocial structure of the mark that it endured substantially unchanged until its convulsive overthrow by Napoleon one hundred and fifty years later. Let us have a closer look at this ordinance officially called the *Landtagsabschied* of 1653.[2]

Every European state with a parliament inherited from the Middle Ages was a hierarchized society of the privileged few and the unprivileged many. While in Brandenburg the ruling classes were, in a strictly constitutional sense, the knights and the burghers, owing to the settled stagnation and resulting poverty of the towns, there was in reality only one ruling class, the knights. It was this fact that the enactment of 1653 heavily underscored, for its main significance may be declared to lie in its setting the knights apart as a distinct and dominant caste. And let it be said in respect to the knights, as already said in respect to the general constitution of the electorate, that the Abschied did not so much introduce novelties as that it gave a more precise formulation to privileges already in possession of the knights and repeatedly confirmed to them by Frederick William's predecessors.

To substantiate this statement it will suffice to refer to the developments recounted in connection with the financial difficulties of Joachim II.[3] By this elector's time, which was also the time of the Reformation, the knights had changed their character and been transformed from medieval warriors into profit-seeking agricultural producers. To employ the expressive German terms indicative of this transformation, they had given up being medieval *Grundherrn,* content to live frugally on ground rents, and become *Gutsherrn,* that is, agricultural entrepreneurs less interested in ground rents than in large-scale production on a capitalist basis. In measure as this transformation proceeded they had been prompted to increase their own land, the demesne, by appropriating the land of the peasants, and to provide themselves with the necessary labor force by increasing the obligatory workdays owed them by the peasants and by making this service permanently

2. For this ordinance (*Rezess* of 1653) see C. O. Mylius, *Corpus constitutionum marchicarum* (Berlin, 1736–41), VI, 427–63.

3. Chap. iv, pp. 90–93.

available by attaching the peasants to the soil. By these encroachments the formerly free peasants had been reduced to a grinding serfdom and what, under pressure from the knights, Joachim, supposed fountain of justice, had done was to forgive them their heaped illegalities by stamping these illegalities with the seal of the law.

In the circumstances one questions why it was that, a century after the decisive concessions they had wrung from Joachim II, the knights should have felt moved to secure their renewal from Frederick William. The answer is not only that renewal is in the nature of insurance but also that it may be utilized for the introduction of additions and clarifications. Conceding such alterations to be present in the Abschied of 1653, we may nonetheless assert that the privileges secured to the knights by Joachim II were not in any substantial way enlarged by it. The document made clearer than before that peasants who had lost their freedom could never again regain it; that in addition to service in the field they owed domestic service as well; and that they were amenable to the lord in his capacity of judge (*Gerichtsherr*), for he presided over the manorial court. While the peasants retained the right to appeal from the court of the Gerichtsherr to that of the elector, the right was nullified in practice by the power of the Gerichtsherr to punish with imprisonment a peasant guilty of preferring a baseless complaint (*mutwillige klage*), the baselessness being left to the judgment of the Gerichtsherr. A final matter worthy of attention was the acceptance by the Abschied of the pretention of the knights to the status of a privileged hereditary nobility, for the document declared that not only were *Lehngüter*, that is, knights' fiefs, immune from every form of taxation but also that they might not pass by sale or testament into other than noble hands. Lands designated as "noble" in 1653 must remain noble and could not come into the possession of commoners.

In the light of this legislation the knights figured as the feudal subjects of the elector, but the peasant serfs, all but completely cut off from contact with the head of the state, figured as the subjects of their lords and were juridically, economically, and financially at their mercy.

That Frederick William had pretty much broken the back of the diet with the settlement of 1653 was made evident with little delay. Two years later the Swedes undertook the drive into Poland which at once threw the whole Baltic area into turmoil. The elector's unhesitating response to the danger in which he found himself was to recruit an army large enough to enable him to become a factor in the situation of sufficient importance not to be contemptuously ignored by the two combatants. By the year 1656 his army had swollen to almost twenty thousand men maintained by supplies wrung from his several dominions by whatever measures served his purpose. Inevitably, on these capricious terms the largest part of the army as well as of the money required for its support had to come from Brandenburg, and as the subsidy granted by the Landtag in 1653 served to satisfy no more than a fraction of the costs incurred, the elector possessed himself of the revenue needed to meet the remaining expenses by the use of force.

For this violence he could claim a measure of constitutional coverage, owing to that loophole touching the defense of the realm which ever since Schwarzenberg's day had served as a means of circumventing the Landtag's authority. To the impassioned outcry of the estates against his arbitrary procedure Frederick William answered blandly that it was his sworn duty to safeguard his territories against the hazards of a war raging along his borders. Exactly as on earlier occasions the estates were at angered pains to point out that it was Prussia, not Brandenburg, that was in jeopardy through the struggle in Poland and that no obligation whatever rested on them to pour out blood and treasure for any territory other than their own. So far had the elector by this time got with his program of a united army serving the total interests of his dynasty that he was able contemptuously to disregard these provincially inspired lamentations.

Deaf to the complaints of the Brandenburg Landtag and to the similar wailings of all his other diets, he traveled the independent way in the Baltic war with which we are familiar. After an agitated early period of wait-and-see, he at last went the length of entering the struggle as a principal and in this capacity fought the great battle of Warsaw at the side of the Swedish king. In these circumstances he was less than ever prepared to reduce his army and less than ever in a position to end his financial exactions. Held fast in the east by the exigencies of the constantly expanding war, he sent orders to his agents in Brandenburg to collect forty and fifty thousand talers a month over and above the contribution to which he was legally entitled. These backbreaking burdens laid on the impoverished inhabitants so soon after the Thirty Years' War were an all but unbearable load, but the elector, while regretting their necessity, saw no escape from their infliction save by sacrificing the advantages he had gained through joining the struggle. And that sacrifice he was unwilling to make.

Before the Baltic war came to an end in 1660 by the Treaty of Oliva the elector must by the rude method of military execution have sluiced some millions of Brandenburg talers into his military coffers; and against this lawlessness the diet never ceased to protest. But that was as far as it got. Not until peace had been rung in and Frederick William had returned to Berlin with an enormously increased reputation did he, simultaneously with the reduction of the army to a skeleton formation, terminate his financial irregularities. His independent conduct of the war through five eventful campaigns left no doubt that he had ceased being a constitutional, and was by now quite visibly on the way to becoming an absolute, ruler. The statement should not be understood to mean that with this increase of the sovereign's prestige the Landtag abdicated its authority and disappeared from the scene. More than once, as we shall hereafter discover, it played a not unimportant part in Brandenburg developments. Undeniably, however, the relations between Landtag and elector had come to a turning. In control of a standing army, he had become the master and could give his attention not only to forging that army into a steadily improved instrument but also to the closely related task of a comprehensive reorganization of the state. These latter labors, which provided Brandenburg with a modernized administration, are reserved for the following chapter.

THE CONFLICT WITH THE DIET OF CLEVE-MARK

It will facilitate our understanding of the constitutional struggle in Cleve-Mark if, at the risk of repetition, we recall the outstanding factors in the local situation and review the main developments since Frederick William's succession in 1640. In every such attempt at a general picture the first item to be set down must be the feeble hold of the house of Hohenzollern on these territories. While by a long list of agreements with the rival house of Pfalz-Neuburg dating from 1614 the considerable Rhenish principality of Jülich had been provisionally divided between the two claimants, the stubborn insistance of each on his exclusive right to the undivided inheritance had kindled a vast animosity and put off the possibility of a final settlement to a remote future. In the absence of such a settlement and under a ruler with a contested title, not only did the Landstände of Cleve-Mark fail to develop toward him the expected loyalty of subjects but also, and not unnaturally, they were encouraged to enlarge their powers at his expense. Add the havoc wrought by the Thirty Years' War with its unceasing incursions into these lands, lying at an important European crossroad, of the armies of all the combatants and we are faced with the decline to the vanishing point of the provisional ruler's authority and with the consequent inclination on the part of the estates to regard themselves as the only effective element of the government.

So utter was the helplessness of Frederick William on succeeding his father that for the first three years of his reign he was unable to do anything to improve his position in his Rhenish territory either in regard to the unfriendly Landtag or to the various occupying enemy forces. Then in 1643–44 there came, with the outbreak of the war between Denmark and Sweden, a transfer to other areas of some of the Dutch and imperialist troops encamped in Cleve-Mark and with it the opportunity for the ruler to repossess himself of some of his fortresses. As this could not be done without soldiers, the momentarily favorable turn taken by the general war became a main reason for the elector's extraordinary effort in these years to recover from his prolonged prostration by creating an army.

As soon as he had an army in hand he employed it, on the mistaken calculation that he would have the backing of the Dutch, in the war of 1646–47 against his hated Neuburg rival. Apart from his failure in respect to his main object, he had the additional misfortune of raising a storm of rabid protest among the members of the Cleve estates. They never tired of reminding him of his derelictions: He had recruited troops, levied taxes, waged war, all without their consent and in flagrant breach of their venerable constitution. Nor did they moderate their tone when, the war over, their young ruler lingered on in Cleve in the hope of coming to an understanding with his critics.

By far the most pressing of the many proposals he kept submitting to them was one for a subsidy which would enable him to maintain a modest defense force in this exposed northwestern corner of Germany. Admirably patient on the whole, he at times gave way, for he was a hot-blooded man, to outbursts of uncontrollable rage. But with neither temperate nor inflamed pleading did he make the slightest impression on his obdurate adversaries; and when at long last a document was drawn up defining the rights, respectively, of ruler and estates, it registered the unqualified victory of the latter. In the Landtagsabschied, dated October 9, 1649, Frederick William confirmed all the traditional privileges of the Landstände, in particular those relating to taxation, the exclusion of foreign (meaning Brandenburg) troops, and the reservation of offices exclusively to natives; and when he at length departed for Berlin, he left behind a territory in which he had failed to advance his position by as much as an inch and of which he was master in hardly anything more than in name.

Two years later, in 1651, on the same fallacious assumption of Dutch aid as in 1646, the elector returned to his quarrel with Neuburg and was even more conspicuously discomfited than on the earlier occasion. At the conclusion of peace he again stayed on in Cleve for many months with the view to making the estates more receptive for his army plan without, however, getting further with them than before, since, owing to the second war and the recruiting of troops and the arbitrary assessment of taxes by which the recruiting had been attended, the estates had become more fiercely aroused against him than ever. In their ungoverned resentment they had gone the length of undebatable treason by appealing in turn to the neighboring Dutch and the Hapsburg Kaiser to take military action against their tyrannical prince; and although their treason miscarried, it was only because the two foreign powers, after weighing the appeal for a while, decided to let it drop. In sum, it is not easy to see how in the years immediately following the second Neuburg war, the war of 1651, the relations between the ruler and the estates could have been worse. Frederick William was the prisoner of the Abschied of 1649, and every innovation he might feel encouraged to introduce brought him up against iron bars.

When, in 1655, the Polish-Swedish War broke out, Frederick William's response to this event was, as we know, nothing short of electric. He at once assembled an army, resolved not to play his father's role in the Thirty Years' War and figure as a shuttlecock knocked about at their pleasure by armed and more powerful neighbors. In Cleve-Mark, as well as in Brandenburg and Prussia, he recruited troops and collected the contributions necessary to their support without giving any heed to the impassioned protests of the several diets. To all three of them he offered the identical justification: Confronted by an instant threat, he was acting under the necessity which knows no law and which was an explicit or implicit feature of the constitution of each of his dominions. Precisely as in Brandenburg the estates of Cleve tossed back the reply that, if a necessity existed, it applied not to them but to Prussia and that Prussia was no more a concern of theirs than the king of Spain or the shah of Persia. Not for a moment did they waver in their stand that their interests were confined to the limits of their duchy and that they would resist with all the strength they could muster the now clearly revealed attempt of their ruler to fuse them with his other territories into a single unit under his absolute dominion.

The acrid debate went on throughout the five years the war lasted. But as the ruler conducted it with soldiers and the estates with words, it is not surprising that the ruler won the argument and remained master of the situation. August von Haeften, who prepared for publication the documents bearing on the crisis, has calculated that during the years in question Frederick William recruited and equipped in his territory of Cleve-Mark and sent thence to the Polish-Swedish War over twenty thousand soldiers and simultaneously squeezed out of the population no less than one and a half million talers.[4] Not until the war closed with the Treaty of Oliva did the exactions represented by these amazing

4. *UA*, Vol. V.

figures cease. And with the return of peace came the inevitable day of reckoning with the aggrieved estates.

Far from avoiding that day, Frederick William met it promptly and with open visor by dispatching to the Landtag for its consideration a proposed revision of the Abschied of 1649 and by announcing his early arrival at Cleve to join personally in the discussion. He could not have picked a moment more auspicious from his point of view since for the time being all the trump cards were in his hands. The part he had played in the recent war had enormously increased his political stature; the ruthless manner in which he had overruled the estates had weakened their confidence and sapped their self-esteem; and the two foreign powers on which alone they could count to check their prince, the Dutch and the emperor, had in the course of the recent war become Frederick William's allies and at this exact turn of affairs cultivated relations with him that put an intervention on their part in behalf of the estates out of the question. Accordingly, when they began the consideration of the elector's constitutional draft, they exhibited an entirely novel moderation and in November, 1660, accepted it, save a limited number of articles adjourned for settlement to his promised early arrival. He came the very next month, and by the following March the new agreement had been perfected to the last remaining detail.

The two enactments of 1660 and 1661, taken together, became and remained the basis of the relations between Frederick William and the estates to the end of his reign. Owing in great part to the personal ascendancy he had achieved, a moderate and even respectful tone henceforth replaced the former violence. This is the more striking as an examination of the new understanding does not disclose many changes; almost the whole roster of traditional privileges, especially such crucial ones as the right to vote taxes and to exclude the foreign-born from office, around which the constitutional struggle had largely turned, were expressly reaffirmed. In point of fact the ruler demanded and was accorded only two distinct concessions. But they sufficed for his purpose. He was granted the right to recruit and maintain troops and to have the body of office-holders take the oath to his person and not, as formerly, to the latest constitutional agreement. The earlier oath, experience had shown, bound the office-holders to the estates and effectively withdrew them from executive obedience. We may sum up by saying that what the Landstände got out of the agreement was the certification of most of their inherited rights and that what the elector got was an army and a civil service under his sole direction. As it is a matter that no one disputes, we may divulge by anticipation that it was these two, army and civil service, which became the companion pillars of the new Hohenzollern state.

But let us be on our guard against exaggeration. Should we, on the basis of the ruler's indicated success, now imagine that the new absolute state had taken definite form, we would be making a grave mistake. The most we may aver is that Frederick William had cleared the path for an organization less feeble and diffused than the state he had inherited and more palpably centralized around his person. He moved forward deliberately, as behooves a successful state-builder, and was at pains not unnecessarily to offend the narrow, complacent provincialism of his Rhenish subjects. Accordingly, in harmony with the recent enactments only native-born were appointed to office and neither administratively, financially, nor judicially was any fusion effected with the pivotal province of Brandenburg. Even the small armed force, which he was privileged henceforth to maintain in Cleve, was in law, if not in spirit, a Cleve army supported by a subsidy which, following the recent pact, the Landstände voted year after year without fail.

Nonetheless, slowly a process of change did set in and, as is usual in all fundamental transformations, it made itself felt in the realm of the mind before taking form in the realm of the law. While continuing to parade their local patriotism, the inhabitants began imperceptibly to take pride in the deeds and growing fame of their prince. If it was not until a hundred years later, in the time of Frederick the Great, that they were content unreservedly to identify themselves with the state designed by Frederick William and completed by his successors, the mental revolution culminating in that identification may be confidently asserted to have begun in the latter half of Frederick William's reign and to have received its main impulse from the heroic legend which the popular imagination gradually wove around his name and person.

A few years later a final settlement with Neuburg made an important contribution to the growing confidence between prince and Landtag. That it was brought about through the initiative of Frederick William is the more surprising in view of his having twice revealed his irreconcilable disposition by levying war on Neuburg. But no man is proof against changing circumstances, and in 1665 events occurred that considerably modified Frederick William's political outlook. When in that year war broke out between England and the Dutch, one of the troublesome little German sovereigns along the Dutch border, the prince-bishop of Münster, took it upon himself to supplement the English attack on the Dutch by sea with an attack of his own by land.

His action set the whole region in commotion and threatened to precipitate a general war. Resolved at all costs to avert this calamity, Frederick William brought military pressure to bear on the cantankerous prince-bishop, thereby obliging him reluctantly to ground arms. But before the prelate gave way France manifested a purpose to bring him to terms by invading Germany; and although this plan was frustrated in the nick of time by Münster's submission, the elector had been filled with such alarm by the heaps of inflammable material piled up in this border region that he resolved to make a personal contribution to their reduction by seeking a settlement of the ancient Neuburg feud. Luckily, for reasons of his own, Duke Philip Wilhelm was at the moment similarly disposed with the net result that on September 9, 1666, a treaty was drawn up that at last terminated the more than fifty-year-old contest between the two claimants. The treaty confirmed in the main the existing partition, that is to say, Neuburg got Jülich and Berg, the larger and richer portion of the disputed inheritance, while the elector received Cleve and Mark with the small county of Ravensberg thrown in for good measure.

The territorial settlement was supplemented by a religious agreement which, challenged in every article by the stubborn Catholic orthodoxy of the Neuburg duke, required over a decade of discussion to bring into port. However, as finally drawn up, it became by its equitable character a model for religiously mixed areas, for it conceded unabridged freedom of conscience and authorized a freedom of worship which, if not absolute, was sufficiently liberal to cancel the most offensive features still firmly imbedded in contemporary religious practice.

Never as yet, owing to the provisional character of Frederick William's incumbency, had the Cleve-Mark estates acknowledged him as their ruler by a formal act of homage. This omission was now remedied, and, a month after the signing of the conclusive Neuburg treaty of 1666, the ceremony took place amidst demonstrations of good will which disclosed that prince and estates had at long last terminated the quarrel that had kept them at bitter enmity ever since the prince's accession to the throne.

THE CONFLICT WITH THE DIET OF PRUSSIA

In passing on to Prussia let it serve as our point of departure that its government of ruler and estates as traditionally organized did not differ greatly from that of Brandenburg and Cleve save in one highly significant particular: It was guaranteed by the king of Poland in his capacity of suzerain and could not be altered without his consent. A consequence of the Polish king's constitutional supervision was that he and the Prussian estates had for generations successfully co-operated to reduce the power of the duke. The most convincing evidence of their team work was that the administration had been intrusted to a board of four noble governors called *Oberräte,* who, although appointed by the duke, exercised an all but independent control. They made their influence felt from one end of the duchy to the other by means of district agents, called *Landräte,* who were of the same noble stratum as themselves. The Oberräte had even got the management of the ducal domain into their hands and, owing partly to careless accounting and partly to illicit favors touching these properties extended to their fellow-nobles, had succeeded in signally reducing the returns to the duke from this, his leading source of income not dependent on the favor of the diet.

We have seen that Frederick William, who was residing at the Prussian capital when his father died, had an acute understanding of his precarious hold on the government and from the day of his advent to power proceeded with the greatest caution in respect to both the hostile king of Poland and the hostile estates. His earliest, necessarily modest, aim was to receive his enfeoffment at the hands of the king and to be greeted as duke by the estates without having to submit to the further weighting of his already unbearably heavy fetters. In this he was by adroit maneuvering measurably successful, not, however, without being brought to a galling realization of his dependence. It will be remembered that even in so personal and intimate a matter as his religion, he had to bow to the exclusion demanded by the uncompromisingly Lutheran Landstände of his own Reformed faith from among the permitted worships of the land.

For the first decade and a half of his reign he accepted the situation with no more than a vivacious upflare of temper whenever the remnant of his rights was threatened with further curtailment. Accordingly, while occasional incidents disturbed his relations with both king and Landstände, they were in every case so quickly disposed of that we may safely characterize the first fifteen years of his reign as a period of relative domestic calm.

It need hardly be expressly said that here, as in every other area under the elector's scepter, the issue bound sooner or later to overshadow every other issue concerned the army. Under the constitution the duchy was provided with a native militia, called by the odd name, probably Polish in origin, of *Wibranzen,* and charged with defending the territory against any attack that might be launched against it from across the border. Although, like all similar establishments of medieval origin, it had long ago fallen into decay, it represented an institution the estates were sworn to sustain, and Frederick William could on this ground undertake to revive it without arousing their opposition. When, in the year 1644, he initiated the army program by which he announced his departure from the purely defensive policy adopted at his accession, he sent Conrad von Burgsdorf to Prussia to reorganize these involuntary volunteers. But, distrustful at the same time of their competence, he had him assemble also a small professional troop to be paid for from the ruler's private income supplemented by a meager subsidy to be wrung from the estates. These were the years of sudden Cossack and Tartar incursions into Poland (and therefore also into Poland's dependency of Prussia) and the members of the diet could only at peril of their private holdings refuse to provide an armed force to protect the border.

Thus was Prussia safeguarded by the revived Wibranzen, aided by a few brigades of mercenaries, without causing overmuch excitement among the estates, since only the latter troop was an innovation and could moreover be promptly got rid of the moment the service it rendered was no longer required. No doubt at all that the estates were as suspicious of their ruler and of that historical instrument of despotism, the professional army, as they had ever been; but they found their duke on the whole so tractable that they persuaded themselves to overlook his obsession regarding the *Defensionswerk* of which he was always talking, especially as there was no denying that the frontiers were in genuine jeopardy. It is a tribute to the elector's intelligently exercised self-control that throughout the period under consideration he trod the narrow, rigidly plotted path between Polish king and Prussian Landstände without rousing to the danger point the wakeful hostility of either of his partners (or shall we call them guardians?) and without sacrificing his own self-respect.

Then, after fifteen years and with the suddenness of a summer cloudburst, the situation underwent a complete change. So little did the change have its start in any action launched by Frederick William that it may much more justly be attributed to that element of chance inseparable from the hazardous affairs of men. In 1655 the king of Sweden attacked Poland, and Frederick William, whose main possessions lay between the two combatants, was inescapably sucked into the maelstrom. We have followed the Swedish-Polish conflict and noted how the elector in turn wavered, plunged, withdrew, and fought and how, in addition, he resorted to every trick in the ancient repertory of diplomacy to make up for his lack of military strength. In the end he emerged from the five-year hurly-burly clinching in his fist as prize the sovereignty of Prussia. Having borne the yoke of the Polish king for fifteen years with the patience imposed by the situation, he had, as soon as events took a favorable turn, boldly staked his all on the attempt to throw it off. The Treaty of Wehlau of 1657, confirmed three years later by the Treaty of Oliva, had set him free.

Free, yes, from the king, but not from the Prussian diet. Its members seized on every available occasion to assert in the most violent language that the sovereignty conceded by the king of Poland would, in order to be effective, have to be confirmed by them and that under no circumstances would they let themselves be persuaded to make a grant that so decisively diminished their importance. During the early years of the recent war the Landstände had, albeit reluctantly, voted certain taxes toward the support of the army. They could not shut their eyes to the fact that the war was not of their ruler's making and that besides, and almost from the first, it flowed irresistibly across the Prussian boundaries. Then when the elector became an active participant, fighting first on one side and then on the other, they were plainly bewildered and revealed their state of mind by tacking to the renewal of their subsidies the childish exhortation to their prince to thrust himself between Poland and Sweden and, waving an olive branch, to persuade them to come to terms. Presently, no longer able to make themselves heard above the deepening din of battle, they dispersed, while Frederick William, fighting for his life, took from the miserable population by military execution whatever moneys he required. That was the cruel as well as lawless situation when the war came to an end. At once and with a single voice the estates demanded that they be called together to be heard on the subject of their violated privileges.

Frederick William knew as well as his adversaries that formally he was in the wrong: That he had collected taxes without authorization; that on abandoning Prussia to fight against the Swedes in Jutland during the last phase of the war he had left behind a Statthalter who overshadowed the Oberräte and for whom there was not a trace of provision in the constitution; that he had brought foreign, that is, Brandenburg and Cleve, regiments into the country; and that he had staffed Prussian regiments with officers of foreign, that is, Brandenburg, birth and worse, if possible, of a forbidden, that is, the Reformed, faith. Over and above everything else he had without troubling to ask the consent of the Landtag altered his constitutional status by raising himself from dependent vassalage to free sovereignty. While he was aware that sooner or later the long roster of these imputed crimes would have to be aired in open debate between himself and the Landstände, he delayed summoning them in the hope that with the passing of time their rage against him might abate and a more reasonable frame of mind gain the upper hand.

Still another consideration caused him to hesitate, filling him with dark forebodings whenever he pondered the conflict that inescapably awaited him. So conscious was he of this particular feature in the situation that he was convinced that the struggle he was conducting and, in the main, had already won with the estates of Brandenburg and Cleve would rank on the level of a lover's quarrel compared with the ferocious nature of the contest that lay ahead in Prussia. Nor was he in any doubt that the difference in last analysis sprang from a source as measurable and unmysterious as geographical propinquity.

The privileged groups of Prussia belonged to a region lying under the political and social shadow of Poland and had to a large degree taken over the outlook of their Polish compeers. The ideal of the average Prussian knight was the unlimited "liberty" of the Polish nobleman, who took no orders from his king and gave to that dignitary what he was pleased to give and not a doit or obeisance more. The ideal of the average Prussian burgher or, more correctly, of the average Königsberg burgher, since Königsberg was the only town of any consequence in the duchy, was the republican "liberty" of neighboring Danzig, a town under the merely nominal rule of the Polish king and in happy possession of all but complete self-government. If we now add that throughout this still undisturbedly feudal region there had not yet come into existence the so potent national sentiment of our day, we shall understand how, without even the faintest sense of guilt, leading members of both the noble and the burgher class should by personal and epistolary solicitation, and even before the war had been brought to a close, have sought to establish contact with the Warsaw government to the end of persuading it to intervene in Prussia and help its ancient ally of the Landtag again to reduce the strutting sovereign duke to the dependence from which he should never have been released.

In the eyes of Frederick William these intrigues of his subjects at a foreign captal had under the new dispensation rung in by the Treaty of Wehlau become plain and unmitigated treason. He was fully informed about them by his capable ambassador at the

Polish court, Hoverbeck by name, but, apart from ordering his representative to be untiringly at the heels of the Polish king with the reminder of the obligation he had assumed at Wehlau no longer to interest himself in Prussia, was content for the nonce to be on his guard. He learned from Hoverbeck that, while the Prussian transgressors were many, the leading culprits, among the nobles, were the Kalcksteins, an unsavory trio of father and two sons, and, among the burghers, a man of a very different stripe, the intelligent and estimable Hieronymus Roth. To all petitioners alike King John Casimir, who was too discouraged by his recent awful drubbing at the hands of the king of Sweden to want to pick a quarrel with his erstwhile vassal, turned a deaf ear. But there was no dearth of high-placed Poles at Warsaw who were of a different mind and never ceased trying to persuade the monarch to recoup his recent losses by an alliance with the Prussian malcontents. All the elector's advisers, especially the trusted Schwerin, regarded the situation as charged with dynamite and certain so to remain until the day the estates had been brought to accept the new status of the duchy and, in unmistakable sign of their acceptance, had taken the oath of allegiance to their prince in his enlarged and sovereign capacity. As this solution would have to be preceded by a settlement with the aggrieved party, Frederick William's advisers were equally agreed in urging him to face the music by calling the estates together. Unable to deny the cogency of their argument, he belatedly made it his own. On May 31, 1661, more than a year after Oliva, the Landtag was formally opened.

Detained by business in the west, the elector sent Otto von Schwerin to Königsberg to fight his battle for him in close conjunction with the imposing but rather easygoing Statthalter, Prince Radziwill, already on the ground for some years past. No sooner was the Landtag in session than it bombarded the two lieutenants of their ruler from the inexhaustible armory of its grievances. Outdoing all its previous efforts, it capped its fiery onslaught with the declaration that its right of seeking redress of wrongs at Warsaw was unchallengeable and unimpaired and would in the future as in the past be employed at its pleasure.

In such an atmosphere the negotiations could make no headway but, though frequently adjourned, were not broken off. As in every sizable assembly there were in the diet both moderates and extremists, and the moderates, particularly numerous at this juncture among the nobles, never abandoned the effort to reach an accommodation. While the extremist leader in the upper class was the aged and authoritative General Kalckstein, the outstanding burgher extremist was the Königsberger Roth; and so hotly and resourcefully did the latter conduct the case against the elector that he became, as the months rolled by, the voice that drowned out and summed up all the other opposition voices in the land. In fact the struggle between Frederick William and the estates took the dramatic turn of a duel between the ruler and a single fearless commoner; and it was gradually made clear that until by one means or another the commoner had been silenced the constitutional battle would go on.

This remarkable adversary of his prince, this Roth christened Hieronymus at the font, belonged to a respected and well-to-do family long established at the Prussian capital. Endowed by nature with an incisive mind and a ready, eloquent tongue, he rose to be *Schöppenmeister*, that is, he achieved the very distinguished position of head of the municipal court. Inherited privilege coupled with superb knowledge and practice of the law prepared the ground for his political role; but he would not have enlisted the interest of posterity, as to a certain extent he has done, had he not also been a man of sterling character ready to sacrifice position and happiness for a cause in which he believed.

From the first moment of the breach between the estates and their revolutionary duke, Roth, strict legalist that he was, took his stand on the platform of the constitution. This gave him an advantage in every argument, for, by completely ignoring the fact that he was by implication setting up as sacrosanct and immutable the privileges of two favored groups, to one of which he himself belonged, he was free to assume the air of an intrepid champion of the law against its ruthless and cynical destroyer. He is adequately described as an honest, dyed-in-the-wool conservative and, more broadly, as an interesting, if minor, example of that type of intellectual fighter who, from a purely legal angle, is in the right in every phase of his struggle but who, viewed in the deeper perspective of the centuries, is nonetheless hopelessly and everlastingly in the wrong.

Against the stand taken by Roth and all others who thought as he did that the historic privileges of the estates could not be canceled except by the estates themselves and that therefore they were intact to the last insignificant flourish, Frederick William held that his sovereignty by having become incorporated in international law had superseded the former vassalage with the result that incitement to intervention by a foreign power, and especially by Poland, was reprehensible, wilful treason. Consequenty, he had been roaring "traitor" every time he had heard from Schwerin at Königsberg or Hoverbeck at Warsaw that Roth or Kalckstein or some confidant or agent of either had put himself in touch with the Polish court. Wholeheartedly seeking a settlement and, as befitted a man so averse to violence, anxious not to add to the existing difficulties, Schwerin for his part consistently busied himself to calm his chief and persuade him to overlook the practices which so enraged him.

Such strictly limited progress as Schwerin made toward an accommodation came to an abrupt end when a particularly flagrant act of Roth's snapped the last thread of the elector's patience. In March, 1662, the Schöppenmeister went in person to Warsaw once again and more pressingly than ever to propose armed intervention in Prussia. Already some months before this open desertion to the enemy the elector had unavailingly suggested to Schwerin and Radziwill that they take action against the bold antagonist. On now hearing that Roth had returned to Königsberg, Frederick William dispatched an order for his arrest without further parley or excuse. But the arrest could not be carried out, as it provoked such a stir among the citizens that the prudent Schwerin wisely stayed his hand.

Events now moved rapidly to a climax. In June, 1662, the united burgher body of Königsberg decided to make Roth's course its own and sent a petition to the king of Poland to come to their aid against an intolerable tyranny. The source of the petition was disclosed beyond a doubt when Roth's son was selected to carry the document to Warsaw. To defeat further communications of the same sort, Statthalter Radziwill ordered the capital to be invested with troops, practically putting it under martial law. In the midst of these multiplying excitements Schwerin, beaten and discouraged, was recalled at his own request. On his arrival at Berlin he drew the picture of a province teetering on the brink of civil war and solemnly warned the elector that nothing short of his own presence would prevent a catastrophe. The baffled prince could not but agree; he would himself have to have a look at the Königsberg bedlam. But instead of the soft-treading measures of conciliation that Schwerin never ceased to recommend, he would apply a more radical cure. What its nature would be was sufficiently indicated when he ordered out two thousand Brandenburg troops and set them marching toward the rising sun. On October 25, 1662, he entered the Prussian capital at their head.

Months before his arrival at Königsberg, Frederick William had convinced himself that what he unhesitatingly called the rebellion of the capital was the work of one resolute man. And he was right; for as soon as he had by a picked company of soldiers laid hands on Roth, the whole agitation died down like a spent fire. With the least possible delay the alleged conspirator was brought to trial and in a procedure replete with irregularities was found guilty and sentenced to lifelong imprisonment. The better to render him harmless he was carried from his native Prussian heath to the fortress of Peitz in Brandenburg, and at Peitz he died, impenitent to the last, some sixteen years after his incarceration. If a martyr is a person who braves suffering and death for his belief, Schöppenmeister Roth must in all justice be hailed a martyr. But to make him also the banner-bearer of a great cause, an authentic hero, as does the one American historian[5] who had tried his hand at a large-scale history of Prussia, is an offense to common sense ascribable to the writer's amazing feat of identifying feudal privilege, calling itself liberty, with the liberty with which he was familiar as the clarion theme of the history of his own country. Rarely has a scholar been tricked into a grosser error by the hypnotizing power of a word.

5. Herbert Tuttle, *History of Prussia* (Boston, 1884), I, 189–90. This is as good a place as any to point out that this chapter rests chiefly on *UA* (*Ständische Verhandlungen*), Vols. V, X, XV, XVI, and *UA* (*Politische Verhandlungen*), Vols. I, IX, and is deeply indebted to the clarifying introductions to these volumes by their respective editors.

Following this ominous intrusion of bayonets into the situation, the debate between the estates and their prince, who wisely decided to stay on at Königsberg and conduct his side of the argument in person, was carried on with less violence of language but not without repeated head-on collisions. After as before the fall of Roth the Landstände were fanatically set on retaining the unimpaired body of their privileges and, while Frederick William for his part declared himself ready to guarantee their traditional rights, he would not do so without first being conceded his two basic demands: his unequivocal sovereignty and a tax appropriation for more than a single year (and therefore presumably permanent), sufficient in amount for the support of no matter how small but indissoluble a fighting force.

The tug of war continued through all the long hard winter months that are the lot of this subarctic province. Not until May 1, 1663, was the diet closed with the usual document of dismissal, the Landtagsabschied. And sure enough, Frederick William was in that document not only awarded his minimum demands but to his intense gratification got something in addition; for, at least to the extent of permitting the adherents of their ruler's Reformed faith to have three churches within the Prussian limits, the narrow Lutheran estates had let themselves be coaxed to depart from their monumental bigotry. To celebrate the conclusion of the hotly fought contest and, at the same time, appropriately to mark the dawn of a new era, there followed on October 18, amidst expressions of rejoicing on the part of the whole reconciled Königsberg population, the impressively staged ceremony whereby the estates did homage to their prince in his now no longer disputed capacity of sovereign.

Frederick William had won. Political—but not social—feudalism had received a death blow. While it is true that it did not expire at once, a situation had been created which assured its gradual replacement by the better co-ordinated and more concentrated system of monarchy. To this monarchist drift the burghers not only of Königsberg but also of the smaller towns accommodated themselves with, on the whole, surprising ease and celerity. Not so the nobles with their Polish hankering for an unlimited freedom of individual action. In spite of Abschied and homage, many of them continued to spin threads across the border in the lingering hope that Poland might yet be aroused to champion their cause. Extraordinarily sensitive in regard to his hard-won sovereignty and fanatically insistent on the cessation of all communications between his subjects and the Polish court, Frederick William was kept informed of these intrigues by his vigilant envoy at Warsaw, the excellent Hoverbeck. However, as they involved no immediate peril to the state, he was content for some years to overlook them. Only when a succession of happenings in the most reckless and brutal of the Junker clans, the Kalckstein family, precipitated a far-reaching crisis, did he take alarm and move into action.

In the year 1667, General Kalckstein, worthless father of two worthless sons, died, and with him passed from the scene Frederick William's oldest but also most dangerous and devious opponent. His title, general, it may incidentally be observed, derived from his service in the Saxon army during the Thirty Years' War. Like every other noble a Kalckstein seeking advancement in those perturbed days took service with any European army that promised honors and good pay. General Kalckstein's two sons also had military handles to their names which, like their father's, derived from another than the Prussian service. While no discredit attaches to them on this score, the fact deserves to be recorded, since it reveals the ready priority the Prussian gentry of the period accorded to their individual fortune over the service of their duke and country.

Well, no sooner had old General Kalckstein departed this life than his two sons and four daughters engaged in a savage battle over the inheritance. The older son and main heir, with whom alone the rest of this story is concerned, was Colonel Christian Ludwig Kalckstein. By his inflated claims to the parental estate his coheirs were stirred to such blind fury that, in order to discredit and, if possible, ruin him altogether, they denounced him to the courts on the charge of his avowed purpose to murder the elector. On his arrest and trial it was established beyond question that he was in the habit of venting his rage against his prince in the most indecent language; but as his precious brother and equally precious sisters were as little able to discipline their tongues and, besides, violently contradicted each other in the witness box, the main charge against the defendant could not be sustained. However, so much dirty Kalckstein linen had been washed in public that the noble associates of the family turned from them in horror and accepted with composure the verdict which condemned the colonel to imprisonment for life.

Hardly had Kalckstein begun to serve his term when the elector, perhaps because he did not believe the culprit had ever entertained the crime imputed to him by his vindictive relatives, commuted the harsh sentence of life imprisonment to a money fine of five thousand talers. Until its payment Kalckstein was to remain a voluntary prisoner on his own estate. Repeatedly he requested and received an extension of the time named for a settlement until the day came beyond which no adjournment would be granted. Thereupon, as the transfer of hard cash from his private to the public purse was a plain reversal of what by him and all his kind was regarded as the divinely ordered course of nature, he took advantage of a stormy night of March, 1670, to steal from his house and, in a vehicle secretly supplied, to rattle over the frozen, rutted roads of his native province until he had arrived at the border. Cleverly eluding the frontier guards, he pushed across and continued his pell-mell flight until he had reached the Polish capital and safety.

The safety was a delusion, the last and fatal error of the colonel's bungling career; for, if Frederick William had been disposed to dismiss the murder charge as insufficiently substantiated and constituting moreover no challenge to his sovereign claim, he was stung to the quick and would never forgive the appeal, implicit in the flight, from his own Prussian justice to the higher justice of the Polish king. Ever since the abolition of the tie of Polish vassalage he had left no doubt that he regarded any appeal to his former suzerain as treason, and at once branding Kalckstein as guilty of this crime, he ordered his ambassador at Warsaw to demand the surrender of the felon. When the Polish government repeatedly refused, the effect on the elector was to confirm him in the suspicion that there was more to this thing than Kalckstein's folly, that it was in all probability a ramified plot against his safety involving, invisibly lined up behind Kalckstein and his royal ally, the whole irreconcilable element of the Prussian gentry. No milder hypothesis than this suffices to explain the succession of deceptions and violences to which he now resorted in order to get possession of his enemy and snuff out his life.

The bare facts of the elector's pursuit of this purpose are lurid enough to satisfy the most devoted explorers of the darker bypaths of history. In order to adhere to the proportions to which this book is committed the author will, to his considerable regret, have to content himself with giving a mere digest of events. When the elector's impetuous demands at Warsaw failed to effect the delivery of Kalckstein, his thought began to turn to other methods until it fixed at last on the plan of having the fugitive kidnapped. In a certain Brandt he found a bold and unscrupulous agent willing to undertake the hazardous business. Thereupon, on a day of late November, Kalckstein was seized, rolled in a carpet, and sped as inanimate merchandise northward by the same road over which he had traveled southward into supposed safety some eight months before. At this rude breach of international law there was a shocked raising of eyebrows throughout Europe and a fierce howl of protest out of injured Warsaw. But the elector pleaded innocence, made excuses, offered reparation, and by these time-gaining tactics succeeded in causing the incident to be gradually forgotten. It supremely touched, after all, only Poland's honor, and the distracted Polish government had long ago arrived at the stage where it was unable to drive along any path whatever with the stubborn resolution necessary for success.

Even after Kalckstein had been tossed into a cell in the solid fortress of Memel, Frederick William required all of two years to effect the execution on which he was bent. The Prussian laws and courts, shaped in the full feudal age with special attention to the safeguarding of noble culprits, simply would not yield the death sentence which the elector demanded. He was reduced to the creation of an extra-constitutional commission which itself balked for months before it bowed to the will of its creator and condemned the defendant to loss of life and goods. And only after another considerable delay did Kalckstein on November 8, 1672, at last lay his head upon the block.

Frederick William might not have carried the Kalckstein affair to this uncompromising conclusion if it had not befallen concurrently with another struggle with his Landtag. Though humbled in 1663, this body had by no means given up the ghost, and when in 1669 the elector renewed his attempt to enlarge his own share in the Prussian administration at the expense of the estates, the states took umbrage at this fresh attack on their privileges and angrily declined to vote the taxes for the support of the army which the elector by now regarded as practically obligatory. The resulting deadlock was particularly embarrassing because the young French king, Louis XIV, had just disclosed that it was his purpose to resume Richelieu's policy of Rhineward expansion, and Frederick William, greatly alarmed at this prospect, was more than ever resolved to have an army in hand ready for every emergency.

Held in the west by the gathering war clouds, the elector, as on earlier occasions, sent orders to his Prussian agents to collect the funds for the army in the diet's despite. It was not an action calculated to smooth the ruffled spirit of the estates, and the situation remained troubled and confused until a momentary easement along the western front enabled the elector to dispatch a few regiments to Prussia to back up his stand with a show of force. Again, as at the time of the rebellion of Schöppenmeister Roth, it was manifested that an undaunted resolution was all that was necessary to bring the estates to heel, for with troops quartered on the capital and countryside they first asked pardon of their sovereign in extremely abject terms and then bowed humbly to all his demands. The fresh submission took place in 1674 at a moment when the French war, begun in 1672 in the form of an assault on the Dutch republic, had expanded to European dimensions. Although we have been exclusively concerned in this chapter with the struggle of Frederick William with his various diets, it is well to let the conjunction of the new Prussian crisis with the French aggression along the Rhine remind us that the constitutional struggle did not take place in the kind of isolation in which we have been obliged to present it and that it was in every one of its phases tied up for both the elector and the estates with the general European happenings unceasingly tossed off the ever revolving wheel of time.

The new defeat of the diet, taken in connection with the grim end, by way of example to his kind, of the rebellious Kalckstein, may be accepted as the end of the systematic resistance of the Junkers to their determined ruler. By slow degrees this headstrong caste accommodated itself to the altered distribution of political power. Not only was there no repetition among its ranks of Kalckstein's treason but by the time Frederick William departed this life it may be declared to have taken the hard yoke of the new system on itself with entire loyalty.

Our last word on the three domestic revolutions may well sound a note of warning. From these struggles Frederick William emerged as victor, since in each case he had brought away with him his minimum requirement: the miles perpetuus and a subsidy for his support. Henceforth no one could doubt that he was moving, slowly, of course, but infallibly, in the direction of monarchy. But to deduce from these successes that he was from now on the master, no longer obliged to take account of his defeated diets, would be a serious mistake. They one and all retained important powers, especially the power of the purse; and perhaps even more decisive, because more subtle and intangible, they exercised a vast, though indeterminate, influence on all the elements of society that instinctively adhered to the set and cherished ways of the past. As soon, therefore, as Frederick William tried to go forward from the position he had gained and broaden the program of reforms, he encountered, if not always open, exceedingly powerful secret, resistance from the members of the estates in both their individual and collective capacity. It is this situation and the net result of his further reform activity that will next engage our attention.

Chapter 9

THE DOMESTIC REORGANIZATION

If in the course of the conflict with his diets Frederick William identified himself more and more confidently with the principle of monarchy, he received, as already pointed out,[1] considerable encouragement from the whole contemporary movement of thought and politics. Royal absolutism was in the air the men of that age breathed, and by the brilliant example set by France, become under this system the leading power of Europe, it was beating down all resistance to its successful advance. Outstanding political philosophers like Hobbes in England, Pufendorf in Germany, and Bossuet in France became its spokesmen; and we may be sure that the ruler of Brandenburg, alertly responsive to every European trend, heartily welcomed the moral and intellectual support which the theorists afforded him in his struggle with an outmoded order.

But while the expositions of leading contemporary writers and most certainly the far-seen French portent had an undeniable weight with the German prince, it would be a mistake to think of him as steering his course by their light. Frederick William was an intensely practical man, who concentrated with all the energy he possessed on his immediate problems and faced them from day to day in an uninterrupted course of struggle and compromise. It was not the haphazard, unsystematic struggle of a man without a purpose; for, if ever there was a man so animated, it was this sovereign who had hardly begun to be buffeted by the storms of office when he became aware that, unless he strengthened his position as head of the three feeble, scattered, and ill-assorted territories to which he had succeeded, he might live to see both them and himself disappear from the map. But such was his earth-bound and unspeculative nature that for him all truly effective guidance

1. Chap. iii, p. 73; v, p. 111.

would have to develop not from philosophic reflection but from the unbroken stream of daily direct experience with the responsibilities of office.

It helps our understanding of the elector's approach to his problems to picture the recurrent scene both in the Privy Council, attended by the full complement of ministers, and in the prince's cabinet, where the weightier decisions were made in consultation with one or two particularly intimate advisers. In either case the issues of his dominions would crowd in all but palpable shape around the conference table making a clamor proportioned to their urgency. They would be sheer countless in number, countless and apparently separate and distinct, and yet on closer inspection delicate threads would be found running from one to the other tying them into an indivisible whole. For sound tactical reasons, however, they could not be attacked as a unified mass, and by what we may call the pressure of circumstances they would range themselves in a definite, if frequently changing, order of importance. Of this the preceding chapter supplied an illuminating example. When the ruler of Brandenburg determined not to be overlooked in the settlement of the Thirty Year's War, he imparted by this decision an overshadowing importance to the problem of the army. The army thereupon became the first link in a long chain of causation. It led to taxes, and these in their turn to the necessity of bending the diets to his tax proposals. Army, taxes, diets, were the closely interlocked elements of the domestic revolution we have just passed in review.

This revolution in its further unfolding gave birth to a whole complex of fresh problems. It was like the rebuilding of an ancient house. Whoever undertakes to make over a wing or section will presently discover that he must make over the interrelated parts of the total structure. Applied to Frederick William's reshuffling of his inheritance, this meant that the revolution he started when he undertook to provide himself with an army imposed a reconstruction of all the services of the state which would, in general terms, take some such course as follows: With a permanent army in hand he would be occupied for the remainder of his days with shaping it into an increasingly effective instrument; the army thus strengthened would call for an ampler flow of revenue; and an ampler revenue return would require a greatly intensified economy together with the setting-up of the appropriate administrative controls. With one reform leading in this way to another the whole public life would experience a gradual and, in the long run, sweeping reconstruction.

Since in this situation it hardly matters at which point of the general flux a start is made, let us begin with finances. As Brandenburg was, after all, the crucial Hohenzollern province and as, furthermore, we cannot afford the space required for the often only slightly differentiated development in the other provinces, no apology is needed for focusing our attention on Brandenburg with the right reserved of widening our inquiry on occasion by drawing on the parallel situation in Prussia and Cleve-Mark.

FINANCES

A. HISTORICAL FOREWORD

The revenue situation of the medieval predecessors of Frederick William reflects the character of medieval society. The margravial revenues derived from two main sources: the domain and the regalia. The domain consisted of an impressive mass of manors amounting in their sum to between one-third and one-fourth of the cultivated land of the electorate. The regalia embraced the road and river tolls, the mint and mines, that is, a body of revenues that either had been freely granted by the emperor or had been appropriated by the margrave in the course of the emperor's gradual decline. The defense of the mark was the duty of the knights with townsmen and peasants making an appropriate contribution in kind or money. It was in return for the military service which they owed the margrave that the knights had been endowed with their fiefs. In case the elector incurred what by local feudal custom was considered a legitimate expense he was free to summon the Landtag to ask for a subsidy.

We have already noted how in the sixteenth century the original system was modified to the elector's disadvantage. More than once Elector Joachim II, having run himself into debt by lavish living, was obliged to throw himself on the mercy of the diet. While this body took over Joachim's obligations, it also took over their extinction by means of taxes which, having granted, it also collected, establishing for this purpose a financial administration under its own control called the Creditwerk. The taxes voted to support the Creditwerk were a tax on beer (*Biergeld*) and a much more important property tax called contribution. If the elector had collected these taxes through his own officials, his authority would have been greatly increased. Collected and distributed as they were by officials of the diet, he fell into a substantial dependence on that body.

In this same sixteenth century occurred a military development which, accelerated in the seventeenth century, stripped the electorate of its traditional system of defense. The feudal army of knights proved ineffective in battle against the better trained and equipped battalions of mercenaries and, falling into desuetude, ceased to be called out. We have already noted the elimination of the knights as the defenders of the mark and need therefore only remind ourselves of its consequences when the Thirty Years' War broke out. Repeatedly the harassed father of Frederick William tried to remedy the defenseless position in which he found himself by recourse to the military system of the day, to mercenaries. His efforts reduced him, financially, to the most painful straits. On the one hand, he was obliged progressively to mortgage his personal wealth, his domain, and, on the other, he had to go perpetually on his knees to the selfish and recalcitrant diet for the money needed to pay his soldiers.

On succeeding his father, Frederick William succeeded also to his father's financial difficulties, and we are aware how throughout the two decades of his rule which lie behind us he continued to be beset by them. In all that time he was unable to improve his position in regard to his heavily mortgaged domain for reasons which we shall set forth when we come to the domain later on. His single notable achievement in the financial field was to wring (1653) a tax, the aforementioned contribution, from his diet, which, in spite of its being voted for a limited number of years, was by both parties to the agreement tacitly assumed to be permanent. Although the permanent contribution guaranteed a permanent army, contribution and army were on so small a scale that the elector neither would nor could be content until both of them had been greatly increased. But while aiming, always with the army in mind, at a larger revenue, he was equally concerned with having the revenue collected by his own officials instead of by the rival institution of the Creditwerk. Thus the elimination of the Creditwerk, which had thrust itself between him and his subjects and was an offense to his monarchical soul, became an integral part of the financial reforms he carried through and which we shall now proceed to examine.

B. THE *GENERAL-KRIEGSCOMMISSARIAT*[2]

During the long Swedish-Polish War the elector had fused the forces raised in Brandenburg, Prussia, and Cleve into a single army, for which he was then obliged to provide by a unified administration. And just as the united army had received a head in General von Sparr as commander-in-chief, so the united administration had been put under Claus Ernst von Platen as *General-Kriegscommissar*, that is, as supreme commissioner of war. Immediately under Platen, who proved to be an administrator of exceptional talent, were commissioners of the separate Hohenzollern territories and under them commissioners of the territorial subdivisions called Kreise—altogether an administrative network which, though hurriedly improvised, proved eminently satisfactory.

With the signing of the Peace of Oliva in 1660 the elector yielded to the clamor of the diet and cut both his army and its administration to the bone. But he was adamant against the demand voiced in the Landtag that he get rid of both in their entirety. Indeed, so little did he conform to this demand that, in the view of many scholars, and certainly in that of Jany, the most recent military historian of the Hohenzollern state, the standing army, as distinct from the wartime army, dates only from this time. According to Jany[3] the army assembled in 1644 was afterward again dissolved and cannot therefore be accepted as marking the creation in Brandenburg of a standing force. That institution was not born until the elector, while greatly reducing the fighting forces

2. *UA* (*zur Geschichte der inneren Politik des Kurfürsten Friedrich Wilhelms von Brandenburg*), I, K. Breysig, *Geschichte der brandenburgischen Finanzen in der Zeit von 1640 bis 1697;* II, *Zentralverwaltung des Heeres und der Steuern.*

3. C. Jany, *Geschichte der königlich preussischen Armee* (5 vols.; Berlin, 1928–37).

got together for the Swedish-Polish War, insisted, nevertheless, on retaining a solid, irreducible nucleus.

Since to keep up even this skeleton army meant money, and to increase it meant more money, it is understandable that all Frederick William's thoughts about the army went on to a lively counterpoint of financial thoughts. Now the tax which supported the shrunken, postwar army was mainly, as we are aware, the contribution. It was a direct tax on property and for a variety of reasons had always aroused a good deal of complaint. In the prosperous Dutch republic there had been instituted an indirect tax on articles of consumption called "excise." In that region of an intense exchange the excise proved so remunerative that it attracted the attention of all the neighbors of the republic and moved some, of whom Frederick William was one, to attempt to introduce it into their own dominions. True, it would fall, if adopted, with disproportionate severity on the poorer classes, but that evil was compensated in the elector's eyes by the ease of its collection and the breach it would make in the hitherto stubbornly maintained tax immunity of the nobles.

For this very reason, however—for this breach of an ancient privilege—a storm of opposition broke out in the diet when the elector presented himself before it with the proposal to replace the contribution with the excise. Not only the knights but also the towns at first rejected the new and unfamiliar tax. But after carefully weighing its consequences for a number of years the towns came around to the elector's plan. In the year 1667 they agreed to raise the share of the contribution for which they were liable by the new method. Since the nobles refused to yield and clung obdurately to the traditional system, a sharp division based on taxation followed between country and town, between the agricultural and the urban classes. The adoption of distinct systems for raising money by the two ruling orders of the state further weakened the already declining diet and helps explain why the resistance to the elector's program of a monarchical transformation of the government grew feebler with every year he reigned.

Precisely as had been the case with the contribution, the towns themselves collected the excise on their first adopting it. But since the returns were delivered to the elector for the benefit of the army, Frederick William claimed the right to put an agent in the towns to review their accounts. This agent, while representing the elector, also represented the war department and, like the camel in the tent, once in the town, took complete possession of it. Not many years after the elector's emissary first presented himself on his innocent-looking errand of review, he began to push the town officials aside and continued his encroachments until he had made the excise his exclusive affair. When that time came, he collected it through his own subalterns, who posted at the town gates the articles of consumption subject to the tax and the percentage of their value due as excise. To give the system its maximum effectiveness, the excise officials were stationed at the gates through which the taxable food and merchandise had to pass. In this manner the sharp division between the towns that paid the excise and the country that had another system was visibly demonstrated to native and foreigner alike.

The electoral agent dispatched to the town bore the designation *Steuercommissar* or *Steuerrat*. When the excise, owing to the country's gradual economic recovery, began to yield a return above the quota for which the town was liable, the Steuercommissar committed a new encroachment. Instead of turning over the collections in excess of the quota to the town authorities, he passed on the surplus to the General-Kriegscommissariat at Berlin to which he was immediately responsible. With these successes to his credit he was encouraged to proceed from one usurpation to another until, before long, and certainly before the end of the century, the whole municipal government had been concentrated in his hands. One gets the impression that the trend toward centralization became so irresistible that the discouraged burghers surrendered to it without making a stand in behalf of their ancient right of self-government. The result was a sweeping urban bureaucratization. That the transformation signified a loss in terms of burgher initiative will hardly be disputed. On the other hand, the superseded local government had been a regime of narrow privilege inherited from the Middle Ages and would have to disappear if the greater concentration of power in his hands at which the elector aimed was to be realized.

Not many years after its adoption the excise had become the

leading revenue item of the state. But even on reaching its highest yield it fell somewhat short—together, of course, with its rural counterpart, the contribution—of meeting the cost of the peacetime standing army. Whenever a war broke out, Frederick William had to strain every nerve to come by additional sources of supply and on such occasions experimented with taxes that had been tried out in the more advanced countries of the west, as, for instance, the poll tax and the income tax. So savage, however, was the objection to them on the part of his economically backward country that he never succeeded in making them stick.

Quite the happiest stroke in the elector's unceasing search for additional funds was his success in fastening a charge on those most hardened and fanatical tax-evaders, the knights. In the year 1663 he issued an edict to the effect that the knights must redeem by a money payment the military service they owed and no longer gave. Tentatively fixed at forty talers per fief, it was thenceforth regularly levied at the outbreak of war and highly valued as a welcome addition to his slender available funds.

But let us make no mistake: Apply the tax screws as the elector might, the returns would at the very best be sufficient for only a short war. Should the war be at all drawn out, there was no escape from the necessity of finding an ally able and ready to pay him a subsidy to help meet expenses. And while such a paymaster would on his appearance be greeted as a heaven-sent deliverer, it would not be long before he would be regarded in the light of a tyrannical bully; for he would bring home to Frederick William the bitter lesson that whenever a large and prosperous state subsidizes a small and impecunious one, it does so in the expectation of an equivalent service and sets up to this end a control that deprives the client of his freedom of action. There is no denying the fact that, since Frederick William never in his life reached the point where he could conduct a war without foreign subsidies, he never succeeded in climbing out of the class of secondary or dependent powers.

Even after the signal rout of the diet in 1653 the Creditwerk, witness of that body's former power, continued to operate. Created to extinguish electoral debts contracted a hundred years before, not only had it failed to do so, but by flagrant mismanagement it had permitted them to increase until by the year 1660 they came to six million talers. Toward this unwelcome institution Frederick William adopted the same policy of subtle encroachment, the working of which we have observed in the case of the towns. Beginning with the claim to a right of audit, he gradually shoved so many of his own officials into the management of the Creditwerk that he came into partial control of it. Then, upon reviewing the debts, he found that some could be slashed in two because they had been fraudulently inflated and that others might be wiped out entirely with a relatively small cash payment. Reducing the obligations in this way to manageable proportions, he won such an ascendancy that by the last decade of his life he had got the manifestly declining institution substantially into his hands. Did he then give it the *coup de grâce?* By no means! Once again we may see that he was an empirical and not a doctrinaire reformer; for, having deprived the Creditwerk of its sting, he did not further interfere with its now harmless existence.

And the upshot of all this unremitting effort effectively to finance his army? Well, the upshot was the creation of that other stout pillar of monarchy, a civil service, which in no respect yields in importance to the army itself. Perhaps it would square better with the facts to speak modestly of the beginnings of a civil service, since even at the close of Frederick William's reign the institution had made no more than a start and still left much to be desired in professional competence and single-minded devotion to the service of the state in process of formation.

Without doubt there were in Brandenburg many difficulties to be overcome before a full-fledged, reliable central administration could get under way. They sprang, in the main, from the still essentially feudal character of Brandenburg society. Back in the Middle Ages it was an unwritten law that the head of a state choose not only the court officials, who waited on his person, but also his political advisers from among his normal associates, the landed nobility. In an earlier chapter we noted that it was only with the coming of such specialized services as the Kammergericht and the Privy Council that the rule was relaxed in favor of men of middle-class origin who by their legal studies had made themselves indispensable. While Frederick William himself was relatively free from the aristocratic prejudices current among his countrymen in his time, he was, however, sufficiently under their sway to incline to reserve the most distinguished posts in his service to men of noble birth. Let us recall that his earliest close adviser was Conrad von Burgsdorf and that Burgsdorf was followed in due course by Blumenthal, Waldeck, and Schwerin, all without exception members of the landlord class. Nonetheless, he made a practice of drawing capable commoners into his service, as is shown by the appointment to the Privy Council of men like Johann Tornow and the brothers Friedrich and Gottfried Jena, than whom there were no more useful agents at his command. Even among his ambassadors, still chosen throughout Europe almost exclusively from the ranks of the nobility, there may be found occasional appointees of humble birth, like Daniel Weimann, who served for years with the greatest distinction as the elector's representative at The Hague.

Admitting that the inherited caste system was in Frederick William's day no longer rigidly maintained, it was still rigid enough to delay the building-up of an effective public service devoted single-mindedly to the prince's interest. And there were other contributory factors, as, for instance, the general demoralization produced by the Thirty Years' War. Before it was over, open and disguised thievery might be encountered at every turn, and peculation in office had become a commonplace practice all the way from the lowest to the highest public officials. The evil situation called for a new uprightness, a new morality, but that would follow only from an extended habituation to a society of law and order and could not be had overnight by waving a wand or by similar sleight-of-hand. A final obstacle not to be overlooked delaying the achievement of an effective bureaucracy was the insufficient education of the common people. It was from them that the mass of the lower officials would have to be drawn, and the common people had not yet achieved the cultural level necessary for the satisfactory discharge of the new responsibilities.

C. THE DOMAIN

Scattered through all the Hohenzollern territories were numerous manors or farm properties belonging to the prince and constituting his domain. The domain in each separate territory was administered from an office called the *Kammer* or chamber, and each chamber, reflecting the separateness of the territory, was an independent unit. In normal times the different chambers produced a profit in the form either of farm products or of money and to the extent of that profit contributed to the support of the prince and his court.

With the outbreak of the Thirty Years' War the times became and long remained abnormal, and the effect on the returns reported by the chambers was disastrous; for, apart from the repeated plundering of the domain by marauding troops, Frederick William, as had his father before him, himself contributed to his growing impoverishment by mortgaging some, and usually his best, properties for the cash always so sorely needed. It was an unhappy device and caused the profit of the respective chambers steadily to shrink. Add that there were years when defaults of nature reduced or totally destroyed the crops, and it might well happen that one or more of the chambers came off with a deficit.

Comparative figures for Brandenburg will assist us in getting the general picture. In 1615, three years before the outbreak of the great war, the Brandenburg Kammer reported a profit of one hundred and sixty-four thousand talers. In 1651, although the war had been concluded three years before, the profit came to fifty-three thousand talers, that is, to less than one-third of the normal pre-war sum. And the war alone does not explain the calamitous shrinkage, although it was far and away the leading cause by reason of the deserted farms it had left behind and the attendant catastrophic reduction of the peasant population. To a certain, not negligible, extent the wretched, postwar showing of the Kammer was owing to something else, to wit, the mournful decline in the standards of common honesty. From top to bottom the administration of the Kammer was honeycombed with knavery and that disordered kind of bookkeeping which in its effects is indistinguishable from knavery.

With our eyes directed, as agreed, on Brandenburg, we learn that the central office of the Kammer at Berlin grouped the electoral properties distributed through the mark in districts called *Ämter* and that each *Amt* embraced anywhere from three to six estates. At the head of an Amt stood the *Amtsschreiber* with a staff proportionate to the size of his responsibility. His duties were numerous and involved. He directed the sowing and reaping of the domain proper, that is, the part of the estate that was worked directly for the account of the elector; and he supervised and regulated the peasants and their work on their own peasant land. The peasant regulation was indispensable since the elector's land was cultivated by the labor service owed him by the peasants, and the financial showing the Amtsschreiber might make depended in good part on the rental payments for their land for which the peasants were liable. They paid to the elector annually and on the average one-tenth of their harvest of grain and hay and one-tenth of their increase of stock. The relation of the peasants within an Amt to the Amtsschreiber was the same as that of the peasants on a knight's estate to the knight. Not only was the Amtsschreiber, as the local impersonation of the elector, the Gutsherr (lord) of the peasants and as such perpetually on their track to get out of them everything (and a little more) that the law allowed, but by the same token he was also their Gerichtsherr (judge) and decided not only the suits that they brought against each other but also the suits, in case they dared bring them (which was not likely), against himself.

While scholars are in agreement that the serfdom of the peasant subjects of the elector was somewhat less severe and also less strictly enforced than that of the peasant subjects of the knights, it presented in both instances substantially the same picture. Exactly as on the fiefs of the knights there were, leaving the almost innumerable minor variations out of account, two kinds of peasants, depending on the amount of land they called their own. The richer peasants (*Hüfner, Vollbauern*) had a hereditary claim to their farms which had never been challenged, although it had clearly been weakened by the recently acquired right of the Junkers under certain conditions to buy them out. The Vollbauern owed their landlord, in addition to the crop tithe, some two or three days' labor service per week. The smaller peasants, the so-called *Kossäthen,* a word we may render as cotters, sat on so small a patch of land and owed so many days' service that they were reduced in effect to the position of day laborers on the lord's estate. The real bitterness of serfdom came to them through their being bound to the soil. Let us not fail to note, however, that the Vollbauern were also bound to the soil. Serfs, like the Kossäthen, they differed from their poorer kin chiefly in owing less labor service and in enjoying a larger return from a more substantial holding.

That Frederick William lamented the meager returns from his domain need not be expressly stated nor that he cudgeled his brain for a remedy. As the decline of the peasant population leaped to view, his first thought after the Westphalian pacification was to look about for colonists to settle on the abandoned properties; and as early as 1650 he entered into relations with some Dutch enterprisers to bring a specified group of farms again into cultivation by means of an imported company of their compatriots. The plan was only partially successful, but it pointed to an attack on his domain problem to which he repeatedly returned.

He was no less persuaded that an improvement could be brought about by reorganization and merger of the various and, let it always be kept in mind, traditionally distinct chambers by which he was served. In the rescript of December 4, 1651, which has the honor of being the first general proposal ever made for unifying his separate territories, the domain was not forgotten, and a committee, composed of his four foremost councilors, Waldeck, Blumenthal, Schwerin, and Tornow, was appointed to work out a reform. But, owing to the absorption of these men with other tasks and perhaps also because of fundamental disagreements among them, their labors came to nothing. Undiscouraged, the elector again and again returned to the problem. Except for occasional slight improvements of a local and circumscribed nature, all his endeavors toward unification proved vain. Whoever patiently follows these efforts will be forced to the conclusion that the difficulty lay deeper than appeared on the surface and that, rooted in the postwar exhaustion of the country, it would not be overcome until a long period of peace had effected a general recovery.

However, experimentation continued through years and decades did at last make clear that what an improved administration could do toward making the domain a more lucrative enterprise reduced itself to three measures. They are so important that they deserve to be set down in order: (1) By overcoming the obdurate provincial and local opposition, the many separate chambers might be advantageously merged into a single organization, a central *Kammerverwaltung.* (2) The individual farms might be taken out of the hands of the bureaucratic Amtsschreibers, who ran them in their own interest, and be leased with increased returns to professional agriculturalists. (3) The loose medieval method of payment in kind, still too usual, might be sweepingly replaced by the more precise system of money payments.

So stout and so obstinate was the resistance to these three reforms on the part of people with vested interests in the inherited abuses that it was not until late in his reign that Frederick William found the man who possessed the drive, tact, and unwearying persistence to overcome the individuals and groups that stood together in solid battle array to defeat reason and reform. This man was Freiherr von Knyphausen, and that he was a native of East Frisia and not a born subject of the elector may serve as additional evidence that Frederick William was quick to detect talent wherever it crossed his path and on the alert to draw it into his service. Not until 1684 was Knyphausen put in charge of the Brandenburg Kammer. When his prince died four years later, the administrative structure based on the three above-indicated changes had already risen into view. Not to exaggerate, not to misrepresent the admirable Knyphausen by making him out a conjurer, let us admit that before his appointment the obstructive traditional system had by continued experimentation already been seriously undermined. And let us add that his leading objective, the unified Kammerverwaltung, was not so far along at Frederick William's death that the historian might list it among the achievements of his reign.

However, since for the decade following the death of Frederick William the invaluable Knyphausen was retained at his post of general administrator of the domains, it came about that the unified Kammerverwaltung had by the end of this period been substantially carried through. Substantially, but not even then altogether, for the Kammer of the most stubbornly separate territory, the Kammer of Prussia, retained its independence for another generation. A gratifying result of Knyphausen's labors had put in an appearance even before Frederick William departed this life. In the very year of his demise, in the year 1688, the Brandenburg

Kammer yielded a profit of one hundred and twenty-five thousand talers as against sixty thousand in the period before Knyphausen took hold. While this represented a heartening improvement, the figures still fell about 25 per cent under those of the year 1615. In other words, administrative wastage had been considerably reduced by the reform but not in an amount sufficient to make up for the loss ascribable to the continued and obstinate economic depression.

For the bringing to completion of the many financial and administrative reforms inaugurated by Frederick William we have to go to the reign of his grandson. His son, Frederick, who cashed in on his father's reputation by assuming the title of king, was a vain, pinchbeck creature of whom the best is said when it is reported that he did not surrender the advances along financial and administrative lines made by his predecessor. But it required the dour and iron-jawed grandson of Frederick William, the first king bearing that name, to carry these interior labors forward to another stage by fusing Knyphausen's Kammerverwaltung with that other financial-administrative service, the origin of which we have traced, the General-Kriegscommissariat. This crowning labor, by which Brandenburg-Prussia acquired the most effective administration of any contemporary state, was performed by King Frederick William I when, in 1723, he set up the *General-Direktorium*. But it is no more than just to insist that the closely unified administration represented by the General-Direktorium is nothing other than the logical culmination of the work begun by the Great Elector.

GROWTH AND ORGANIZATION OF THE ARMY

We have learned that because the armies assembled to wage the two Neuburg wars of 1646–47 and 1651—comparable rather to violent meteorological disturbances than to wars—were again dissolved, Frederick William's standing army dates from the preparations which he began in 1655 in order not to be flattened out between the Swedish hammer and the Polish anvil. We have also learned that simultaneously an army administration (General-Kriegscommissariat) was called into being and that, on the conclusion of peace, army and administration were indeed reduced but not then or ever afterward again discharged. The taxes (contribution, excise) paid into the coffers of the war commissariat sufficed to maintain a force of about eight thousand men, which according to an estimate drawn up in 1667 by the elector himself constituted his army in that year.[4]

By a device already tried out in an earlier period a certain portion of the troops he was obliged, after the Peace of Oliva, to dismiss was held in reserve subject to call when the need should arise. This reserve embraced such soldiers, both infantrymen and cavalrymen, as, in return for the remission for a number of years of the contribution and other usual obligations, were willing to be settled on deserted farms of the domain. An inquiry of the year 1663 showed that former soldiers settled on these terms came to two hundred and nineteen in the Altmark, one hundred and fifty-two in the Havel area, and a proportionate number in every other district of the electorate.[5] The double advantage must have tickled the heart of so thrifty a soul as the elector; for, in addition to giving him a trained wartime reserve, the device promoted the repopulation of the depleted countryside, ever one of his most stubbornly pursued aims.

The twelve years lying between the Peace of Oliva and the outbreak of the war with Louis XIV in 1672 were, in spite of numerous small disturbances, substantially a peace period throughout which the army may be considered to have remained at approximately the strength the elector himself attributed to it in 1667. The point to remember is not so much the army's size as the fact that, supported by all the as yet legally separate and distinct Hohenzollern lands, it had become an organic unit and was both symbol and pledge of the monarchical state in process of formation.

However, far from being a national army as we understand the term today, it was still largely the familiar mercenary army of the Thirty Years' War. At its head was a group of superior officers who, engaged directly by the elector, lived in a relation of trust and intimacy with him. They were not attached to specific regiments but constituted and were called the General Staff. Having inherited

4. *UA*, XII, 725–26.

5. Jany, I, 194.

no commanding officer of note from his father, Frederick William picked these superior officers from the outstanding armies of the time and by his excellent selections gave evidence of his instinctive feeling for military endowment. To substantiate this statement, we may call attention to his two most distinguished appointments. As early as 1651, at the time of the mock Neuburg war, he put at the head of his armed forces Otto Christoph von Sparr, who, though a Brandenburger by birth, had risen to eminence in the service of the Kaiser. Then, on his engaging on his next and very real war, the war between Poland and Sweden, he made Sparr commander-in-chief (*General-Feldmarschall*) and, impressed with Sparr's considerable organizational gifts, retained him in that post until his death in 1668.

On the occasion of this same Polish-Swedish War, Frederick William appointed to a position under Sparr an Austrian-born commoner, Georg Derflinger by name. Derflinger, a Protestant by birth, had left his home at an early age in order to escape religious persecution and had taken service as a simple soldier with the Swedes. His considerable military gifts enabled him to overcome the heavy handicap of a lowly origin and achieve a high rank among his Swedish employers. Attracted as the elector was toward talent of every kind, he lured Derflinger out of Swedish into his own service, gave him his entire confidence, and on Sparr's death raised him to the supreme command in Sparr's stead. Derflinger's is one of the rare cases reported in this aristocratic century of a commoner's reaching the topmost rung of the military ladder. The undivided credit goes to himself, of whom the story circulated that he had started life as a tailor's apprentice. But it should not be overlooked that Frederick William, confronted with this fine specimen of the soldier's craft, was big enough to overcome the bias of his generation in favor of men of noble birth, of which he himself was by no means free.

The unaltered mercenary character of the army appears clearly when we come to the heads of the regiments, the colonels. In the practice of the age a colonel was both a soldier and a businessman, for, on the strength of a contract made by him with the head of a state he undertook for an agreed sum to provide a regiment of a stipulated size. As his first step toward the execution of the contract he appointed the required complement of captains and lieutenants. Thereupon these officers, in association with their subalterns, took to the road to recruit the regimental rank and file from every station in life and every country of Europe.

The system, conferring a dangerously disproportionate power on the colonels, was neither to the advantage nor to the taste of the elector. The best he could do was to seek gradually to modify it in his favor. He tried, for one thing, to bring the officers of lower than colonel grade into a more immediate dependence on himself and, for another, to build up the rank and file in increasing measure from his own subjects. While striving throughout his reign to realize these aims, he only very partially achieved them. He did however bring it about that the colonels agreed to submit the list of their subofficers to him for approval and thus at least got a veto power on unreliable elements. Also, in selecting the colonels charged with the creation of regiments he more and more gave preference to men who had been born his subjects. And, finally, to make provision for a more strictly native body of officers, he founded, not long after the Peace of Westphalia, a military academy at Colberg in Pomerania. It was projected on a small scale and grew slowly, if at all, for even by the end of the reign it provided training for no more than some twenty to twenty-five cadets.

As for the privates still lured into service by the rude methods of recruiting squads roaming through every country of Europe that did not expressly bar them, the rule for the Brandenburg regiments came to be to draw chiefly on Brandenburg territory and in this way to give them an increasingly native composition. The success achieved is evidenced by a regiment for which we have the exact figures for 1681, that is, for a relatively late year of the elector's reign. The regiment in question with a muster roll of eleven hundred men was made up to half that number from sons of Hohenzollern lands, while two-thirds of the remaining half were at least Germans of various allegiances. However, the presence in appreciable blocks of Danes, Swedes, Poles, Czechs, and other European groups confirms the statement of the still essentially mercenary and nonnational character of this and every other electoral regiment.

When the Franco-Dutch War of 1672 broke out, the elector rapidly increased his army to twenty thousand men and before that long struggle was over expanded it to the almost unbelievable figure for so small a state of forty-five thousand men. The details touching these enlargements will be noted when we get to the events that produced them. The purpose pursued in this chiefly technical section will have been satisfied if we conclude with a word on such features as equipment, tactics, and relative strength of infantry, cavalry, and artillery. How these matters stood at the time of the Swedish invasion of Poland has been set forth in an earlier chapter.[6] For the later years of the reign there are no startling innovations to report. The cavalry continued to be regarded as the decisive arm of combat and in preparation for battle was drawn up as a right and a left wing with the infantry, covered by the light artillery, in the center. The infantry continued to figure chiefly as a defensive troop with its maneuvering unit, the brigade, composed two-thirds of musketeers, one-third of pikemen. By 1680 the bayonet was coming into use and also the flintlock musket in place of the musket precariously lighted with a fuse. These two inventions made the musket a more effective instrument than it had been and prepared the way for the complete elimination of the pike. However, so far as Frederick William's army is concerned, at the time of his death the pikemen still figured with the musketeers in the old proportion.

Passing on to the artillery, we note that the destructive power of this arm captured the imagination of the leading strategists of the age to such a degree that the number of cannon of all calibers attached to the European armies mounted with each new decade. But it cannot be said that their quality notably improved within the span of Frederick William's life. The identical apparel of the gunners, the uniform, did not either in their case or in that of the infantry and cavalry become a prescribed feature until the time with which we are concerned, that is, the second half of the seventeenth century. Abundant evidence would seem to justify the claim not only that the Brandenburg army was among the first to impose the uniform on all ranks but also that the uniform it adopted afforded an unusually neat and attractive appearance.

The sensational military event of the elector's closing years was the rise to the premier position in Europe of the French army. This

6. Chap. vii, p. 166.

pre-eminence it owed in large measure to the immense resources a France economically and financially reconstituted was able to devote to the upbuilding of its armed forces. Not to be overlooked, however, was the emergence at this same moment of a brilliant array of daring and original strategists, like Turenne and Condé, and of an impressive school of mathematically trained engineers headed by the admirable Vauban. The French military advances were not lost on Frederick William, but it was left to his successors to incorporate in the Brandenburg army such improvements, especially in siege operations and engineering tactics, as had made the French army the envy of all the other armies of Europe.

A later development in both the administrative and military reorganization treated in the foregoing pages must at least be briefly noted at this point because, as the feature which more than any other characterized the Brandenburg-Prussian state in the period after Frederick William, it has become associated in every reader's thought with the aspect assumed by this state in the eighteenth, nineteenth, and twentieth centuries down to its total breakdown under the impact of World Wars I and II. This outstanding development has to do with the taking over by the Junkers of the elector's two centralizing and unifying departments, the army and the civil service. Doubtless the country squires began to enter them immediately on their creation, but since the two services did not, as we have been at pains to show, achieve their full development during the reign of their founder, the story of their appropriation by the Junkers belongs to a later period and is glanced at here merely to satisfy a legitimate curiosity arising from their later history.

The fact clamoring to be noticed is that it did not take the Junkers long to become aware that new avenues of employment and power had been opened to them by the creation of a standing army and a widened public service. Consequently they, or at least their younger sons, began to offer themselves at Berlin as candidates for the new posts. At first no more than a trickle, by the eighteenth century a steady stream of ambitious youth poured from the landed estates, on the one hand, into the openings created by the expanding central administration and, on the other hand, into the officer positions made available by the gradual transformation of the original mercenary into a standing national army. We have in this book made acquaintance with the Junkers as the passionate opponents of these two monarchical innovations; but, faced by them as the irreducible minimum demand of their indomitable chief, they began to examine them in a more sober spirit and discovered that they offered originally unsuspected opportunities of a profitable livelihood and a heightened social status. In short, the Junkers stayed to worship where they had formerly cursed and by this opportune conversion regained the political ascendancy that they had apparently lost when the elector struck the formidable weapon of the diet from their hands.

We have repeatedly referred to Frederick William's novelties of a unified army and a unified administration as the companion pillars of his new state. But when, in consequence of an attraction that neither he nor anyone else could have foreseen, the originally hostile Junkers adopted these pillars as their own, they became, as it were, their living counterparts and thereby the chief sustainers of the monarchy in process of formation. Thus absorbed into the leading institutions of the new state, they experienced a revival of their traditional devotion to the head of these institutions. It was the consequent intimate co-operation between the sovereign and his feudal dependents, the Junkers, that accounted for much of the vigor shown by the Hohenzollern monarchy in the era after Frederick William; but it is no less true (and the truth became increasingly manifest with each succeeding generation) that the close union, feudal in its origin and spirit, constituted a towering and, ultimately, perilous anachronism in a world rolling on to a bourgeois and industrial expression of its energies that neither would nor could be stopped.

THE NAVY AND THE BID FOR COLONIES

Sea travel and commerce are the foremost pillars of a state.[7]

Among the unforgotten impressions of Frederick William's apprentice period in the Dutch republic was the sea as an inexhaustible source of wealth and power. The memory counted heavily in his long resistance during the negotiations at Westphalia to

7. Statement by Frederick William in an official communication of the year 1684. In the original it reads: "Seefahrt und Handlung sind die fürnehmsten Säulen eines Staates."

the Swedish demand for the port of Stettin and the mouths of the Oder. Already at that time it had become his settled opinion that it was indispensable for landlocked Brandenburg to win an outlet to the open sea lanes. And though he was obliged to yield to the might of his Scandinavian neighbor, his thought never afterward drifted toward Stettin without quickening the hope in him sometime, somehow, to get back what he had been wrongfully deprived of.

Ten years after the Treaty of Westphalia he found himself, after a successful campaign at the side of Poland and Austria, standing on the shores of Jutland and straining his eyes in the direction of the Danish islands. On one of them lay Gustavus X of Sweden with a small army, and there he might have been captured and a new situation been created in the Baltic, if only the elector had possessed a fleet. As his maritime impotence precluded his coming to close quarters with his enemy, the campaign led to no results, and in the peace negotiations at Oliva that followed the Swedes were restored to the Baltic hegemony which for a fleeting moment had seemed to be slipping from their grasp.

It throws a sharp light on Frederick William's wakeful intelligence that long before he had been confronted with this particular situation he had attached to his person as adviser in all matters pertaining to the sea a Dutch colonial expert, Gysels van Lier by name, formerly high in the councils of the Dutch East India Company. However, owing to his lamentable lack of funds, the elector could do no more for a long time than pore intensely over a succession of projects put out by the indefatigable Van Lier for the development of a Brandenburg oversea trade; and, for the same unanswerable reason, he was obliged resolutely to pigeonhole Van Lier's hopeful proposals on the related subject of a Brandenburg fleet. Building a state not for the present only but also, and preeminently, for the future, Frederick William instinctively recognized the importance of the sea and the necessity of acquiring both a merchant marine and a navy. But his situation was unhappily such that he was obliged to give prior consideration to the many land issues that crowded more immediately upon his attention.

Then, in 1675, came a new war with Sweden to be treated in a later chapter. All that concerns us about it at this point is the manner in which Frederick William met the issue of a navy that with the renewal of his conflict with the dominant Swedes promptly came again to the front. Gysels van Lier had by this time been succeeded as maritime adviser by another Dutchman, Benjamin Raule; and Raule, characteristic product of the resourceful capitalism that had established itself in the Dutch area, had a brilliant idea. He proposed—and must have made the elector gasp with pleasurable unbelief—to fit out a fleet ready to confront Sweden on every sea without its costing the chronically exhausted Brandenburg exchequer a single penny. The amazing plan was for Raule, in association with other enterprisers of his homeland, to provide ships, fit them out with cannon, hire sailors and soldiers, and according to circumstances employ the vessels either as dispersed privateers operating against Swedish shipping or as a united navy prepared to engage and, if possible, to defeat the navy of the enemy. All that the associated capitalists asked Frederick William to contribute to the venture was his flag and his blessing, neither of which would figure appreciably in the expense account. It will not occur to anyone to imagine for even a moment that the so accommodating Dutchmen were thus putting themselves at the elector's service for the love of his blue eyes. They were businessmen and reckoned on a handsome return for their investment from the sale of the ships and cargoes captured by the privateers.

The arrangements must have proved satisfactory to both parties, for they were repeatedly renewed and were still effective when the war came to an end some four years later. In the course of the long struggle Frederick William captured from the Swedes not only the coveted harbor of Stettin but the whole Swedish-Pomeranian coast, and to these successes the hired fleet of warships, a curiosity making its first appearance in European annals on this occasion, notably contributed. True, the fairly astonishing victory of the elector over the Swedes was nullified in the end by the intervention of all-powerful France; however, that blow did not alter the fact not only that the Swedes had been badly beaten but that for the first time since the existence of a Brandenburg state its flag had made an appearance, and a victorious appearance, too, at sea.

Frederick William therefore continued to lend his ear to the ingenious Raule, and when the Dutchman now returned to the proposals of his predecessor, Gysels van Lier, and invited the elector to emulate his prosperous neighbors by reaping the bounteous harvest of the sea, he let himself be persuaded. Why, sang the tempter in ever new variations of the same tune, should not Brandenburg come in for a share of the huge profits the Dutch and the English drew from their colonial enterprises? In this way it came about that no sooner had peace (1679) rung down the curtain on the first chapter of the naval history of Brandenburg than the first step was taken in the related colonial field.

Raule's specific proposal was for the elector to seize a portion of the Guinea coastal area for the establishment of a trading post, and he proved his own faith in the project by offering to finance the first and purely exploratory expedition. Accordingly, late in the year 1680 two ships undertook the voyage, and after repeated unpleasant encounters with the Dutch, who claimed the whole Guinea coast as their exclusive property, the leader of the expedition signed a treaty with a number of Negro chiefs by which his master, the elector of Brandenburg, was conceded the desired foothold. Encouraged by this success, the elector now chartered the African Trading Company and invited subscriptions, with the disappointing result that the only sizable sums came from Raule and himself. Clearer evidence could not have been furnished that his Brandenburgers were still landlocked mentally as well as physically and that, besides, and for good measure, they disposed of no capital reserves.

In these circumstances it is surprising that the company fared as well as it did. A settlement protected by a fort was effected on what had been optimistically advertised by earlier explorers as the Gold Coast. Called Grossfriedrichsburg in honor of the elector, it developed a modest export trade in such articles as gold (in infinitesimal quantities), ivory, and slaves. As slaves constituted by far the most profitable ware supplied by Africa to the trade of Europe at this time and as the leading market for African slaves was in the West Indies, the company sought and acquired from the Danes a trading post at St. Thomas, one of the Virgin Islands. This was a movement in the right direction from a trading angle; and another profitable modification of the original plan was the transfer of the seat of the company from Pillau (Königsberg) in distant Prussia to

Emden, not far from the Dutch border and nearer the center of German population. Of course, Stettin would have been the logical choice for a Brandenburg trading company, but, alas, captured in 1677, it had, two years later, to the indescribable anguish of the elector, been given back to the Swedes. We may say without hesitation that only Frederick William's invincible spirit coupled with his willingness to make financial sacrifices for a venture which glowed temptingly beyond the horizon's edge kept the company alive.

Thus supported, the African Trading Company flourished modestly in the elector's time. It waned perceptibly, but did not die, on the accession of his son; for his son, in spite of his very imperfect comprehension of his father's work, took an erratic pride in the colonial establishment on the African Gold Coast and refused to let it disappear. It was the closefisted and exclusively military-minded grandson of the elector, King Frederick William I, who, sorrowfully viewing the long succession of deficits that had by the time of his advent to the throne been piled up by the sick company, was moved to be rid of it. With the contemptuous judgment: "I have always regarded this trading nonsense as a chimera," he offered the African enterprise to its envious rival, the Dutch West India Company, for a sum so small that it must have invited the derision of the purchasers. The bargain was clinched in 1721. Therewith ended in ignominy what most historians agree was a premature attempt on the part of Frederick William to launch upon the Seven Seas his little dinghy of a state alongside the majestic galleons of England, France, and the United Provinces.

In view of all the circumstances, in view, above all, of the material and mental backwardness of Brandenburg, the judgment may be allowed to stand. But a speculative consideration, based on the way in which men of genius have frequently set an apparently impossible goal for themselves and their followers, must be conceded a passing word. If Frederick William had been succeeded by one or two rulers of the same temper and breadth of outlook as himself, it might well have come about that the mental obstructions of the agrarian population over which they ruled would have yielded ground and that a direction would have been given to their awakened will which would have made them a seafaring folk against every reasonable calculation and in their own despite.[8]

ECONOMIC RECONSTRUCTION: AGRICULTURE, INDUSTRY, TRADE, COMMUNICATIONS

The elector was in no doubt at all that a sound economis basis was necessary for his proposed monarchical state. The expensive tool, the army, could not prosper unless its economic understructure prospered also. It happened that at this very time a school of politicoeconomic thinkers was coming to the front in Germany who made a new and stimulating analysis of the material resources of society. They are usually grouped together as cameralists, and the name is very well chosen since they made the supply of the prince's treasury or camera the starting-point of their investigations. Mainly interested in increasing the returns of the prince from taxation, they advocated the increase of the wealth of his subjects by stimulation under state direction of the many activities connected with agriculture, industry, and, especially, trade. Since the leading trading nations of Europe, the Dutch and the English, had manifestly become also its wealthiest nations, it may be that the German cameralists overstressed the trade factor in the contemporary social structure. In so far as this was the case they revealed their close kinship to the contemporary economic thinkers to the west of them, the so-called "mercantilists."

It is not likely that the elector concerned himself much with the often painfully academic and mortally dull brochures of the cameralists. But he did not have to study their books to become himself a cameralist of sorts since the issues they discussed and attempted to illuminate thrust themselves on his attention every day of his life. We may say sweepingly that throughout his reign he concerned himself ardently with methods for carrying to a higher potential the economic activities of his people. Herein, in the manner of initiators, he scored both successes and failures, whereof at least a brief account is indispensable in a review of his efforts directed to material betterment.

On considering the depressed condition of agriculture his first

8. The naval and colonial story is presented in detail and with supporting documents by R. Schück, *Brandenburg-Preussens Kolonial-Politik unter dem Grossen Kurfürsten und seinen Nachfolgern (1647–1721)* (2 vols.; Leipzig, 1889).

thought was not directed to larger harvests but to more peasants, that is, to new settlers to fill the yawning gaps made in the farm population by the war. We have already heard how immediately after Westphalia he negotiated with Dutch contractors to establish sizable bodies of their compatriots on his abandoned lands. Although the experiment did not work out very well, he issued a kind of standing invitation to Dutch farmers to come and settle in his dominions and was heartily seconded in these endeavors by his electress, who, a princess of the house of Orange, had a natural bias in favor of her countrymen. However, it may be contended that on purely objective grounds the Dutch took precedence over all possible competitors since they had developed a notable technique for draining and cultivating swamplands. In addition, they had become the leading cattle-raisers and dairymen of Europe and had acquired special and outstanding skill as gardeners and orchardists.

Among the many regions benefited by a planting of Dutch colonists an estate to the north of Berlin, presented to his wife by the elector and renamed in her honor Oranienburg, deserves particular mention. With the aid of the immigrants she transformed this property into a model for the backward native cultivators round about. So good a manager did she prove herself that Oranienburg threw off a handsome profit which, since she was also a good wife, she employed toward the redemption of some of the heavily mortgaged properties of her husband's domain. Brandenburgers of a later age never forgot that it was she who introduced into the mark the potato, which soon became, and to this day has remained, a leading item of the people's diet. Frederick William himself specialized rather as an orchardist than as a general farmer and, like most enthusiasts, was convinced that his hobby called for universal imitation. Not long before his death he issued an edict worth citing because of its patriarchal and cameralist flair. It required pastors of the state church to refuse to give their blessing to a new couple until the bridegroom had submitted evidence of having improved six fruit trees by grafting and of having set out an equal number of seedlings.

Not only from the Netherlands were peasants invited to the mark but also from various parts of Germany, and, as in the case of the Dutch, they were lured across the Hohenzollern boundaries by the remission of dues for a number of years and with, on occasion, the added inducement of a free gift of farm tools and cattle. Nonetheless, in spite of these replacements, the agricultural situation improved very slowly. This is not difficult to understand if, to the wounds struck by the Thirty Years' War we add the grave handicaps of an incurably thin and sandy soil and the low educational level of both the native and the immigrant peasantry. Do what the elector would, the farm population was at his death still far below what it had been before the Thirty Years' War. To give only one example: In the Uckermark, a section of the electorate which is not known to have been subjected to worse devastation than its neighbors, a count made in 1687 showed there were still twenty-nine hundred unoccupied holdings of either Hüfner or Kossäthen rating.

Exactly as in the case of agriculture, Frederick William attacked the industrial stagnation by trying to draw craftsmen to the depleted towns with the offer of a variety of favors. Behind this effort was the hope of reviving the many manufacturing enterprises which the war had destroyed. Because the desired revival was irritatingly slow in putting in an appearance, the impatient elector would at times himself play the entrepreneur by subsidizing establishments for the production of such necessary articles as glass, tin, and iron tools. To encourage these and whatever other infant industries came to life, he employed the several measures familiar to this mercantilist age, more particularly the grant of monopoly rights and the imposition of a protective tariff on imported goods.

In spite of these encouragements production continued to lag. The many difficulties inherent in the situation were not overcome. We may sum them up as an almost total lack of capital on the part of the war-stripped townsmen, coupled with a corresponding contraction of their mental outlook. In point of fact the urban ruling class, the burghers, still dwelt industrially in the Middle Ages and clung with stolid tenacity to the guild system, which guaranteed them, together with a meager livelihood, the maintenance of their social and political privileges. At one time an effective method of production, the guild system had latterly degenerated into an industrial monopoly for the benefit of a body of self-perpetuating masters and had all but put an end to the spirit of free enterprise. This spirit had, however, come once more into its own among the seafaring nations, the Dutch and the English, and was the principle underlying the system of capitalism that ruled their economy. Had Frederick William possessed the power, he would probably have broken the back of the guilds on the convincing ground that they were an obstacle to free enterprise and to increased production; but since they were too firmly intrenched to be overthrown and, furthermore, because there was as yet no spirit of enterprise abroad in his lands on which he could lean, he had to be content with leaving the situation pretty much as he found it.

His greatest disappointment occurred in connection with the woolen industry. In evidence of an earlier industrial vigor in the now stagnant towns they had once boasted a not inconsiderable production of cloth; and since, as soon as the war was over, the electorate had again begun to produce wool, though in diminished quantity, the ever sanguine elector concluded that a revival of the woolen industry ought to follow as a matter of course. Nonetheless, it made little headway for the identical reason that proved fatal to the elector's other industrial hopes: Brandenburg had an immobile burgherdom without capital savings, constitutionally timid, and of a rock-ribbed conservatism. In conclusion, it deserves mention as sounding a more hopeful note that the burghers did not prove to be permanently paralyzed. By the time the elector's grandson, King Frederick William I, came to the throne they had sufficiently overcome their lethargy to bring the so long and so hopefully awaited Brandenburg woolen industry back again to life.

The only economic area in which proud and indisputable successes were achieved was trade and communications. That will not cause surprise when we recall that Brandenburg was by decree of nature a land of transit. The most favorable single factor was that the leading channel of communication for eastern Germany, the river Oder, flowed for a large part of its course through Brandenburg territory. But there was a difficulty. The two foremost trading centers along the Oder were Breslau on its upper course and Stettin at its mouth, and neither of them was under Brandenburg control. From Breslau, a leading emporium for the products of eastern Europe, goods might go by boat down the Oder to Stettin but did not to any considerable extent do so, owing to high tolls and physical difficulties along its course. The Breslau goods went in far greater volume overland to Leipzig, still overland from Leipzig to the Elbe, and thence by river to the open sea at Hamburg.

From an early time it was Frederick William's intention to provide this important Breslau-Hamburg exchange with a water route through Brandenburg by digging a canal between the Oder and the upper reaches of the Spree. The canal dug, the rest would be easy, for the Spree connected with the Havel, and the Havel emptied into the Elbe. Undertaken in 1662, the canal, named for the elector, was completed six years later and, besides vitalizing Brandenburg by endowing it with a water route thenceforward given preference by the merchants of Breslau and Hamburg over the longer and more expensive alternative land route, had the added advantage of making Berlin an inland port. Its population, long stagnant, now picked up rapidly with the result that, hardly in Frederick William's lifetime, it is true, but by the end of the century, the capital of the by then fairly unified Hohenzollern territories had gained a recognized position as a north German commercial center.

An additional satisfaction in connection with the new waterway was that a measurable fraction of the Oder traffic was deflected thereby from the port of Stettin to that of Hamburg. As long as Stettin remained in the hands of the Swedes, the elector had no interest in contributing to its prosperity. In line with his recognition of the suitability for his lowland realm of water travel and his resolve to develop it, he reduced the customary tolls at Lenzen on the Elbe and also at various points along the Rhine with the happy effect that, instead of experiencing a shrinkage, they registered a considerable increase due to increased volume.

A unique achievement was the Brandenburg post, of which he may be acclaimed the originator, since nothing of the kind worth mentioning had existed before his day. While it is true that the great distances between his scattered provinces made the post an urgent necessity, it is also true that a less alert ruler would not have responded to the need or would have responded to it much less energetically. The first postal service he instituted joined up Berlin and Cleve at a time, early in his reign, when circumstances obliged him to pass a number of years in his western dominion. A service between Berlin and Königsberg followed. Thereupon, hardly a year passed without the electoral postal net being extended by the addition of a new route.

The elector was fortunate in finding in a certain Michael Mathias a technical adviser and postal administrator on a par with those other two administrative finds, Platen and Knyphausen, responsible, respectively, for the unified army administration and the unified domain. As early as 1649 Mathias consciously set himself the task of creating a post embracing all the elector's territories, and, laboring at this enterprise until his death in 1684, he brought it to a remarkable degree of fulfilment. Starting with the limited program of providing the ruler with a speedy and reliable means of communication among his widely separated government centers, Postmaster Mathias soon extended the service to the public by offering to carry letters, packages, and passengers and to multiply facilities according to demand. Then, after providing the widely scattered Hohenzollern lands with as complete a system as the unfavorable conditions permitted, he struck boldly across the Hohenzollern boundaries into the adjoining states, and, though only after often long-drawn-out and vexatious negotiations, succeeded in extending his lines until they embraced such leading centers of trade as Danzig, Hamburg, and Leipzig, thereby effectively covering the whole north German plain.

It need not be expressly said that the extensive postal net proved a great stimulus to trade. In measure as its services were improved, the time of travel was cut down until the journey from Berlin to Königsberg was effected in four days. To a record so miraculous the astonished contemporaries responded by acclaiming the Brandenburg service as the "flying" post. In brief, the postal system set up by the elector gained the confidence not only of his subjects but of the German public in general and was looked up to as a model by all the neighboring states.

RELIGION: ORTHODOXY VERSUS TOLERATION

In the seventeenth century, religion still engrossed as large a place in the life of Western man as in the Middle Ages, and the fact that over considerable stretches of the European area the older Catholic had been replaced by the newer Protestant worship made no difference in this respect. The religious attitude of Frederick William was therefore of the highest importance to his subjects, especially as the *jus reformandi,* the right to impose either Catholicism or Protestantism accorded to the German princes in the Treaty of Augsburg of 1555, was solemnly reaffirmed to them in the Treaty of Westphalia.

We have already learned that the elector distinguished himself at Westphalia by being largely instrumental in winning legal recognition for the Reformed faith to which he and a minority of German Protestants adhered, and we have also been apprised that, like his father and grandfather before him, he declined to make use of the conceded right to impose his particular religion on his subjects. This self-restraint may have been the consequence less of personal choice than of hard necessity, since his subjects, especially in the main territories of Brandenburg and Prussia, were overwhelmingly and ardently Lutheran and might have responded to an attempt forcibly to convert them with a general uprising. The fact remains, however, that there is no evidence that he ever even contemplated such an enforced conversion; and a fact no less important is that, doctrinally at least, he refused to regard the two competing versions of Protestantism as in serious conflict with each other. And why should he, seeing that their doctrinal differences reduced themselves, in the main, to the two issues of predestination and the Lord's Supper? As for the predestination or election by grace dogma of his own Calvinist belief, the elector regarded it as too abstruse a teaching for his lowly, secular intelligence to grasp. Refusing to wrestle with it, he referred it to the realm of the higher mysteries, to which also he assigned the equally unfathomable doctrine of the Lutherans which touched the presence of the actual body and blood of Christ in the bread and wine of the Eucharist and was called "consubstantiation" by them in dialectic, hairsplitting distinction from the "transsubstantiation" of the Catholics. Thus we may see that the same practically directed and matter-of-fact attitude that characterized his approach to the problems of government marked also his religious approach. Theological subtleties had no appeal for him, and he was content to conduct himself as a simple evangelical Christian, who diligently read the Bible, began and ended each day with prayer, and regularly and with sincere devotion attended divine service.

But the Lutherans in neither Brandenburg nor Prussia were willing to grasp the hand he held out to them. They, meaning not so much the unlearned congregations as their rigidly orthodox, stubborn pastors, denounced and cursed the adherents of the Reformed faith in the most unmeasured terms and, when rebuked by the indignant elector, would as their utmost concession withhold their thunder for a short breathing space. Undiscouraged, he again and again renewed his plea for mutual toleration, until at last in 1662 he took the bold step of calling a conference of leading representatives of both faiths at Berlin to the end of bringing them, if not to doctrinal agreement, to a cessation of the outrageous pulpit warfare.

The sessions extending over half a year got nowhere. So palpably did the blame for the failure fall on the stiff-necked Lutheran ministers that the elector's long-withheld wrath finally overflowed and he took active measures against them. Not only did he prohibit students of theology henceforth to repair for study to the Saxon University of Wittenberg, cradle and stronghold of unbending Lutheran orthodoxy, but he issued (1664) an edict of toleration forbidding all further name-calling from Brandenburg pulpits and obliging the pastors of both confessions to signify their submission in writing or forfeit their appointment.

While the larger part of the incumbents signed as required, a zealous Lutheran minority refused to bend the knee to what it denounced as religious persecution and, in spite of the heated support it won from such official bodies as the Brandenburg diet and the Berlin municipality, was forced out of office. It helps the present generation to a better understanding of the obsessed nature of this stark orthodoxy to learn that the most admired of the Berlin divines, a man of great learning and exemplary piety, chose to take his dismissal rather than forgo the right of warning his congregation against the soul-destroying teachings of his Reformed colleagues. The divine was Paul Gerhardt, who in the course of a long and devoted service in the pulpit produced some of the most moving hymns of the whole Protestant literature of song. Difficult though it may be, it is not possible to doubt his utter sincerity when he declared: "Ich kann die Calvinisten nicht für Christen halten" (I cannot regard the Calvinists as Christians).

After some months of deeply disturbing domestic conflict Frederick William reached the conclusion that his so-called "toleration edict" contained too many features suggestive of intolerance. Ceasing to enforce it, above all, canceling the acceptance in writing of the edict by the ministers of both faiths, he invited the greatly revered Gerhardt to return to his pulpit. But the preacher and poet preferred to accept a call which enabled him to breathe the more congenial atmosphere of neighboring Saxony, where Lutheranism enjoyed an unchallenged ascendancy.

In Prussia the elector met an even tougher opposition than in Brandenburg from the Lutheran chuckleheads. It will be recalled that his own Reformed worship remained obstinately taboo to the inflexibly orthodox Prussian Landtag until the adoption of the constitution of 1663, when that body graciously relented so far as to permit the holding of the Reformed worship in a total of three churches throughout the duchy! Only in his western territory of Cleve-Mark did his toleration policy come to something approaching fruition. And if it did so, it was to a large extent because his persistent personal pressure was supplemented by a situation favorable to his irenic aims. It was a situation identical with that which afterward, and often long afterward, caused the new principle to overcome opposition to it in country after country of Europe. Throughout the Westphalian area Lutherans, Calvinists, and Catholics were so inextricably mingled that they had it perforce brought home to them that there was no alternative, if they were to live together as a peaceful civil community, but to let each group worship God in its own way. No attempt to define the elector's attitude toward the total religious problem of his day can improve on the statement found in the testament of the year 1667 which he wrote with his own hand. After warmly recommending his practice of toleration to his son and successor, he exhorted him in no case to employ force, for, warned he, "no potentate is so powerful that he can coerce the conscience."

It remains to consider Frederick William's attitude toward Catholics and Jews. In view of the fact that the Brandenburg Landstände never met without putting themselves on record as irreconcilably opposed to their own ruler's Reformed faith, we will feel no surprise at their periodically voiced savage denunciation of Catholicism. Having over a hundred years before the elector's time been ejected from the mark, the Roman worship no longer commanded more than a few sporadic adherents. Consequently, the diet's frequently renewed exclusion of the mass cannot be said to have caused widespread hardship. Possibly for this reason the elector was at no pains to bring that body round to a more reasonable attitude. However, it may also be that in his secret heart he approved of the prohibition of Catholicism since he was inalterably suspicious of what he regarded as the consistently aggressive policy of the Roman church. It is worthy of notice that, in spite of this innate hostility, his fundamental tolerance asserted itself in the public declaration that individual Catholics should enjoy full freedom of conscience and should not be personally molested. As for the Jews, in the anti-Semitic convulsion which attended the coming of the Reformation that much-persecuted people had been expelled (1573) from the electorate. Almost exactly one hundred years later Frederick William's liberal disposition secured them permission to return and engage in barter and money-lending subject to certain restrictions of residence and the payment of a protective tax (*Schutzgeld*).

A sweeping summation of Frederick William's relation to religion, still a central concern of European society standing hesitantly on the threshold of an era of rapidly accelerating secularization, reveals that he was a devoted adherent of the radical Protestantism identified with the Reformed faith. Nonetheless, he insisted that his Reformed brethren constituted with the Lutherans a common evangelical body which it was his pleasure and duty to defend at every point at which it was threatened. By this unfaltering attitude he came to be regarded throughout the German world as the champion of the common Protestant cause, ready at all times to ride into the lists in its behalf. But an open and loyal, not a contentious and embittered Protestant, he had, a thing rare indeed at that time, a sincere respect for every other honest religious conviction. By this breadth of outlook he rose above every other ruler of his age and became the advocate of a toleration still deeply abhorrent to the generality of Christian worshipers but destined in the long run to establish itself as a fundamental principle of the modern world.

Chapter 10

PERILS OF THE REICH BETWEEN THE TREATY OF WESTPHALIA AND THE RISE OF LOUIS XIV

THE subject matter of this chapter will be the perils of the German Reich in the post-Westphalian period; and since our state of Brandenburg was a leading member of the Reich, the perils of the Reich will inescapably figure also as the perils of Brandenburg. However, they were not all on the same level for the emerging northern electorate, since, being also a distinct sovereign state with a body of distinct interests, it was moved to range the perils in an order of importance according to their pressure on its separate existence. This ambiguity, as we may call it, characterized the policy of every other member of the many-headed Reich and therefore also that of Austria. For the past two or three centuries Austria had played the part of the foremost German state and, because of the recurrent election of its head to the imperial office, was more visibly tied up with the empire than were any of its German associates. But only visibly and, as it were, for show, since Austria for centuries back had never failed to subordinate the interests of the Reich to its own interests and in large part owed to the successful pursuit of this policy the great authority its dynasty had attained in the European world.

Every profitable examination of the perils of the Reich after 1648 must start with the assumption that its members would regularly set their distinct and separate interests above those of the dying federation to which they belonged. This much established by way of guidance through the political confusion of the age, we can enter on our inquiry and agree that the most immediate perils of the empire stemmed from the foreign victors in the recent war, from France and Sweden. Having won a lodgment, respectively, in western and northern Germany, they had become free to resume their aggression whenever the occasion served. To these undebatable perils staring everyone in the face was added some ten years after Westphalia an unexpected peril which advanced upon the Reich from the southeast. It carried the name of the Ottoman Empire. A generation and more before, this once martial state, which in the fifteenth and sixteenth centuries had repeatedly threatened the existence not only of Austria but of Germany itself, had fallen into such a torpor that it was generally held to have ceased being a danger to its neighbors. However, under the energetic direction of a reforming family of grand viziers it confounded this hope and resumed its interrupted forward march against the hated Christian world. By the early sixties it had become clear that the Reich and Austria, the eastern bulwark of the Reich, were facing a fight for their lives.

While both Vienna and Berlin directed an ever watchful eye on all three of the enumerated perils, it followed from the principle adopted for our guidance that each cabinet assigned to them an order suited to its interests. The Austrian cabinet, for reasons equally of geography and of history, was pressingly concerned with the Ottoman and French perils and regarded the spatially more remote Swedish peril with relative indifference, while the Brandenburg cabinet for identical reasons was feverishly agitated by the Swedish and French perils and looked on the Ottoman advance as too distant a threat to provoke undue excitement. In the manner of all such threats they were often withdrawn or rested and were active only intermittently. Whenever one or the other or, as might happen, all three of them together darkened the sky of the Reich, they produced a quickened exchange of notes between Vienna and Berlin to the end of working out a common policy of defense. At once the opposed viewpoints springing from divided interests surged to the front and presented so many obstacles to agreement that, if reached at all, it would in all likelihood fall quickly to pieces over the disputes attending its application.

Let us now turn to the Reich itself. It was, theoretically considered, the agency most immediately concerned with the perils to which the German community was exposed. But against the theory the naked fact stood out that the Reich had been so weakened and disrupted by the Treaty of Westphalia that it had lost its last elements of cohesion and been reduced to a shadow. That circumstance was, however, not immediately apparent to the Germans of that generation, especially as the treaty itself had expressly rehabilitated the leading institution of the Reich, the Reichstag. For a period preceding by some years the outbreak of the Thirty Years' War and extending throughout its duration the Reichstag had been inoperative and for that long span of time had not once come together, owing to the inability of the savagely embroiled Catholics and Protestants to take peaceful counsel together. With the most cantankerous differences between them accommodated in the Treaty of Westphalia the more than a generation old deadlock was broken. Not only did the treaty resurrect the Reichstag but it assigned to the restored institution the task of bringing the Reich itself back to some semblance of vigor.

What little national sentiment still existed when the German civil war first irrupted had completely disappeared in the course of the insufferably prolonged conflict. Nonetheless, when peace at last quieted the domestic turmoil, it experienced a faint revival and inspired such individuals and groups as were still accessible to patriotism to greet the return of the almost forgotten Reichstag with lively hope. It was, after all, in name at least, the central authority of the nation, and it was from its renewed activity, if from any source whatever, that the federal government might be expected to be again invested with enough vitality to turn it into something better than the mockery it had proved itself to be.

THE REICHSTAG UNABLE TO REFORM THE REICH

To all dreamers of a Reich brought back to a vigorous existence by action of the revived Reichstag a long succession of disappointments was in store. To begin with, instead of coming together, as the treaty provided, within six months after exchange of ratifications among the signatories, the call to the two-hundred-odd members of the Reich to assemble was not issued by the emperor until well over three years later. Nor could the delay be charged exclusively to the Kaiser, although it is true that he repeatedly adjourned action in the matter and failed at any time to exhibit enthusiasm for a parliament composed of princes who, theoretically his vassals, in practice regarded him, as they had his predecessors before him, as their footstool. Much more than to the emperor the depressing delay may be attributed to the insecurity and confusion which continued to reign in Germany long after the hostilities had been brought to a formal close. There were fortresses and territories to be evacuated by enemy troops, armies to be paid and disbanded, boundaries to be drawn, properties to be restored; and in almost every instance sharp differences of opinion had to be adjusted before even the simplest arrangement laid down in the treaty could be carried out.

Nor is that the full story of the difficulties of the hour. After so grueling a war fought over religious differences Catholics and Protestants found it difficult, even after the settlement of the main issues between them, to come together in genuinely amicable conference. To the abiding religious irritation was added an all but universal political tension due to the claim of each Reichstag member to sovereign status. It caused every prince to look on all the other princes, but especially on those who were his immediate neighbors, as rivals and prospective enemies and to be perpetually on his guard against them. There was no blinking the fact that in this war-churned, post-Westphalian Germany there existed hardly so much as a measurable modicum of that good will that holds societies together and that each selfish state, mindless of the welfare of the nation, recognized no higher law than its own advantage.

And with what thoughts and feelings did the members of the Reichstag look toward their official head, the emperor? This was Ferdinand III, prize product in his time of the airtight Jesuit educational system and, consequently, the fanatical champion of the church of Rome. Emperor since 1637, when he succeeded his father, Ferdinand II, he had filled so large a role in public life that his mind and policy lay like an open book before the world. It followed that in religious matters the Catholic princes indorsed him as decidedly as the Protestant princes suspected and feared him. However, when the issue was not religious but political and constitutional, Protestant and Catholic rulers alike promptly forgot their aversion for each other and stood shoulder to shoulder against their chief. Come what may, they were determined to hold fast to the power which they had wrested from the Kaiser's predecessors and to block every move on his part to recapture the lost ground.

Nor was their alertness on this score unjustified. Like his father before him, Ferdinand III had throughout his reign nursed plans of imperial restoration, which, except for the intervention of France and Sweden in the German civil war, might have been at least partially realized. Was it not probable that Ferdinand was still the man he had ever been and ready at the first opportunity to resume the program he had been obliged to abandon? Another question: Was he prepared to employ the little actual power he still exercised as Kaiser in the interest of Germany or surreptitiously and against his oath of office in the interest of his dynasty? As everyone only too well remembered, he had monstrously dragged out the war in its last and dying phase for no other reason than that he would not separate his fate from that of Spain and the older Hapsburg line. And when he was forced at last by accumulated disaster to dissociate himself from his Iberian ally, he had not lived up to the obligations assumed at Westphalia, for he had given, and at the time the Reichstag was preparing to come together was still giving, help to the Spanish armies in their continuing struggle with France. This was double-dealing, and very dangerous double-dealing, since it exposed the barely pacified Reich to the risk of a renewal of the war.

Such were some of the tensions gripping the German world when on June 30, 1653, the long-overdue Reichstag at last began its sessions at Regensburg on the Danube. The Kaiser attended in person together with his son, another Ferdinand, who to the father's unbounded relief and joy had just been named as his successor by the college of electors, thus securing the imperial crown to the house of Hapsburg for another generation. Over the impressive ceremonies connected with the younger Ferdinand's coronation as successor under the traditional title, king of Rome, there was a renewed upflare of national sentiment coupled with a revival of hope for the achievement of federal reform. It shone bravely for a few weeks, died down, and then with a faint sigh guttered out. For about ten months the Reichstag dragged out its sessions until, unable longer to bear up against a gathering sense of futility, it welcomed the adjournment pronounced by the emperor, himself tired to death of a debating ground, whereon, despite an uninterrupted downpour of words, no tiniest sprout of awakening green ever rewarded the eye.

Let us once more review the reasons why it was folly and delusion ever to have expected an outcome other than this. In name the assembly of the nation, the Reichstag was in point of fact the meeting place of several hundred sovereigns, who, as lords temporal and spiritual, were distributed among the two houses of the electors and the princes. The third house, that of the free cities, exercised no measurable influence and may, for practical purposes, be omitted from consideration. As for the sovereign lords, they held themselves to be Germans to the marrow of their bones and rarely lost an opportunity to vaunt their conviction in ringing declamation. However, when it came to diminishing their cherished sovereignty by again handing over an infinitesimal fraction thereof to the refashioned federal institutions, they as ringingly denounced the idea as inacceptable and monstrous. If the German people, if, more particularly, the German middle classes, had been powerfully stirred by national feeling, they might conceivably have changed the course of events, even though they were represented in the Reichstag by only that third house, so slavishly submissive to the other two. But the middle classes, sapped economically and morally by the exhausting war, were a depressed social order and throbbed but feebly with the masterful emotion that constituted their strength in Holland, France, and England. In consequence the decision regarding German federal recovery was made exclusively by several hundred princely beneficiaries of the federal decline. To retain their sovereignty, always their primary aim, they rejected the secondary aim of national revival, and from this pursuit of a blindly selfish policy they were not deflected by the agitation of an organized middle class, for none existed.

In support of this judgment it will be profitable to have a look at the labors with which the Reichstag occupied itself through the ten months of its life. Vain as the labors of Sisyphus, they were in outward appearance, if not in inward reality, almost as onerous. With the reform of the Reich the acknowledged purpose of the sessions, the leading heads of discussion were necessarily three in number: the raising of money for national defense, the organization of that defense, and the rendering more effective the supreme court created over a hundred years before, the Reichskammergericht.

So little were the first two items, taxes and an army, to the taste of the sovereign princes that they never got further along with them than a verbal salute. No territorial lord in his senses would seriously lend a hand toward the creation of instrumentalities by which his own luster was bound to be dimmed. No doubt some prince now and then impulsively favored the strengthening of the Reich defense. On second thought, however, he would always join the majority in the deep and undoubtedly correct persuasion that any sort of executive rejuvenation was certain in the long run to advance the cause of the emperor. The moment the argument swung around to the emasculated head of the federation, every, even the slightest, difference of opinion disappeared. The loss of virility he had suffered was the measure of the vigor of his vassals, and the support of proposals to re-establish his manhood was instinctively recognized as dallying with suicide.

The only reform undertaken with any show of sincerity was that of the Reichsgericht. Since on its creation in the reign of Maximilian I this court had been withdrawn from the control of the emperor, it was possible to discuss its improvement without imperiling its settled dependence on the Reichstag. Furthermore, the Treaty of Westphalia had already laid down the norm by which it was to be reorganized, and all that was left for the Reichstag to do was to arrange the details. In order to promote religious good will, the lack of which had proved such a blight to the nation, the treaty had declared for the equal representation in the supreme court of the land of Catholics and Protestants. To meet this provision the Reichstag decreed that henceforth the court should be constituted with fifty assessors equally divided between the two opposed faiths. With this much comfortably settled, two issues remained: to provide the required funds for the enlarged legal staff and to find a way to reduce or to get rid in its entirety of the enormous backlog of cases that had been accumulating since from before the outbreak of the war.

Both of these measures were dealt with in a manner affording an illustration that would be tragic, if it were not so grotesquely farcical, of the doddering imbecility of everything connected with this bankrupt empire. Although the insignificant taxes for the agreed number of assessors and their clerical aids were duly voted and allocated, they were so irregularly paid by the member-states, on which, owing to the absence of an effective executive organ, no pressure could be brought to bear, that the court remained starved and undermanned and unable to dispose with even approximate dispatch the suits carried to its bar. Before long it was years and, finally, decades in arrears. As for the backlog, which had piled up for over half a century and become completely unmanageable, the Reichstag dealt with it by appointing a commission charged with clearing the intolerable mess out of the way. The commission was ordered to begin work in November, 1654. Unbelievable as it may sound, it held its first session in May, 1767, one hundred and thirteen years later!—with which appalling detail we may bring to a close our story of the "reforming" Reichstag of 1653–54. It should leave no doubt in anyone's mind that the Reich was unreformable by means of the Reichstag, a body composed of sovereign princes who throve on the weakness of the Reich. Nor can there remain any reasonable doubt that, unreformable by its Reichstag, the Reich never would be reformed until that organ itself had been swept from the scene either by the violence of a revolutionary leader or the rising of an outraged middle class or by both of them in combination.

THE SWEDISH PERIL

Even before the Reichstag session of 1653 had made it clear that Germany was not going to be saved from further encroachment on the part of Sweden and France by the strengthening of its central government, the expected aggression had materialized. However, the aggressor was not France, as might have been concluded from its greater dynamism. When France made peace with Germany in 1648, it did not at the same time come to terms with Spain, wherefore the war between the Bourbon monarchy and the Spanish Hapsburgs continued unabated. Furthermore, since in the very year of Westphalia serious civil disturbances broke out in France familiar under the name of the Fronde, the hitherto victorious Bourbon government experienced a grave setback and, with France in the altered circumstances repeatedly invaded by Spain, it looked as if this declining state might yet turn the tables on its enemy. One of the main objects of the Frondist rebels was to rid France of Prime Minister Mazarin, and twice their pressure forced him to abandon the country. But, a tough as well as a buoyant spirit, he twice came back; and, on finally re-establishing himself at the helm, he sought and won the friendship of the Lord Protector Cromwell and with the help of his English ally loosed such a concentrated mass of warrior might upon Spain that that already groggy power was at last pounded into submission and obliged to sue for peace.

By reason of the continuing Spanish conflict France paid little attention to the Reich in the years immediately following Westphalia. Wherefore Sweden, unthreatened on its northern throne and swelling with a feeling of invincibility, took the lead against the helpless federation and, more directly, against such of its member-states as lay within convenient reach. We have already recounted how Queen Christina's government refused for five years to hand over eastern Pomerania to Brandenburg as it had obligated itself in 1648 to do. The distressing episode may be regarded in the light of a notice served to the many small German states bordering on the sea that Sweden was not done with expansion at their expense and that it would hold them all in a state of perpetual alarm by keeping them guessing as to which of their number it would single out as its next victim.

As it befell, next after Brandenburg it was Bremen's turn. At Westphalia, Sweden had acquired, in addition to western Pomerania and the mouths of the river Oder, the secularized bishoprics of Bremen and Verden lying between the great seaports of Hamburg and Bremen. The two territories gave the northern kingdom a controlling position along the mouths also of the rivers Elbe and Weser without, however, handing over to it the two nearby seaports. For an expanding power like Sweden, Hamburg and Bremen, lying within easy reach of the Swedish lion's paw, were desirable morsels; and hardly had the Westphalian document been filed away in the Stockholm archives when the government turned on one of them, on Bremen, with the demand that the city forthwith take the oath of allegiance to Queen Christina. Now not only had the city of Bremen been expressly exempted from transfer to Sweden in the section of the treaty enumerating the Swedish gains, but Bremen was and had been for centuries a free imperial city with representation, like other cities of this class, in the Reichstag. The demand of the queen's government therefore rested on no better warrant than that of the sword, and the magistrates of Bremen, supported by a unanimous citizenry, indignantly refused to comply with the outrageous order.

After repeated rebuffs the Swedish government resorted to force and began its campaign by choking off the land and sea approaches to Bremen in order to starve the town into surrender. By the time the blockade was well under way the Reichstag of 1653 had begun its sessions and, aroused by the Swedish violence, warmly interceded in behalf of its threatened member. While the tough-minded militarists at Stockholm can hardly be supposed to have been frightened by the bark of this ancient and toothless watchdog, they recognized that their action might alarm Bremen's neighbors and draw them into a league of mutual support. While anxious to subdue Bremen, the Swedes were not anxious at that moment to unleash a general German war and therefore, checking themselves, moved more cautiously. It contributed to their hesitation that the abdication of their queen, Christina, which occurred at this critical time, made a large-scale conflict look like too grave a risk. Then, when Christina was succeeded by Charles X, this sovereign showed at once that he had his own idea as to the section of the northern world to which it would be most advantageous to apply the Swedish lever. From the moment of his elevation to the throne in 1654, he began preparations for that attack on Poland, the tremendous developments of which have already passed before our eyes. In order to clear the decks for the Polish action, which took precedence with him over everything else, he declared his willingness to give up the attack on Bremen. Accordingly, in December, 1654, a treaty was signed between the two parties which brought the war and blockade to a close.

Let it be well understood, however, that Charles X in that treaty did not renounce the Swedish claim to the homage of the ancient seaport. He merely withdrew the claim from sight with the idea of bringing it forward again when he had finished with the temporarily more urgent Polish business. Since, as we are aware, he died in 1660, still up to his neck in the developments that followed his plunge into Poland, he did not realize his expectation. Though thus perforce adjourned, the claim on Bremen was not forgotten. In the year 1666 it was revived by the Swedish regency acting in behalf of the boy-king, Charles XI, in an impulsive order to the government of the free city that it take the oath of allegiance without further delay.

More quickly than on the first occasion and in far greater number the German neighbors of Bremen, with Frederick William of Brandenburg leading the way, rallied to its support. Even two non-German states, Denmark and the United Netherlands, both active trade and maritime rivals of Sweden, joined the German helpers of the threatened seaport. So powerful was the coalition that sprang promptly and spontaneously into being that the alarmed regency agreed to treat rather than face the dangers of war. The negotiations led to a second accommodation much more favorable to Bremen than the first. In fact, a few face-saving concessions apart, the Scandinavian power suffered a distinct defeat, for it was obliged to acknowledge Bremen's unimpeachable status as a free, self-governing city (November, 1666).

Before we drop the Swedish peril to consider the shape that had meanwhile been assumed by the French and Turkish perils, it will prove enlightening as to the much-debated quality of Frederick William's German patriotism to examine an episode of the Swedish-Brandenburg enmity of the years covered by the just-recorded events. It befell when the war which Charles X of Sweden launched against Poland had taken the turn of a powerful combination of neighbor states to overwhelm the king and thus set a term to his insufferable arrogance. Gradually closing in on him, the allies planned, among other features of their strategy, to drive him out of Germany and allotted the leading role in this particular enterprise to Frederick William. Nothing could have given the ruler of Brandenburg more satisfaction than this assignment, since its successful achievement would have put him in possession of western Pomerania, withheld from him, as he unshakably believed, against every consideration of right and justice. We shall not review the story of the Brandenburg campaigns of 1658 and

1659 further than to remind the reader that they might have been crowned with success, had not France, in the person of Cardinal Mazarin, interfered and in the Treaty of Oliva of 1660 insisted on the full restoration to Sweden of all its German holdings.

Now when, in the year 1658, Frederick William took over the task allotted to him by his allies of ousting the Swedes from Germany, he recognized that his chances would be measurably improved if he could persuade the Reich to align itself at his side. Admittedly, the stricken Reich would strongly resist taking action and prove itself of small military value even should it do so; but there was no reason why the attempt to overcome its massive inertia should not be made and why, by way of preliminary, an appeal should not be issued to the slumberous but not entirely extinct patriotism of the German people. Could this be sufficiently mobilized, it might create a general sentiment conceivably powerful enough to raise the tired Reich from its sickbed and push it into action against the presumptuous northern conqueror.

Accordingly, Frederick William prompted a member of his Privy Council, possibly the nobleman, Otto von Schwerin, more probably the commoner, Friedrich Jena, to compose a pamphlet for general German circulation under the catch phase: *Bedenke dass Du ein Teutscher bist* (Remember that you are a German). Written with unusual feeling for that age of grave and leaden public documents, it exhaled a warmth that can still be felt after all the intervening years. Its master-theme was the degradation of Germany which stood revealed to all the world. Lingering particularly over the country's lost control of its rivers, it indignantly cried out: "What are Rhine, Weser, Elbe, and Oder other than foreign nations' prisoners?" And in concluding its call to action it summoned every German to weigh well his duty in connection with the current crucial struggle for the honor of the German name.

Let us agree at once that the appeal proved vain: The Reich did not come to the elector's help, and Pomerania was not recovered. Nevertheless, as throwing light on Frederick William's position touching the issue of whether or not the Reich was to have a foreign policy and an army of its own to enforce it, the pamphlet may not be overlooked. Not for the first time on this particular occasion, but before and afterward as well, the elector held to the view that the Reich must be aroused to a sense of its dangers and be brought to take action in regard to them. He was, of course, aware that the divided counsels of its members would always hinder it from playing a decisive role, but he saw no reason why it should not add its modest contribution to the wholehearted effort of a member-state like Brandenburg to eject an invader from the country's soil. Since such was his deeply implanted conviction, it fully justified him in thinking of himself as a German patriot. Wherefore it is inadmissible to regard the pamphlet of the Swedish war, as has been done in some quarters, as nothing other than a shrewdly calculated diplomatic maneuver for a purely personal advantage. A much more reasonable interpretation is that it reflected the ambiguous position in which he found himself throughout all the days of his life: He wanted to serve Germany but he could not help giving a much intenser service to the small state which he was engaged in nursing to greatness. Therefore, the appropriate last word on the pamphlet is that, though it voiced a sincere love of country, it would never have been published had not Brandenburg been in a political jam from which it was hoped that the pamphlet would in some sort bring it relief.

THE FRENCH PERIL: MAZARIN AND THE RHEINBUND

It testifies to the elector's sound political intuition that, although plagued in his early years chiefly by Sweden and practically not at all by Sweden's ally, France, he was never in doubt that, so far as the Reich was concerned, the Bourbon monarchy was much the more dangerous enemy. However, not under such immediate pressure by France as he was by Sweden, he adopted toward France the policy of keeping as far as possible in the background, content to conduct an intermittent polite exchange of views with this most formidable state of Europe. Throughout the first half of his reign his relations with France sounded a note of respectful caution.

Not that moments were lacking when the two states had found it mutually profitable to draw somewhat closer together. One such moment had occurred during the prolonged negotiations that preceded the final drafting of the Peace of Westphalia. In the hope of ranging the elector among the French clients he was engaged in assembling beyond the Rhine, Mazarin interceded in the elector's behalf with his ally, Sweden, and was largely responsible for Sweden's reducing its Pomeranian claim to the western half of that province. In spite of this service, Frederick William had successfully evaded making any definite commitments to France. Unaccustomed to rebuffs, Mazarin would doubtless have promptly manifested his resentment had not the outbreak of the Fronde and the consequent confusion in France dropped more pressing issues into his lap.

The check administered to the already achieved preponderance of France in Europe by the rising of the Frondists was, as we are aware, overcome after a few troubled years. At once Cardinal Mazarin, restored to his post of authority, resumed the intrigues in Germany which pursued as their main object the undermining of the power of the house of Hapsburg. The core of the plan, already revealed by his pre-Westphalian courtship of Frederick William, was the formation among the German princes of a dependable French clientage beyond the Rhine utilizable as a check upon the Hapsburg emperor. Such progress as had been made with the plan by 1648 was canceled by the rebellion of the Fronde and the attendant overthrow of the prime minister. On his return to power he had to build up his German program, as it were, from scratch and had the good fortune to be at once confronted with a German event than which it would have been impossible to create a happening better suited for his purpose.

On April 2, 1657, occurred the death of Emperor Ferdinand III. Since his son, elected in 1653 to succeed him, had preceded him in death, an interregnum now occurred which would continue until the college of electors had met and agreed on a successor. This signified the troubled waters in which foreign powers had in the past ever delighted to fish, and Cardinal Mazarin made haste to follow the established precedent. In private negotiations with the electors, he brought forward as his candidate for the imperial office the elector of Bavaria. This young man, being a Catholic, could, thought Mazarin, be made acceptable to a majority of the electors who were themselves Catholics; and being a member of the house of Wittelsbach, the rival of the neighboring and stronger house of

Hapsburg, he would, if raised to the throne, be obliged to lean on France for support. The bold project was defeated by the refusal of the cautious Bavarian to let himself be used as Mazarin's pawn; and when, after the usual long delay, the electoral college met at Frankfurt on the Main, the Hapsburg candidate made a runaway race of it. This candidate was Ferdinand III's second and sole remaining son, Leopold, who, when on July 18, 1658, he received the unanimous vote of the electors, had just passed his eighteenth birthday. Thus was the wily cardinal balked by a combination of circumstances, among which figured, besides the good sense of his Bavarian candidate in refusing to serve as his stooge, the imponderable prestige of the house of Hapsburg.

However, a diplomat of Mazarin's caliber always has a reserve arrow in his quiver, and immediately after having failed to defeat the Hapsburg candidate for the imperial office he laid his hands on an instrument admirably suited for the prosecution of his relentless war on the Austrian house. In the course of the election campaign that ended in the victory of Leopold the three archepiscopal electors of Mainz, Cologne, and Trier had begun a correspondence with a view to creating an association calculated to promote their interests. Fully agreed that the house of Hapsburg should, in the person of the youthful Leopold, retain its traditional headship of the Reich, they were equally determined that certain alarming practices which had characterized the rule of Ferdinand III should not be continued by his successor. A line of action followed by the late Kaiser against which they had constantly but vainly protested in his lifetime was to give help to the Spanish branch of his house in its continuing war with France, in spite of his having assumed the obligation in the Treaty of Westphalia to cease all traffic with his wartime ally. Although the help was given under cover, the whole world knew about it, and France, angered by the flagrant breach, repeatedly threatened to renew the war. This was a frightening prospect to the three archbishops whose territories lay along the Rhine directly facing France, and they were resolved that Leopold should not be permitted to perpetuate his father's evasions.

To this end they formed a league, which they invited as many princes as shared their alarm to join. The league's program was twofold: first, to draw up a pre-election agreement by which Leopold would forswear the criticized practices of his father and to which he would be constrained to put his signature prior to his elevation to the imperial purple; and, second, to provide a league army by which Leopold would be forcibly kept from breaking his promise after his election. As finally constituted, the league boasted a considerable roster of both secular and ecclesiastical princes, but as most of them hailed from the Rhine area, the organization came to be known as the *Rheinbund.*

In spite of its laudable central purpose of maintaining the peace consecrated by the Treaty of Westphalia, the Rheinbund quickly gained an unsavory reputation, which for fervidly nationalist Germans it has retained to the present day. That was owing to an additional signatory, who in a special ceremony put his name to the Rheinbund agreement the day after the German members had signed. He could not but ominously overshadow his dwarfish associates, for he was the ambassador of the king of France.

And so we come to the story of how the subtle Cardinal Mazarin insinuated himself into the Rheinbund, with the origin of which he had had nothing to do. As soon as the news reached him that certain German princes were planning an organization to oblige Leopold to discontinue his father's practice of underhand succor for Spain, he could hardly contain himself for joy. The planned action would bring the Spanish war, in which France, following the dispersal of the Fronde, was again piling victory on victory, to a speedy, happy conclusion. In his elation the cardinal dispatched his congratulations to the original sponsor and presiding official of the Rheinbund, the archbishop and elector of Mainz, and followed them up with the request that France be admitted to membership.

Such an application from an enemy country might well have given the archbishop and his associates pause, especially as they never ceased asserting their German patriotism and their pursuit of a strictly German purpose. Past history revealed, however, that it was usual for German princes, who in the eyes of the law were the vassals of the emperor and bound to him by oath, to feel alarmed for their own safety whenever they took action against him. Consequently, they would welcome diplomatic support from any likely quarter, and in the ruling European situation there was no support remotely comparable to that of France. True, they quieted an uneasy conscience by insisting that France was to be a member of their union on a precise par with the German signatories. But that such an assumption was pure self-deception was disclosed with very little delay, for, when the Rheinbund set up at Frankfurt a sort of Reichstag of its own, the delegate from France dominated the sessions as the sun does its satellites and effectively dictated all the Bund's major decisions.

To Frederick William, who had a way of seeing through political shadow-dancing to the hidden manipulator behind it, the Rheinbund was from the day of its formation in August, 1658, a tool of France and therefore an abomination. His critical attitude grieved the German members, who interpreted it as a denial on his part of their patriotic pretensions. It also, though for other reasons, grieved Mazarin; and, after Mazarin's death in 1661 it grieved the young king, Louis XIV, who, following the cardinal's departure from the scene, took the government into his own hands. Content at times to shrug their shoulders over the hostility of a distant north German prince so feeble as to be negligible, at other times Mazarin and, more particularly, Louis would change their tune and warmly court him. They adopted this alternative policy because they were secretly convinced that the elector had no match among the princes of Germany and that their fine engine for German control, the Rheinbund, would not work at top capacity until he had been made a part of it.

For almost a decade after 1658 the Rheinbund remained the center around which the relations of France and Brandenburg revolved. Attempts were not lacking on both sides to come to a closer and better understanding. But either they were abandoned as soon as France brought forward its inalterable demand that Frederick William join the Rheinbund or some incident occurred which showed the French government so congenitally ill-disposed to either himself or the Reich that he angrily rejected the idea of cultivating a greater intimacy with this western neighbor.

The first such estranging incident was Mazarin's injection of himself into the closing phase of the Polish-Swedish War. He gave Sweden, threatened with overwhelming defeat at the hands of its enemies, his undivided backing and not only saved the northern kingdom from threatened territorial loss but even re-established it on a broader base than it had ever before enjoyed. The cardinal's purpose herein was perfectly transparent: He was resolved at all costs to maintain the political system consecrated by the Thirty Years' War, whereby the German Reich was held as in a vise by simultaneous pressure from the west and north. To take this stand was to turn a face of stone to any demand of Brandenburg to be rewarded for its victories with even as much as a purely token payment from Swedish Pomerania. The upshot was that the Oliva settlement of 1660, inspired in all its decisive paragraphs by Mazarin, obliged Frederick William to abandon every inch of the coveted Pomeranian soil which he had succeeded in occupying during the war. While French diplomacy gloated over his discomfiture, hoping that he had learned his lesson and would henceforth be more amenable to French guidance, the elector was thrown into a rage which did not burn itself out for a long time.

It blazed up again when, three years later (1663), the Turks began their advance against Austria, and the Rheinbund, instead of contributing its support as part of the aid voted by the Reichstag, insisted on putting in the field its own independent force. While this was ostensibly the decision of a group of German princes, Frederick William, and all the world besides, knew that it was an idea originating in Paris. But abandoning for the present the episode of the Turkish war, we shall give it the treatment it deserves when, a little later in this chapter, we consider the Turkish peril in its entirety.

Hardly had the Turk war ended in August, 1664, with the Treaty of Vasvar, when the Rheinbund took action even more disturbing to the elector's peace of mind. It dispatched an army against the town of Erfurt in Thuringia, the heart of Germany. Erfurt belonged to the archbishop of Mainz, whom the French, finding him properly submissive, had prudently refrained from displacing from the presidency of the Rheinbund. Without possessing the status of a free imperial city, Erfurt had from as far back as the fourteenth century been self-governing with little or no interference in its affairs from its archepiscopal lord. Swelling with importance as head of the Rhenish union and assured of the support of all-powerful France, the archbishop, Johann Philip von Schönborn, resolved to reduce Erfurt to obedience; and when it refused to open its gates to his officials, he set the Rheinbund army, largely composed of Frenchmen, in motion against it. Accordingly, in the autumn of 1664 Germany was afforded the disconcerting spectacle of a French army of four thousand men crossing the border of the Reich and marching halfway across its width to lay siege to the recalcitrant town. Thus beset, Erfurt promptly capitulated and yielded its ancient liberties into the archbishop's hands.

Frederick William was greatly chagrined, especially as he was much too weak to think of halting the march of the aggressors. The French contingent in that so-called German army caused him to explode with ever renewed wrath. By what right had those four thousand men at a time of complete peace between the Reich and France entered Germany and laid siege to a German town? Certainly the Reich had not authorized the double breach and, in the absence of the Reich's consent, was not the presence of the French on German soil a sign that they had become its masters?

In a system of unscrupulously competitive states like that of seventeenth-century Europe we must be prepared for a ceaseless change of position, especially on the part of its weaker members struggling to survive amidst hazards that often threatened instant destruction. Even thus forewarned, the reader can hardly avoid being startled by our next piece of news, to wit, that at the very height of his concern over the mounting subservience to France of the Rheinbund, Frederick William joined it! After many years he finally yielded to the pressure the French put on him, since, anxiously searching the horizon for a helper against them, for the moment at least he stared into vacancy. That his inner opposition to the Rheinbund remained unbroken was revealed when, after making his verbal submission to the French late in 1664, he did not take the required next step of applying for admission to the Rhenish union until a year later, in November, 1665.

Yet he did join!—to the intense satisfaction of Louis XIV, who was free to believe that he had therewith set the keystone in his German arch. However, since the elector did not give up his French fears and remained as suspicious of Louis XIV as before, the French sovereign can hardly be said to have taken much profit from his diplomatic victory. In short, the elector continued to go, warily, of course, his independent way, whereof conclusive evidence was afforded by his injection of himself into the Münster war within a few months of his tardy obeisance to the great Louis.

The Münster war resulted from an attack of megalomania suffered by a small Westphalian neighbor of Frederick William, the bishop of Münster. In the year 1665 there broke out a war, essentially a trade war, between the English and the Dutch, and the bishop of Münster, who nursed a long-standing rancor against his Dutch neighbors, undertook to support the action of the English navy by attacking the Dutch from the land side. His lunge across the border produced a turmoil throughout northwestern Germany which Frederick William resolved to abate by threatening the inflated bishop wth an army mobilized on his flank, in Cleve. While his action was visibly directed against the episcopal troublemaker, it was partly prompted by his secret fear that France would seize on the Dutch-Münster disturbance as a pretext for marching an army into the Reich. It is a safe conclusion that by obliging Münster to sign a peace with the Dutch (April, 1666), the elector thwarted an impending French intervention. The incident must have brought home to King Louis that, although he had drawn the elector into the Rheinbund, he had not succeeded in chaining him to the French chariot.

THE REDUCTION OF MAGDEBURG

Plainly, the restoration of peace in northwestern Germany was a prestige-enhancing success for the elector, but it had been won at the expense of a mobilization which never failed to embarrass his finances. Bethinking himself, like the thrifty householder he was, of how he might get some return for the unwelcome outlay, he was no sooner assured of having brought the self-willed bishop to terms than he ordered the army of fifteen thousand men which he had assembled under General Sparr to march on the city of Magdeburg. With that name we are introduced to a minor but difficult chapter of Frederick William's history dating from the Treaty of Westphalia. The treaty had given him, among other benefits, the *expectancy* to the city and territory of Magdeburg, which meant that they were to revert to him on the death of the actual incumbent, a younger member of the house of Saxony, August by name. The arrangement was a typical example of the confused relationships that were an unhappy specialty of the decaying Reich.

Two years after the Treaty of Westphalia had been signed, in the year 1650, Frederick William ordered the Magdeburg town and countryside to take the oath of allegiance to him as the eventual heir; and, while the countryside readily complied, the town refused, alleging that certain documents in its possession established that it was a free, self-governing commonwealth. Although these papers, on being submitted to the Reichstag for verification, were formally pronounced spurious, the town persisted in its stubborn refusal to make submission to either Saxon August or Brandenburg Frederick William. The outraged elector might have appealed to arms but for two considerations: He had his hands full of more immediately pressing business and he was given pause by the town's almost impregnable position on the middle Elbe. While he let the issue rest, he never for a moment lost it from sight, since both as a military outpost and as a leading emporium of middle Germany it would prove an invaluable addition to the growing Hohenzollern dominion.

Not until some fifteen years had passed did the opportunity beckon for which Frederick William had been patiently waiting. In 1666 the army mobilized to exercise pressure on the bishop of Münster became available for any other useful Brandenburg purpose with the result that the master of that army directed it against Magdeburg, persuaded that its considerable size of fifteen thousand men would cause the surprised townsmen to yield without a struggle. And so, indeed, it befell. On June 8, 1666, the town authorities signed a treaty, whereby they agreed to do homage both to Prince August, the actual ruler, and to Frederick William, his designated successor. To make their submission irrevocable, they further agreed to receive and support at the town's expense a Brandenburg garrison. Since Prince August did not die until 1680, it was not until then that the Magdeburg lands were incorporated with the Hohenzollern state. But the presence of a garrison in the town after 1666 gave Frederick William effective control of it from that year.

Throughout the long crisis thus resolved by military action

Magdeburg boasted as its leading citizen one of the most famous physicists of the age, Otto von Guericke. His outstanding achievement in his chosen field was the invention of the air pump. A patriotic member of his community, he had honorably and repeatedly served it as burgomaster and ambassador and had been a potent factor in its stubborn resistance to Frederick William's claim to sovereignty. However, intelligently awake to the advantage accruing to a commercial center like Magdeburg from its association with a strong and growing state, on the morrow of the accommodation with the elector he became the loyal subject of that prince. Nor can a later generation doubt that an ampler future awaited the city on the middle Elbe through its integration with the Hohenzollern dominion than if it had remained an isolated unit beset on every side by rival polities.

THE TURK PERIL

By the time Magdeburg had been brought into camp the Reich had already had its first experience of the revived Turk peril. It cannot be well understood without briefly rehearsing the whole story of the Asiatic assault on the Christian world.

It was in the year 1453 that the Ottoman Turks captured Constantinople, the gateway to Europe, and entered on a career of conquest which for many subsequent generations kept the west in a perpetual state of alarm. Refusing to be content with the famous city on the Bosporus, they turned next to the subjugation of the Balkan Peninsula and, when this had been effected, under their most ambitious sultan, Solyman the Magnificent (who reigned from 1520 to 1566), inaugurated a powerful westward drive by both the land route of the Danube Valley and the water route of the Mediterranean Sea. In the Mediterranean they encountered and steadily pushed back the colonial might of once sea-proud Venice, and along the Danube, on issuing from the mountain gorges at Belgrade, they faced across the river the low-lying Hungarian plain.

In 1526 the chivalry of Hungary, with young King Louis at its head, went down disastrously before the Turks in the fateful battle of Mohacs. On the death of Louis without direct heirs the Hungarian crown was claimed by Ferdinand, archduke of Austria and younger brother of Emperor Charles V, on the strength of his marriage with the late king's sister; but when Solyman followed up his victory by flooding the great mid-Danubian plain with his conquering host, it was only the western and northern fringes of Hungary on which Ferdinand was able to maintain his hold. Resolved to crush the Austrian sovereign's resistance at its source, Solyman pushed on, three years later (1529), to his capital, Vienna, from where, manfully repulsed by the united energy of soldiers and citizens, he was obliged to beat a retreat. The siege of the great city on the Danube was the high-water mark of Solyman's westward sweep, for, though he never gave up the hope of ultimately capturing the Austrian capital, he was for the remainder of his days too occupied with other problems ever to return to the attack. And promptly on his death the Ottoman army and administration lost their vigor and passed into eclipse.

This is not the place to examine the causes of the Turkish decline further than to point out that, in keeping with the strictly military character of the Ottoman Empire, it had waxed great under a succession of active warrior-sultans and decayed as soon as a breed of rulers came to the throne who let themselves be beguiled into do-nothing idleness by the corrupting, self-indulgent life of the imperial seraglio. The passage from action to passivity set in with Solyman's son and successor and continued with occasional breaks down to the final extinction of the Ottoman Empire three hundred and fifty years later at the close of the first World War. The recurrent revivals, essentially no better than arrests in an uninterrupted process of decay, were usually the result of the seizure of power by a vigorous chief minister or grand vizier. Such a one made his appearance in the year 1656, almost a century after Solyman's death, in the person of Mohammed Kiuprili.

Mohammed Kiuprili, an energetic, stern, and puritanically minded follower of the Prophet, far advanced in years, purged the administration and the army of their worst plunderers and then set about reviving the martial tradition of the state. His purpose was facilitated by the circumstance that he found himself confronted on his advent to power with the revolt of the easternmost province of Hungary, called Transylvania. He put the revolt down not without difficulty and then guarded against its repetition by reducing the province to a much stricter dependence on Constantinople than before. The Transylvanian uprising aroused the sympathetic concern of Emperor Leopold, who had recently (1657) succeeded his father, with the result that he gave the rebels at first secret and, finally, open support.

To this explosive point had the situation developed by the year 1661, when the grim old reformer at Constantinople came to the end of his days. He was succeeded as grand vizier by his less puritanical but equally able son, Ahmed. Accepting Leopold's interference in Transylvania as a challenge, he resolved to punish the audacious meddler and in the spring of 1663 led his Janissaries up the Danube with the plan of overruning the parts of Hungary still in Hapsburg possession, preparatory to a renewed assault on Vienna itself.

Although amply warned of the coming of the Ottoman host, roughly calculated at one hundred and twenty thousand men, the Austrian government failed to make even remotely adequate provision for the approaching conflict. The main reason for its failure was without doubt that it was still suffering from the exhaustion resulting from the Thirty Years' War. It could count on some help from the Hungarian feudal militia; but, made up of habitually rebellious, though courageous, troops, it was a force incapable of sustained effort. The government also succeeded in raising two small Austrian armies and put them in action, respectively, in northern and western Hungary. They did what they could to turn back the incursions into Austrian territory of the swift-riding horsemen of the Moslems but were far too feeble to venture on a battle with the main Turkish host. As a result, Grand Vizier Ahmed was able to occupy and plunder large sections of Hapsburg Hungary before he went into winter quarters. Thus ended the campaign of 1663. In the campaign of the following year Ahmed planned to complete the conquest of the Hungarian kingdom and dictate peace under the walls of Vienna.

The extreme gravity of the situation caused the Austrian court to strain every nerve to get ready for the decisive struggle. It added as many regiments as its means permitted to the existing field force; and to its enormous relief it succeeded in winning the support of the German Reich. This, in view of what we know of that paralytic body, was a feat so extraordinary that it must needs be viewed a little more closely. Its explanation lies in the fear of the Turk which had won lodgment in the blood of the Germans a hundred years before, in the days of Solyman the Magnificent, and which, although more or less dormant since, had never been entirely expelled. The renewed advance of the Turkish flood caused the fear to come again to life and clamorously call for all possible aid for the threatened Austrian outpost. When, in January, 1663, at Emperor Leopold's summons the Reichstag met at Regensburg to consider the Turkish peril, as yet only a tiny black cloud on the horizon, the youthful sovereign heard more encouraging words than the feudal dependents of the German chief of state had spoken in many a generation. While this was an agreeable change of tune, it was attended, as soon as the question arose of how to convert words into deeds, by the cautions and delays so characteristic of Reichstag procedure. The never slumbering jealousies that so sharply divided these petty sovereigns persisted in the very face of an onrushing doom. Nevertheless, after a year of bickering and, though late, in time for the campaign of 1664 it was resolved that the Reich should mobilize an army of its own and send it to fight against the Turk shoulder to shoulder with its Austrian brothers.

The army voted by the Reichstag was calculated at a total of thirty thousand men. But a surprise awaited it promoters, whereby it was reduced to little more than half that number; for, prompted by their sponsor, the king of France, the German princes of the Rheinbund, refusing to contribute their required military quotas to the common Reich army, insisted instead on assembling and operating them as an independent force. Their offer was not without a certain surface generosity. They would supply seven thousand troops and, with their most powerful member, France, matching that number, the proposed Rheinbund army would be about as large as the Reich army diminished by the Rheinbund subtractions and, because of the solid character of the French contingent, several times as efficient. When Emperor Leopold was informed that he would have to accept the Rheinbund army in its independent and French-dominated form or renounce it altogether, the distraught ruler, after a hard struggle with his pride, yielded to necessity. In this strange manner he received help from the Reich in the double form, first, of a Reich army and, second, of what we may call a Reich secessionist army and experienced an evaporation of much of the joy wherewith he had originally greeted the proffer of German help. The idea of France fighting alongside a group of German princes in semirebellion against their liege was gall and wormwood to him.

The Austrian army, the Hungarian irregulars, the Reich army, and the Rheinbund army reached a total strength, if not as great as that of the Turks, sufficiently impressive not to be afraid to risk a battle. Accordingly, on August 1, 1664, the two hosts met at St. Gotthard on the Raab River, and the result of a long and bloody encounter was that Ahmed Kiuprili, though not exactly routed, was obliged to retire from the field. St. Gotthard was celebrated throughout Germany and Europe as a Christian triumph; but, while it saved Austria from invasion, it did not in the least shake the Ottoman hold on Hungary. The general expectation was, therefore, that the victorious Christian host would now drive against the Moslem position on the middle Danube. However, in place of news of this happy event the European public was shocked to hear instead that, ten days after the St. Gotthard success, Austria had patched up a peace with Grand Vizier Ahmed which left the situation between the two combatants exactly where it had been when the war began.

The Viennese government negotiated the surprise Peace of Vasvar for many reasons, chief of which in all probability was the situation in the Hapsburg section of Hungary. The real power in that ancient kingdom still rested, as had been the case from the beginning, with the feudal magnates, and they, a self-willed race of men comparable in their political outlook to the Polish nobles, bore the yoke of their Hapsburg ruler with the greatest distaste. They objected to the presence on Hungarian soil of Austrian troops, fearing in them an instrument for their own subjugation; and, being, in part, of the Protestant faith and in their vast majority favorable to religious toleration, they passionately resented the Austrian policy of religious persecution in the interest of Catholicism. In the recent campaign not only had the magnates at a highly crucial moment withdrawn with their militia from the field, they had also not scrupled to conduct secret negotiations with Ahmed looking to the betrayal of their Hapsburg sovereign in return for an Ottoman guaranty of religious liberty. Their treason so greatly outraged Emperor Leopold and his Viennese advisers that they seized on the earliest possible opportunity to end the war in order to be free to deal with the rebellious Hungarians.

Treasonable relations with the Turkish grand vizier were not the whole story of Hungarian misdemeanor. As every helper against their Hapsburg ruler was welcome, they were not slow to discover the potential value for them of the king of France and successfully to establish contact with his diplomatic service. The underhand negotiations spun by the Hungarians in the direction of both Constantinople and Paris must henceforth be steadily kept in mind. Fate had placed Austria, and with Austria the German Reich, of which Austria was the leading state, between two great and aggressive powers, the Ottoman Empire on the east and the French kingdom on the west. And either of them could at its pleasure start an insurrectionary fire almost at the gates of Vienna by encouraging the anti-Hapsburg Hungarian magnates to rise against their ruler. Pursue what course it would, Austria faced untold perils in the time ahead, and every peril of Austria would inescapably be also a peril of the chaotic Reich to which Austria was bound by hoops of steel.

A last feature of the Peace of Vasvar remains to be listed. Called a peace, it was by its own express declaration no more than a twenty-year truce; and, with the situation along Austria's eastern border as disturbed and fluctuating as we have found it to be, it was most unlikely that it would last out even its twenty-year term since, as soon as in the aggressive career of Louis XIV the hour should have struck for him to advance against Austria and the Reich, it could be taken for certain that he would play all his diplomatic trumps and bestir himself, first, to persuade the Turks to start a sympathetic war on the emperor's eastern flank and, second, to encourage the Hungarian noblemen to raise the banner of revolt against him.

Consequent to the Peace of Vasvar the Reich army was disbanded in the late summer of 1664 and each parti-colored contingent made its way back to its separate home. Outstanding among the returning contingents was that of Brandenburg. The excellent account it had given of itself throughout the fighting filled the master who had dispatched it to the eastern front with justified pride. Indeed, Frederick William was strongly persuaded that in this crisis precipitated by the Ottoman attack on Austria and the Reich he had comported himself as an exemplary German patriot. For one thing, no sooner had the question been raised of a Reich army to be mobilized in support of Austria than he had given it his enthusiastic backing; and, for another, he had anticipated by many months the laggard action of the Reichstag on this head by dispatching a well-equipped Brandenburg corps of twenty-five hundred men to serve with the Austrian army under Austrian command. While it is understandable that the elector was disgusted with the Austrians for breaking off the campaign before a decision had been gained, his vivacious criticism of his ally did not diminish the patriotic satisfaction with which he viewed his own share in the Ottoman episode.

AGAIN THE FRENCH PERIL: LOUIS XIV INAUGURATES A CAREER OF CONQUEST

Promptly on Cardinal Mazarin's death in 1661 young King Louis XIV announced to his assembled cabinet that he would henceforth be his own prime minister, and to the surprise of a skeptical world he lived up to his word. As long as he ruled, which was well into the next century, he and none other shaped the policy of France, pointing it with a resolution that never faltered to the domination of Europe. Nevertheless, it would be misleading to think of his plan as complete in every detail on the day that he took up the burden laid down by the cardinal. First to remember, it was a plan which unfolded by stages, and, second, it was already implicit in Mazarin's policy, from which it sprang as surely as the lion grows from the cub.

To support this position, let us go back to the Peace of the Pyrenees of 1659 by which Mazarin triumphantly concluded the war with Spain. Perhaps its most important article in the cardinal's eyes was the one which arranged for the marriage of the oldest daughter of King Philip IV of Spain to young Louis XIV. The Spanish king was at the time without male offspring, and, although his daughter, Marie Thérèse, on the occasion of her marriage solemnly renounced all claims to the succession in Spain, the shrewd Mazarin was privately persuaded that he was with this marriage clearing a path to the Spanish heritage for his sovereign.

Two years later, in 1661, a male late-comer was born to Philip IV so feeble in mind and body that his anxious parents lived in daily expectation of his death. Almost miraculously he lived, succeeded his father in 1665, and, as the childless Charles II, dragged out an unbelievably wretched existence until his death in 1700. The long-delayed demise, when it at last took place, precipitated the fourteen-year-long agony known as the War of the Spanish Succession, lying well beyond the scope of this book. Throughout Charles II's invalid existence the disposition to be made of the Spanish empire at his death feverishly occupied all the chancelleries of Europe. More especially it held the attention of Louis XIV, whose thoughts from the day of his marriage to Marie Thérèse were irresistibly drawn to the almost incalculable benefits which he might hope to extract from that connection.

So anxious was Louis to begin the appropriation of these confidently expected benefits that he was hardly well wed when he opened negotiations with his father-in-law for the peaceful cession to him of the Spanish Netherlands. Quickly and sternly rebuffed by Philip IV, on hearing a few years later, in 1665, of the death of the unwilling negotiator, he turned from persuasion to threats. On a legalistic pretext such as can always be dug up by expert crown lawyers and into the intricacies of which it would be sheer waste of time to go, he claimed the Spanish Netherlands in right of his Spanish wife and demanded their surrender without further demur. When the Spanish government acting for the boy-king emphatically denied the justice of his demand, Louis mobilized his army and in the spring of 1667 sent it under the famous Turenne into the coveted territory. The war, thus begun, is commonly designated the War of Devolution from an ancient feudal ordinance, called *droit de dévolution,* on which Louis based his territorial claim.

The daring invasion produced a tremendous repercussion, which continued unabated as Turenne, encountering only weak resistance, took fortress after fortress in the region immediately adjoining France. Completely taken by surprise, Europe was too disunited for concerted, countervailing action. England and the Dutch republic, the two powers most likely to take alarm over the French aggression, were engaged in one of their periodic trade wars, although negotiations had been started between them looking toward its termination. The Reich, hardly alive at best, found itself completely paralyzed by the influence exercised by France through its membership in the Rhinebund. As for Emperor Leopold, Louis adroitly pledged him to neutrality with the promise that, when the time came for the partition of the Spanish empire, the lion's share should fall to the younger branch of the house of Hapsburg.

Nevertheless, the shock of Louis's unprovoked attack was so widespread that resistance to it began gradually to take form. The English and Dutch hurriedly completed their peace negotiations and happily succeeded in associating the Swedes with themselves in a triple alliance pledged to keep France in check. When the spokesmen of the three powers confronted Louis with the demand that they be accepted as mediators between himself and Spain, he took umbrage at their interference but ended by graciously accepting it. At a congress held at Aachen in western Germany the war was brought to a close in May, 1668, by Spain, now manifestly in full decline, paying the price for the stay afforded it against destruction by the cession to Louis of a border strip of its Netherlands territory.

By a legal fiction, which had survived all the recent disasters of the Reich, that part of the Netherlands which was Spanish was still a territory of the Reich, whereof it constituted the Burgundian Kreis or circle. Louis's unexpected descent on the Spanish Netherlands alarmed Germany, as it did all his other neighbors, and provoked an outburst of anti-French feeling. When the Spanish governor at Brussels took advantage of this state of affairs to remind the Reichstag of its duty to come to the aid of its Burgundian circle, a rousing tocsin was sounded in that usually drowsy assembly. But it did not frighten Louis, as he knew only too well that it would not be followed by action. The mere fact that the German princes nearest the scene, the Rheinbund princes, were not only allied with France but in French pay was a clear warrant that Louis would not be hampered in his Netherlands venture by German interference. An unexpected consequence, however, of the king's raid across the Netherlands border was that it put an end to the tool that had so conveniently served French policy. So deeply shocked were the members of the Rheinbund by the highhanded action of their French partner that on the expiration of the Rheinbund agreement, which happened to fall in the very year of the Netherlands invasion (1667), they failed to renew it.

Thus, after an existence of nine years died a league which, formed to keep Kaiser Leopold true to his oath to maintain the peace, had totally against its original purpose become a means for enabling the French king to set foot in the German house. The burglary committed upon the Spanish Netherlands had aroused the princely clients of Louis to a consciousness of the threat hanging over every German state along the western frontier. Permitting the Rheinbund to lapse may therefore be set down as evidence of the continued existence of a German national conscience. But whether that conscience was vigorous and general enough to resist fresh attempts at expansion by the French king remained to be seen. If, though the Rheinbund had died, its spirit lingered, as there was excellent ground to believe was the case, Louis XIV would not fail to continue to find ready helpers in Germany to support his future aggressions.

Chapter 11

POLISH INTERLUDE: FREDERICK WILLIAM FACES EAST

When, in the spring of 1667, Louis XIV set out to conquer the Spanish Netherlands, no German ruler was filled with greater consternation than the elector of Brandenburg. He promptly and vehemently communicated his alarm to his German fellow-princes as well as to every European state within the range of the striking power of France. At the same time he evolved a plan calculated to meet the French challenge; for, as far as his voice carried, he advocated as inclusive a league as possible to stem the swollen Bourbon power. We have already noted that the general European situation at the moment strongly favored France, since the two states of great-power rank most likely to take umbrage at the French advance, England and the Dutch republic, were at war and since French control of the Rheinbund put an early movement on the part of Germany out of the question.

While Frederick William was not cheered by the swift creation, in response to his diplomatic clamor, of a defensive league, anti-French action gradually did get under way. The two fighting sea powers composed their differences in the Treaty of Breda (July 10, 1667) and then at an exasperatingly slow pace set about forming an alliance into which they succeeded in drawing Sweden. The three powers thereupon agreed on a line within the Spanish Netherlands beyond which French aggression should not be permitted to go. Deeply concerned over the emerging program of intervention, Louis XIV bestirred himself to keep it from so enlarging its range that it would include the Reich or any of its individual members. Within the whole German area he had in simple fact only Frederick William to fear, for the elector alone among German rulers was seriously engaged in urging a defensive alliance against the French king. In an access of prudence Louis therefore resolved to placate Frederick William and had him privately informed that he had reduced his claim to the Spanish Netherlands to a modest border strip and that peace on this basis had already been accepted in principle by Jan De Witt in the name of the Dutch government. This comforting news he supplemented with the expression of his desire for a general peace and of his willingness, in case the elector abandoned his agitation and gave an undertaking to remain neutral in the pending conflict, to support Frederick William's Polish policy.

Greater even than the elector's astonishment was his delight over this surprising approach. It was the first time in his dealings with the grandiose Louis that he had had the honor to receive from him a proposal wherein the two contracting parties appeared in the light of equals. For what was asked of him? Nothing more than that he give up pressing for war in an issue already as good as settled on relatively favorable terms by private negotiations between Louis and the Dutch government. And for the proposed abandonment of a cause which he, a small German prince, lacked the means to influence in any decisive way he was offered nothing less than the invaluable prize of French co-operation in Poland. A ruler of feeble Brandenburg would have had to be of unsound mind to refuse such a bargain as that. If the elector, nonetheless, gave the appearance of holding back, it was not for lack of eagerness but merely to avoid giving the impression of indecent haste. On December 15, 1667, at Berlin he signed with the French ambassador a treaty embodying the above-indicated terms.

A NEW ELECTION CRISIS IN POLAND

Thus suddenly confronted with Poland, we must briefly explain Frederick William's special concern with that kingdom at that particular time. We have in an earlier chapter dealt with the political chaos which had overwhelmed Poland by reason of the selfish policy of its ruling class; and we have also glanced at some of the resulting evils, such as ever recurrent civil war, bloody risings among the Cossacks, destructive invasions by Tartars, Turks, Russians, and Swedes. In the reign of King John Casimir (1648–68) the evils rose to a nightmare climax that carried Poland to the brink of destruction. We have treated in some detail Poland's devastating war with Sweden, which ended better than might have been expected from its early course, but which, on its conclusion at Oliva (1660), nonetheless cost the republic the province of Livonia, handed over to Sweden, and the sovereignty of the duchy of Prussia, conceded to Frederick William. A concurrent war with Russia was not terminated until January, 1667, by the Treaty of Andrussovo. By its terms Russia acquired the eastern part of the Ukraine and the Smolensk district, thus inaugurating a policy of encroachment which foreshadowed the total extinction of Poland effected a hundred years later.

A constitutionally indolent man, manifesting zeal only in connection with his religious devotions, King John Casimir was so cast down by the difficulties of governing a state and society clearly marked for destruction that he would have succumbed to the burdens of office had it not been for his beautiful and vivacious queen, Louise Marie, a princess of the Italian house of Gonzaga but, through her Gallic mother, of frankly French sympathy and culture. Because the royal couple had no children, it was but natural that the question of the succession should have weighed heavily on their minds. Immediately after the blow of Oliva the resolute queen proposed to settle it by having a successor elected by the diet in her husband's lifetime.

Being the politically minded and ingenious lady she was, she had, of course, a candidate for the Polish honors concealed from the world under her royal mantle. This was no less a personage than the celebrated prince of Condé, a marshal of France and a younger member of the ruling house of Bourbon; and in Condé's default she was ready to give her approval to his son, the duke of Enghien. Unfortunately for her plan both Polish law and custom forbade the election of a successor during the life of the reigning sovereign. On this account the mere proposal of the queen produced such violent commotion among the nobles, insanely jealous of every smallest privilege they had usurped, that she had regretfully to give it up.

Hardly less violent than among the Poles was the disturbance produced by the queen's proposal among the neighboring courts. Sweden, Austria, Russia, and Brandenburg surrounded enfeebled Poland like so many hunters gathered for the kill and, though snarling and snapping at one another, were prompt to make common cause against a fifth party rudely elbowing his way into their company. Besides, since the intruder in the present instance was a Bourbon prince, his candidature, if successful, would mean the extension of Louis XIV's influence, already dominant in the west, to the European east. While this was a gravely disconcerting prospect for the sovereigns of all the states immediately bordering on Poland, it was particularly alarming to Frederick William. Already hard pressed by France on the Rhine, he would with the establishment of that country on his Prussian border be gripped in a suffocating embrace.

In politics, as in chess, there is for every move a countermove, and Frederick William, become by this time an expert political chess player, resolved to meet the announcement of a French candidate for the Polish throne as the successor of John Casimir by bringing forward a Polish candidate of his own. For this candidate he hoped to obtain the backing of one or more of the other interested states and, when the hour of the election struck, a majority of the Polish diet. While the queen's plan of a premature, illegal election had failed, there would nonetheless, in view of John Casimir's precarious health, be an election in the not too distant future, and it was the part of wisdom for all the interested parties to prepare for it. The candidate who in Frederick William's view would command the strongest support among neighbor states and native Poles alike was his old Neuburg enemy, Philip Wilhelm; and when, in 1666, he effected with him that final settlement of the Jülich inheritance of which we have already taken note, the Polish throne was probably the decisive bait by which he drew his stubborn adversary to an accommodation. As Sweden and Austria for reasons of their own seconded the Neuburg candidature and a large Polish faction gave private assurance of support, the Condé-Enghien bid for the succession encountered gathering opposition, and with each passing month the contest between the French candidate and him whom Brandenburg and Brandenburg's associates favored grew more intense.

In the light of these developments in neighboring Poland the extreme excitement of the elector over Louis XIV's sudden descent in 1667 on the Spanish Netherlands will become more understandable. He found himself threatened by Louis on two sides, openly in the west, underhandedly, but no less seriously, in the east; and he could think of no more effective way of meeting the danger than by a general anti-French coalition. Although his efforts in this direction proved unavailing, they so greatly impressed, nay, disturbed the French king that he made his adversary the offer of a Polish-Netherlands bargain which completely altered the situation. By the terms of the proposal Louis, to be sure, was to come away with a modest booty in the Netherlands but—and what unspeakable relief that must have brought the anxious elector!—he agreed in the Polish election affair to withdraw the Condé candidature and throw his support to Frederick William's candidate, the Neuburg duke.

As the spirited Queen Louise Marie had died a few months before the signing of the Berlin treaty of December 15, 1667, the Polish situation, with her influence removed, took a new turn. Worn and weary John Casimir, deprived of the only prop that for these many years had sustained his courage, insisted on renouncing with the least possible delay a diadem which for a long time past had been to him no better than a crown of thorns. In September, 1668, he effected his purpose, and in the following May the assembly of nobles met at Warsaw, in accordance with custom, to elect his successor.

According to the pre-election agreements drawn up among the interfering foreign powers they should now have put their united strength behind Philip Wilhelm of Pfalz-Neuburg. Characteristically, they played one another false, or Austria and France played Frederick William false, for as soon as the Polish delegates streamed into the capital, the French ambassador, secretly, of course, revived the candidature of Condé, and the ambassador of Austria, a little more openly but no less deceptively, recommended consideration of the duke of Lorraine, whom the Viennese government had reason to think more subservient to the house of Hapsburg than Pfalz-Neuburg. Intrigue and double-dealing were running riot at Warsaw, when, suddenly, to the delight of the ironic gods looking down on these indecent proceedings, the bribery, deceit, and fraud by which the outsiders had been for years attempting to fortify their selfish interest in Poland were scattered as dead leaves by the sudden rising of a wind. Enraged beyond endurance by the attempted domination of their diet by designing foreigners, the lesser nobility united as with one voice on a native Pole, Michael Wisniowiecki, as their candidate and, howling down the magnates, who for clinking metal had espoused the cause of strangers, raised Michael to the throne. Austria, France, Sweden, Brandenburg, deceived deceivers all, had been beaten by an uncontrollable outburst of national resentment.

Unfortunately for the stricken country this act of spontaneous self-assertion was not followed up. The country remained divided as before, and poor Michael I throughout his short reign (1669–73) presented the same picture of a paralyzed executive as had his unhappy predecessor. We have already heard of his feeble intrigues with the turbulent element among Frederick William's Prussian nobility. Having no settled policy nor permitted by the domestic crosscurrents to have one, he alternately encouraged and discouraged the Prussian rebels in their opposition to their prince, and when Frederick William had their leading representative, Colonel Kalckstein, brutally kidnapped (November, 1670) under the king's very nose at Warsaw, Michael roared out his protest like a lion, only to temper it after a few months to the murmur of a sucking dove. The episode is here recalled to establish the fact that the explosive election of a native-born king accomplished nothing whatever toward fortifying Poland's executive power or remedying its woeful general anarchy.

For Michael's final discomfiture the Ukrainian Cossacks once again raised the banner of revolt against their Polish overlords and did not scruple to appeal to the Turks for aid. In the war that followed the Poles were so badly worsted that Michael was obliged in 1672 to buy peace by declaring the Polish section of the Ukraine independent under an Ottoman protectorate. Utterly crushed by the disgrace of this settlement, Michael died in the following year. The Polish diet thereupon raised to the throne John III Sobieski (1674–96), a fierce fighter and able general, who resumed the war against the Turks and succeeded in somewhat redressing the balance. But the ever resurgent divisions among his countrymen prevented him from getting much good from his victories gained in the field. He did, however, in his lifelong contest with the Ottomans inscribe his name on one of the most shining pages of Christian story, for it was he who, in 1683, led the composite army of Germans and Poles which went to the relief of Vienna and broke the Moslem siege of that town.

Chapter 12

HOW LOUIS XIV MADE WAR UPON THE DUTCH AND FREDERICK WILLIAM TWICE PLUNGED INTO THE MÊLÉE

THERE is something insatiable about conquest. Once begun, it goes on and on until it is at last stopped by the cumulative resistances which it itself creates. So it has been through the ages and so it is still—a recurrence so constant as to suggest a historical law. Thinkers of a religious turn have tended to explain it by the presence of evil in the world and by its unclean habit of feeding on itself. Biologists or biologically influenced historians have offered as their clue that nature, a reservoir of inexhaustible energy, runs to excess in everything in innocent, total disregard of any moral order man, the dreamer, may be moved to invent for it. Anthropologists have not failed to put in their word. Covering with their investigations the many thousands of years of man's slow ascent from savagery, they have singled out as the motivating force of his advance the urge to mastery and cannot conceive his giving it up until he gives up being man.

Reflections of this nature are unavoidable when one is confronted with the vast and disturbing phenomenon which will be found to lie at the heart of the developments covered by the remainder of this book—the will to conquest of Louis XIV. This will he first clearly revealed on launching in 1667 the War of Devolution. From one viewpoint that war was a French success and served to sharpen the king's appetite; from another it was, if not a failure, at least a disappointment, since Louis had looked forward to a much ampler territorial dish. Of this expectation he had been cheated when the Triple Alliance of the Dutch republic, England, and Sweden intervened and obliged him to come to terms with his helpless victim, the once formidable power of Spain.

Now the guiding spirit of the Triple Alliance was Jan De Witt, who as head of the Dutch government had, in checking the French king, taken the course imposed on him by his passionate desire to safeguard the Dutch state and people. True, like his allies, England and Sweden, the grand pensionary had been at great pains to avoid going to war with France and in the negotiations over a peaceful settlement had obliged Spain to make the full complement of sacrifices constituting the French minimum demand. Nevertheless, when all was over, Louis harbored a passionate resentment against the man who had had the audacity to take the lead in stepping between him and his designated victim. The king had been balked, in itself no light offense, and balked, on closer view, by whom? By the republican head of a republican community of merchants, roundheaded, potbellied mynheers, whose talk was of figures and profits, who dressed in sober black, disdained the fine feathers and elegant manners which were the boast of the French court, and had nothing to recommend them in the eyes of a ruler by divine right save their estimable moneybags. Believing with the unreasoning force of instinct in kingship and aristocracy, the Bourbon sovereign had needed only the check administered by De Witt to bring him round to the view that the step toward continental mastery precedent to all others was the destruction of the republican abortion that nature had spawned at his doorstep and that impudently pretended to the right of saying to his marching hosts: So far and no farther.

But his disappointment over the Treaty of Aachen and his monarchical disdain are not the whole story of the royal wrath. The king did not dwell at so great an altitude above his French subjects as to be unaware that they were the source of all his grandeur; and should he ever have been inclined to forget it, there at his elbow was that excellent man and councilor, Jean Colbert, prompt and eager to remind him of the lowly origin of his power. Colbert was Louis's minister of finance. Not only had he on his advent to office performed the heroic labor of sweeping the Augean stables of the treasury clean of the rubbish piled up by Mazarin's slipshod financial regime but, as head of the administration, he had also, and perhaps for the first time in French history, projected a material development for the country according to a coherent economic program. As everybody knows, Colbert was the outstanding spokesman in his day of that mercantilism of which Frederick William within his narrower compass was also an exponent and which was a system neatly suited to the outlook of an absolutist age, since it fostered as its central concern the expansion of the power and revenues of the ruler.

Let us look a little more closely at the workings of the Colbertian system. While stimulating agriculture and performing a notable service to communications by a greatly expanded network of roads and canals, Colbert was resolved, and perhaps chiefly, to develop French industry and for this purpose determined to protect the home market by discouraging the importation of foreign manufactures. As many of these came from the Dutch republic, it was Dutch importers who chiefly complained when, in 1664, Colbert inaugurated his industrial nursing-plan by a steep and comprehensive tariff. Even so, more Dutch goods poured across the frontier than Colbert relished, and by the still steeper tariff of 1667 he proceeded to raise his customs wall to an unscalable height. When the Dutch ambassador now boldly charged that this latest measure was contrary to existing treaties, Louis interpreted his intervention as just another instance of that merchant insolence with which he was at that very time becoming only too well acquainted in the political field. He sincerely hoped it was true, as the envoy alleged, that the Dutch were suffering incalculable injury from the French exclusion policy.

They could not suffer enough to please him, for his gathering wrath had by now carried him to the resolution of their total ruin. In pursuit of this aim he had, immediately after bowing to the Treaty of Aachen, inaugurated a diplomatic campaign to break up the Triple Alliance. The core of his program was to deprive the Dutch of every friend they had in the world and, having effected their complete isolation, to pounce upon and swallow them at one gulp.

The Europe-wide diplomatic preliminaries of Louis's planned attack on the Dutch have elicited a stupefied admiration on the part of historians which would seem to be somewhat excessive in view of the fact that the Triple Alliance was not the well-cemented structure it appeared to be and that the men at the head of the governments of Europe in this particular period were more amenable to bribery than ever before or since. Having already, though still a young man, experienced at every hand the venality of rulers and ministers of state, Louis was not restrained by feelings of delicacy from approaching them frankly, purse in hand. He inaugurated his campaign by negotiations with the king of England and promptly scored an amazing success. Five million livres were required to persuade this improvident, pleasure-loving monarch not only to drop the Triple Alliance and abandon the Dutch but to effect a complete turnabout by becoming Louis's helper in his contemplated war on the republic.

This English king was the restored Stuart, Charles II, undeservedly celebrated as the Merry Monarch, unless merriment be conceived as a form of gaiety totally divested of conscience and honor. The treaty by which Charles shed his Dutch ties and committed himself to fight his discarded ally at the side of Louis was signed in the greatest secrecy on June 1, 1670, at Dover. The promised attack on the Dutch in return for the above-indicated cash is the only section of the agreement that concerns our immediate story; but as throwing light on the frivolous spirit prevailing at the English and many another contemporary court and therefore as revealing a character of the age not to be overlooked, we must at least mention the monstrous betrayal of his own people by their sovereign for which the Treaty of Dover was intended to clear the way. In due time after the prime purpose of that document—the elimination of the Dutch as a political power—had been attained, Charles was, with the help of Louis, forcibly to bring England back into the Catholic fold.

If on turning his diplomatic guns on De Witt's other ally, Sweden, Louis did not achieve so swift a triumph, the only reason for the delay was the confusion then reigning at Stockholm. The government rested with a regency which ruled in the name of the boy-king, Charles XI, and among the regents there were both pro-French and anti-French members. It was the anti-French group which had committed Sweden to the Triple Alliance. Not for a moment did the French foreign office, which had held Sweden in leading strings ever since the Thirty Years' War, doubt that it could bring the pro-French group back into control as soon as it was prepared to follow up its verbal arguments with persuasions of a more material kind. Sure of itself and feeling no need to hurry, it delayed bringing the northern kingdom into camp until the very eve of the Dutch War. In a treaty signed in April, 1672, Sweden agreed, in return for a liberal subsidy, to mobilize an army with which to attack any German state which might venture to come to the aid of the Dutch. While there was no express mention of Brandenburg, it was as clear as if it had been set down in black on white that the treaty delegated Sweden to act as a check on the elector in the event that the known sympathies of this ruler should get the better of his judgment.

As Spain no longer counted at more than a pawn's value on the diplomatic chessboard, the only other possible interference with his Dutch plans that Louis needed to reckon with was from the emperor and from an occasional German state exercising its recently gained sovereignty. The union of the German states, the senile Holy Roman Empire, had fallen into such decrepitude that the king could with good reason look upon it as self-eliminated. But the emperor? First and foremost to remember, he was not the empire. He was a Hapsburg, the head, moreover, of a house whose duel with the house of Bourbon had been the central theme of European history for the last one hundred years and who could hardly be expected to brook the vast increase of strength accruing to his rival from the overthrow of such an imposing power as the Seven United Provinces. Louis recognized the difficulty of getting the emperor to agree beforehand to the annihilation of the Dutch, but he was not the man to admit failure until he had played his card and lost. The recollection of what had happened in the recent War of Devolution must have greatly encouraged him at least to make the attempt. He had on that occasion taken the measure of the shy little inmate of the Hofburg by successfully persuading him, even though it was his Spanish relative who was under assault, to keep his arms grounded in exchange for a promissory note of very dubious value drawn on the Spanish heritage.

We are driven to conclude that not only Emperor Leopold but also his chief advisers were smitten with a blindness and plagued with a confusion at this time that almost pass belief. Unsteadily wavering between conflicting courses, they comported themselves as though politics were a game on the mental level of blindman's buff. The only constant element in their perpetual vacillations was the inveterate Hapsburg religious intolerance, and it was to this that Louis's representative at Vienna cleverly made his appeal. Leopold's dull eyes lighted up at the thought of the promised destruction of the solid cornerstone of Continental Protestantism and, seduced by this pleasing prospect, he agreed in the treaty of November 1, 1671, to play the neutral onlooker whenever Louis got ready to snuff out the heretics. He did, however, sufficiently remember the traditions of his dynasty to stipulate that the French armies were to limit themselves to fighting the Dutch and that they were strictly to avoid giving offense either to Spain or to the Reich.

Parallel with the negotiations with the emperor ran those with such German princes as might be regarded as carrying some weight in a prospective Franco-Dutch war. Two of them, indeed, were not only important but, in view of the location of their territories, definitely decisive. They were their ecclesiastical graces, the bishop of Münster and the archbishop of Cologne. Their states bordered on the Dutch republic, and since Louis was pledged to the emperor not to violate Spanish, that is, Spanish Netherlands territory, Cologne and Münster afforded the French armies their only available road of invasion. However, since Louis was also pledged not to violate the Reich, we might conclude that his entrance into Dutch territory via Cologne and Münster was equally ruled out were we not aware of the chaotic condition of German constitutional law since the Treaty of Westphalia. Was the Reich invaded when a prince, become sovereign in 1648, made a treaty permitting a foreign power to send an army across his territory? It was, according to most experts in the field, a debatable issue, but not according to Louis. He held the two bishops to be, in principle, as sovereign as himself, and when in the year 1671 they signed agreements to join him—for a cash consideration, of course—as allies in his proposed war, he considered himself to be legally authorized to lead an army headed for the Dutch republic right across the northwestern corner of Germany without offense to either Kaiser or Reich.

However, to procure the smooth movement of French troops over German soil, Louis needed also the consent of the duke of Cleve to pass through his territory, and the duke of Cleve was the elector of Brandenburg. We learned in the previous chapter that during the War of Devolution, King Louis, abruptly changing his estimate of the elector, had signed (December, 1667) a treaty with him on a strictly "something-for-something" basis. As a result Frederick William had not joined the Triple Alliance and the close of the war had found the two rulers on the friendliest terms they had ever so far achieved.

Now no sooner had Louis developed his Dutch invasion plan than he set about getting Frederick William to join him in its execution. Since the elector's Calvinist and Dutch leanings were well known at Paris, the negotiations not only called for a good deal of delicacy but, at least in their early stages, for complete concealment of the king's ulterior purpose. Consequently, the French agent at Berlin approached Frederick William with talk only of the *Spanish* Netherlands and on December 31, 1669, got him to agree to support Louis's claim to this territory with an armed force whenever the demise of the imbecile Spanish king would toss that fearful apple of discord, the Spanish succession, among the growling European powers. In return, Frederick William was promised a subsidy in support of his army and a certain rather more than trifling territorial reward along the lower Rhine.

With the first step toward Frederick William's seduction thus successfully taken, it seemed safe, after the passing of more than a year, to take the second and final step. By this time Louis's Dutch plan was one of those secrets which are shouted from the housetops, and a new French ambassador, the comte de Saint-Géran, dispatched to Berlin in the winter of 1671–72, no longer lost time beating about the bush. He came with the avowed purpose of negotiating the terms of Frederick William's participation in the proposed extinguishment of his Dutch neighbors. However, in case the elector could not be won over to so drastic a course, the ambassador was charged at least to render him innocuous by his commitment to a pact of neutrality.

The demonstrative French courtship gravely embarrassed the elector. Now that Louis's vindictive program was out in the open, Frederick William knew instinctively and without debate not only that he would have no part therein but that, on the contrary, he would do what lay in his power to defeat it. He was no sentimentalist, but he was capable of sentiment; and where his religion was concerned his sentiment ran deep. At the French court ultra-Catholic circles had already given voice to aims and designs which foreshadowed the later, revolting Huguenot persecutions. When these same circles now spoke elatedly of the coming war against the Dutch in terms of a crusade, Frederick William could not but be filled with alarm, and not for the Dutch alone. In the chambers of his mind began to echo the powerful old tocsin: Protestantism in danger! And with his nerves tingling with this threat an insurmountable barrier raised itself between him and the French envoy who had come to Berlin to capture him for his king. But let us make no mistake: Now no more than before or after did considerations of sentiment dwell in his bosom unattended by the grosser promptings of self-interest. His sound estimate of political forces which rarely forsook him imposed the conviction that the fall of the Dutch republic would put him and, with him, the whole German Reich at Louis's mercy. Whatever the future had in store, it was in these perilous circumstances unthinkable that he should play the French game.

But how tell this to the comte de Saint-Géran, thereby at once drawing the French Jove's lightning on his head? That winter was for the elector a succession of dark and anxious weeks broken happily by a ray of light when, on a cold February day, the coach of a Dutch diplomat, Mynheer van Amerongen, rolled into the capital. His coming could mean only one thing: that the Dutch, belatedly aroused to their danger, had at last launched a diplomatic counterattack and proposed to draw the elector of Brandenburg to their side. From the very beginning of his reign Frederick William had given repeated evidence of his desire to be friends with the Dutch, but they, instead of warming to his approaches, had been almost at pains to treat him contemptuously. To illustrate their attitude it will serve to recall a situation particularly painful to the elector. By the spring of 1672 more than twenty years had passed since the close of the Thirty Years' War, yet the troops of the republic still occupied the half-dozen towns in the duchy of Cleve which they had seized during that struggle, and Dutch officials still collected the Rhine tolls of the occupied areas as partial payment on the fabulous Hofyser debt contracted by Frederick William's grandfather more than half a century before. Ever since the assumption of control at Amsterdam and The Hague by De Witt and the burgher party the relation between the two governments had become steadily worse, for the oligarchs looked upon the elector, who was the uncle of the young prince of Orange and one of his legal guardians, as practically a public enemy. The unhappy fruit of these clashes and misunderstandings was that De Witt and the elector had become all but completely estranged, and it was this distressing situation that explains the mixed surprise and pleasure with which Frederick William greeted the arrival at Berlin of a Dutch ambassador come to beg for assistance in the no longer avoidable conflict with the French king.

Not until April, when Louis was on the point of opening the campaign, did the crestfallen French envoy acknowledge his defeat and take his departure from Frederick William's court. It was by this time perfectly clear that the elector would close with Amerongen as soon as a few remaining differences had been ironed out. By early May the treaty was duly perfected, and by its terms Frederick William unequivocally took his stand at the side of the Dutch as their ally in the looming war. It is worth noting that in adopting this course he set aside the advice of his ministers who by a large majority urged neutrality as the safer measure. Neutrality did not accord with his impetuous temperament, and besides, having at the very beginning of his reign given it a disastrous trial, it had left a bitter taste in his mouth. Sweeping it and its partisans aside, he boldly sought the thick of the fight. Against the payment of half of his expenses by the Dutch he promised to mobilize and lead into the field an army of twenty thousand men. It was a generous, even an overgenerous concession on his part to accept a full half-share of the necessary military outlay, since his slender resources would with all but certainty prove unable to sustain the strain. In the elation of the moment he was not counting the cost, for a war was about to be engaged, which, while directed at the Dutch, in his settled opinion involved also Brandenburg, the Reich, nay, Europe, and was, besides, another ordeal by fire of his beloved Protestant cause.

THE DUTCH WAR: THE FIRST PHASE

By the time the Dutch-Brandenburg alliance had been signed the world was already ringing with the din of war. Aligned with the French against the Dutch were the English, the Swedes, and the German bishops of Münster and Cologne. In a passive sense the emperor and the many other German princes who had signed neutrality agreements with Louis were also aligned with the aggressor. In short, so well had the king wrought diplomatically that the Dutch faced the onset of an overwhelming coalition alone and unaided, except for such support as might be given by the one and only, and certainly far from formidable, helper they had been able to recruit, the elector of Brandenburg.

With the odds thus heavily against the Dutch the French invasion, which followed, as planned, the line of the Rhine, went forward with extraordinary speed for those days of cautious and deliberate warfare. Nonetheless, the feeble nature of the resistance it encountered on the part of the Dutch aroused general astonishment; for now only was it clearly revealed that the ruling burgher party embraced no more than the relatively small body of great merchants of the single province of Holland. Holland, to be sure, included most of the large Dutch cities, above all, Amsterdam. Moreover, it paid 57 per cent of all the taxes levied for public purposes. But, after all, there were six other provinces in the commonwealth, the voice of which could not be suppressed forever. And these six, together with the common people even of Holland, were strongly Orangist in sympathy. They looked forward to reinvesting as soon as possible young William III, who had just arrived at his majority, with the great offices of state to which his forebears had given luster and of which he had been deprived by Jan De Witt and the burgher clique. De Witt himself, latter-day historians are agreed, commanded a fine intelligence and a cultivated spirit and was far from being a mere party wheelhorse. In the course of the critical months preceding the French attack he went as far as he dared to conciliate adverse public opinion by clearing the way to his ancestral honors for the disinherited prince. It was his misfortune that he could not go the whole way without wrecking the republican regime with which he was identified and which had been built up in conscious opposition to the monarchical tendencies identified with the house of Orange.

The worst that can be justly charged against De Witt was that he refused for months and even years to put faith in Louis XIV's rumored designs against the Dutch state. But it cannot be charged that, when he could no longer ignore them, he failed to advocate as the only feasible countermeasure the creation of an adequate army. In this, however, he met with resistance from the Republican party, perhaps even with a certain inner resistance from himself, for the army was and had ever been the leading locus of Orange sentiment, and to increase it was equivalent to smoothing the path for the restoration of the deposed house. In this predicament De Witt adopted the half-measure which is regularly foredoomed to failure. While enlarging the army, he failed to enlarge it sufficiently to enable it to meet the French in the field. Consequently, when in the month of June the invasion began in full force, the French, meeting with no effective resistance, quickly spread over the eastern, inland provinces and confidently looked forward to ending the war in a few more weeks by overrunning the crucial seaboard province of Holland.

At this point the enraged Dutch army, egged on by the panicky masses of the threatened towns, rose in revolution. An irresistible public sentiment forced the restoration of William III to all the civil and military offices of his ancestors. With him as leader the government thereupon adopted the heroic measure which will be celebrated in prose and verse as long as men honor undaunted courage and self-oblivious sacrifice. It issued the order to return the country to the dominion of the sea by the cutting of the dikes. Regardless of the cruel destruction wrought upon the Dutch themselves, the command was spiritedly carried out. Holland became a waste of waters islanded here and there with populous cities lifted above the raging flood because built on higher ground.

At once, as if by magic, the situation was reversed. The advancing French army, helpless against the conquering ocean, was stopped in its tracks. The province of Holland remained unsubdued, and, with Holland free, the Dutch cause itself was safe. The single stain that sullied the valiant uprising of the people may not be veiled by silence. In its savage resentment a mob of his excited countrymen foully murdered the least guilty of the ruling oligarchs, Jan De Witt.

FREDERICK WILLIAM'S FIRST PLUNGE INTO THE DUTCH WAR

While these stirring events were holding the hypnotized attention of Europe, what of the single friend and ally of the Dutch, what of Frederick William? It was not expected that his army, which had first to be recruited and equipped, would be ready for action until the late summer. He had, therefore, time to look about him, and, as he did so, the caution that always asserted itself on the heels of his impulsiveness demanded a hearing. Why should he not be able to get German, particularly Austrian, help against Louis XIV? Had not the French sent their army through Cleve? And if they might—falsely thought Frederick William—claim that they were not breaking the peace of the Reich in passing through the territory of allied Münster and Cologne, they were beyond dispute doing violence to that peace in not only passing through but actually seizing and holding Cleve against its ruler's declared will.

The French campaign had got no farther than the Rhinelands of Cologne, Münster, and Cleve when the elector carried the issue raised by the invasion to the bar of the emperor and, perhaps not without surprise, discovered a certain readiness on that sovereign's part to take action. By an agreement negotiated before the month of June was out the emperor undertook to send an army of twelve thousand men into western Germany which, joining with a Brandenburg army of the same strength, was to serve as a watch along the course of the threatened Rhine. But, unfortunately, the two parties to the contract were from the first in hopeless disagreement regarding the precise purpose of the watch. The elector, committed to his Dutch ally, wanted passionately to fight the French; Emperor Leopold, committed to neutrality, had no stomach for the war and wished to avoid it, even though, with many reservations, he had taken the field because the presence of a French army on German soil had begun to trouble his sleep. So much regarding their different intentions was in the open between the two allies. But there was worse, much worse, which each kept to himself. Leopold's secret thought was to have his army tag along with that of Brandenburg in the hope of preventing it from attacking France; and Frederick William, for his part, proceeded with the undisclosed purpose of throwing himself so boldly at the French that he would sweep the reluctant Austrians along with him, thus overcoming their caution and catapulting them into the war on the Dutch side.

In these circumstances the campaign, worse than a failure, proved an outrageous hoax. The two German armies effected their junction in September, 1672, and then, with the elector impatiently clamoring for action and with the Austrian general, Montecuccoli, an able officer hamstrung by his instructions, perpetually applying the brakes, the united forces slowly rolled forward toward the middle Rhine. This was the miserable compromise arrived at by the two leaders, of whom one aimed at the lower Rhine in order to effect a junction with the Dutch, and the other at the upper Rhine to be as far away as possible from the actual scene of conflict. Arrived at the great river, the elector was for crossing at all hazards; but as that signified the war with France which Montecuccoli had been ordered to avoid, nothing but hot words between the commanders came of the several halfhearted attempts made to force the stream.

In these distressing circumstances the originally fairly respectable Austro-Brandenburg army reeled planlessly from point to point over the middle Rhine countryside until, bedraggled and disheartened, it had degenerated to no better than a military rabble. Of course, the Dutch observer, who on behalf of his government attended the elector, violently protested against these futilities with the result that as early as October his disgusted superiors cut off the stipulated subsidy payments. For a period of three months the Brandenburg army, unwilling to detach itself from its Austrian ally, wandered with that ally over western Germany as aimlessly, as one biblically versed Dutch critic put it, as the children of Israel over the desert. Then, toward Christmas, hoping to find in Westphalia the laurels that had not sprouted for it on the Rhine, it abandoned the Austrians and moved northward, resolved singlehandedly to drive from Westphalia a French army of occupation led thither by Turenne. But that great strategist, for reasons of his own, refused battle, and after some further weeks of disruptive maneuvering in the dead of a particularly hard winter, the elector was forced to conclude that the only way to save the shrunken remnant of his army was to lead it into winter quarters in the comparative safety of the zone beyond the Weser River.

Begun with such high hopes, the campaign for the relief of the Dutch had come to nothing. It was an unqualified fiasco. What use to blame the emperor who would not fight or the Dutch who would not pay? And the worst was not behind but in front of the elector, for, totally lacking the financial means any longer to supply his army, he was obliged to prostrate himself before the triumphant Louis XIV and sue for peace. His former great enemy, the Neuburg duke, who since the recent settlement (1666) of their bitter inheritance dispute had become his friend, offered to act as intermediary. He could perform this service without offense to Louis because, officially committed to neutrality in the matter of the Dutch War, he was numbered among Louis's obedient German clients.

So graciously did the French king receive his discomfited opponent's plea that we are obliged to conclude that, having been balked, at least for the present, of his Dutch prize, he was anxious to narrow his field of operations by getting rid of all other opponents. Be that as it may, Louis demanded no more of the humbled Frederick William than that he abstain from giving further help to the Dutch and show his good faith by keeping this army beyond the Weser River at a safe distance from the Dutch scene. The king even agreed, incredible as it sounds, to restore to Frederick William most of the fortresses he had seized in passing through Cleve and further, in somewhat ambiguous terms, consented to the exercise of the right on the part of the elector of again taking up arms in the event of a declaration of war against France by the German Reich. On these conditions hostilities between Louis and his allies, on the one hand, and Frederick William, on the other, were terminated by a document signed on June 6, 1673, at the king's camp at Vossem.

A craven peace climaxing a craven campaign. Such was the universal view of an action which the elector had undertaken with magnificent audacity against the practically unanimous advice of his councilors. His wretched showing made his enemies, who were many, rejoice and his friends, who were few, grieve. Unquestionably it cost him a large measure of the favorable opinion which he owed to the steady rise of his fortunes during the last twenty years. But he himself was far from a broken man. His unfailing spiritual resilience enabled him to greet each new day as a new opportunity, and his ripened experience informed him that as long as the war continued, unexpected events and changing political alignments would throw other chances his way, provided always that he stood alertly on guard and kept his powder dry.

In this expectation of early novelties the elector was not mistaken. In fact, they came so soon and so fast after the disgrace of Vossem that he must often have regretted his withdrawal from the war as overhasty, the more so as his attitude toward the two antagonists had undergone no change: After as before Vossem he looked on the Dutch with sympathy, on Louis and the French with distrust and aversion. If the Bourbon sovereign entertained any illusions on this score, he could not have entertained them for long, as he was abundantly informed concerning the consistently anti-French sentiments of the Berlin court by the new ambassador he had dispatched thither as soon as peace had been signed.

This envoy, Verjus by name, had it impressed on him before leaving Paris that his presence in the northern capital had no other purpose than to convert the master of the country from the neutral bystander he had become by the recent treaty to an active ally. It is in the light of this design that the surprisingly favorable terms which Louis conceded to the elector at Vossem become more intelligible. But on this, as on the occasion of the mission of Verjus's predecessor, the calculations of the crafty roi soleil went askew. So systematically did Frederick William drag out the negotiations over the alliance project and so studiedly did he avoid admitting Verjus to a personal interview that the irritated and despairing ambassador repeatedly asked to be recalled. His wishes were not met, for Louis, having persuaded himself that Brandenburg was the pivotal German state, had become convinced that if its ruler could be brought to range himself actively on the French side, all danger to his Dutch plans from the direction of Germany would disappear. Consequently, Verjus was ordered to be ever at Frederick William's heels and to pester him with a distasteful proposal long after the envoy had obtained the most positive evidence that the elector was already deep in negotiations with the enemies of France and making barely concealed preparations for swinging again into action.

THE DUTCH WAR: THE SECOND PHASE

What chiefly encouraged the elector to consider his renewed intervention in the war was the way the unforeseen and unforeseeable post-Vossem developments had changed the European situation. That act of desperate Dutch heroism, the cutting of the dikes, which went back to the summer of the year 1672, had given the initial impulse to the transformation. Men and not web-footed waterfowl, the French had been obliged to retire from a large part of their conquests, and the campaign had come to an all but complete standstill. In their chagrin they began to turn their attention once more from the Dutch to the Spanish Netherlands, which, bordering directly on France, had for generations been accepted as the foremost objective of French foreign policy and which by his former war, the War of Devolution, Louis had joined his predecessors in so designating. Agitated like a hunted hare by every military move of France, the frightened government of Spain had been filled with dismay by the invasion of its Dutch neighbor, and, as might have been expected from its moral caliber, had followed a wavering and ambiguous course. While officially proclaiming its neutrality at Madrid, it had permitted its governor-general at Brussels to give unofficial military assistance to the Dutch.

Not until it had become clear that the French were making ready to compensate themselves for their failure against the northern Netherlands by returning to their first love, the southern Netherlands, did Spain sufficiently rouse itself from its apathy to look around for help. Naturally, it turned first to the already fully engaged Dutch. Aware that the French sword hung suspended over all the Netherlands and not over just their own seven provinces, the Dutch were, of course, eager to enter into a close alliance. In the spring of 1673 negotiations were initiated which may be regarded as a first step toward a more general movement of resistance to French aggression. A second step followed soon after, when the Madrid government succeeded in persuading its Hapsburg branch office at Vienna to take advantage of the brightening situation to retrieve the prestige which Emperor Leopold had all but destroyed; for, although he had through his treachery in the campaign of 1672–73 brought shame on his ally, Brandenburg, he had also, inescapably, heaped it on himself. Never had the credit of the imperial name sagged to a lower level than under the impression of the aimless migrations over western Germany of that blundering Austro-Brandenburg host. In one of those emotional revulsions to which timid minds are particularly exposed Leopold gave eager ear to the proposals of the Dutch and Spanish envoys at his court, with the result that on August 30, 1673, he entered into agreements with them by which a new and certainly far from negligible coalition against the French bid for supremacy in Europe saw the light of day.

The inaugural successes of the coalition were beyond expectation and proved extremely gratifying to all the enemies of France. An Austrian army, displaying an unwonted energy, pushed down the Rhine Valley and, effecting a junction with a Dutch and Spanish force under the command of William of Orange, laid siege to the city of Bonn and in November captured it. As Bonn was the main Rhine base of the French for their campaign against the Dutch, its loss obliged them to retire from Dutch soil, save for a few fortresses along the border. It was the open admission to the world that their great plan had miscarried. While the Dutch War went vigorously on, it was, after the loss of Bonn, no longer fought over the question of the existence or nonexistence of that embattled people. Louis had taken his hand from their throats. They were out of danger.

The surrender by the French of their original purpose signified the abandonment by them of the German princes along the lower Rhine whom they had persuaded to join them in the Dutch enterprise. Following the capture of Bonn, the victorious allies flooded the territories of Cologne and Münster and obliged their cowed episcopal rulers to make peace. This was no mean success, but a far greater one followed. In February, 1674, the English gave up their alliance with Louis and came to terms with their Dutch opponents.

At no time since the war began had they done the damage to their old trade rivals that Louis had counted on in hiring them for the ignoble enterprise. The Dutch fleet, under Admiral de Ruyter, one of the ablest captains that ever scoured the ocean, had proved more than a match for the combined Anglo-French navy and not only had made a successful stand against it at sea but also, and repeatedly, had frustrated its attempts to effect a landing on the Dutch coast. However, it was not his unimpressive showing in the naval war that persuaded Charles II to retire from the French partnership. To the parliament as well as to the broad trading classes Louis XIV had in the course of the struggle revealed himself as the real danger to English aspirations in both the political and the economic fields, and they brought their sentiments to their king's notice in such a storm of protest that he was reluctantly obliged to bow to their will.

That the tide was, for the time being at least, running strongly against the French was further indicated by the adhesion to the coalition of numerous German princes, some of whom had until recently been Louis's allies. As final evidence of the gathering anti-French sentiment we may record that in May, 1674, the Reich, that most venerable but also most decrepit of governments, so far overcame its habitual paralysis as to join the allied front by a declaration of war against its western neighbor. Coming from a bedridden invalid, it was so helpless a gesture that Louis was justified in regarding it as of little consequence. And yet it was not quite so inconsequential as the haughty monarch imagined, since in simple truth the Reichstag declared war on France under pressure of public opinion, and the existence of that pressure indicated that German patriotic sentiment was capable of coming at least spasmodically to life. Its appearance in the spring of 1674 had nothing mysterious about it. It sprang from the wave of resentment which washed headlong over the land at the news of the outrages perpetrated in Germany by the French armies in connection with the shift of direction of the French war effort from the Dutch to the Spanish Netherlands.

The shift first revealed itself when Louis inaugurated his 1674 campaign. His opening move was to invade the isolated, Spanish-owned Franche Comté (the Free County of Burgundy) and to set about capturing its garrisons and fortresses. In order not to be disturbed in this enterprise by a diversion from the direction of the upper Rhine, he ordered a brutal devastation of all the German territory on the left bank of the river and particularly of the fertile Palatinate. The idea was to create a desert, where a German army, dispatched to discommode him in the Franche Comté, would be unable to find nourishment. The task was entrusted to Turenne and, in spite of the distaste this great and honorable man may be supposed to have had for it, was systematically carried out. It was the savage fires set in the German villages that, by lighting answering fires in German hearts across the Rhine, were chiefly responsible for the revived patriotism of which we have taken note and of the consequent declaration of war against France by the all but defunct Reich.

FREDERICK WILLIAM'S SECOND PLUNGE INTO THE DUTCH WAR

To no one did the action of the Reich bring greater satisfaction than to the elector of Brandenburg. First, it accorded with his own patriotic indignation over the French excesses in Germany, but, more immediately important, it opened the loophole through which he was able to escape the passivity imposed on him by the Treaty of Vossem. It will be recalled that he had pledged himself to neutrality in that document, saving only his duty to the Reich. It would take a bold, indeed a very bold, man positively to affirm that the elector would have been content to play the onlooker had he not won release from neutrality through the Reich's declaration of war. Frederick William was a ruler with many irons in the fire, and it accorded with his usual procedure that by the time the Reich spoke out he was already up to his ears in negotiations with agents of the coalition sent to Berlin to solicit his adherence to their cause. Unquestionably, however, the Reichstag's bold stand was most welcome, since he could now allege a moral justification for his change of sides and could, besides, invoke the cause of patriotism in making ready to take his headlong second plunge into the mêlée.

Not until July 1, 1674, was the treaty signed by which the elector joined the anti-French coalition. By its terms he agreed to put an army in the field to be maintained half at his expense and half at that of the Dutch and Spain. The size of the army he was to lead into action was set at sixteen thousand men, as Spain and the Dutch refused to furnish funds toward the support of a larger force. By his own decision and at his own charge Frederick William raised the army to twenty thousand men, since in his view that was the minimum strength which would enable him to perform the work he had mapped out for it. He re-entered the war in the same high spirit as two years before and with the same energetic resolve to find and, if possible, destroy the enemy. His high expectations were again destined to be blasted, for he encountered the same adverse conditions as on the previous occasion and suffered a similar, if not quite so crushing, disaster.

Although these adverse conditions were brought out in connection with his first plunge, it is worth while to glance at them again, since they considerably reduce his responsibility for the blight that quickly settled on the new campaign. While his army of twenty thousand men constituted a considerable force, it was not large enough to operate independently and, at the urgence of the coalition chiefs and with his own hesitant consent, was dispatched to the upper Rhine. Here the Austrians, reinforced by the many small contingents of the Reich army, had for some months past been facing the French under their most resourceful general, the famous Turenne. Although the elector on his belated arrival on the upper Rhine was given the formal command of the combined German armies of this area and was consequently held responsible for their conduct by the German princes and public, he was in point of fact subjected to the kind of chicanery inseparable from a coalition force and was obliged to bring every proposed military move before a council of generals, who modified or rejected it at their pleasure. With this fatal handicap he confronted Turenne, the first soldier of the age, who mapped out his campaigns under his own exclusive direction, enjoyed an undisputed unitary command, and could throw his army into action with the inestimable advantage of sudden surprise and swift execution which a multiple command regularly sacrifices.

Even before the elector had joined his German allies, their numbers exceeded those of Turenne, thereby obliging the Frenchman to retire from the right to the left bank of the Rhine. On the heel of this move and under command of the Austrian general, Bournonville, the Germans had in September crossed the Rhine at Strassburg, still at that time a free city of the Reich, and had carried the war into Alsace. It was here that Frederick William came up with them toward the middle of October. His arrival swelled the allied armies to some fifty thousand men and gave them so decided a numerical advantage over their adversaries that the elector resolved to attack without delay. Rushing forward with his Brandenburgers, he opened battle, which to his unbridled indignation he was obliged to break off when Bournonville refused to bring up the Austrians to his assistance. When Turenne, under cover of night, beat a retreat from a position too hazardous for him to continue to hold, Frederick William's battle plan was fully justified, but it was now too late to carry it out.

It was an unhappy curtain raiser. The fighting season, as reckoned in those days, was about over; and when Turenne now took up winter quarters in an inaccessible position in lower Alsace, the Germans followed suit by distributing themselves in loose cantonments over upper Alsace. However, they made the mistake of not reckoning with the offensive spirit of the great strategist, whose army after its rebuff had received reinforcements sufficient to bring it approximately to the German total. Leaving some of his troops in their winter quarters in lower Alsace as a blind, he retired in December with the bulk of his army into France behind the curtain of the Vosges Mountains in order, as the Germans thought, to win a winter rest beyond any possible chance of disturbance.

Nothing was further from the enterprising general's mind than such seasonal hibernation. Moving swiftly southward behind the shelter of the Vosges, he suddenly, just before the new year was rung in, burst into upper Alsace through the famous gap in the mountains at Belfort. While some of the German units, taken completely by surprise, were annihilated, the majority, in a shaken state not far removed from panic, managed to effect a northward concentration. At Türkheim, on January 5, 1675, they tried to stop the forward-pressing French and, although they made a rather better showing than might have been expected in the circumstances, were obliged to continue their retreat. A week later they recrossed the Rhine at Strassburg and, thoroughly disorganized by the successive mishaps they had encountered, sought winter quarters in southern Germany, whence there was good reason to expect that they would not again be routed. Upper and lower Alsace, reconquered, remained in the hands of the French.

Not even yet had Frederick William's fortunes touched their nadir. At the height of the disorderly retreat from Alsace he was met, after the manner rather of a tale of romance than of authentic history, by a breathless rider on a foaming steed. He was the last of a succession of mounted couriers dispatched by the government at Berlin to break the news to him that the Swedes had put an end to their watchful waiting just across the border and had broken in force into Brandenburg.

Chapter 13

POMERANIA WON AND LOST

THE CAMPAIGN OF 1675: RATHENOW AND FEHRBELLIN

By twice plunging into the thick of the struggle precipitated by Louis XIV's attack upon the Dutch, Frederick William had twice abandoned the Baltic area to which he primarily belonged by the gravitational pull of the mass of his territories and interests. The transfer of his always limited forces to the Rhine had obliged him to strip Brandenburg and Prussia of their defenders, thereby exposing them to attack by their hostile neighbors, Poland and Sweden. Fully aware of the attendant risks, he had resolved nonetheless to face them on the calculation that Poland, involved at the time in a losing war with the Turks, was not in a position to take on another adversary and that Sweden under a divided regency would prove incapable of decisive action. While his judgment turned out to be correct so far as Poland was concerned, he was to learn to his sorrow that it was mistaken in regard to Sweden.

It will be recalled that in April, 1672, on the eve of his attack on the Dutch, Louis XIV signed a treaty with Sweden by which its government pocketed a considerable bribe, euphemistically called a subsidy, on the understanding that it would go into action against any German state which might venture to side with the Netherlanders. When Frederick William, alone in all Europe, presently put an army in the field in support of Louis's victims, the Swedes had not exactly refused to meet their obligations but had found so many excuses for delay that Frederick William was forced to his knees at Vossem (June, 1673) before the regency had given marching orders to its army. The elector's withdrawal from the conflict was received with great satisfaction at Stockholm, since it removed every reason for Sweden's participation in an uncongenial war.

A year later, to the deep chagrin of the Swedish government, the elector's strong distaste for the French king's domination of Europe caused him again to enter the fray. The inevitable consequence was that the French foreign office reminded Stockholm of its obligation to come to the aid of its ally by an attack on Frederick William; and when the many-headed regency, completely devoid of the martial spirit that had characterized the previous one-man governments of the country, again resorted to one lame excuse after another for its continued inaction, the French ambassador lost patience and threatened to end his subsidy payments. The gesture was effective, although, even so, the Swedes consumed the whole latter half of the year 1674 in getting ready. Then, precisely at Christmas, as if to celebrate the return of the season of good will on earth, the regency dispatched an army of fifteen thousand men across the frontier into the Uckermark. Their commander, General Wrangel of Thirty Years' War fame, underscored the allegedly harmless character of the invasion by informing the inhabitants that the only reason for his presence was the necessity of finding winter quarters for his troops.

Having crossed the border in search of supplies, Wrangel was obliged to spread over ever more and more territory and in the course of the winter and spring of 1675 sent his plundering columns through all the eastern and northern districts of the mark. On departing for the Rhine, Frederick William had appointed his brother-in-law, John George, prince of Anhalt-Dessau, as governor of Brandenburg, and the prince, having only a few garrison troops at his disposal, was forced to sit idly by as the Swedish cavalry foraged impudently right up to the gates of Berlin. Then in early June, Wrangel began to move westward toward the Elbe. To all appearances the plan, dictated by the French paymaster, was for the Swedes to take up a position beyond the Elbe in northwestern Germany, from which they could either operate against Frederick William, should he ever return from the upper Rhine to defend his dominion, or proceed to the lower Rhine in support of French action in that quarter. As there was no foe immediately in sight and also perhaps because Wrangel was now an old man heavily handicapped by the fashionable malady of the age, by gout, he carried out the march to the Elbe with the greatest deliberation.

At this point the topography of the Mittelmark and, particularly, of the region west of Berlin must receive our attention, as it played a capital role in the events that followed. The region in question was the Havelland, a low-lying district of moors traversed leisurely by the river Havel, whose many windings frequently broaden out into placid, reed-grown lakes. The moist lowlands are rimmed by lines of pine-studded dunes which provide the necessary means of communication and along which are located the meager villages and insignificant towns the ill-favored district is able to support. Somewhat past the middle of June, Wrangel, with the advance guard, had arrived at the town of Havelberg, the point at which

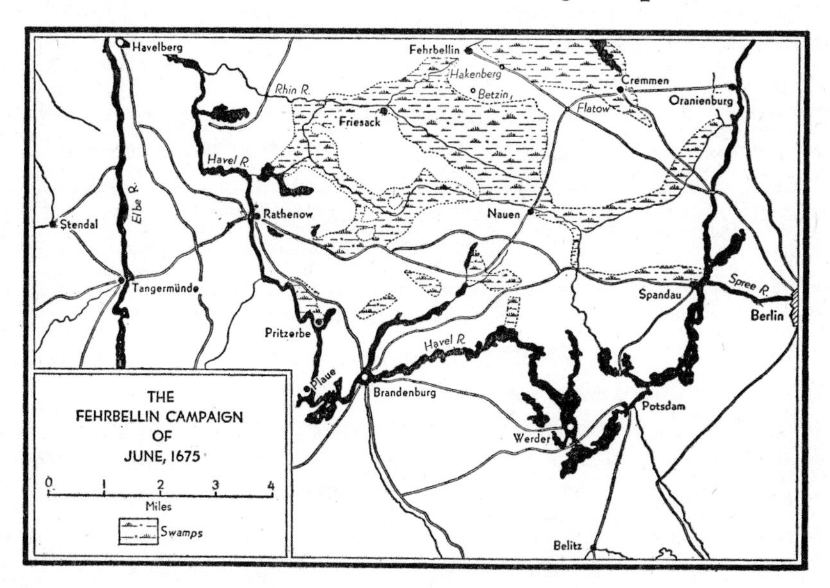

he intended to cross the Elbe. His troops were strung out loosely behind him all the way to Brandenburg, the ancient town on the Havel from which, back in the Middle Ages, the mark had received its name. The bulk of the Swedes still lingered at Brandenburg, whence they were preparing to move to Rathenow, also on the Havel and the halfway station on the road to Havelberg.

On the morning of June 25, like a bolt from the blue, the news fell both on the too leisurely advancing Wrangel at Havelberg and on his equally unconcerned younger brother commanding at Brandenburg that electoral troops in a night attack had stormed and taken Rathenow. The capture prescribed to the Swedes a single undebatable measure: Their line having been broken at its precise middle, the only chance of saving the army was by a swift retreat with a view to effecting a rearward junction of the two separated halves.

The little miracle, for thus in the light of the prestige of Swedish arms the Rathenow incident was regarded throughout Europe, was the happiest military stroke yet accomplished by Frederick William's young army. But in his own eyes it was no more than the curtain raiser to a struggle which, now that the Swedes had broken the peace, he was resolved to carry through to the complete liberation of Pomerania and for which he had begun systematic preparations as soon as, following the unfortunate campaign in Alsace, he had found himself in safe winter quarters in Franconia. As for his fighting force, its reconstitution had been a relatively easy matter, since it had held well together even under the strain of its disastrous retreat. But, regardless of its readiness, he had to let months roll by while he waited patiently for the coming of the season that would permit him to lead it across the rough Thuringian hill country into action in the north.

Let us once more recall at this point that winter campaigns were still generally avoided in this age and on the most unanswerable grounds. European roads were, with few exceptions, not yet hard-surfaced and were consequently impassable in the season of alternate slush and ice. Their condition signified that even if the army managed somehow to push and splash its way along, it was impossible to send the wagon trains after the army with the indispensable supplies. Moreover, as tents were not yet a prescribed item of military equipment and the men slept under the open sky wrapped in their cloaks, campaigning in the season of hard frosts was a feat beyond human endurance. Particularly grave was the problem of feeding the horses. In the growing season they could be pastured along the wayside, but to put them in motion with the country buried under a blanket of snow was tantamount to sentencing them to death by starvation.

For these reasons Frederick William had been for many months immobilized in his winter quarters in southern Germany. But that does not mean that he had been idle. Indeed, he had been exceptionally busy; for, aware that in meeting the Swedish challenge he was engaging a power much stronger than himself, he was anxious to leave no stone unturned in getting ready, first of all, by fortifying his position diplomatically. His earliest and most urgent appeals were directed to Austria, Denmark, and the Dutch republic. Since these states were members with himself of the coalition against France, his plea met with a favorable reception. But refusing to be paid with facile phrases when it was deeds he needed, he attached himself to the three governments until he had wrung from them the promise not only to declare war on Sweden but also effectively to support his campaign against that power, in the case of the emperor, with troops; in the case of Denmark and the Dutch, with ships. He was particularly insistent on naval co-operation, since the bitter experience of his earlier war with Sweden had taught him that land action unsupported by action at sea would not force the Scandinavians to their knees.

Pondering the coming campaign, he became so convinced of the inescapable necessity of sea power that he made the plunge he had long considered but had always been hindered from taking by his miserable impecuniousness. Even though his treasury was as yawning a void as ever, he procured himself a navy, or at least the beginnings of a navy, with the help of the accommodating Dutchman, Benjamin Raule. The story has already been told how Raule brought a small Brandenburg fleet into existence at no greater expense to the elector than the loan of the Brandenburg flag and the issue to Raule's hired Dutch captains of letters of marque and reprisal.[1]

Since, in the elector's eyes, the Dutch were still the world's leading sea power, he rated the presence of their fleet in Baltic waters as the probably decisive factor in the coming campaign. To leave no measure untried to secure its support, he resolved to seek an interview with William of Orange and in the month of March took on himself the fatigue of the long journey to The Hague. Arrived in his duchy of Cleve, he was laid low by an attack of gout, which with advancing years—he was now fifty-five—was paying him ever more frequent and harassing visits. On this occasion the painful ordeal confined him to his room for more than a month. Not until May did he reach the Dutch capital, where his nephew's as yet

1. See chap. ix, p. 240.

unbroken ascendancy won him a response on the part of the States-General as close to enthusiasm as that restrained body ever permitted itself to go. Hurrying back, with freshened confidence, to his army in Franconia, on June 6 he gave the order that started it, long chafing with impatience to be off, on its northward march.

Two weeks later the army had mastered the difficult Thuringian terrain and, fifteen thousand strong, had arrived at the elector's own fortress of Magdeburg on the river Elbe. Here Frederick William was informed by messengers of that careless disposition of the Swedes along the Havel, of which we have taken note, and at once resolved to crumple their front with a surprise attack. With his cavalry of six thousand men supported by twelve hundred infantry loaded on wagons to enable them to keep up with the cavalry, he directed his course straight at the center of the Swedish line at Rathenow. The rest of the infantry, too slow of motion for the contemplated surprise, had to be left behind. Traveling at top speed and without pausing for rest, the vanguard under Field Marshal Derflinger appeared at the bridgehead of Rathenow, precisely as planned, in the dead of the night of June 25. Old Derflinger himself, who at the smell of gunpowder was always able to slough off some thirty or forty of his sixty-nine years, led the assault. Not so much as a whisper of the Brandenburg approach had reached the Swedish regiment of dragoons that held the town. Roused from slumber by the wild shouts of the sentries, they found, on tumbling from their bunks, the Brandenburgers already in the streets. In spite of their bewilderment they made a brave stand but by the time the rising sun gilded the housetops had been either killed or captured.

Since it was clear that the Swedish army, thus split in two, would have to seek a rearward junction, Frederick William promptly formed the plan of cutting off the retreat of the main enemy force massed to his right at the town of Brandenburg. But the enemy was as quick as he. No sooner did the Swedes at Brandenburg learn of the break at Rathenow than, reversing their direction, they struck north toward Fehrbellin, where a bridge over the Rhin, a crawling tributary of the crawling Havel, afforded the only available escape from the treacherous marshland. While the elector moved forward as fast as he could to keep on the heels of the enemy, he at the same time sent a small scouting party under Colonel Henning to Fehrbellin by a direct, cross-country route. The plan was to destroy the bridge at that point, thus closing the trap on the foe.

This Colonel Henning is worth having a closer look at. Born a peasant, he is the rare example of a member of that class to attain officer rank. Following the 1675 campaign, he was even ennobled. Owing to the reputation he had gained as a partisan, he was the elector's own choice for the Fehrbellin mission. Cutting his way northward through the swamps by trails known only to the natives, he seized and destroyed the crucial bridge but, having only a few horsemen at his disposal, could not hold the position. When on the morning of June 28 the Swedish army with the Brandenburgers in close pursuit reached the vicinity of Fehrbellin, the bridge, although by now again in process of repair, was not yet ready for the passage of troops. The general in command, the younger Wrangel, quickly saw that to keep his men from being pushed into the sluggish, reedy Rhin he would have to risk a battle. He was nothing loath, since, although he had little more than half as many horsemen as his adversary, he commanded some seven thousand infantry as against no infantry whatever among the Brandenburgers whose foot soldiers had been left behind in the course of the hot pursuit. In these circumstances, Wrangel argued, Frederick William might not venture to attack at all; but, should he do so, to hold him off for a few hours would suffice to complete the bridge and assure an unmolested crossing during the night.

As soon as the leading pursuit squadron of the Brandenburg cavalry made contact with the Swedes drawn up in battle array, it rode to the attack without regard for the disparity of numbers. Sharp on their heels came the elector and Derflinger. They dragged with them—it was the hardest kind of going in the sandy wastes above the marshes—some twelve light cannons which with quick decision they planted on a low dune commanding the right wing of the Swedes and in their haste left unoccupied by them. When the shelling from the height began, Wrangel felt obliged to silence the artillery. To this end he first ordered an infantry regiment to storm the position and, when it failed, sent some squadrons of cavalry against the height, which also failed. That was the whole battle, if battle is not too lordly a designation for an action which, while sustained by all the available Brandenburg cavalry to a total of some six thousand men, involved no more than the threatened right wing of the Swedes.

If the Brandenburgers then and afterward celebrated the battle of Fehrbellin as a victory, they were fully justified, for they had held their ground against several vigorous assaults of the enemy. Repeatedly, the attacking cavalry almost penetrated to the cannons which they were ordered to spike, whereupon friend and foe became locked in a shouting, sweating, indistinguishable mass. Frederick William, sharing the day and its dangers with his men, was more than once encircled by the enemy and toward the close of the battle missed death by a hairbreadth when a shot from a Swedish cannon killed his faithful equerry, Froben, at his side. With the unsilenced cannons continuing their devastating play, Wrangel broke off the fight by ordering a general retreat. It was conducted without confusion and with little interference from the Brandenburgers, too exhausted to engage in more than a feeble pursuit. Since leaving Magdeburg five days before, the saddles had not been lifted from the horses' backs, and horses and riders alike had come to the end of their tether.

In a sense the Swedes, too, might have claimed the victory, for they had with their delaying action successfully covered their retreat. By nightfall of the day of Fehrbellin the bridge had been repaired, and they crossed in safety to the other side. In point of fact, however, it never occurred to them to blow the trumpet over the recent action, for the general trend of the campaign spoke too heavily against them. Not only had they suffered considerable casualties through the collisions at Rathenow and Fehrbellin, they had been weakened even more substantially by loss of equipment and soldier desertion along the difficult line of retreat. Ever since their first arrival on German soil back in the period of the Thirty Years' War the Swedes had made a practice of getting their recruits to a large extent from the German population; and on the rare occasions when disaster overtook them, these Germans, tied to the invader only by their pay, simply faded out of the ranks. When the younger Wrangel rejoined his brother, the field marshal, a few days after Fehrbellin, the Swedish army stood at little more than half its original figure. Too shaken in its morale to face another attack, it continued its retreat until, after a few weeks, it was back in Swedish Pomerania, whence it had set out some six months before.

Between June 24, when the Brandenburg army crossed the border of the mark, and July 2, when the last Swedish soldier abandoned its soil, lay a little more than a week. That brief time had sufficed to rout the invader from the elector's dominion. It was a *veni-vidi-vici* sort of victory, a kind to which the leaders of war as practiced in that age no longer even aspired, if we make exception of the great Turenne. In that stirring last week of June there had been two bloody encounters but, a far more important matter, there had been a unified campaign of which the encounters were merely the outstanding incidents. Although ill-wishers and enemies of the elector might refuse to be impressed with Rathenow and Fehrbellin because they were, after all, only small-scale actions, the most critical contemporary was obliged to admit that the campaign as a whole had been masterfully planned and executed.

For years Frederick William's reputation had been rising in Europe and particularly in the narrower German world to which he belonged. But against such successes as he had hitherto won there had always been enough setbacks to leave behind doubt as to the real solidity of both himself and his achievement. This lingering skepticism the lightning-like campaign culminating in Fehrbellin put to complete and final rout. No recent German ruler had performed a comparable feat; no recent German ruler had by his own strength alone ever scattered an army belonging to either of the two arrogant Westphalian victors. Elatedly the name of Frederick William began to pass from mouth to mouth, especially among the common people, until the general enthusiasm found vent in a commensurate title. Shortly after Fehrbellin he was spontaneously hailed by encomiasts in both verse and prose as the Great Elector. The lofty appellation stuck, and as the Great Elector he has passed into history.

Frederick William followed the retreating Swedes as far as Mecklenburg and then, for well over two months, the campaign came to a halt—certainly not because such was his pleasure, but wholly and undebatably because his allies failed to furnish him the stipulated support. It will be recalled that, on joining the anti-French coalition in the summer of 1674, he had been promised precisely fixed subsidy payments by Spain and the Dutch. Then, when six months later the Swedes fell on his rear, he had not deluded himself with thinking that he could meet them in the field without important aid of a military nature. By a journey to The Hague he had persuaded the Dutch to promise to dispatch a fleet into the Baltic; and at the same time by continued ardent solicitations at Vienna he had induced the emperor to agree to swell the Brandenburg army with a substantial Austrian contingent.

Each and all of these prospective helpers had proved remiss, not from ill will, as the impatient elector occasionally charged in his wrath, but owing to the exigencies of the grinding war. By the summer of 1675 exhausted Spain had entirely ceased its payments; the overburdened Dutch, besides paying only intermittently, failed to send their fleet; and the anxiously awaited battalions of Austria did not appear. Left without money to purchase supplies and pay his troops and unable to assemble the strength on land and sea required for a successful offensive, Frederick William could do nothing but camp idly at the gates of Pomerania and relieve his nettled feelings from time to time by hurling passionate remonstrances at his laggard allies.

His enforced unhappy inaction obliges us to throw a glance at the progress of the general war. Although it is not our business to unfold the ups and downs, the chances and mischances of the vast European conflict, we cannot without making ourselves familiar with at least its main vicissitudes grasp the closely related contemporary occurrences in the Baltic area. Now while the 1675 campaign was, in its two main theaters of the lower and the upper Rhine, going unevenly, the balance was patently in favor of the French. This was particularly apparent in the Spanish Netherlands, to which, beginning with the previous year, the French had shifted their attack. Pushing along the northward flowing rivers, they had captured so many fortresses that the areas immediately along the border passed into their control. Paralyzed Spain was doing less and less to stem the French tide, and while the Dutch under William III fought with the determination he had succeeded in rousing in them, they were not able to hinder the capture of ever new ground by the admirably equipped and captained armies of the French king. However, on the upper Rhine the outlook for Louis was far less rosy. There he faced the army of the emperor strengthened by the contingents of the Reich; and there on July 27, 1675, he was dealt a blow more severe than a whole succession of defeats. On that day, at the battle of Sassbach, a chance cannon ball ended the life of the ablest of his generals and the leading soldier of his day, Turenne. In dismay over this irreparable loss the French army broke off the conflict, withdrew to the left bank of the Rhine, and did not for many a month thereafter recover its offensive spirit.

Weighing these events, we can readily understand why the hard-pressed Spaniards and Dutch failed to meet the obligations they had assumed toward Frederick William. However, in the light of the emperor's improved situation along the upper Rhine his failure to keep his engagement is less explicable. His dereliction sprang from a very special feature of his complex situation. We learned in an earlier chapter that it was his unhappy lot, while threatened by France on his western border, to be equally pressed by the Ottoman Empire along his eastern frontier and that in 1664 he had gained a precarious security against the latter enemy by the Peace of Vasvar, in reality no peace at all but merely a twenty-year truce. We also learned that he signed this unfavorable document in order to get a free hand against the native opponents of his rule in Hungary.

These opponents were the self-willed feudal magnates, who to retain what they called their "liberty" had not scrupled to enter into treasonable communications with the sultan. Shortly after Vasvar their long-simmering rebellion against their Hapsburg sovereign boiled over and, in spite of occasional insincere accommodations between themselves and Vienna, threw Hungary into confused turmoil for well over two decades. It will be admitted without debate that the vigorous and persistent Hungarian insurrection must have gravely hampered Leopold's effort throughout the war with his western enemy, the French, and that also it could not fail to delay his meeting his obligation to help Frederick William against the Swedes. At no time did Leopold repudiate the elector's claim upon himself; he merely moved at the dragging tempo which marked all Austrian action in this age. But until the stipulated imperial corps had arrived on the scene, the elector would not feel strong enough to begin the assault on his enemy.

In this exasperating state of uneasy waiting the first relief came to Frederick William, though not until September, from the ally by whom he had been least inclined to set store, from Denmark. The king of Denmark, Christian V, as violently anti-Swedish as Frederick William himself, did not have to be belabored with heated arguments to recognize that the occasion was favorable for undoing the disastrous treaty with the Swedes of 1660. He therefore reached a settlement with the elector, whereby the two sovereigns agreed to split and thus weaken the Swedish forces in Germany. While he, Christian, threw himself on the Swedish fortress of Wismar in Mecklenburg, Frederick William undertook to invade Pomerania.

From the nature of the case the elector's Pomeranian objective would be Stettin. But since an attack on this harbor city, which the Swedes had converted into an impregnable fortress, was out of the question until it had been cut off from the sea, he directed his immediate attack on certain vantage points in the Stettin vicinity. With the aid of an Austrian contingent, which had at last put in an appearance, he succeeded in occupying the town of Wolgast below Stettin and the islands of Usedom and Wollin in the Oder estuary. With these strictly limited gains winter had arrived and, as usual, military action ceased.

The Danes got further along with their part of the program, for they obliged Wismar to open its gates to them. At the same time the dukes of Brunswick, made covetous by the weakness shown by the northern kingdom, threw themselves on the Swedish territories of Bremen and Verden and, after little resistance, successfully occupied them. Throughout their German conquests the Swedes had shown such feebleness and distraction that their enemies jubilantly looked forward to their early complete collapse. Thus ended the campaign of 1675.

THE CAMPAIGN OF 1676: CAPTURE OF THE APPROACHES TO STETTIN

Instead of the expected Swedish collapse, the new year brought an astonishing revival, due mainly to the fact that the young king,

Charles XI, now took over the reins of government. Animated by the traditional Vasa spirit, he was firmly resolved to retain his foothold on the southern shore of the Baltic and, aware that he must not disperse his limited energies, settled as his leading purpose on the retention of Stettin and Pomerania. He cashiered the famous Wrangel, grown old, gouty, and imbecile, and appointed in his stead the energetic Königsmark, who had received his military schooling under such famous masters as Swedish Charles X and French Turenne. In order that Königsmark might enjoy an undivided authority, the king wisely made him both civil governor of Pomerania and commander-in-chief of its armed forces.

It was not long before Frederick William learned that the situation had undergone a radical change. He had thought, and was justified in thinking, that he could devote the coming campaign to the siege of Stettin, but the brilliant Königsmark shattered the plan. With characteristic audacity he took the offensive, partly undid the elector's work of the previous year, and then kept the Brandenburg army, numerically superior to his own by virtue of its Danish and Austrian contingents, so busy mastering the difficult sea and land approaches to Stettin that winter had arrived before the siege could be started. It had consequently to be postponed to the following year. The disappointed elector had to comfort himself with the thought that it could not again be interfered with, as an event at sea had deprived the Swedes of the possibility of coming to the aid of Stettin from that quarter. In the spring of the year the Dutch had at last made good their promise of sending a fleet into the Baltic. Effecting a junction with the Danes, the combined fleet on June 11 had encountered the Swedish fleet off the island of Öland and had practically annihilated it. It was no small satisfaction to Frederick William that three vessels of the young Brandenburg navy had fought alongside the victors.

The long delay in the capture of Stettin proved fatal to the elector's Pomeranian hopes. He went on fighting and, as we shall see, in the end won military laurels beyond, if that was possible, even his own sanguine expectations. But the disastrous developments in the main theater of the war, the theater of the Spanish Netherlands, gradually obscured his prospects and finally nullified his victories.

To this theater it is therefore imperative to turn. The head of the anti-French forces in this area was, as we know, William of Orange, who commanded the army of the Dutch republic, strengthened by such contingents as Spain, the emperor, and the Reich were able to furnish. William, a stubborn but consistently unlucky fighter, had not been able to hinder the enemy from capturing fortress after fortress of the invaded territory. By the end of the 1676 campaign the aid furnished by anemic Spain had become negligible, and the harassed emperor was subjected to so many drains upon his resources that he was obliged to curtail rather than to increase his contribution to William's drooping cause.

In the eyes of the heavily burdened Dutch people, particularly of the unmartial merchant class, the distressing outlook gave birth to a waxing desire for peace. The republic itself was no longer the immediate object of Louis's attack, and when the French monarch now let it be known that he was going to be moderate in his demands on his Dutch enemies, the clamor for a cessation of hostilities became so strong that the government could no longer ignore it. Even William, though strongly opposed to a peace which, concluded at that juncture, would undoubtedly leave France the master of Europe, had to bow to public opinion so far as to agree to the summoning of a congress of the warring states at Nimwegen in order to explore the possibilities of a settlement. When the allies of the war-weary Dutch hesitated to fall in line, they had their resistance broken by a Dutch ultimatum to the effect that unless their representatives appeared at Nimwegen before November 1, 1676, the Dutch would begin separate negotiations with the enemy.

Now Frederick William's political instincts correctly told him that if the Dutch, the leading power among the allies, signed a separate peace, the French would dominate the situation so unquestionably that he, Frederick William, would come off empty-handed. Therefore, while bowing to the Dutch threat and dispatching ambassadors to Nimwegen, he instructed them to bend all their efforts to frustrate the peace drive and keep the war agoing. Pomerania had yet to be won, and unless he came to the peace table with this Swedish pledge in his possession, no amount of moral or any other kind of indignation would hinder the bland ignoring of his demand. Luckily for him the emperor, unwilling to give up to Louis the large slice of the Spanish Netherlands which he was sure to exact, was also against peace; and, more important yet, the frequently defeated William of Orange, although now no longer the worshiped idol of his countrymen, still carried enough weight to balk the appeasement program championed by the ancient foe of his house, the burgher party. The negotiations conducted through the winter came to naught; and, though the congress retained just enough vitality to continue a kind of dummy existence, with the coming of the spring of 1677 hostilities were resumed wherever the opposing forces stood arrayed against each other.

THE CAMPAIGN OF 1677: THE CAPTURE OF STETTIN

Frederick William was delighted at this turn, for it freed his hands for his main objective of the war, the capture of Stettin. He did not underrate the task and assembled for the enterprise an artillery park that came to the, for that age, extraordinary total of one hundred and eighty cannons. Owing to the weakening of the Swedish fleet effected in the previous year, his small Brandenburg navy sufficed to shut off the encircled city from the sea even without Dutch help, which was no longer given. A Brandenburg army posted along the strategic Peene River some thirty miles north of Stettin was prepared to frustrate any attempt at relief from the direction of Stralsund, the Swedish key position directly on the Baltic coast.

Despite these measures isolating the harbor city, its siege obliged Frederick William to strain his resources to the utmost not only because Stettin was a veritable showpiece of advanced contemporary engineering science but also because the garrison, aided by a stubborn citizenry, offered magnificent resistance. Only by gradual stages could the siege lines be pushed close to the walls. Even so, the town had been reduced to the utmost misery, had, indeed, largely gone up in flames from the icendiary cannonade with which it was showered, before the shrunken remnant of the garrison agreed to surrender. The event took place on December 27. The siege had lasted all of six agonizing months.

Heavy as the elector's own losses had been, he floated on that

December day along the summits of existence, for he had achieved the dearest purpose of his reign. Now at last he was free to launch his inland state upon the oceans that were the highways of the world and to bring it into competition with the prosperous seafaring communities to his west. From early youth he had nursed this dream, and with each passing year of his rule it had taken an ever stronger hold on his mind and heart. In the course of this war it had finally become a fixed idea. Nothing short of an utterly obsessed state of mind will account either for the fierce energy with which he conducted the Pomeranian struggle or for his attendant blindness to the presence of forces in the world certain in the end to render his frenzied efforts vain.

In the Netherlands theater the campaign of this year had been the same old story: William of Orange had been defeated, and the French had continued their penetration of the Spanish Netherlands. The prince himself confessed to the elector's agent at his court that he could no longer hold out against the popular demand for peace. Then, a last hope dawned for him and his allies in the war through the acceptance by Charles II of England of William's suit for the hand of Princess Mary, daughter of the duke of York and eventual heir to the throne. William crossed the channel and was married to the princess amidst the general acclaim of the English people. In consequence of the steadily increasing French preponderance the subjects of Charles had become passionately anti-French and their king, unwilling to risk his throne, consented to mollify them by giving his blessing to the union between his niece and the leading adversary of the dominant Bourbon monarch.

However, the hope which the marriage aroused among the members of the anti-French coalition was no more than a shooting star in a summer night, for the union did not mean, as these members were pleased to imagine, that England was preparing to add her strength to their own. It did not even mean that Charles II would henceforth give diplomatic support to the coalition, since, secretly, he continued precisely as pro-French, and for the same ignoble reasons, as he had ever been. The most to be said for the Anglo-Dutch match was that it gave fresh authority to William, on the strength of which he was able to persuade the Dutch government to engage in one more campaign against the ever vic-

Engraving by R. de Hooghe (Bettmann Archive)

SIEGE OF STETTIN WHICH SURRENDERED DECEMBER 27, 1677

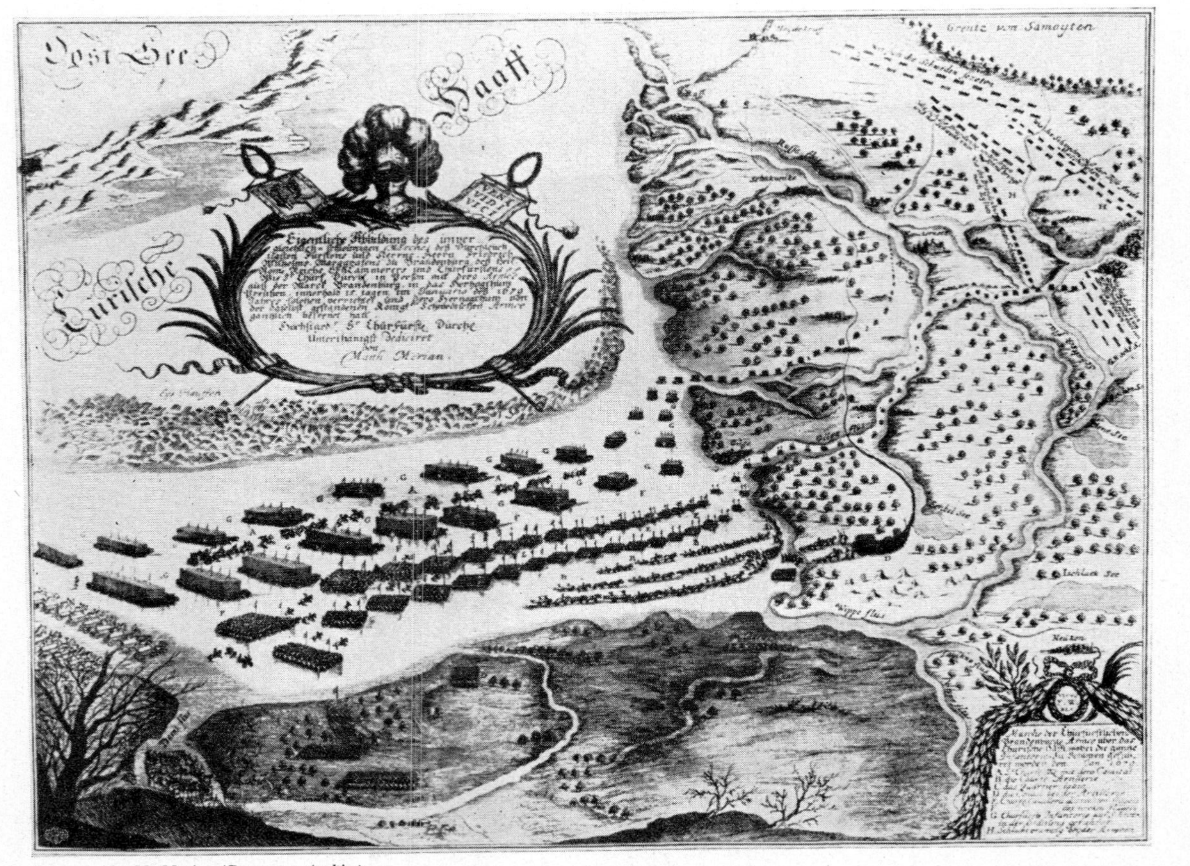

Engraving by M. Merian (Bettmann Archive)

MARCH OF THE ARMY OF THE GREAT ELECTOR ACROSS THE ICE OF THE KURISCHES HAFF IN JANUARY, 1679

torious French. While getting ready for it, he did not fail to make it clear to the emperor, to the various German princes committed to the struggle, and, above all others, to Frederick William, by now far and away the most powerful of the German princes, that only if they contributed the largest possible contingents to the army he would lead against the French could he hope at last to turn the tide and wring from King Louis not a victorious peace—that would be too much to expect in any circumstances—but a peace not wholly unendurable.

Thus the outcome of the winter hesitations and debates was another campaign, and the decision accorded in every respect with Frederick William's hopes and interests. Nevertheless, satisfactory as the prospect was in itself, it plunged him into a grave predicament. William of Orange, his nephew, friend, and ally, was about to make a last and superhuman effort against Louis and urgently demanded his uncle's help—the whole Brandenburg army by preference but, if that was impossible, the largest fraction thereof that could be spared. For the elector, however, the immediate foe was not, as for William, France; it was Sweden; and while he had recently captured that priceless treasure, Stettin, he had not yet by any manner of means finished with the enemy. He had not done so because the indomitable Königsmark held the coast around Stralsund and would be sure to move to the recapture of Stettin the moment the elector relaxed his vigilance. Fresh evidence that the Swedish general was sleeplessly on the lookout was dropped right into the interallied discussions of the winter, when it was learned that in January, 1678, he had made a surprise attack on the island of Rügen, too carelessly held by the Danish allies of Brandenburg, and had captured it.

The representatives of Frederick William's allies at his court and camp did not hesitate to urge him to sign a truce with the Swedes on the basis, in contemporary diplomatic language, of *uti possidetis* (to hold what you have) and, thereupon, relieved of pressure in Germany, to march his army westward right into William's camp. As if the Swedes, the puppets of their French masters, could have been brought to sign an agreement having no other purpose than to permit the allies unitedly to bear down on those same masters! Frederick William had too clear a perception of the realities of the situation to invite rebuff by such a proposal.

Besides, to lay all the elector's cards on the table, the proposal went against what had become by now the deepest conviction of his nature. Even could the Swedes have been won over to the outlined truce and have left Stettin in his possession, he had worked himself into a state of mind that made him unwilling to accept any such merely provisional solution of the Pomeranian problem. Let us, to plumb his sentiments to their bottom, go back for a moment to the winter of 1675 when, while campaigning in the upper Rhine region, he had been informed by courier of the Swedish irruption into the mark. Confronted with this unprovoked assault, he had promptly decided to remove once and for all the sword perpetually hanging over him and had written as follows to his most intimate councilor, Otto von Schwerin: "I can assure you that I am resolved to revenge myself on the Swedes. . . . . Now that they have left me no more than my life, I shall persist, come what may, in ridding myself of their neighborhood. The Almighty in whom I have put my trust since my youth and who has miraculously saved me from innumerable dangers will not desert me now."[2] So little was the sentiment here expressed a passing impulse that he sounded it again and again through the subsequent months and years until it had hardened to a dogma beyond the range of debate. As he saw the situation during the diplomatic fencing of the winter of 1677–78, it would require one more campaign to drive the Swedes from Stralsund, Rügen, and the few other Pomeranian strongholds still in their grasp. That was the task to which he had committed himself three years before; that was the task from which he would not let himself be deflected by any interested argument. He was sorry for Dutch William and did not deny him the Brandenburg contingent which he had regularly committed to the prince's orders during the preceding campaigns. But with his main strength required for the Pomeranian operations he was unable to increase his nephew's support. Willam would have to fend for himself.

2. *UA*, XVIII, 826.

THE CAMPAIGN OF 1678: COMPLETION OF THE POMERANIAN CONQUEST

Admitting that the decision sharply divided him from his allies and lent credibility to the charge that he thought only of himself, let us weigh for a moment what effect his acceptance of the Dutch proposal may be conceived to have had on the outcome. Leaving an army of observation behind in Pomerania, which might or might not have been able to hold off Königsmark's Swedes, he could have dispatched as the largest possible figure some ten to fifteen thousand men to the Netherlands. Now this increase would not have enabled William to stop the French, who had resolved by a final supreme effort to bring the war to a close. They mustered for the new campaign a total of three hundred thousand men, whose main mass they discharged on the Spanish Netherlands against their leading opponent, against William. Armies of such size had not been heard of thus far in the wars of Europe, and William had nothing comparable at his disposal. The addition to his ranks at most of some fifteen thousand Brandenburgers would not have altered the existing hopeless disparity. Matters standing thus, Louis was able practically to inundate the Spanish provinces with his troops, and when now he determined to achieve peace by splitting the allies and again offered the Dutch terms more favorable than in their evil plight they had any reason to expect, they fairly snatched at them. Through his representatives at the continuing congress of Nimwegen, Louis proposed to leave the republic in possession of its undiminished territory and to concede besides—and what a bait that must have been for the burgher appetite!—a highly favorable commercial treaty.

As early as May the separate Franco-Dutch treaty was practically ready. But as the diplomatic decencies required that the Dutch inform their allies of their intended desertion and give them at least the chance of abandoning the war simultaneously with themselves, it was not until August 10 that the two powers came officially to terms. A month later Spain followed the Dutch lead and dropped out of the war. That the once-proud monarchy lay helpless on the ground was evidenced by the fact that it meekly accepted its role of scapegoat of the Franco-Dutch settlement; for the two contracting parties were in full accord that Spain, and

Spain alone, should pay the price for the French victories by handing over to Louis the Franche Comté and sixteen fortified towns along the Netherlands border.

On the day the Dutch signed the separate peace with the French, Frederick William lost Pomerania. This is not just a facile, after-the-event reflection, for even then it was perfectly clear that, deserted by the Dutch and the Spaniards, the emperor and the Reich would also come to terms and that in all these treaties there would recur a stipulation calling for the return of Pomerania to Sweden, the ally of victorious France. Such was the will of Louis, and Louis was supreme in Europe. So indisputably did Frederick William's fate turn about this supremacy that it would be superfluous to insist on it, were it not that many historians, in its despite, have argued that if the elector had but managed to get his hypnotized mind off the Swedes and to take his stand unreservedly at the side of the Dutch, things might have turned out differently. In the present writer's opinion the suggestion is no better than unmitigated delusion. It is his view that in the prevailing circumstances there was no conceivable course Frederick William might have taken that would have ended other than the one he took. Louis XIV had decreed that the elector was not to have Pomerania or any part thereof, and from the moment he had succeeded in splitting the allies he was sure to have his way.

As Frederick William refused to see the situation in the light of the political realities, he went on obstinately with his Pomeranian campaign; and although we know by anticipation that his labors went for naught, they so considerably enhanced his warrior reputation that we cannot pass them by. The campaign of 1678 was slow in getting under way, as, owing to his chronic financial straits, was the case with all his military undertakings. In the course of the winter he had quietly tightened his alliance with his steadiest helper in this war, with Denmark. Consequently, a force of Danes joined him in the action with which he inaugurated the new campaign and which had as its goal the reconquest of Rügen, the island guarding the great land and sea fortress of Stralsund. So skilfully did the versatile Königsmark contest this undertaking that it was not until September that Rügen was cleared of the Swedes and the way opened for the investment of Stralsund. Not until the end of October did Stralsund capitulate. And November had all but slipped by before Greifswald, the last remaining Swedish stronghold, opened its gates to the conqueror. An arduous four-year enterprise had been brought to a close and Pomerania delivered into the hands of him who from the day of his accession to the Brandenburg heritage had considered himself Pomerania's rightful owner.

THE WINTER CAMPAIGN OF 1679: HOW A BRILLIANT VICTORY CAME TO NAUGHT

Whatever happened now, the fighting at least seemed to be over. And yet it was not over. The beaten Swedes had still one more arrow in their quiver, a most defective arrow it is true, but, unwilling to accept defeat, they resolved to discharge it blindly at the enemy. In their province of Livonia, to the north of Prussia, they possessed a last, over-aged and under-equipped army commanded by General Horn. With this the government at Stockholm resolved to strike a blow at its tormentor by invading his Prussian duchy. Its desperation must have been great, for winter had come and campaigns in that age, as we know, were not conducted in snow and ice and, least of all, in the characteristic subzero temperatures of that northern latitude.

It was late in November when General Horn, at the head of sixteen thousand second-rate troops, crossed the Prussian border. With the duchy practically stripped of defenders, he quickly overran its northern and eastern districts. When Frederick William, who had just ended the Pomeranian campaign, was informed of the attack, he did not hesitate for a moment to accept the challenge. Speeding General Görtzke eastward with five thousand men to cover the capital city of Königsberg, he outfitted to the best of his ability an added force of nine thousand men for the cruel physical trials that awaited them and, a month later, followed Görtzke's advance guard. While the army was, as usual, under the command of Field Marshal Derflinger, the elector would not be dissuaded from going along with it, even though sorely plagued at the time by the complicated ailments which had by now become almost inveterate and made every bodily jolt a torture.

What now unrolled itself before the astonished eyes of his contemporaries was the elector's last but also his most arduous, original, and triumphant campaign. When on January 20 of the new year his army on its long eastward tramp had crossed the Vistula, it ceased traveling by land and took the short cut to its Königsberg objective over the solidly frozen lagoon, the Frische Haff. Along this unobstructed highway the cavalry and horse-drawn artillery were able to move at such high speed that to keep the infantry from being outdistanced the elector loaded them and their equipment into sledges, providently assembled for the purpose. The bold and unexpected movement filled General Horn with panicky apprehension. Unwilling and unable to face the approaching army, he ordered a retreat without even attempting a delaying action. He really had no other choice, for, commanding only loosely organized local levies, he did not dare to send them against the seasoned veterans of Brandenburg. But the elector was not minded to let the invaders escape, if he could help it. Once more, to head them off on their northbound course, he pushed his army across the ice, this time of the second great Prussian lagoon, the Kurische Haff. Only by plunging into the frozen wilds of Poland did the fleeing Swedes escape complete destruction. Harried by the unceasing assaults of the pursuers and decimated by cold, hunger, and desertion, they had shrunk to a hunted remnant of three thousand men when, toward the end of February, they at last succeeded in catching their breath behind the protecting walls of Riga. The retreat had been a story of unintermittent battling without anything that could be fairly called a battle. The absence of that climactic feature did not alter the fact that a Swedish invasion had been repulsed and a Swedish army ruined in the process.

When Frederick William returned to Königsberg from the pursuit of the Swedes, he was felled as by a blow from a battle-ax with the news that, on February 5, emperor and Reich had in their turn made peace with Louis XIV at Nimwegen. Although he must subconsciously have expected the event, he had right up to its announcement refused to accept it as credible. The new settlement practically re-enacted the Treaty of Westphalia. That meant, as far as Pomerania was concerned, that emperor and Reich had subscribed to Louis XIV's demand that the conquered province be returned to Sweden. Already the breath of a new spring was in the air, the spring of 1679. It brought with it a new era of peace between France, on the one hand, and the emperor and members of the Reich, on the other—with a single startling exception. Between the king of France and the elector of Brandenburg the state of war continued, and the elector was left to the devastating reflection as to what that might mean to him and his little state.

The opinion has been voiced in some quarters that in his blind rage Frederick William was at first resolved singlehanded to carry on the struggle—Brandenburg against France! Occasional passionate words that escaped his lips might be adduced to support the opinion, but these explosive outbursts were native to his manner and did not mean that he had lost possession of his reason. Deep down in his heart he knew from the first moment that he would have to yield to the all-powerful Louis, although it is true and understandable that he was unwilling to swallow Louis's terms without first resisting their imposition to the limit of his powers. These terms, the return of all his Pomeranian conquests to the Swedes without the subtraction of a meadow or a frog pond had been long known to all the world. Directly or indirectly, they had been incorporated in the several Nimwegen settlements. Pursuing the only course left him in his cruel predicament, Frederick William sent one of his most skilful diplomats, Franz Meinders, to Nimwegen to see whether some concession could not be wrung from Louis and the outcome of a four-year successful war not be made to sum up precisely to zero.

Absolutely unyielding in substance, Louis was patience itself in manner. Inviting Meinders to present his case at Paris instead of Nimwegen, he agreed to put off the threatened crushing invasion of Brandenburg until the middle of May. On the expiration of the truce Meinders had not yet been authorized by his self-tortured master to meet the French demands and, accordingly, a French army under Marshal Créqui crossed the Rhine and headed for Berlin. A small Brandenburg force posted in Westphalia tried as best it could to impede the progress of the French. Not until the invaders had reached the banks of the Weser did Frederick William bring himself to admit that the game was up. Thereupon on June 29, 1679, Meinders signed at Saint-Germain the peace from which there was no escape. At the news Marshal Créqui promptly halted his advance. The month-old war was over.

It should not be overlooked that Louis did, after all, slightly soften the blow of Saint-Germain by making two tiny concessions. He permitted Frederick William to retain a few inconsiderable localities on the right bank of the Oder and, instead of continuing to share the sea tolls collected in his own eastern Pomerania with the Swedes, henceforth to enjoy their undivided possession. Louis could do this without departing from the inalterable norm by which he insisted that he was ruled in his negotiations with all the members of the Reich. This norm was the Treaty of Westphalia. Applied to Brandenburg and Sweden at Saint-Germain, it permitted the two indicated rectifications since they represented Swedish usurpations beyond the strict Westphalian letter. Without departing from his professed Olympian detachment the French Jove could therefore impose a slight fine on his ally and confer an insignificant benefit on his foe. The solemn judgment had the further merit in the eyes of its deliverer that it taught Swedes and Brandenburgers alike that the last word in their affairs pertained to the king of France.

The tragic failure of Frederick William's Pomeranian conquest precipitated a complete turnover of the political system by which he had hitherto been ruled. From the beginning of his reign he had consistently, though from an understandable, healthy caution not always openly, adopted an anti-French orientation; and as soon as, on the occasion of the Dutch War, an apparently effective coalition had been formed to stop the French advance, he had made common cause with it. Then, when Sweden sided with France and fell on Brandenburg during the elector's absence on the Rhine, he had accepted Sweden as his allotment in the common enterprise and in four campaigns of superhuman energy and sacrifice had triumphantly carried out his mission. And the result? One ally after the other had made a separate peace with Louis XIV and treacherously, in his opinion, deserted him. His lashing-out at them in uncontrollable fury may have relieved the tension of his spirit but did not alter the fact of his fatal abandonment. Left to fight it out alone with the French king, he was obliged, in order not to be annihilated, to drop meekly to his knees and present Pomerania to the conqueror as a peace offering.

When the humiliating episode was over, Frederick William was done with his allies. And not just done with them either; he would, if justice reigned on earth and there was a God in heaven, be revenged on them too. He would henceforth take his stand at the side of Louis XIV, who, by the unwavering support which he gave to Sweden, had proved that he was a man who kept his word. At the center of his hot mood smoldered another consideration of a more strictly political order. Since it had proved impossible to win Pomerania against the will of France, the clearly indicated way to obtain it was with the approval of that state. That he had lost Pomerania did not rid him of the Pomeranian dream. Indeed, more than ever following its loss, his reflections revolved around this object of his lifelong striving. If it could somehow be brought about that Louis would permit Brandenburg to be substituted for Sweden in connection with the French plan of German control, Pomerania might yet be his. It was a chance, no more, but had not his life been an uninterrupted succession of chances? The immediate, practical step would be to seek close association with the French king and bring it home to him that his late enemy, now no longer his enemy, proffered himself as the king's friend and ally.

Chapter 14

STRANGE INTERLUDE: THE GREAT ELECTOR IN FRENCH LIVERY

THE TREATY OF ALLIANCE OF OCTOBER 25, 1679

NO SOONER had the Treaty of Saint-Germain of June 29, 1679, ended hostilities between France and Brandenburg than the elector pushed forward to his next goal, nothing less than an alliance with his erstwhile enemy. In point of fact, so headlong was his humor that he would have been pleased to achieve the alliance simultaneously with the peace; and it was only because King Louis distrusted his motives, and justly so in view of his shifty conduct toward France in the late war, that he was obliged to be content with the peace until the suspicious monarch had familiarized himself with the elector's proposal and explored its possible benefits.

Inevitably the party to a negotiation who cannot conceal his eagerness to have the bargain concluded is at so great a disadvantage that the final agreement will be virtually dictated by the opposite party. This truth is strikingly illustrated by the secret alliance that France and Brandenburg signed with, after all, little loss of time on October 25, 1679. Like the preceding peace it was negotiated by Councilor Franz Meinders in behalf of Frederick William, and, also like that peace, it was drawn up at the seat of the French court at Saint-Germain. As might have been expected from the elector's precipitancy, it was in the main an enumeration of the advantages secured by Louis in return for an undertaking to defend Frederick William against his enemies. While it is true that the elector had enemies, indeed a rather formidable roster of them, it is also true that they did not immediately threaten him and that Louis in offering his protection was not assuming a heavy burden. Pressed to do something more substantial, he tossed the too eager suppliant a subsidy of one hundred thousand livres per annum, a sum more like a bountiful tip than a subsidy, since it did not much exceed the gratuity wherewith the magnificent monarch was in the habit of rewarding the services of the bribed minister of a rival ruler.

In contrast to these negligible favors extended to Brandenburg, Frederick William assumed toward Louis obligations so extraordinary that the human reason hesitates to credit them. But there they are staring at us from the printed text and must needs be accepted as fact.[1] At the next imperial election Frederick William promised to cast his vote for Louis or for Louis's heir, the dauphin; should the election of either prove impossible, he agreed to vote for the candidate favored by the French court; when the next election for the Polish crown took place, he pledged his support to the French candidate; and, finally, he agreed to permit French troops at their request to pass through his territories and, should the need arise, to take shelter in his fortresses.

Never since his reign began had Frederick William been willing to garner no matter how attractive-seeming an advantage at the cost of anything suggesting a personal humiliation, and yet here he was pusillanimously submitting, in return for nothing better than Louis's loftily bestowed patronage, to a whole series of them. The only explanation that makes the contradiction plausible has been offered in the previous chapter. He wished, regardless of what it might cost, to convince Louis that Brandenburg could be substituted for Sweden in the French political system; and he hoped further, that, as soon as the king had been brought round to the idea, he would in his grandiose manner concede the transfer of Pomerania to Sweden's adversary.

In simple truth, however, never for even a fleeting moment did Louis, invariably and sharply indisposed to practice his vaunted magnanimity in a power issue, identify himself with the elector's view and never, in spite of serious difficulties with Sweden, of which we shall presently hear, did he withdraw his protection from the Scandinavian kingdom. Consequently, as might as well be divulged at once, five years of playing flunkey to Louis XIV, for that is the span of Frederick William's fatal aberration, failed

1. See Moerner, where, too, all the other treaties mentioned in this chapter may be consulted.

to bring him a foot's length nearer his Pomeranian goal. In registering the negative result of the unhappy interlude we must not fail to bracket with it the positive injury which it brought on the German Reich, for which, though it came but haltingly in his affections after his native Brandenburg, he nevertheless had a genuine devotion.

Perhaps the most startling single feature of the October treaty was the article that disclosed Louis's plan to succeed Emperor Leopold and become the head of the Reich. How long he had been dallying with the idea can no longer be accurately made out; but in no case was it original with him, since Mazarin, who wielded the sovereign power during Louis's minority, had already entertained it in his royal ward's behalf. Let the fact be given due weight that Louis's avowal of intention was not a commitment; it was not even an open, public avowal, since the document containing it was a secret treaty and, in distinction from most treaties carrying that label, was kept so closely under cover by the parties concerned that it was not disclosed to the world until a browsing scholar stumbled on it in the archives some two centuries later. Granting, therefore, that Louis's candidature for the headship of the Reich was probably more a desultory than a fixed feature of his policy, we can, nonetheless, not fail to be impressed with the fact that it accords strikingly with the stage of European domination *le grand roi* had achieved with the Nimwegen settlement.

THE CHAMBERS OF REUNION AND THE OCCUPATION OF ALSACE

The two decades that had passed since Louis's personal rule began had involved him in two wars of aggression. They both had been directed against the Spanish Netherlands, even though the second war is commonly called the Dutch War and in its origin had taken the form of an attack on the Lowland republic. The net result for Louis had been that he had so substantially strengthened his northeastern or Netherlands boundary that he might consider himself secure in this direction and let his attention swing instead to his eastern or German boundary. While this had been much improved during his minority by the foothold acquired at Westphalia in the border province of Alsace, the treaty contained so many ambiguities and involved the distribution of territory and authority between France and the Reich in so many uncertainties that a clarification of the muddled situation had long been a leading demand of French foreign policy. The continuous involvement with the Spanish Netherlands had caused the problem to be adjourned. But when with the Peace of Nimwegen, Louis's hands were freed, he faced sharply eastward toward Alsace, resolved to utilize the partial cessions of 1648 as a springboard for the occupation of the whole province. The crude but forthright procedure would have been at once to overrun Alsace with his irresistible army, ordering it in every town and village to replace the eagle emblem of the empire with the lily banner of the house of Bourbon. To such depths had the authority of the Reich dropped in consequence of its latest defeat and so helplessly divided were its weak and innumerable constituent members that there was little reason to fear that the invasion would have aroused an organized resistance. Still there was always the chance of an explosion, and as Louis had just finished fighting a long and costly war and wished, at least for the present, not to embark on another, he resolved to substitute for open and avowed aggression a sly and indirect attack conducted under the mask of law.

In accordance with this plan he set up juridical commissions, called Chambers of Reunion, at certain border towns like Metz, Besançon, and Breisach and ordered them not only to "interpret" the double-meaning clauses of the Peace of Westphalia but also to search out the "dependencies" of the ceded territories which, although unnamed in the crucial document, might by legal sleight-of-hand be held to have been made over to the French crown together with their principals. Let it be recalled in this connection that Alsace had been for centuries a region of superlative feudal atomization and that every tiny lordship had at one time or another been tied up with a dozen others. The black-robed, bewigged judges of the Chambers of Reunion went at their work with antiquarian gusto directed and magnified by patriotic zeal. Throughout the year 1680 and well into 1681 they pored over musty repositories of worm-eaten parchments, some of which went back all the way to the already fabulous Merovingian and Carolingian days, and then in the ponderous, circumlocutory language of their kind solemnly handed down the decisions dictated to them by the very form of their appointment by their master, Louis. The next and last step was for the French soldiery to execute the court order by occupying in the name of the king the territories designated as legally his and—Alsace had passed in its entirety under French rule!

And yet not quite in its entirety. There remained the great Alsatian city of Strassburg, the condition of which, exceptionally, had not been enveloped in confusing verbiage in the settlement of 1648. Strassburg, for centuries a leading free city of the empire, had been expressly and unambiguously guaranteed its historical status at Westphalia. Turn and twist the matter as they would, the ingenious pundits of the Reunion Chambers were unable to find a legal pretext on the strength of which the ancient city might be declared a French possession. However, with the countryside and small towns of Alsace taken over by Louis, he could not conceivably let its metropolitan center slip through his fingers, and, therefore, force, naked and unashamed, had after all to be resorted to. In the early autumn of 1681 an army of thirty thousand Frenchmen was set in motion against the town which habitually employed a troop of four hundred mercenaries for its defense. Resistance was out of the question; and to escape bombardment and destruction, the city magistrates on September 30 surrendered at discretion.

While with its ancient liberties extinguished Strassburg quickly sank to the level of a French provincial city, in the matter of religion it received rather better terms than might, in view of Louis's bigoted Catholicism, have been expected. Overwhelmingly Protestant since the early days of the Reformation, it was confirmed in the free exercise of its faith and worship. From only a single concession to his Roman fervor was Louis not to be deflected. The cathedral, a noble and outstanding monument of the great Gothic building period, was at his behest handed over to the bishop of Strassburg as his episcopal seat.

Decreed by partisan French courts, the Alsatian "reunions" spread consternation not only through Germany but over Europe as well. By revealing that even in a period of official peace Louis was pursuing the policy of aggrandizement with which he had inaugurated his reign, they blasted the general hope that Nimwegen would prove the gateway to an era of rest and recovery. While the German Reich, the immediate victim of the reunions, was swept with patriotic resentment, it was still too exhausted by the long Dutch War even to think of a new conflict. In any case, resistance would have had to be initiated by the emperor, and at the moment the emperor was even more effectively hindered from taking action than the lesser members of the Reich. Not only did the stubborn Hungarian rebels oblige him to devote his none-too-robust energies to their suppression but they were once again getting help from the Turks. While this support continued for some time to be given secretly, there was always the likelihood that the Ottomans would in the end openly ally themselves with the insurgents and resume their march on Vienna. Outraged, like all other Germans, by the reunion violences, the emperor, like them, had to admit that, for the present at least, they had to be suffered in patience.

In every other region of the European Continent on which the eye might light the same helpless timidity prevailed. In the kind of daze that overcomes the victim of a boa constrictor everyone sat stunned awaiting his doom—with a single exception. This was William of Orange, who, back in 1672, had, like the shepherd David, resolutely stepped forth to challenge the French Goliath brazenly planted on Dutch soil. True, the enthusiasm kindled by the young champion's courage had not lasted, and as soon as Goliath, baffled but not felled, had directed his attack elsewhither, William's war-weary countrymen had clamored for the peace which, in the teeth of their leader's protest, they had then concluded at Nimwegen.

However, at no time had William been more than a passively consenting party to that peace. To scrutinize him closely is to become aware that his was not the inspired leadership that commands an intoxicated and unwavering following. Although a prince of ancient lineage, he was in mind and bearing not so much the born aristocrat as the admirable compendium of the virtues of the solid Dutch society from which he sprang, laborious, incommunicative, enduring, valiant. Persuaded that the recent war was merely the first round in a fated struggle between Louis XIV and the rest of Europe, he refused to relax his watchfulness after Nimwegen in the assurance that the French king would presently commit the fresh aggressions which there would be no way of meeting save by reconstituting on a firmer basis the European league which the French had pounded into division and surrender.

WILLIAM OF ORANGE AIMS TO REVIVE THE DISRUPTED ANTI-FRENCH ALLIANCE

William did not have long to wait to have his sinister view of Louis confirmed, for the hypocritical reunion seizures followed with a minimum of delay on the heels of the Nimwegen settlement. Automatically, the wakeful prince responded by sending impassioned pleas in all directions urging a common stand against the incorrigible aggressor. It was unfortunate that, although still the foremost figure of his nation, he had lost the political control to his opponents of the burgher party and that he could be silenced by the response that, before asking others to expose themselves to Louis's vengeance, he would be doing well to commit his own country to an unambiguous resistance to the offender. In these circumstances he was unable to overcome the fear either of the German princes or of any of the other neighbors of France.

Not until the reunion policy was in its second year did William score his first success. Having by that time persuaded his own timid Dutch government to take a somewhat bolder stand, he was able to draw Charles XI of Sweden into negotiations over what the contracting parties agreed to call a Treaty of Association. It was a harmless enough document that in October, 1681, saw the light, for it did not go beyond declaring the interest of the two signatories in maintaining the status quo. But as a first step toward a revived front against Louis XIV it produced something of a stir, the repercussions of which made themselves heard throughout Europe.

That a king of Sweden should thus openly abandon his tested French ally aroused considerable comment at the time but was not so surprising as would seem at first blush. While it is undeniable that it was exclusively owing to Louis's intervention in his behalf that Charles XI had got back Pomerania, the recipient's gratitude had been killed in the bud by the highhanded way in which he had been excluded from the negotiations with Brandenburg at Saint-Germain. Louis obviously intended to impress on Charles that he was not so much the ally as the client of the French king. Then, when the reunions began, King Charles suffered a second, even greater humiliation. Duke, by virtue of a German ancestor, of the little territory of Pfalz-Zweibrücken, he awakened one day to learn that Zweibrücken had been incorporated in France and that he was now, in respect of this territory, the vassal of the unloved Louis. On being at this emotional juncture approached by William of Orange, he joined with him in that Treaty of Association which less created than foreshadowed a new league against France. However, in spite of its cautious wording, the treaty was a sufficiently definite declaration to encourage the many ill-wishers of the Bourbon monarchy, and before the close of the year 1681 the emperor and the king of Spain took a bolder stand by adding their names to the document.

But in strict point of fact what did the alliance thus taking shape amount to? Apart from its terror-ridden members refusing to commit themselves to a strong line of action, they constituted, with the exception of manifestly declining Sweden, the very powers whom Louis had struck to their knees in the recent war and who could by no stretch of the imagination be conceived to be a match for him in a new encounter. That the Continent had become unbalanced in Louis's favor was so generally recognized that, even before Nimwegen had made his ascendancy plain to all eyes, William of Orange, Frederick William of Brandenburg, and other equally penetrating observers had come to the conclusion that only by England's throwing her weight into the scales of the anti-French bloc could the disturbed balance be again redressed. But of this there was not even a remote probability so long as Charles II sat at the controls of the English ship of state. Still secretly the Catholic who hoped with the aid of Louis XIV to bring his people back to the Roman fold, he was also still the weak voluptuary dependent on the bounty of his friend across the channel for the funds required for the uninterrupted pursuit of his pleasures. William of Orange, who in 1677 had married Charles's niece in the hope of thus winning Charles to his cause, had long ago been obliged to admit his signal miscalculation. But the Dutch leader's disillusionment did not alter the fact that, until by some unforeseeable turn England should have been won over to the allied side, the pre-eminence of Louis would remain unshaken.

UNCOMPROMISING HOSTILITY OF THE ELECTOR TOWARD HIS FORMER ALLIES

Such headway as William of Orange succeeded in making with his anti-French design came to an abrupt halt at Berlin. No amount of stern appeal or subtle flattery directed to his offended uncle diminished that relative's fierce resentment against one and all of his former allies. They had broken faith with him, and for all he cared they might now drink the cup of humiliation to the lees. Not content to turn a cold shoulder to them and their spineless Treaty of Association, he never ceased to badger them with his demand for the subsidies which by his reckoning they still owed him. Spain had been particularly remiss; in fact, owing to its confessed bankruptcy, it had, very early in the recent war, repudiated its treaty obligations. In order to even scores Frederick William in his wrath at last resorted to an extreme measure. He ordered his little navy, product of the late war, to capture a number of Spanish merchant ships and to dispose of the cargoes for whatever they might bring. Outraged Spain vociferously threatened reprisals, but the elector, aware that he was dealing with a decadent power now practically toothless, refused to be turned from his course.

With his estranged Dutch allies his relations took on a hardly less exacerbated form. From the Dutch, too, he demanded subsidy arrears which they obstinately disallowed, and while this difference of opinion over a money issue made for bad blood, it was as nothing compared with the upflare of ill will over the colonial venture on which the elector had embarked immediately after the twin disaster of Nimwegen and Saint-Germain. The episode has been reviewed in an earlier chapter[2] and notice taken of the envious Dutch opposition to the Brandenburg enterprise along the African Gold Coast. It reached a climax in the seizure of a Brandenburg vessel and the stubborn refusal of the captors to accede to Frederick William's demand for its surrender. Let us turn, finally, to the emperor. When this onetime friend and ally followed William of Orange's example and tried his luck in effecting a rapprochement, the elector mockingly responded by intoning the ancient and

2. Chap. ix, p. 241.

annoying chanty about the disputed duchy of Jägerndorf—and the negotiations were halted in their tracks. In short, every call to Frederick William to join the anti-French ranks fell on deaf ears.

THE FRENCH ALLIANCE BECOMES A LOVE FEAST

While well aware that the elector had rallied to the side of Louis XIV, his former allies were far from appreciating the completeness of his commitment. Let us never forget that the alliance of October 25, 1679, was a carefully kept secret. Regarded by both signatories as no more than an invitation to better acquaintance, it led to a period of the greatest intimacy between them. To cultivate the almost gushing friendship that now came to life, Louis early in 1680 dispatched an outstanding member of his diplomatic corps, Count Rébenac, to Berlin. Rébenac, a good example of the contemporary *grand seigneur,* saw his life's purpose in the establishment of French ascendancy in Europe and brought gifts to the service of the cause which did not fall far short of the exceedingly high estimate put on them by himself. His eager initiative is attested by the fact that he so promptly made himself the leading intermediary between the two courts that, after his arrival at Berlin, negotiations between France and Brandenburg were no longer conducted as in the past at Saint-Germain but under Rébenac's guidance on the Spree.

A year after his coming to the elector's capital, on January 11, 1681, Rébenac drew up, with Councilors Jena and Meinders acting for Frederick William, a second treaty of alliance. It was a far more binding instrument than its predecessor since it provided in case of attack on either of the contracting parties for the military assistance of the other. Thus openly reckoning with war, it increased the Brandenburg subsidy from the former paltry one hundred thousand livres to one hundred thousand talers, that is, to a sum three times as great. As to the event prompting this considerable advance in team work we can be in no doubt. The Alsatian reunions were in full swing, and innumerable European voices had been demanding that they be resisted. Minded to harvest his gains without the hazards of a war, Louis resolved to utilize his newly found friend to that end. With Brandenburg bound to him by a military convention no German action on account of the Alsatian usurpations had even a chance of getting started. For Frederick William, on the other hand, the treaty, its subsidy feature apart, undeniably signified another heavy sacrifice to the French alliance, for its clear implication was that the elector accepted the reunion policy. No one will affirm that that could have been an easy concession for him to make. But he had no other choice. Having embarked on his French course in the hope and expectation that somehow, sometime, it would yield him the Pomeranian prize, he had to continue moving in step with France until the day when heaped-up disappointments would at last convince him of his error.

A third treaty, dated January 22, 1682, reflected the progress of events in the intervening year. Louis was still the master of the situation, but William, his unwavering adversary, had launched his Treaty of Association; and although it constituted only a feeble threat, Louis was sufficiently disturbed by it to moderate his procedure. The evidence is contained in the new web spun by Rébenac, for therein the French sovereign pledged himself to Frederick William to discontinue the reunions and to be satisfied with whatever he had appropriated up to August 1, 1681, with the city of Strassburg, occupied two months later, thrown in for good measure. What may we deduce from this royal self-restraint? This: that the elector, never other than uneasy over the peacetime appropriations of Reich territory, had begun to develop so much irritation over their indefinite extension that he had perforce to be placated. Therefore, while signifying in the new agreement his acceptance of the Alsatian thefts already effected, he was by way of compensation given the promise that they would be discontinued.

The concession was a distinct gain over the uncertain situation hitherto prevailing; indeed, it was so considerable a gain that Frederick Willam could afford to make himself the spokesman before the German princes and the Reichstag of a peace to be concluded with Louis on the proffered terms. He could argue—and there was an undeniable cogency in the argument—that it was the part of prudence for the Reich to surrender what it had been unable to defend in return for a guaranty of the preservation of all the rest that had been spared.

But all the elector's pleading with his compatriots in behalf of the peace proposed by Louis dropped on barren ground. The indignation over Louis's violences burned too hotly for Frederick William to garner anything but hatred for his sinking to the level of accomplice to the burglar who had broken into the German house. True, largely under pressure of the elector negotiations looking to the accommodation proposed by Louis were duly opened between representatives of France and the Reich, but they did not get far before they were completely deadlocked. No authoritative German voice, always excepting that of the lord of Brandenburg, was raised in their behalf.

Throughout this latest turn taken by the reunion issue King Charles of Sweden continued to align himself with the enemies of France and not unnaturally became thereby the target of Louis's waxing resentment. Than a Franco-Swedish breach nothing more to the liking of Frederick William could be imagined, and he had no difficulty persuading himself that the hour for which he had been confidently waiting had at last arrived. With his usual energy he began *sub rosa* preparations for war and by way of strengthening his hand effected (June 8, 1682) an alliance with that other implacable foe of Sweden, Denmark. With these preparations made, he approached France, since without the permission of France an attack on Sweden was out of the question; and for once, we must conclude, he caught the usually circumspect Rébenac off his guard. Perhaps, too, owing to the ambassador's strong personal desire to punish the Swedish ruler who had dared to cast off the customary French harness, on April 30, 1683, Rébenac put his signature to still another treaty of alliance, by the terms of which France promised to guarantee Brandenburg and Denmark against attack by any envious neighbor as soon as the two confederates should renew the struggle which none other than this same France had brought to a close some four years earlier by obliging them to return to Sweden every foot of land they had conquered.

When this frankly bellicose treaty was forwarded to Louis for ratification, he promptly and angrily rejected it. Rébenac in his view must have been out of his mind to draw it up, for here in unmistakable terms he was committing his master to a policy diametrically opposed to a leading French interest. True, Louis had filled Rébenac with his own deep resentment over the anti-French turn taken by Swedish policy, but even in his most explosive moment the king was not prepared to go the length of contributing to the ousting of Sweden from Germany. On the contrary, the presence of Sweden on the German Baltic coast was in his, as it had been in Mazarin's, view the necessary counterpart of the presence of France on the Rhine. Nor did the encouragement of Brandenburg to go to war with Sweden exhaust the sour ingredients of Rébenac's disgusting diplomatic concoction. As the probable consequence of the Brandenburg-Danish attack on Sweden the treaty envisaged a general European war, from which the only benefit specifically enumerated for France was to be the ratification of the Alsatian seizures already safely in French hands. Since Louis was set on obtaining this ratification from the Reich without war and solely by continued diplomatic pressure, the projected war ran directly counter to his fixed policy. Accordingly, the misguided ambassador got the appropriate instructions, the treaty became a diplomatic casualty, and Frederick William, already far advanced in his war preparations, had, to his immense disgust, again to abandon them.

This should have opened his eyes to the uselessness of the French alliance for the end he had in view. The most that can be said on this score is that the rebuff he suffered started a process of disillusionment. That it only slowly gathered momentum is proved by his letting two more years pass before he freed himself, and even then not unconditionally, from his voluntarily assumed French bonds. With the obstinacy that was an essential part of his character he continued to hope, though doubtless with diminishing confidence, that the European situation woud yet take the turn that should permit him with French connivance to win the incomparable Pomeranian jewel. Then, at the moment of his deepest disappointment over Louis's refusal to sanction his projected Swedish war, an event occurred that temporarily eclipsed for the Reich, the emperor, Frederick William, and even Louis himself the rancorous issue of the reunions.

THE SIEGE OF VIENNA AND THE RESURGENCE OF AUSTRIA

The event that in 1683 magnetically drew the attention of Europe was a happening of ecumenical scope: the siege of Vienna by the Turks.

We have learned that the chief reason Emperor Leopold did not more wholeheartedly commit himself to William of Orange's program of resistance to Louis XIV's Alsatian encroachments was the dangerous rebellion of the Hungarians made doubly dangerous by secret Ottoman support. In the course of the year 1682 this support revealed itself as the curtain raiser to an assault on Austria itself, which then was duly launched in the following spring. Under the Ottoman grand vizier, Kara Mustafa, an army of some two hundred thousand men, of whom the famous Janissaries constituted the fighting core, made its way up the Danube and without wasting time, as twenty years before, over the capture of the outlying fortresses, struck straight at Vienna.

Owing to his preoccupation with the French problem, Leopold had been anxiously hoping to escape war on his eastern front and had neglected to prepare for the Turk attack until it was all but upon him. He then sent out frantic appeals for help which in a Europe still sharply conscious, in spite of its political and religious divisions, of the common Christian tie, met with a heartening response. The pope emptied his well-filled purse into the emperor's lap; the German princes, whether Catholic or Protestant, with, let us not fail to note, the conspicuous exception of the elector of Brandenburg, volunteered a generous measure of assistance; and John Sobieski, king of Poland, famed throughout Christendom as the "Hammer of the Ottomans," hastened to declare his readiness to throw an army of his redoubtable countrymen into the fray.

However, long before these helpers could join the Austrians the Turks were swarming toward Vienna, and, unable to meet their vast numbers in the open field, the emperor with his main army retired up the Danube toward Bavaria, leaving behind for the capital's defense a garrison of barely ten thousand men. At the Bavarian border Leopold planned to await the promised contingents from Germany and Poland in order, on their arrival, to set the united Christian host in motion for the relief of his beleaguered residence. The success of this strategy depended not only on the timely appearance of the allies at their upper Danubian rendezvous but also, and above all, on the undaunted resistance to the Turk assaults of the Viennese garrison. Despite its courage this numerically feeble body would infallibly have been overwhelmed by the vast horde of the besiegers had it not been devotedly seconded by the citizens, high and low, rich and poor, fused into an indivisible, dynamic whole by the awful fate suspended over them. More than any other single circumstance it was the action of the Viennese population, men, women, and children, which has thrown an aura of heroism around the historic siege. Begun by the Turks around the middle of July, it was marked by attacks which the Janissaries conducted with such reckless bravery that more than once they were stopped within the already partially breached walls.

After two months of ever more desperate fighting even the most sanguine defenders despaired of holding out much longer, when on September 11, in the nick of time, the lookout posted on the high tower of the Cathedral of St. Stephan's caught the glitter cast by the helmets of a troop of cavalry descending from the western hills. It was the vanguard of the Christian host which on the next day under the supreme command of the king of Poland fell upon the surprised besiegers. In the ensuing savage battle, which for many anxious hours swayed indecisively to and fro, the Mohammedan resistance was at last broken and the remnant of the beaten foe driven in headlong flight down the Danube into Hungary.

The Ottoman debacle of 1683 marks a turning point not only for Austria and Germany but also for Europe. The defeat suffered at Vienna was so catastrophic that it disrupted the whole Turk administrative structure. Even the meagerly endowed Emperor Leopold could not fail to see that an unexampled opportunity had been given into his hands to rid himself of the ogre which, planted along his eastern marches, had for generations and centuries darkened the outlook of his dynasty and people. He therefore resolved to pursue the fleeing enemy with all possible dispatch. Then, locked in combat with him in Hungary, he determined not to rest until he had ousted him from every stronghold of that kingdom which he occupied. This required, because of the resilience which the Turks had not yet lost and the recurrent exhaustion of the imperial resources, a war that lasted all of sixteen years. Not until 1699 did the Peace of Carlowitz bring to a close the first indisputably successful land war ever fought by a European state against the Ottomans. By its terms the sultan surrendered to the house of Hapsburg the province of Transylvania together with all of Hungary except a small strip along the Danube. It was a triumph by virtue of which the younger branch of the Hapsburg dynasty emerged from the shadow that had descended on it with the Treaty of Westphalia and stood forth in the luster of an unmistakable rebirth.

THE TWENTY-YEAR TRUCE BETWEEN FRANCE AND THE REICH

Our first reflection touching Louis XIV's response to the investment of Vienna by the Turks is likely to be that he must have welcomed it as an opportunity to wrest concessions from his hard-pressed Hapsburg enemy. Although undoubtedly inclined to utilize the situation in this sense, he was kept from doing so by the powerful bond of Christian fellowship which, as already noted, continued in his time to characterize Western civilization. So distinctly was Europe still a single religious unit that it viewed the attack by an infidel group on a part of itself as an attack on the whole. Consequently, volunteers from Catholic and Protestant countries alike streamed to the Austrian colors with the fervor of their medieval ancestors going on crusade. The numerous Frenchmen among them revealed the lively Christian sentiment of the country ruled by Louis and make clear the reason why that monarch, responsive to public opinion as even an autocrat must be who wants the continued support of his people, found himself constrained not to hamper Emperor Leopold during the crisis of the siege.

Nonetheless, an advantage beckoned that Louis was unwilling to forego, especially as he could present it in the light of a favor to his imperiled Christian fellow-sovereign. For two years he had been unsuccessfully pressing Leopold and the Reich to make peace with him on the basis with which we are familiar, that is, the acceptance of the Alsatian reunions up to August 1, 1681, with the free city of Strassburg thrown in as his reward for moderation. Instead of the definitive peace he had been demanding, he now, under the influence of the Ottoman crisis, offered to be content with a Twenty-Year Truce; but it was not until after Vienna had been relieved and the excitement over its possible fall had died down that the revived proposal was pressingly presented to Kaiser and Reichstag. It then rapidly led to a new crisis by Louis's ominous attendant threat that, unless his generosity as evidenced by his modified terms be accepted promptly, he would feel free to resort to other, more martial means to arrive at a settlement.

In order to bring to bear on the Reich every ounce of available influence, Louis once again had recourse to his Brandenburg satellite and on October 25, 1683,[3] signed with him another and, every reader will be relieved to hear, the last of the treaties that regulated the collaboration of Louis and Frederick William during the black period of their partnership. In return for an increased subsidy and some vaguely indicated advantages the elector agreed to advocate of the Twenty-Year Truce both at the Viennese court and before the Reichstag sitting at Regensburg. While it is not recorded that he had any greater success than before in winning converts among his countrymen to the French plan, developments along the eastern front came to his rescue by playing into his and his ally's hands. Emperor and Reich were now fighting the Turks in Hungary and, committed with all their resources to this struggle, they would have had to be stark mad to embark on another war on the western front with a foeman far more powerful than the sultan. Nonetheless, so greatly had German national sentiment become aroused over the reunion injuries that it was only after long debate and hesitation that the emperor and Reichstag could be persuaded even to consider Louis's proposal.

To accelerate the German submission, Louis now took a final and characteristic step. In March, 1684, he struck, practically out of a clear sky, at the great fortress of Luxemburg in the Spanish Netherlands. It was an act of war, as bold a fresh challenge to distracted Europe as can be imagined. But Spain from feebleness and the Dutch ally of Spain from fear failed to respond to it. William of Orange, as might be expected, pleaded for action with all the zeal at his command, but the comfortable burghers of the coast cities set greater store by their discretion than by his valor. Unavoidably, however, the unprovoked attack on Luxemburg

3. The real date of the treaty is January 18, 1684. It was dated back to October by mutual agreement.

deepened the apprehension that the outbreak of war by a sort of spontaneous combustion was not improbable. Luckily, the event was adjourned, and when on June 4, 1684, Luxemburg fell before the engineering skill of the famous Vauban, Louis's opponents recognized that, for the time being at least, they were beaten and impotent. Separately, as at Nimwegen, they scurried to accept the proffered Twenty-Year Truce with, of course, conquered Luxemburg added to the mass of earlier French demands in punishment for the prolonged refusal of submission.

In accordance with a by now well established custom the Dutch were the first to cry quits. On June 29 they not only accepted the Twenty-Year Truce for themselves but agreed to oblige their good friend, Charles II of Spain, also to accept it and yield up conquered Luxemburg into the bargain. On August 15 the prematurely withered last offshoot of the family tree of the Spanish Hapsburgs obeyed the orders from The Hague; and on the same day at Regensburg, Kaiser and Reichstag in their turn swallowed the bitter medicine. Nowhere was there any rejoicing over the averted war with France. To every responsible contemporary it was clear that Europe had escaped the threatened general conflict by an act of abject submission and that the settlement dictated by Louis XIV had left that monarch the unchallenged master of the field. It was therefore as sure as any event hidden behind the veil of the future can ever be that the king would continue his encroachments either by the sly, legalistic reunion method or by the direct action employed at Luxemburg and that in this manner he would hold the Continent in effective thralldom until such a time as its disunited governments should join in a resolute action for their common liberation. In the summer of 1684, the summer of Europe's deepest humiliation, even a confirmed optimist might have doubted that such a movement could ever be brought to pass.

FREDERICK WILLIAM THROWS OFF THE FRENCH LIVERY

The substantial agreement among recent German historians that Frederick William's heart was never in the French alliance is not above suspicion, since it may be conceived to have been inspired by their wish to save his German reputation and thus salvage him for the pantheon of German nationalism. However, when both the French scholars who have made the Great Elector the object of their admirable researches, Waddington and Pagès,[4] voice the same opinion, our distrust of the claim of their German colleagues begins to give ground. The fact is that no attentive reader of the diplomatic correspondence of the Berlin court can escape the impression that Frederick William never ceased being uneasy, restless, and even secretly conscience-stricken over the French connection. Let us agree at once that into his unhappy state of mind the issue of nationalism in the modern sense did not enter. A nationalism of this kind had not yet come to birth anywhere in Europe and least of all in Germany. The contemporary sentiment most closely related to it was patriotism, and German patriotism in the Great Elector's time was capable of considerable transitory fervor but quite incapable of resolute persistence. The fact has been repeatedly brought out in the course of this history, as has also its cause, which was that the natural focus of patriotism, the Reich, had become too pitiful a ruin to enlist a sustained enthusiasm.

Now Frederick William had from the day of his accession to the signing of the calamitous Treaty of Saint-Germain, that is, for a period of thirty-nine years, been a Reich patriot, which means that he had been minded throughout that stretch of time to support the Reich and even to have this support put him to some cost, provided always that he was not expected to sacrifice a solid Brandenburg interest for the formless, jelly-like institution the Reich had become. In no case had he ever been disposed to stand idly by while the Reich was being plundered. All of which was the exact reverse of the attitude imposed on him by his alliance with Louis XIV. Nay, more: The alliance obliged him formally and unequivocally to accept the Alsatian reunions which in his as in every German's eyes were nothing short of outright thefts of Reich territory.

The elector's course after 1679 was therefore in the sharpest conceivable contrast with his earlier course and can be accounted for on no other ground than that already adduced: his purpose, first, to possess himself of Pomerania with, instead of against, French consent; and, second, to be revenged on the allies who

4. A. Waddington, *Le Grand Electeur Frédéric Guillaume* (2 vols.; Paris, 1905–8); and G. Pagès, *Le Grand Electeur et Louis XIV, 1660–1688* (Paris, 1905).

had obliged him to renounce his Pomeranian conquest. His indulgence in the latter sentiment was so incompatible with what is and has ever been accounted good statesmanship that we are forced to admit that, in measure as he yielded to it, he declines sharply in our political esteem. And his failure to acquire Pomerania through subservience to France presents his statesmanship in an equally unfavorable light; for nothing can be more certain than that an even approximately correct estimate on his part of Louis XIV's true relation to emperor and Reich would have saved him from the error of believing that the king would ever consent to the ejection of the Swedes from Germany.

As the elector himself at last came round to the opinion that he had been following a will-o'-the-wisp, we need not hesitate to qualify his delusion in uncompromising terms. However, even when the light did break, it was only after he had clung for some five years to the unprofitable association. In so far as it is possible to indicate the particular occasion which convinced him that he must revise his political system, we may with considerable confidence name the enforced acceptance by the Reich of the Twenty-Year Truce. In connection with that nationally humiliating event the reflection was unavoidable that he had served as the tool of the French court and that he had not received any remotely comparable value in return. In his bitterness he blurted out to Rébenac one day in his impulsive manner that he was well aware that it was none other than the king himself who stood between him and Pomerania.

There was another, hardly less pressing reason for his waxing uneasiness over the French connection. If there was a lodestar by which he had never ceased to steer his course, it was the Reformed faith, and at the very time he entered upon his compact with the king of France, his ally had inaugurated the last and culminating phase of his persecution of Frederick William's spiritual kin, the Huguenots. Beginning in 1681, one royal decree after another deprived these Protestant worshipers of some right secured to them by the Edict of Nantes of 1598 and in steadily increasing measure handed over themselves, their children, their schools, and their churches to the mercy of the king's officials. As many as had the means to escape began to make their way to foreign lands, a considerable stream directing its course toward Protestant Germany and particularly toward Brandenburg. Not only did the elector welcome such refugees with open arms, but he had the temerity to lodge repeated remonstrances with his good friend, Rébenac, and to insist that they be transmitted to his sovereign without any blunting of their edge. Of course, to no avail. Egged on by the fanatic Catholic hierarchy of France, Louis had formed the inalterable resolution to extirpate the Protestant heresy from his kingdom by the peacemeal destruction of the heaped safeguards conceded by the fourth Henry, the famous first sovereign of the Bourbon line.

As alarmed by Louis's religious intolerance as chagrined for having so long been his political dupe, Frederick William resolved to renew friendly relations with that power, the Dutch republic, for which he had always had a special predilection, to no small extent for the particular reason that it shared with him his own Reformed faith. For the last five years his nephew, William of Orange, for whom through all the estranging events that had occurred he had maintained an unwavering personal regard, never ceased, albeit unsuccessfully, to ply him with requests to return to his old allegiance. Then, in the winter of 1684–85 to William's agreeable surprise his apparently implacable uncle turned to him of his own accord, indeed, not only to him personally but also to that curious Dutch government which could neither ever quite persuade itself to do without the stadholder nor bring itself fully to accept his guidance. Before long, negotiations between Berlin and The Hague were in full swing. They looked in the private thought of both the prince of Orange and his Brandenburg relative to an alliance against French preponderance, but before that goal could be reached the considerable grievances Frederick William had accumulated against the republic needed to be cleared away.

On February 6, 1685, occurred an event which greatly speeded up the cautiously inaugurated exchanges. On that day died Charles II of England, and although he had been no more than a nominal Protestant at best, he was regarded by the Continental Protestants as belonging, though with disappointing reservations, to their party. On his being succeeded by his brother, James II, an open and avowed Catholic, Protestants the world over became alarmed and no one more so than the ruler of Brandenburg. To him the event added incalculable strength to that mounting tide of Catholic intolerance, of which the persecution by the emperor of the Hungarian Protestants and Louis's violent repression of the Huguenots furnished frightening evidence. Protestantism everywhere was in danger and the drawing-together of its threatened ranks the only assurance of survival. And who in the nature of things would have to head the movement of resistance but he and William of Orange, the two outstanding Protestant princes, now that the new sovereign of England had gone over bag and baggage to the enemy?

Interesting evidence of Frederick William's concern over the possible defection of the English people themselves from the Protestant ranks is supplied by his suggesting to his nephew at this early date the saving of the situation by that invasion of the island kingdom for which William himself did not think the time had arrived until three years later. His religious fervor notwithstanding, the elector had no thought of letting himself be hurried into a new engagement with the Dutch without due regard to necessary safeguards. He had become a very sharp bargainer, perhaps to no small extent owing to his lifelong dealings with these same Amsterdam merchants. Had they not from the day of his accession to the throne plagued him with the unconscionable Hofyser debt?[5] It had appeared on the agenda of every negotiation between him and them since that time, obstinately defying settlement until the last year of the recent war. On March 8, 1678, only a few months before the Dutch signed their separate peace with Louis XIV, they renewed their defensive alliance with him and, in return for certain financial and territorial concessions on his part, agreed at last to regard the ancient claim as canceled. While, therefore, the Hofyser ghost graciously omitted reappearing when the electoral and Dutch plenipotentiaries sat down together to renew amenities, so numerous were the other matters that called for an accommodation that many months were consumed in tangled discussion.

Not until August 23, 1685, was the new treaty of friendship perfected. By its terms the Dutch conceded to Frederick William a

5. See chap. v, pp. 121–22.

liberal settlement of his claim of unpaid subsidies. In addition, he was indemnified for the ship which had been seized by the Dutch West India Company on the African Gold Coast and given a promise—never carried out—of an early adjudication of the irritating territorial dispute between him and this same trading concern. However, the treaty's center of gravity did not lie in these adjustments, important as they were. It lay in an article which, after renewing the earlier defensive alliance, affirmed the interest of both signatories in maintaining the peace of Europe against potential disturbers. Cautiously but unmistakably it was pointed at France.

As the significance of the treaty escaped neither the alert Rébenac nor Rébenac's highly sensitive master, their relation with the court of Berlin now suffered an autumnal chill. When, a few months later, on October 18, 1685, Louis set the crown on his persecution of the Huguenots by formal revocation of the Edict of Nantes, the chill hardened to a frost. As in simple fact the Edict had already been revoked by a series of over one hundred preceding decrees depriving the adherents of *la religion prétendue reformée* of one right after another, the act of October 18 came to no more than a contemptuous consigning to the rubbish heap of the remaining husks of a once-solid mass of Protestant guaranties and privileges. Nonetheless, it made final and complete the outlawry of something less than two million Frenchmen who constituted a vital segment of the economic and cultural life of their country. The event sent a shock of horror through the Protestant and even a considerable part of the Catholic world. The indignation of Frederick William knew no bounds, and in a public proclamation issued at Potsdam on November 8 he openly identified himself with his coreligionists by inviting them to take refuge in his territories.

The bold Potsdam counterblast almost but not quite brought down the already undermined edifice of Franco-Brandenburg friendship. While turning his most disdainful frown on his refractory client, Louis cannily refrained from terminating the alliance, pending the substitution for it of an equally effective means of exercising French influence in the Reich. Frederick William for his part was every whit as eager to keep up an appearance of good relations with the dominant power of Europe until the time came when the anti-French coalition, as yet no more than in process of formation, had achieved a dependable strength. But in spite of cunning weasel words neither side any longer deceived the other: Still officially yoked together, Louis and Frederick William had come to the parting of the ways.

Arrived at this point, the elector turned to Sweden. No action could have served better to indicate the primacy which by this time religion had acquired in his outlook than this holding out his hand to his lifelong enemy. Charles XI had proved himself to be a sincere Protestant, and in the face of the dangers threatening the Protestant cause Frederick William renounced the strengthening of the Catholic opposition which was the unavoidable consequence of the maintenance of his feud with a fellow-believer. Having made up his mind that in the altered situation he would have to surrender the territorial aspiration of a lifetime, he did so, despite the gnawing compunctions that long held him back. On February 20, 1686, he and Charles XI signed a defensive treaty directed, like the recent Dutch treaty, secretly, if not frankly and publicly, against France.

All that now remained to bring Frederick William's political conversion full circle round was his reconciliation with Austria. It was duly effected a few weeks after his alignment with Sweden. So great is its importance and so numerous are the complications in which it involved him that it may be said to have constituted the political substance of the two remaining years of his life. Before launching on these concluding labors of his reign we shall briefly turn aside in order to become better acquainted with him in his private capacity as head of a family and court and as promoter of the lagging culture of the still backward people under his rule.

Chapter 15

FAMILY, COURT, AND CULTURAL ACTIVITY OF THE GREAT ELECTOR

IN THE story of a statesman that aspires not to lose sight of him as a human being it is imperative at some point to interrupt the account of his official doings in order to have a look at him in his private capacity and to realize that he did not pass his days exclusively among tedious administrative reports, the bickerings of rival councilors, an uninterrupted stream of diplomatic correspondence, and the agitating issues of peace and war. To present him as an actor perpetually pacing the stage, mounted on the high cothurnus and speaking through the hollow-sounding mask of a character in the old Greek drama, is to run the risk of transforming him into a cloudy legendary figure bereft of all marks of human identity. Only by viewing him also as a man steeped in the interests and activities shared by all our kind will he lose the abstract quality conferred on him by a too exclusive concentration on his public role and be invested with the flesh and blood that draw him within range of our immediate sympathy.

FREDERICK WILLIAM'S FIRST MARRIAGE

Although intent by preconceived plan on Frederick William's public career, we have not avoided mention of his personal affairs whenever they happened to impinge on business of state. We have thus given attention to his marriage in the year 1646 to Louise Henriette of the house of Orange, since it developed from a specific political situation.[1] In reporting the event we seized the occasion to sketch the solid character of the young Dutch princess and to note the close and enduring union she achieved with her husband. While she realized to a striking degree the seventeenth-century ideal of the self-obliterating wife, she must not be understood to

1. See chap. v, pp. 119–20.

have renounced that subtle intervention in personal issues which her sex has always regarded as its peculiar province. Court gossip did not hesitate to attribute the favor and disfavor of ministers to her secret influence, and although court gossip gave her more than her due, there can be no doubt that her judgments, even in matters of state, carried much weight with the elector. At times, indeed, they were pressed with such unrelenting, quiet persistence that they provoked him to an angry explosion. He would then, it is reported, dash his electoral bonnet at her feet, inviting her, as it were, to pick it up and wear it in his stead.

Admitting that Burgsdorf fell from the eminence he enjoyed during the first decade of the elector's rule because of delinquencies in his conduct of office, an at least subsidiary reason for his disgrace was the disgust with his deep oaths and coarse camp manners which the pious, delicately reared electress was never at pains to conceal. On the other hand, she felt herself strongly drawn to the high-minded Otto von Schwerin, and while his unbroken, lifelong employment by his master may be attributed in the first place to his character and talents, it is not a negligible circumstance that Louise Henriette was always prompt to smooth out any differences that might arise between her husband and his leading minister.

In short, she served as a link between the two men, a view that is fully borne out by her correspondence with the Pomeranian nobleman.[2] It has the further interest of testifying to the deep and lasting friendship which the two correspondents felt for each other. From our repeated reference to the electress's manor of Oranienburg, which, by the way, was only one of several estates her husband made over to her, we were permitted to deduce that she had a head for affairs and achieved an intelligent command of the problems of agriculture. The letters interestingly support this view, for they apprise us that, while she herself developed the plans for her various properties, she intrusted their execution to her serviceable friend. As the elector likewise consulted him in regard to the many questions connected with his own vast assembly of estates constituting his domain, we get the agreeable picture of

2. "Die Briefe der Kurfürstin Louise Henriette an den Oberpräsidenten Otto von Schwerin," *FBPG*, VIII, 176–206.

the leading public official living in such close familiarity with the sovereign couple that they were moved to apply to him for advice in their private concerns as well.

When the electoral prince, Carl Emil, having passed his sixth birthday, had, according to custom, to be provided with a *Hofmeister* charged with superintending his education, another and still more powerful strand was woven to strengthen the established union; for husband and wife at once agreed that no one would do for the new post but the steady and deeply religious Schwerin, and so in the year 1662 the preceptorial burden was piled on top of those he already carried. Since, shortly after, the Hofmeister's authority was extended also over the second son, Frederick, we are not surprised to observe that a new note of anxiety and tenderness crept into the communications which the mother of the princes addressed to their governor. He for his part discussed with her the tutors to be appointed for the diverse fields of study, reported the progress made by his charges, and, a conscientious Christian although a courtier, honorably recorded the occasional derelictions of which especially the older and livelier prince was guilty.

A curiosity of the letters deserves mention, especially as it reflects on the lax schooling afforded in that day to women even of the highest level. The letters are in French, the native speech of the electress, since it was the language of the home in the Orange family. Her words are poured out in a steady stream as they might have fallen from the princess' lips, with small respect for syntax, with none at all for spelling, and with a positively sovereign disdain for punctuation. Here was a soul so superior to rules of language that it suggests kinship with that medieval emperor who, on having his attention called to a faulty gender in his Latin address, waved it aside with the lordly pronouncement: "Caesar sum et super grammaticam." If we add, to complete the record, that the lady never by any chance attached a date to her communications, we may hardly in fairness ascribe this particular failing to her defective training since it continues to be a practice common to her sex down to our own day. However, the point of this enumeration of her epistolary lapses is not to visit contempt on a princess whom her contemporaries held to be unusually alert but to bring out that such formal education as she may have received neglected what we would reckon as the primary elements of schooling and that her case was so little singular that it may be regarded as that of all contemporary womankind.

If the impression has been created that Frederick William was content to leave the education of his sons to his wife and leading minister, a correction is imperative in the light of the abundant evidence to the contrary supplied by his own correspondence with Schwerin.[3] An even more striking witness is the *Instruktion* he drew up for Schwerin's guidance on first confiding his heir to the hands of his friend. So far as this writer is aware, no professional educator of the age, with the single exception of that pedagogic genius, John Amos Comenius, to whom no one listened in his day and with whose revolutionary views our own age is only just beginning to catch up, has laid down a more original and enlightened program. Some of its features have a distinctly modern ring, unless it be more correct and less presumptuous to accept them as the elements common to the pedagogy of the truly wise teachers through the ages. Among its proposals are the demand that the two foreign languages incorporated in the curriculum, French and Latin, are to be learned exactly as the mother-tongue, that is, by ear and use; that geography and history, which figure prominently among the prescribed studies, are to be taught with the visual aid of globes and maps; and that the instructor observe due moderation in order not to create a spontaneous aversion in his pupil for his books and studies ("Solche Moderation zu gebrauchen dass derselbe keinen Ekel vor den Büchern und Studien bekomme").

Naturally, the bulk of the document was concerned with the acquisition of those qualities of mind and body essential to a seventeenth-century German Protestant prince. Here, too, a certain freshness of statement raises the Instruktion far above the conventional level. When we recall Frederick William's intense devotion to his faith, we shall not be surprised that religion stood at the very head of the curricular requirements and that he demanded that it should be earnestly and continuously inculcated. On the

3. *UA*, VIII, 737–43; IX, 823–64; XII, 917–52; XVIII, 779–841. See also the article by F. Hirsch, "Die Erziehung der älteren Söhne des Grossen Kurfürsten," *FBPG*, VII, 141–71.

occasion of the morning and evening prayers passages were to be read from the Bible, more particularly from the Psalms, and hymns were to be sung and memorized. The Reformed catechism was to be learned by heart and carefully expounded twice a week. And since we are in the full absolute age, how could it be that this important environmental datum should not find expression in the elector's handbook? There was, therefore, strong emphasis on carriage, gestures, and speech. Not only must the scholar learn to bear himself in a truly princely manner (*echt fürstlich*), but he must also become a master of eloquence, "since eloquence is a great ornament for a prince and at the same time very useful." The stressing of the utility of an otherwise decorative trait is peculiarly characteristic of this hardheaded ruler turned pedagogue.

Since in Frederick William's own upbringing health and exercise had held a place which he never ceased to approve, he also made them prescriptive for his sons. Riding and fencing, as obligatory skills of the European privileged classes, were to be systematically taught under specialists, and shooting was to follow as soon as the princes were old enough to attend their father on the chase. It was not long before hunting became such a passion with the older and more vigorous prince that his governor lamented to the elector that this enthusiasm had been awakened at too early an age and diverted attention from his sedentary studies. It is plain that the scholarly Hofmeister wanted his charge to become not just a soldier and Nimrod but a cultivated Christian ruler.

A puzzling feature is the emphasis on dancing. Dancing, it is true, was as much the mark of the cavalier of the period as the expert use of sword and pistol, but its daily practice, as required by Frederick William, is unusual. It may well be that he thought of it chiefly, and wisely enough, as physical exercise.

Louise Henriette presented her husband with six children, three of whom died in infancy. Of the three survivors, all of them boys, we have just heard of the two older ones, Carl Emil, born in 1655, and Frederick, born two years later, in 1657. Carl Emil, designated as his father's successor under the title *Kurprinz,* was a wide-awake, exceedingly active lad, often in trouble with his parents and, afterward, with his Hofmeister because of his quick temper and headstrong resistance to discipline. When he reached the age of nineteen, his father invited him to win his spurs in the war against Louis XIV. The occasion was the unfortunate Alsatian campaign of 1674. After little more than a month in the field the young prince contracted dysentery. Carried to nearby Strassburg, he died in that city on December 7, owing at least as much to the excessive cupping administered by the ignorant physicians as to the malevolence of his disease.

That he was succeeded as electoral prince by Frederick was in many respects a misfortune for both Brandenburg and Frederick himself. A fall due to a careless nurse when he was a babe in arms had injured his spine and left him permanently, though not repulsively, disfigured. His twisted body made him ashamed and shy, and although he was by no means unendowed mentally, his vigorous, military father could not always conceal the regret he felt over this misshapen, unmilitary successor. The cloud over the relation with his father increased the sensitiveness and timidity that had become Frederick's second nature, and since environment and education alike inculcated the impropriety of these attitudes, he attempted to conceal them under a false affectation of grandeur. It would not have evidenced much foresight to have prognosticated a future clash between father and son which then did not fail to appear.

The third son, Ludwig, was born in 1666, almost ten years after Frederick. He died at the early age of twenty-one before he had had a chance to prove his caliber. The somewhat mysterious circumstances of his death precipitated a serious family crisis which will receive attention in due time. Louise Henriette survived the birth of Ludwig for less than a year. She had always been in delicate health, which was not improved by her many childbirths. With Ludwig she exhausted her last reserves of strength and on June 18, 1667, hardly forty years old, slipped quietly from this life. Like so many other Scripture-saturated women of her time, she felt that she was called to play her part in life as wife, mother, and guardian of the hearth. If she wandered at times beyond this narrow range, it was only because she sensed that some force from beyond the precincts of the home was gathering strength which she went out to meet before it could discharge itself against the family group over which she had been set as protectress by her Calvinist God.

FREDERICK WILLIAM'S SECOND MARRIAGE

A year after the death of Louise Henriette, on July 4, 1668, the elector contracted a second marriage, with the thirty-one-year-old widow of a Brunswick duke. Dorothea by name and a member of the Lutheran church, she accommodatingly passed over to her husband's Reformed faith shortly after her marriage. Perhaps this ready submission to her dominating partner supplies the leading clue to her character, although it is well to remember that the acceptance of the husband's religion by the prospective bride was the almost prescribed procedure of that age. True, the elector's close neighbor, Sophie, duchess (afterward electress) of Hanover and mother of George I, who in 1714 mounted the English throne, saw Frederick William's successful second-marriage venture in a light less flattering to his reputation. She was a witty, temperamental lady, who, touched prematurely with the rationality of the coming Age of Enlightenment, saw much that amused her in an old-fashioned figure of proved solidity like that of Frederick William. She liked to aim her shafts at him, mocked at his piety as affectation, and caught in his swelling account of his campaigns the accents of a mere *miles gloriosus*. While she could not deny the deep attachment to him of his two wives, she was pleased to ascribe it less to their willing self-surrender than to his uxorious tyranny.

Be that as it may, the new electress lived for her husband's service, and whether it was a question of attending him on the hunt or sharing a hazardous campaign or nursing him in the many illnesses that afflicted him in his declining years, she was ever at his beck and call. Far inferior to her predecessor in intelligence and distinction, she had the good fortune to surpass her to the same degree in bodily vigor. There can be no doubt that the affection which the elector never ceased to manifest for his robust mate—proclaimed by her contemporaries, owing to her feats in field and forest, as a veritable amazon—was greatly strengthened by her presenting him in the course of time with seven children, four boys and three girls. Having throughout his early years been the sole representative of the older Hohenzollern line, he had come to attach an understandable importance to a goodly flock of descendants.

But this particular source of Dorothea's credit with her lord was destined to precipitate a serious domestic crisis, since, developing into as blindly devoted a mother as she was a wife, she became concerned about the future provision for her brood and inevitably permitted an ugly jealousy of the children of her predecessor to take root in her bosom. Gossips and backbiters, of whom there are always more than enough at every court, before long charged her with an active enmity against them and toward the close of the elector's life succeeded in producing so grave a disturbance in the family circle as actually to threaten it with disruption. While recent investigations have completely cleared the electress of the monstrous designs against her stepsons, stories of which were spitefully circulated against her by her ill-wishers and widely given credence in her day, it cannot be denied that her exaggerated maternal zeal was a leading factor in the unhappy domestic upheaval. The episode will be examined in detail in the following chapter when we resume our narrative of events.

To complete the family census, let us recall that Frederick William on mounting the throne had two sisters. They were Louise Charlotte and Hedwig Sophie, who in the first decade of his reign were married, respectively, to the inconspicuous duke of Curland and the considerably more important landgrave of Hessen-Cassel. As they hardly thereafter entered his life, we may dismiss them with a mere mention.

That may not be done with Johann Georg, prince of Anhalt, who, married to a sister of Electress Louise Henriette, was Frederick William's brother-in-law. A good-looking, honorable man of average endowment, Anhalt wielded much influence at court as long as Louise Henriette lived. It declined sharply on the elector's second marriage, since Anhalt, Orange-tinctured by reason of his own marriage, saw fit to take umbrage at the second electress, who had no part in the Orange tradition. Although sovereign lord of the small German territory of Anhalt-Dessau, he had entered the service of his brother-in-law and had risen to high rank in the army. That he was also named Statthalter of Brandenburg was less important, since this appointment had a purely honorary character, save during the elector's absence from the mark. During the critical period of the French alliance Anhalt headed the Austrian party at court, not to the entire displeasure of Frederick William, who utilized him to maintain a tenuous connection with their common suzerain, the emperor.

THE COURT, THE CASTLE, AND THE CAPITAL

The life at court, whether during the reign of the first or the second electress, was, except for rare festival occasions, extremely simple. It fell in with the grandiose notions of the age to make a display before a visiting stranger, especially if he was of high degree. An expensive show was then put on with prancing, plumed horses, ornate coaches splashed with gilt, innumerable liveried servants, and a table laden with every conceivable beast and fowl and sauce and culinary wonder set out in lustrous silver dishes. In sharp contrast with this explosive splendor there ordinarily prevailed an almost Spartan regime, in part because ettiquette and splurge were not a congenial element to Frederick William, in even greater part owing to his incurable lack of funds. His poverty touched its lowest ebb in the earliest period of his reign but even after the peace of 1648 continued for another decade to press so cruelly upon him that he had again and again to adjourn even the most urgent repairs of the dilapidated *Schloss* at Berlin.

The Schloss or castle lay to the west of the municipality of Berlin, in the originally separate municipality of Cöln, an island area completely encircled by the meandering Spree. It was a vast and haphazard complex of buildings and courts housing not only the reigning family but also the main governmental offices. Than this combination of functions no better demonstration could be imagined of the fact that the state of Brandenburg had its beginning in the exercise by the feudal ruler of his patrimonial rights and that the original condition of its officials was that of personal servants incorporated in the margravial household. Not until about the time of the great turning-point in his career marked by the Treaty of Oliva (1660) did Frederick William find himself in sufficient funds to begin the long overdue, thoroughgoing renovation of the castle. This will explain why even the fitful displays of an expensive elegance, in which the elector felt he owed it to his station to indulge from time to time, belong chiefly to the latter half of his reign. During this more prosperous period the Schloss was at last repaired and even considerably enlarged and beautified in its continuing capacity of both residence and office building. Before, but not long before, the elector's death it had become a habitation comparing favorably with the similarly compounded structures of the German princes of his rank.[4]

Once embarked on residential improvements, the elector gave his attention to the swampy area in the bend of the Spree to the north of the castle and converted it into a pleasure ground. Starting modestly with paths among flower beds (for delight) and vegetable beds (for use) the *Lustgarten,* as it was called, expanded by degrees into a handsome and instructive botanical preserve, with a fountain in the center and statues of marble or metal half hidden among the ordered shrubbery. The venture was largely the creation of Louise Henriette and, as might be expected, was laid out according to the mathematically precise Dutch taste of the period.

Berlin itself long presented the same decrepit and expiring aspect as the castle. Throughout the decade following the Peace of Westphalia it remained the shrunken town of from six to seven thousand starving inhabitants to which it had been reduced by the havoc of war. The pickup that, exactly as in the case of the castle, dated from Oliva gradually converted it into the fairly respectable capital of a leading German ruler. The roaming pigs, which long functioned as the bankrupt municipality's only scavengers, were banished to the countryside; the rutted streets were paved and kept clean by a specially instituted service; and, in measure as trade revived along the roads and waterways of the north German plain, immigrant merchants and artisans reoccupied the deserted houses.

Presently it even became necessary to lay out new suburbs to the west and southwest of Cöln. The earliest of them, Friedrichswerder, was followed in the 1670's by Dorotheenstadt. Projected by the second electress, it was properly named for her. It was she, too, who was responsible for its broad main artery which, planted

4. An interesting ground plan of the enlarged Schloss appears in A. Waddington, *Le Grand Electeur Frédéric Guillaume* (2 vols.; Paris, 1905–8), II, 15.

with four rows of linden trees, grew, although not until the next century, into the impressive metropolitan thoroughfare familiar to travelers of our day as Unter den Linden. Before Dorotheenstadt could take shape, much draining and clearing had to be done, since its site, like so large a part of the environs of this city on the crawling Spree, became during the winter months an impassable bog. The broad, linden-lined avenue led westward to the Tiergarten, originally a wooded hunting ground of the elector's ancestors but converted, at least in part, in his time into a park dedicated to the health and pleasure of the townsmen.

The capital's growth called, in view of the martial times, for an effective, modernized circumvallation. This, as projected by the elector's engineers, comprised, together with Berlin, the two suburbs of Cöln and Friedrichswerder. The omission of Dorotheenstadt from the walled area proves that this development was at the time still in a rudimentary stage. Owing to the eternal problem of money, the new fortifications were long in process of erection but, when at last completed, presented with their thirteen bastions and six monumental gates a proud and warlike appearance. In 1688, the year of the elector's death, they sheltered some twenty thousand people, of whom one thousand were garrison troops. It meant that Frederick William's capital had trebled in number since the miserable beginnings of his reign. Even so, it was no better than a petty provincial center compared with such great western capitals as Paris, London, and Amsterdam. Yet for a city of the backward Reich it had made notable strides and was now close on the heels of such comparable inland rivals of northern and eastern Germany as Leipzig and Breslau.

THE RETREAT TO POTSDAM

It is an arresting circumstance that about the time that the castle at Berlin and Berlin itself began to shake off the disastrous effects of the war, the man who had chiefly supplied the impetus to their revival disclosed a preference for another habitation. Shortly after the close of the Polish-Swedish War we hear of Frederick William's resorting with increasing frequency to the quiet village of Potsdam, tucked away among the low, forested hills through which the Havel threaded a winding, picturesque course.

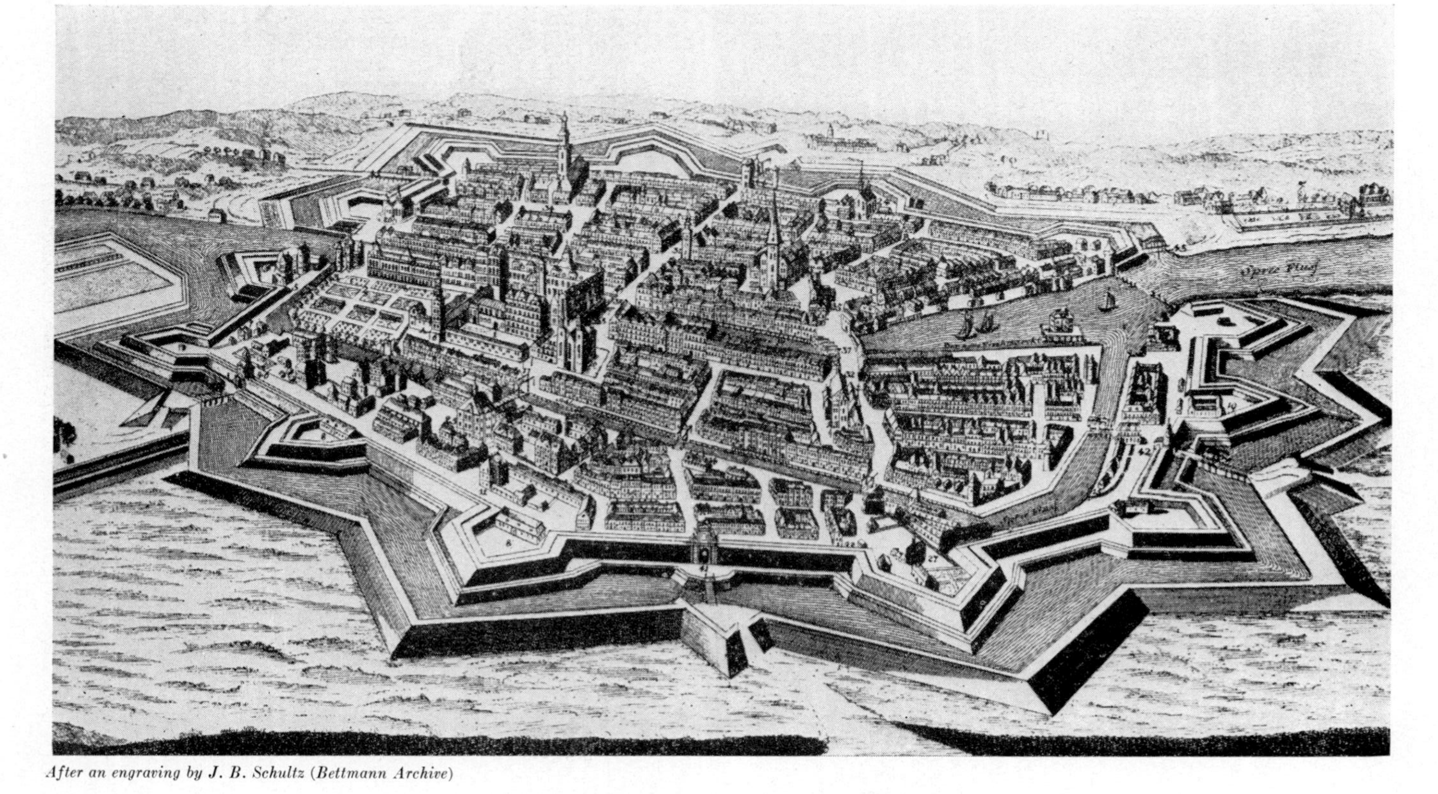

After an engraving by J. B. Schultz (Bettmann Archive)

VIEW OF BERLIN IN THE YEAR 1688

From Callot's "Misères de la Guerre" (*Bettmann Archive*)

SOLDIERS ASSEMBLED IN THREE BATTALIONS. AT LEFT, PAYMASTER

Potsdam lay about fifteen miles to the west of Berlin and with its environs of reedy lakes and lush meadows rose like an oasis among the barren and monotonous Brandenburg sands. This idyllic retreat the elector found so much to his taste that he built himself a modest country house on the edge of the village. It must not be identified with the *Stadtschloss* of the present day which is an ambitious reconstruction carried out by the elector's successors in the course of the following century. By its subsequent enlargements Frederick William's original building, which a French ambassador contemptuously described to his royal master as a *ménagerie,* that is, an establishment no better than a farmstead, has been all but completely obliterated.

What the elector pre-eminently liked about his Potsdam retreat was the escape it afforded from the hubbub at the Schloss and the leisure it gave for a more concentrated reflection on his affairs. He was with the second half of his reign entering on the era of domestic reform, the difficult problems of which called for close and diligent study. But there was yet another reason for his growing love of seclusion. He had during the grinding Polish-Swedish War suffered his earliest attacks of what was called gout in that age but what physicians of our day would be more likely to diagnose as rheumatism or arthritis. In any case, this gout of his became recurrent, and after he had passed his fiftieth milestone would clamp him to his bed or chair for a week or more several times each year. Then, after his sixtieth birthday, it became, complicated with asthma, a torturing affliction which visited him with growing frequency and for ever longer periods and during his savage bouts with which he refused to see anyone except his wife, a devoted body servant named Kornmesser, and, for the dispatch of urgent business, one or another of his councilors. As the attacks could be more easily borne away from the stir and gossip of Berlin, we need not wonder that as he entered his last decade he became so attached to the seclusion of his country hermitage that the capital never caught more than an occasional fleeting glimpse of him.

So ingrained were the working habits which the elector formed at his accession and of which we took occasion to speak at that time that he never abandoned them. He required little sleep, rose at six o'clock and, following his morning prayer, partook of a frugal breakfast. Consisting originally, as throughout the European north, of beer, it shifted in the course of his reign, as everywhere else, to the imported delicacies of the colonial areas, to coffee, tea, or chocolate. He was now ready for work with his councilors, sticking to it as a rule, right up to the main and traditionally heavy midday meal. The afternoon was usually given to outdoor exercise, which not infrequently took the form of an inspection of the field and garden projects under way at Berlin or Potsdam. Unless some pressing matter required the resumption of labor with his councilors, he passed the evening with conversation and games in the family circle.

That his periodic physical torments increased the impulsive and irritable upflares that were natural to him is comprehensible. Rébenac, the French ambassador, who achieved almost the status of a crony during the Franco-Brandenburg alliance period, has left ample evidence on this head. But on one point the too-cocksure Frenchman, who flattered himself that he saw to the very heart of the ruler on whose watch he had been set, went radically astray. Observing that Frederick William at Potsdam was in touch with only a few persons, who, moreover, were constantly about him, he developed the theory that these intimates determined the elector's policies and that the certain way to maintain his country's ascendancy was to attach them to the French interest by bribes, politely disguised as "gifts." Accordingly, he paid out considerable sums—the records have been published by Hans Prutz[5]—to the frequenters, including the electress, of the Potsdam sick chamber. While in our eyes and by universally accepted present-day standards the recipients of these favors besmirched their honor, it is no more than fair to remark that their conduct accorded with the general practice of the age and, within limits, was not considered reprehensible. The proved fact of the French "gifts" is of less importance than their substantial lack of effect. Except the self-deceived Rébenac, no man of his or of a later age whose judgment carries any weight has ever shared the ambassador's view that Frederick William's political decisions were the whispered suggestions of his Potsdam intimates or has held any other opinion than

5. In the Beilagen to his *Aus des Grossen Kurfürsten letzten Jahren* (Berlin, 1897).

that the elector remained the sole shaper of his policies to the end of his days.

To affirm the continued control of his affairs is not to deny an altered procedure in his method of arriving at decisions. We noted at the time of his coming to power his adoption of the practice of debate in Council to the end that the issues constituting the order of the day might be illumined from every conceivable angle. With the lengthening periods of withdrawal to the Potsdam seclusion this early system fell into disuse. The Council sitting in the castle at Berlin would then thrash out a matter by itself and, upon reaching a conclusion, forward it to the absent master. Besides imposing delays of which the Council never ceased to complain, the method of written, in place of spoken, exchange impersonalized the ministers and left the final decision to the sovereign unaffected by debate and in consultation with no more than the one or two carefully selected councilors who shared his retirement. Of course, these intimates were greatly envied and, on their arrival at Berlin with the elector's resolutions in their pockets, caused the court habitués almost to crack the hinges of their backs in fawning obeisance to the favorites. But it may be doubted that they contributed any more than the councilors serving at Berlin to the decisions of which they were the bearers.

It must not be understood that the Council debates under the elector's personal direction were completely abandoned. They did, however, become the exception where they had once been the rule. While we are free to hold that the elector was the loser by removing himself from the stream of discussion, we cannot lay our hands on any conclusive evidence to prove the contention. All that can be asserted with any degree of assurance is that if even in the days when he listened to the opinions in Council of such dominant personages as Burgsdorf, Waldeck, and Schwerin he steered his own course, he steered it more decidedly than ever during the latter half of his reign when Council debates under his presidency had become rare and he was confronted with the opinions of fewer men commanding smaller consideration.

In sharp contrast to the situation in the first half of his reign the less weighty advisers of the later period were more likely than not to be commoners. While diplomacy and the army continued to be the preserves of the nobility, the high posts in the administration, the ministries in other words, had become so specialized that they called for men trained in the law, and such men came usually from the middle class. Let us recall that the outstanding councilors before and around 1660, Burgsdorf, Blumenthal, Waldeck, Schwerin, were all born noblemen. In the succeeding period the leading councilors (always excepting Schwerin, who died in 1679), such as the two Jenas, Meinders, Fuchs, were all born commoners. However—and the fact supplies significant evidence of the deeply aristocratic bias of this society—the commoners were without exception ennobled by the elector, apparently on the silent assumption that they were not fit company for their august master until they had attached the invaluable prefix "von" to their names.

Taken together, the bourgeois councilors of the later period must be held to have been a competent professional group. Each shone in one field or another and possessed a distinctive silhouette. Friedrich von Jena was called to the Council from a professorship of law at the University of Frankfurt. A sober, precise man of sharp intelligence, he neither invited nor received the love of his colleagues. Just the same, by mockingly dubbing him *der Doktor*, they involuntarily revealed their respect for his contribution to their labors. His hardly less capable younger brother, Gottfried von Jena, served for over twenty years as the elector's representative at the Reichstag at Regensburg and made himself formidable there as leader of the anti-Austrian party. His all-too-successful opposition to the emperor cost him his official head when, toward the close of his reign, his master abandoned the French alliance and swung over to the Austrian side. Admittedly the administrative equal of the two Jenas, Franz von Meinders greatly surpassed them in amiability and social grace. He rose to prominence as an advocate of the French connection and negotiated, as we have seen, the alliance of 1679. His favor with the elector remained unimpaired until the rise of the star of Paul von Fuchs. He, too, had been a professor of law before he was called to his sovereign's service. Endowed with a supple, ranging mind, he succeeded in making himself indispensable to the ageing anchorite of Potsdam. Unfortunately, his character was not on a level with his talents; for, as soon as he sensed his master's growing distate of the French bondage, he switched to the opposite side. He then became in the Council, Fuchs the Austrian, ever ready to lock horns with his one-time friend and ally, Meinders the unwavering Frenchman.

THE CULTURAL BACKWARDNESS OF BRANDENBURG

In an earlier chapter we took account of the elector's effort to revive the agriculture, industry, and commerce of his territories prostrated by the war and noted at how dishearteningly slow a pace the recovery proceeded. The fact could not be blinked that, compared with the societies of Holland, England, and France—which, planted along the Atlantic seaboard, had been quickened by the commercial penetration of the newly discovered continents of Asia, Africa, and America—not only Brandenburg but the German lands without exception were but a stagnant backwater. Only by forcibly channeling an outlet for themselves into the world stream could they hope to draw abreast of their western neighbors and, in view of their lack of unity and consequent political impotence, there was in the seventeenth century not even a distant prospect of such an event. Germany, and Brandenburg with it, was in the time of the Great Elector not absolutely, of course, but in effect an economically static society.

And if economically static, then also culturally, since culture invariably waits on socioeconomic change. As soon as, on now turning to the cultural picture of Brandenburg, we remind ourselves that the mark was a particularly immobile sector of immobile Germany, we shall be advised to keep our expectations within very modest limits; for what, socially examined, was this Brandenburg but a still prevailingly medieval country dominated by its landowners or Junkers? Rooted for centuries in the soil, the Junkers had undeniably acquired from this stimulating attachment a notable social and moral vigor. However, it was not readily convertible into culture values, which have to do with the refinements of living and manifest themselves most convincingly in the idealistic projections of the arts. Culture in this sense has always been an urban phenomenon for the persuasive reason that only large aggregations of men present a challenging diversity of occupations and concentrate at a single point the material goods and human aspirations whose sharp interaction produces the cultural stimulus. If Holland, France, and England achieved a high culture contemporaneously with their commercial expansion, it was because the growth in the volume of goods exchanged was attended by a comparable urban transformation. Resorting once more to the argument from analogy, we may confidently declare that Brandenburg neither would nor could achieve a similar development until its townsmen had overcome their lethargy, multiplied their wealth and numbers, and boldly challenged the traditional ascendancy of the Junkers. And since nothing in the contemporary situation even suggested a turnover of this sort, our cultural review cannot yield better than a very slender harvest.

While we are, in the case of Brandenburg, dealing with a nobility which was culturally negligible, we are not representing nobilities in general as having that rating. On the contrary, their contribution may be of the greatest importance, as the French and English nobilities of the very period we are treating conclusively prove. But, observe: Both the latter, or rather the sections of both that counted in this matter, were court nobilities. That means that their members had established residence in their country's capital, that they constituted a leisure class living on rents from estates, of which they were the absentee landlords, and that, materially unhampered, they were free to cultivate the refinements of social intercourse and to exercise a fructifying patronage of the arts.

The Brandenburg nobles were of a different and far humbler kind. In fact, rather than nobles of the French and English variety, they constituted an order of relatively impoverished, fixedly conservative, and, often enough, coarse-minded country squires. The individual squire owned in general no more than a single manor, the cultivation of which he superintended in person. Not only was he too poor to own a townhouse, he had no desire to pass his time, except perhaps for a brief visit, either in town or at court, for he was passionately attached to the bit of soil which he called his own and, besides, was obliged diligently to attend to the various labors imposed by the revolving seasons or find himself at the end of the year a debt-laden bankrupt.

These practicing, small-scale landowners constituted an exceptionally vigorous body of men who lived scattered and in isolation over the whole mark and whose highest conception of social intercourse was an occasional uproarious reunion of neighbors marked by an unchecked consumption of food and drink. The drink was beer, brewed on the estate, although moralists of the age noticed with apprehension that a potent *schnapps* extracted from the recently imported potato was beginning to replace the traditional, milder beverage. The food, too, was native: rye bread, potatoes, turnips, mutton, beef, fish, and game, of which last-named article there was always an abundance, since the chase was the leading diversion of these tough, hard-riding descendants of the medieval knights. A few of their more wealthy members might travel abroad, more particularly in France, and on their return might pioneer in the introduction of more gracious forms of association and in the dispensing at their tables of more delicate dishes; but such occasional innovators did not greatly alter the established character of the group. The one art in which they were likely to have an interest growing out of the actualities of their life as country gentlemen was architecture. By its means a landowner might provide himself with a residence which flattered his dignity and at the same time added a more than purely transitory luster to the family of which he was the temporary head.

Frederick William himself was, as an individual, a fair representative of the culture of his age and, as a ruler, a believer in his obligation to further it by his efforts. He took a keen interest in architecture and sculpture, less in painting, and practically none at all in music. Apart from choir and congregational singing, the only kind of music heard around Berlin and Potsdam in his time was the unrelieved cacophonous fury of military bands. In so far as native-born practitioners of the arts were available, he made it his business to call upon their services; but as both his narrow Brandenburg and his wider German countrymen rarely rose in this period of national decline above the level of skilled craftsmen, he was obliged to have liberal recourse to foreigners, chiefly Dutchmen and Frenchmen. Considering the scantiness of his means he had a surprisingly large amount of work carried out at his orders, which, if it did not succeed in making Brandenburg an artistic center, created a tradition that did not again die and that yielded not unimportant dividends as early as his successor's reign.

There was little imaginative literature in Germany in the elector's day and, such as it was, it had no appeal for him. Science and history were a different story. Both of these fields of knowledge attracted his interest, and in the dilettante manner of many leading men of his time he even occasionally dabbled in laboratory experiments. The inventor of the air pump, the physicist Otto von Guericke, enjoyed his friendship and dedicated to him his important treatise on the vacuum. The elector's lively sense of the historical importance of his own work and period is attested by his appointing, though late in life, the leading German follower of Clio, Samuel Pufendorf, official court historiographer. Pufendorf's work, entitled *De rebus gestis Frederici Wilhelmi magni,* was not completed until the following reign. From its appearance in 1695 it held the field as an invaluable source book on the elector's rule and was not superseded in this respect until the issue in our own day of the great official publications of the Prussian state listed in the Foreword.

Neither the elector nor any other ruler of this aristocratically colored century gave much thought to popular education. But higher education enlisted his active and unintermittent interest. He saw to it that his various territories were provided with so-called Gymnasia, that is, with institutions that furnished young men with the current humanistic groundwork of the ancient languages, logic, and mathematics; and he endowed as liberally as he could afford, but skimpily enough, the universities dedicated to the cultivation of the learned professions of theology, law, and medicine. To the two universities of Frankfurt and Königsberg, already in existence at the time of his accession, he added for the benefit of his Rhenish lands a third university at Duisburg. Not unnaturally his favorite among them was and remained the original Brandenburg University of Frankfurt on the Oder, to which in a burst of fervor he once referred as *ein grosses Kleinod.* Reflecting the low intellectual condition of Germany in general and Brandenburg in particular, the electoral universities were neither well attended nor can their faculties be said to have shone among the circumambient darkness with more than a feeble candle's light.

Libraries, too, as the indispensable storehouses of past learning, enjoyed the elector's support. While he could not expand those attached to the universities in the way he would have wished, he did succeed in establishing a fine central library at Berlin, which he housed in the Schloss and made accessible to the public. At the time of his death it had swelled to the impressive total of eighty thousand volumes.

THE HUGUENOTS

Although Frederick William highhandedly carried through in his dominions an important *political* revolution, no one will think of him as the promoter of *social* revolution. The very idea seems absurd in view of the fact that never in his long reign did he take the least step toward modifying the tight class system prevailing in his territories. And yet in so far as he attempted to improve the economic condition of his subjects, he must be credited with stimulating change and therefore unconsciously, if not consciously, with initiating a gradual social transformation. The repeatedly asserted thesis that the mark was essentially a static society does not quarrel with the statement that by his measures of material improvement he imparted a certain modest movement to it. The most important of all his acts carrying this implication belongs to the close of his reign and is associated with the Huguenots.

When, following the Revocation of the Edict of Nantes, Frederick William on November 8, 1685, issued the bold Edict of Potsdam, he was not just acting on the spur of the moment and impetuously offering sanctuary to his persecuted fellow-believers. He entertained also an economic program which, communicated in outline in the original invitation, promised to Huguenot noblemen employment in the army; to agriculturists farm land on easy terms; to merchants and artisans houses, tools, exemption from taxation, and similar advantages. Heartened by these prospects, Frenchmen of these various classifications began to make their way to the electoral lands. When Frederick William died three years later, the migration was in full swing and is calculated to have brought a total of twenty thousand settlers to the electoral dominions by the end of the century.

And what settlers! These latest newcomers were not the peasant groups, largely lowly serfs, with whom the elector had in his earlier years tried to fill the gaps in the population left by the Thirty Years' War. Men and women who for conscience' sake took the stony road of exile, they came from every station in life and, from an ethical point of view, represented the highest type of contemporary civilization. Following their chosen occupations, as did the Reformed in general, with incomparable devotion, they represented also the highest contemporary type from an economic angle. Certainly in their own France they had no peer in this double respect, and government officials of understanding, like the great Colbert, never ceased to protest as far as they dared against the king's policy of persecution and freely acknowledged the invaluable energy imparted by their hunted fellow-countrymen to the French body politic.

When we now raise the question as to how the colonists fared in the country of their adoption, we may begin with the smallest group, the noblemen, and note that they were largely absorbed into the army. Most of them had been officers at home, and the transfer was therefore effected with comparative ease. The agriculturists were more numerous but still not plentiful, since it was a peculiarity of the Reformed faith throughout Europe that it found its adherents chiefly in urban communities. Such countryfolk as responded to the elector's call were in the main landscape gardeners and vegetable growers and were settled in the suburbs of Berlin and other expanding towns. There they cultivated the vegetables, such as lettuce, beans, and peas, which French industry had brought to a notable development and which were now for the first time advantageously grafted on the traditional bread-and-meat diet characteristic of northern Europe. The French kitchen gardens became a much-noted ornament of the Berlin environs and retained their fame for several generations.

Far and away the largest Huguenot colonial group was made up of industrialists and industrial workers, and this from the point of view of the host country was an altogether fortunate circumstance, since, though Brandenburg lagged behind western Europe in every economic department, it was particularly backward in manufactures and the artistic crafts and stood in crying need of just such skills as the Huguenots were able to supply. In many instances the immigrants brought money with them or household valuables convertible into money. However, when their only capital was their hands, the government, faithful to its promise, furnished on liberal terms the tools and raw products required for the many enterprises the fugitives set agoing.

The manufacture most commonly established was that of woolen cloth, of which some of the finer varieties were now produced for the first time in Brandenburg. But almost every article in current use seems to have been put out by these skilled foreigners, for we hear of their setting up as dyers, tanners, glovers, hatters, hosiers, and tapestry weavers. The electoral dominion was fructified throughout its whole extent by their activity, since they were planfully settled in towns lacking in industries all the way from Cleve on the Rhine to Königsberg on the Pregel. Quite the largest group, however, was magnetically drawn to Berlin. To such numbers did the refugees swell in the capital that at the turn of the century they were calculated to have constituted one-fourth of the population.

At Berlin, too, as was natural, congregated the preachers, the physicians, and the artists who composed the cultural élite of the newcomers. While, doubtless, they stirred somewhat the dull pools of German intellectuality, the effect was not immediately apparent, as they formed a closed society which long retained an exclusive character through the continued use of the French tongue. This had been steadily gaining ground in Germany since the middle of the century and, even before the coming of the Huguenots to Brandenburg, had begun to supplant German as the language of diplomacy and polite society. With the invasion by the refugees of the upper social levels of the capital their language gained such an ascendancy in these circles that it gradually became an indispensable adjunct to the native idiom.

Indeed, in certain extreme instances French all but completely supplanted the use of German. It will suffice to point out in this connection the amazing case of Frederick William's great-grandson, Frederick II, commonly called the Great. Educationally and intellectually the product of the Huguenot circles of Berlin, he accepted the French language as his normal medium of expression and in the use and mastery of his country's speech never, as he himself almost proudly confessed, rose above the coachman level. The statement may find a place in this record as a final tribute to the influence wielded by the refugees. However, it concerns us only indirectly, since the Great Elector himself remained to the end of his days a stalwart German, who befriended the Huguenots for both religious and material reasons but who felt no prompting whatever to divest himself of his nationality under the seduction of their superior culture.

Chapter 16

THE HOME-COMING

THEIR COMMON NEED DRAWS AUSTRIA AND BRANDENBURG TOGETHER

As soon as Frederick William had begun to detach himself from the French alliance it was as good as certain that he would find his way into the Austrian camp. His Dutch and Swedish commitments, to which we have carried the story of his breach with France, were in the nature of preparatory measures. The affronted Louis promptly sensed them as evidences of a beginning defection, and since he was sure to end by regarding their author as his enemy, the safest course for the prospective enemy was to align himself with the king's one certain and inalterable foe. That was, as matters stood toward the end of the seventeenth century, the emperor, head of the younger branch of the house of Hapsburg. Under the pressure of logic and necessity alike Frederick William was bound, on beating a retreat from Paris, to take the road to Vienna.

Fortunately, sentiments favorable to an accommodation with the estranged elector had already for a long time dominated Emperor Leopold and his advisers. Held as in a vise between France and its Alsatian encroachments on the west and the Ottoman Empire with its program of Danubian conquest on the east, the emperor was threatened with suffocation and in his distress lifted his voice for help to every quarter of the heavens. Never since the Chambers of Reunion had set to work had he ceased entreating Frederick William to join him in resisting them. How unavailingly, we have been abundantly informed. Then, after three years, in 1684, the Twenty-Year Truce had adjourned, though by no means closed, the issue. If the Austrian court had bowed to that inconclusive settlement, it was because the Turks had meanwhile unloosed their hordes on Vienna and, following the Turk repulse, the war against the infidels had been automatically carried into Hungary. The unforeseen offensive held out such brilliant prospects of removing once and for all the century-old Ottoman threat that the government could not afford to abandon it, especially as the Reich, carried to an unusual pitch of enthusiasm by the defeat administered to the sultan at Vienna, was supporting the Austrian action with substantial contributions of men and money. However, the contribution of him very generally regarded by now as the leading German prince was conspicuously missing, and Emperor Leopold continued to address a spirited and pained summons to the laggard Frederick William to do his duty by a cause which he himself had on innumerable occasions declared to be not only that of Austria but of the whole German fatherland as well.

In point of fact the elector had never answered the emperor's plea for help against the Turks with an outright rebuff. But whenever he and his suzerain had begun negotiations touching the auxiliary force which Brandenburg was asked to contribute, the many controversial matters that had piled up through the years immediately injected themselves into the discussions, and the conference ended abruptly with a fresh flare-up of ill will.

In the course of the year 1685 the war-harassed Austrian court resolved to make another and supreme effort to draw Frederick William into its system. It dispatched Baron Fridag, one of its most skilful diplomats, to Berlin and was delighted to hear from him that he had been made heartily welcome. His good reception was due, as may be readily surmised, to the elector's having already begun to free himself from his five-year-old dependence on France and to the perhaps as yet merely subconscious persuasion that an accommodation with Austria was imperative. Ambassador Fridag's instructions set forth two objectives as the purpose of his mission: first, the dispatch of a solid body of Brandenburg troops to fight in Hungary against the Turks, and, second, a defensive alliance against France pledged to resist any new seizure of Reich territory.

At once the Brandenburg grievances were again spread on the table before Fridag, with just this difference: In Frederick William's softened mood they were no longer represented as unnegotiable demands. Even so, each side had come to regard the other in the course of their long disagreement with such settled suspicion that the exchanges between them were often halted for weeks at a time. Nonetheless, they were never again broken off, among other reasons because there was now a group of Austrian partisans at Berlin headed by no less a personage than the electoral prince. Although long courted by the insinuating Rébenac and not indifferent to his flattery, young Frederick had at last plumped frankly and decisively for Austria. True, his distrustful father was not in the habit of consulting him, and he exercised little or no direct influence, but he was, after all, the heir apparent and together with such older men as the prince of Anhalt and Field Marshal Derflinger, who had never at any time subscribed to the French connection, constituted a solid Austrian nucleus on which Fridag could always fall back for support. But the most valuable assistance of all came to him from Privy Councilor Fuchs. Throughout the elector's last period Fuchs was closer to his master than any other adviser and, although originally as favorable to France as his sovereign, with the typical courtier's unhesitating response to his sovereign's changed mood he had successfully metamorphosed himself into an adherent of Austria.

AGREEMENT ACHIEVED ON THE TURK WAR (JANUARY 4, 1686)

That Fridag nonetheless had a hard struggle becomes clear when we learn that it took almost a year to reach an agreement regarding the first and less contentious of the two objects of his embassy. On January 4, 1686, a treaty on the Turk war was perfected whereby Frederick William promised to come to the aid of the emperor with a body of seven thousand men; and the emperor, for his part, agreed to make a contribution to the elector's expenses in the sum of one hundred and fifty thousand talers. Accordingly, as soon as spring had arrived, the admirably accoutered Brandenburg *Hilfscorps* was assembled at Crossen on the Oder, and there, before starting for the Danube, it was reviewed by the elector in a brilliant spectacle attended by the whole court. Its command was intrusted to General Schöning, owing doubtless to the distinction this officer had gained in the famous winter campaign in Prussia in 1679. Admittedly a capable soldier, he must be listed as one of the less admirable characters among the men who had come to the top under Frederick William. Long afterward it was revealed that before starting on the Danubian expedition he had accepted a considerable bribe from the French ambassador in return for an undertaking not only to keep his paymaster duly informed on the progress of the campaign but also to pick a quarrel with his Austrian allies at every opportunity. His case, since as a military man he had sworn a special oath of devotion to the elector, was far more heinous than that of the many bribetakers among the councilors and arouses the suspicion that the standards of conduct among the servants of this as yet imperfectly consolidated state still reflected the moral disorders of the Thirty Years' War.

Despite Schöning's disloyal commitments, the Brandenburgers greatly distinguished themselves in the 1686 campaign. They were attached to the army assembled to reduce the fortress of Buda, the pivotal stronghold of the Turks in their Hungarian dependency, and were singled out for special praise by their Austrian superiors when, after a strenuous siege, Buda was at last taken by storm.

THE SILESIAN DISPUTE

The discussions looking to a defensive alliance against France, which from the first ran parallel to those touching the Turk help, ran into so many snags that it repeatedly looked as if they would have to be abandoned. The main obstructions were Frederick William's territorial claims. More than once in the past we have run into the elector's pretension to the small Silesian duchy of Jägerndorf and the refusal of the Viennese court to give it serious consideration. Then, during the Pomeranian war, in 1675, to be precise, the Jägerndorf claim was augmented by a claim to three other Silesian duchies, Liegnitz, Brieg, and Wohlau. The new issue sprang from the death in that year of the last duke of these territories whose heir Frederick William declared himself to be by virtue of a reciprocal treaty of inheritance (a so-called *Erbverbrüderung*) drawn up in 1537, more than a century before, between the then reigning heads, respectively, of Brandenburg and Liegnitz. The duke of Liegnitz (lord also of Brieg and Wohlau) was, like all holders of Silesian territory, a vassal of the king of Bohemia, and the king of Bohemia at the time of the 1537 treaty was a Hapsburg who afterward became Emperor Ferdinand I. His action is important: Whether or not authorized by current feudal law to do so, he had promptly declared the Erbverbrüderung to be null and void. Consequently, when the last duke of Liegnitz died in 1675, Emperor Leopold, a successor of Ferdinand I, stood by his predecessor's decision and, disregarding the Erbverbrüderung, took over the vacated duchies under the law of escheat. The counterclaim advanced by Frederick William ran to the effect that the 1537 treaty was no concern of the Bohemian overlord and that Leopold's seizure of the duchies was not in accordance with the feudal custom governing the case.

Let no reader expect a pronouncement by the present writer on the merits of either the older Jägerndorf or the newer Liegnitz claim. We have seen how in comparable cases—such as the Jülich inheritance, contested for half a century between Brandenburg and Pfalz-Neuburg, and Louis XIV's claim to the Spanish Netherlands in right of his Spanish wife—claim and counterclaim thickened to so impenetrable a legal jungle that no responsible historian has ever affirmed that he has succeeded in cutting his way through it. Nor has he felt pressed to do so, for the cases in question were not of the sort that are carried to court and argued before judge and jury by opposing attorneys. They were political, that is, power issues and like all similar issues since the world began could be settled only by the method either of war or of negotiation ending in compromise. And that was precisely the alternative Brandenburg and Austria faced throughout their heated and long-drawn-out debate over Frederick William's four Silesian claims.[1]

Since, however, the two governments at no time gave consideration to the method of war and since, further, each, under pressure of the situation in which it found itself, could not get along without the other, they were inescapably directed to the alternative of compromise in respect not only of the Silesian but also of every other issue between them. It thus came about that a loss at one point was traded for a gain at another until the slate was

1. It may be that some reader touched with antiquarian curiosity may want to look into the older and probably more valid of these claims. It is the claim carrying the name of Jägerndorf. In *UA*, XIV, 60–62, he will find a summary which should satisfy an even extreme predilection for historical bypaths.

gradually cleared of every contention save that of the four duchies. And here, contrary to what we might be led to expect from his stubborn nature, it was Frederick William who yielded. Nor are his reasons difficult to uncover. For one thing, in measure as, during the Berlin exchanges, the breach between Brandenburg and France continued to widen, the need for an accommodation with Austria became more pressing; for another, it fell heavily into the scales that the elector's health was declining so precipitately that he was obliged to reckon with the probability of his early death. What more natural than, before departing this life, to try, even at heavy sacrifice, to steer the passionately loved state he had founded into what he had become convinced was its only safe haven? Considerations of this kind adequately explain how it came about that this abnormally land-hungry ruler surprised Fridag one day with the offer to surrender all his Silesian claims in exchange for the single district of Schwiebus. Schwiebus was a small Silesian locality almost completely inclosed within Brandenburg territory, and its fame had traveled so little afield that the unusually well-informed Fridag was obliged on transmitting the Schwiebus proposal to his government to confess that he had only the vaguest notions regarding the suggested *quid pro quo*.

There can be no doubt that when the elector's offer was communicated to the Viennese councilors it was received with astonishment and gratification. But still it was not enough. In the view of Leopold it was beneath his imperial dignity to make a concession, however slight, to a vassal in a territorial dispute, and a majority of his council ended by supporting his position. Fridag was instructed to sound his mildest notes in informing the elector of the rejection of his proposal. But now Frederick William mounted his high horse. To give up his four-duchy claim without at least a tiny territorial compensation signified an intolerable loss of face, and he planted himself before the uncompromising Kaiser in an identically uncompromising posture.

While it may be conjectured that one or the other would in the end have given way, that solution was made unnecessary by a device excogitated by the labyrinthine brain of the shrewd Fridag. He had from the first been supported in his efforts by the electoral prince, eager to the point of precipitance for the Austrian alliance.

When Fridag now suggested, oh so delicately, to the prince that it lay in his power to break the deadlock over Schwiebus and bring home the invaluable treaty, he was invited to explain and was not rebuffed when he proposed that the emperor commit himself to deliver Schwiebus to Frederick William on the understanding that Frederick William's son sign a secret agreement to give it back on his accession.

Fridag does not seem to have needed to employ much persuasion to bring the heir apparent to an acceptance of his scheme. We may conjecture that the young man justified himself before his own conscience by his conviction that the Austrian alliance was indispensable to the welfare of the state; but it is beyond conjecture with what excuses to himself he justified the deception practiced on his father and sovereign. Twenty-nine years old, he was no longer a child and must be charged with full responsibility for his action. An additional discrediting circumstance not to be overlooked was that he let himself be eased into acceptance by a handsel from a grateful Kaiser in the sum of ten thousand ducats. Admitting that Fridag played the part of the tempter in barely disguised horns and cloven hoof, it passes understanding how even the most prejudiced Prussian historian can blind himself to the fact that Frederick invited temptation—and fell.

THE SECRET TREATY OF RENUNCIATION AND THE OPEN TREATY OF ALLIANCE

In this manner all barriers to an Austro-Brandenburg agreement were at last removed. But as Fridag was not the man to take any chances, he insisted before giving it its final touches that the electoral prince formally commit himself to his pound of flesh; and, accordingly, in a very secret meeting at the house of the prince of Anhalt in Potsdam, Frederick on March 10, 1686, put his name to the document whereby he bound himself to return Schwiebus on mounting the throne. Thereupon, on April 1, the treaty of alliance was signed in its turn. The tiny nubbin, Schwiebus, to which the sizable Silesian apple of discord had shrunk in the course of debate was grandly handed over by a generous Kaiser to his unduly voracious vassal, causing the deluded recipient's heart to swell with satisfaction. Nor did his contentment, one is pleased to note, ever turn to bitterness, for he died two years later without the remotest inkling of how he had been duped by the Kaiser, ignobly seconded by his own son and heir.

To complete the record, we may note that Frederick kept his promise and returned the grubby little molehill that discussion had puffed up to a mountain. But observe: His act had the effect of reviving the Silesian issue that the Great Elector imagined had been disposed of at long last by way of compromise. Since it developed that it had not been compromised, it automatically reverted to its original status of an unsettled power question. Thereafter it was entirely possible that at some time in the near or distant future the complainant in the case, who was Brandenburg, might seek a solution by the alternative method of war. Which is exactly what happened; for when, in the year 1740, Frederick II, called the Great, mounted the throne, he took this course with results which, as everybody knows, permanently altered the distribution of power within the framework of the cracked-up old Reich.

To return to the defensive treaty between the two leading German states: While the cession of Schwiebus assumed a conspicuous place therein, it was in point of fact a minor element of the many-articled agreement. Its leading feature was the wholly unambiguous avowal that it was directed against France. To make their alliance effective, the two contracting parties agreed to resist any new violence against the Reich; they promised an equally vigorous resistance to a new attack on the Spanish Netherlands; in the event of an attack on one of them, the other agreed to come to his support with a precisely specified force; and to enable the elector to maintain his army at full strength, the emperor agreed to pay him a subsidy. While these items sketch a close partnership, it was left to two further articles to proclaim the elector's unqualified return to the Austrian allegiance: On the occasion of the next imperial election he pledged himself to give his vote to the emperor's son, and in the matter of the threatening conflict over the Spanish succession he agreed to support the claims of the house of Hapsburg.

NEW ENCROACHMENTS BY LOUIS XIV GIVE BIRTH TO THE LEAGUE OF AUGSBURG

So exact were the commitments and so unusually tense was the language of the Austro-Brandenburg Alliance that it must have been concluded under the apprehension that war with France was just around the corner. And, indeed, expectation of its early outbreak was general through the length and breadth of the Reich; for, in spite of the Twenty-Year Truce of 1684, Louis XIV had not abandoned his aggression. A particularly flagrant case had occurred within hardly more than half a year of his signing that standstill document. When, in May, 1685, the elector palatine, Karl, the last male representative of the reigning Simmern line, had died, he was followed by the head of the younger Neuburg line. This was none other than our old friend, Philip Wilhelm, duke of Jülich, whose succession was unchallengeable under the laws of the Reich. That, however, did not hinder Louis XIV from putting in a claim on behalf of his brother's wife, the duchess of Orléans, who was a sister of the defunct elector. Her name was Elizabeth Charlotte (Lise Lotte for short), and she was through her rare vigor of character an outstanding personage in her day. Although as a loyal member of her house and nation she was opposed to Louis's stand, she was set aside by that monarch and obliged to let him have his way. On the strength of the legal hocus-pocus so general in that age and by now only too familiar to us, the French ruler claimed such large sections of the Palatinate for his brother in right of that brother's overruled wife that, if surrendered, there would have been very little of his electorate left for the new incumbent. True, Louis exercised sufficient self-restraint not at once to seize by force what he demanded. In distinction from the earlier reunion procedure he appealed his case to the Reichstag; but as that body would go no further than to agree to investigate, and Reichstag investigations notoriously never yielded a judgment there was always the chance that the impatient king would at some least expected moment resort to arms.

So outrageous in the opinion of the German princes and people were the French king's pretensions to the Palatinate that they released a vast indignation. It culminated in a general demand for preparedness, which naturally delighted the head of the Reich, the emperor. He summoned a congress of princes to the city of Augsburg, where in July, 1686, a league of resistance, called from the place of meeting the League of Augsburg, saw the light. All the more important heads of German states accepted membership, with the one notable exception of the three ecclesiastical electors along the Rhine. Dwelling in the immediate shadow of France, they kept aloof, in the case of Cologne out of devotion to Louis, in the case of Mainz and Trier out of a wholesome fear of him. Even Sweden and Spain added their signatures to the Augsburg pact in behalf of the Reich territories respectively in their possession, western Pomerania and the Spanish Netherlands.

In the eyes of Louis the League of Augsburg was a challenge, and he reacted to it in characteristic manner. He had thus far successfully encroached on the Reich without war, and he preferred to hold to this course as involving both less expense and less danger than open conflict. Instinctively and correctly he interpreted the League of Augsburg as a declaration by emperor and Reich that further impairment of German territory would not be tolerated; but though pretending to be alarmed, he was not really troubled, for with the German states already engaged to the limit of their strength in a war with the Ottoman Empire, he was persuaded that they could not afford to undertake a second and far more exacting war with himself. He had hitherto refrained from falling on his neighbor across the Rhine because in the prevailing European frame of mind he did not care to invite the charge of being the ally of the infidels. There was nothing, however, to hinder him from applying at Vienna and Regensburg the kind of pressure which without abandoning the customary diplomatic amenities carried with it a veiled threat of war. His precise procedure was to direct his German agents to declare that the time had come to convert the Twenty-Year Truce into a definitive peace. To emperor and princes acceptance meant a return to the policy of appeasement with which they had broken, and they firmly refused. The consequence was a nervous tension which steadily spread and deepened with every fresh clash between members of the two opposed groups into which Europe had by this time fallen.

THE FAMILY CRISIS OVER THE GREAT ELECTOR'S TESTAMENT

Frederick William followed the many developments pointing to an early war with France with a troubled spirit. But great as his public anxieties were, every whit as disturbing were the agitations of a private nature that came to a climax at this time. While they slowly gathered to a sheer inextricable maze of intrigue and misunderstanding, they had their origin in as simple an event as that second marriage which the elector contracted in 1668. His second electress, Dorothea, presented him in rapid succession with seven children, four of them boys. It was her natural motherly instinct to urge her husband to make substantial territorial rather than purely pecuniary provision for her sons, and in a testament drawn up in 1680 he did so. Not being on the best of terms with his successor, Frederick, who with a younger brother, Ludwig, constituted the surviving descendants of the first wife, Frederick William unwisely, we may unhesitatingly say, left the heir apparent in the dark regarding the territories with which his half-brothers were endowed in that document. Rumor at once pounced on the undisclosed testament, and spiteful tongues took pleasure in alarming the thin-skinned and not overly intelligent Frederick with whispered intimations that such considerable areas had been given away that he would be left with a sadly diminished inheritance. At the same time the rumormongers enlarged on the sinister role in the transaction of the prince's stepmother, the electress Dorothea. She was represented as having taken unfair and deceitful advantage of her husband's devotion to her and as having been, and still being, tirelessly at his ear with demands favoring her own sons and injurious to her predecessor's offspring.

Although neither Frederick nor his brother, Ludwig, were so simple-minded as unquestioningly to swallow these malicious insinuations, they effected a sufficient lodgment in their minds to create suspicion and, in the long run, to bring about a complete estrangement between the two young princes and their father's second wife. Court opinion, which for reasons of its own was hostile to Dorothea, cast her in the role of the wicked stepmother of German fairy-tale lore and so successfully blackened her character that all the efforts of latter-day historians to show the essential baselessness of the charges against her have not to this hour succeeded in destroying the traditional picture. A relatively early disclosure that should by itself have served to exculpate the electress was that Frederick William had made a considerable number of testaments prior to that of 1680 and that in all of them, *including those antedating his second marriage,* he had never failed to make territorial provision for younger sons.[2] It was this feature of the 1680 testament that was at the bottom of the current malicious gossip. That a man who with rare single-mindedness had labored for a lifetime to construct a strong and unified state should at the close of his days be willing to lop off sizable portions of it was held to be impossible, except through some powerful personal influence like that of a beloved wife. However, if an influence of this nature is to be given credence in the case of the electress Dorothea, it must in the light of the devisements of the earlier testaments be predicated also of the electress Louise Henriette. In short, should such sway as Dorothea may have exercised over her husband be attributed to her as guilt, the same guilt would have to be laid at the door of her historically unsmirched predecessor.

The simple truth, however, is that we do not have to assume an undue influence on the part of either wife to account for the elector's repeatedly documented impairment of his unitary state. Let us agree that his bringing himself to do so comes with as sharp a surprise to us, who have followed his arduous upward climb, as it did to the courtiers who then maliciously nursed his departure from an apparently unwavering course into a family scandal. But when we look a little more closely into the contemporary state of the ancient succession issue among German ruling families, our surprise begins to evaporate. It will be remembered that the principle of primogeniture and the indivisibility of the electorate were not conclusively affirmed for the house of Hohenzollern until the family pact of Gera of 1598.[3] While that meant the recognition of the state as a living, continuing organism, it did not at once kill the earlier patrimonial notion that it was the personal property of the ruler which he might on his demise distribute among his male heirs. Now among all the German rulers of the seventeenth century, including Frederick William, there was, in spite of a general veering to the principle of primogeniture, a lingering persistence of

2. The matter of the testaments is very complicated. Particularly worth consulting are: J. G. Droysen, *Geschichte der preussischen Politik*, IV, Part IV, 129–203; H. Hallmann, "Die letztwillige Verfügung im Hause Brandenburg," *FBPG*, Vol. XXXVII; and L. Tümpel, *Die Entstehung des brandenburgisch-preussischen Einheitsstaates* (Breslau, 1915). The important testament of 1667 has been published by G. Küntzel and M. Hass, *Die politischen Testamente der Hohenzollern*. Droysen in the above-indicated volume has published the final testament of 1686.

3. See chap. ii, pp. 39–40.

the patrimonial conception. Even the Gera pact, after making its significant antipatrimonial declarations, weakened them to the extent of permitting a ruling elector to devise to younger sons any territory which may have been newly acquired by him. And this was precisely what Frederick William did! In the testament of 1680 he left certain territories added to the Hohenzollern mass in his lifetime to his younger sons. It was these deductions which, magnified by rumor and ascribed by her ill-wishers to the electress, sowed the perilous seeds that threatened the family cohesion.

By the time the Austro-Brandenburg Alliance of 1686 was under discussion the once-firm family structure was already so undermined that, as we have seen, the electoral prince departed so far from his filial obligations as to nullify by secret treaty his father's settlement of the Silesian controversy. While still in the midst of this indefensible intrigue and before his commitment to the emperor, he was alarmed by the whispered information that his father had replaced the offensive testament of 1680 with a document even more injurious to his prospects. This was the testament of 1686, which, as the last of the series, represents Frederick William's final disposition of his effects. Had the father called the son into his cabinet and given him the new testament to peruse, the subsequent upheaval might possibly have been avoided, for in this newest declaration Frederick William arranged, or at least tried to arrange, for the preservation of all his dominions as an unbroken political unit. True, he reaffirmed to his younger sons the districts already allotted to them in the testament of 1680, but he now provided with the utmost care that, in respect to their foreign policy and internal administration, they should remain in the essential control of Frederick, designated in unambiguous terms as the universal heir.

In April, 1687, the mounting tension between father and son reached a climax through the sudden and mysterious death of twenty-one-year-old Prince Ludwig. On returning from a dinner in the castle at Potsdam the young man fell violently ill and died a few days later in the conviction that he was the victim of poison administered either by his stepmother or a member of her circle. The ignorant doctors, who had reported to the anxious elector that Ludwig's illness was not serious, were sternly commanded to perform a post-mortem examination and in order to save their reputations gave credence to the poison theory. No member of the court who halfway kept his balance during the attendant wild commotion put any faith in the idea, but that did not hinder the numerous unbalanced individuals who swarmed at Berlin and Potsdam from entertaining and circulating the most atrocious suspicions about the electress and her "wicked" entourage. Among the unbalanced group were, unhappily, the electoral prince and his far more intelligent wife, Sophie Charlotte, a princess of Hanover, famous in her later, more mature, years as the friend and correspondent of the philosopher Leibnitz. We must assume that the miasmatic fog that had become the normal atmosphere of the court had eaten into her marrow and temporarily dimmed her naturally brilliant mind. How else explain that she used the compelling influence she exercised over her pliable husband to push him into an insanely irresponsible course of action?

In the midst of the furor attending Prince Ludwig's sudden death the young couple withdrew to the Bohemian watering-place of Carlsbad, ostensibly in search of health. When, in June, the time came for their return, Frederick informed his father by letter that as neither his nor his wife's life was safe at court, they were resolved to establish residence in the security of distant Cleve. Frederick William, always a choleric man but now a sick and suffering invalid into the bargain, almost went out of his mind with rage, in part over the affront to his paternal authority, in larger part over the all but openly formulated criminal charge against the electress. The alarm was voiced in some quarters that he might attempt to disinherit his son, but even when his wrath was at its acme he cannot be seriously charged with having entertained this extreme step. Some neighboring princes, friendly to both parties, intervened between them, and after a few months of restless travel over western Germany the runaway young couple reappeared at court, forgiven and reassured by the elector and inwardly ashamed of the silly panic to which they had given way.

No doubt, too, the son was moved to compunction by the wasted appearance of his father, who by the winter of 1687 had manifestly arrived at the final stage of his slow decline. Rarely now did he leave his Potsdam bedchamber, and the gout that racked his weakened body no longer gave him respite for more than a brief interval. Spiritually softened by his approaching end, he was anxious not only to let bygones be bygones but also to help prepare his even now not particularly loved son for the heavy responsibilities that lay ahead. He had Frederick preside at the Council in order to familiarize himself with current business, and he empowered him to sign documents in the invalid ruler's name. The terms of the final and crucial testament were no longer withheld and were apparently accepted by the electoral prince, too happy over the new cordiality with his dying father to register an open protest.

However, privately the protest persisted with consequences which, for the sake of completeness, may not be omitted from our story. No sooner, following his father's demise, had Frederick acceded to the throne, than he quashed the contentious document on the ground that it violated the Gera family pact of 1598. While this was only generally, not literally, correct, nobody was prepared to argue the case against the new ruler, especially as the privy councilors to a man shared his opinion. Consequently, the annulment was not seriously questioned in any quarter. His four half-brothers were offered and, after some hesitation, accepted annuities in exchange for the lands they were obliged to surrender, and the whole critical episode was brought to a close not only with the minor good of the preservation of the family peace but also with the major and incalculable benefit of the reaffirmed and strengthened unity of the state; for, though, as already stated, the Great Elector had made as careful provision in the canceled testament as lay within his power for the continued subjection of his younger sons to their older brother's control, they were nonetheless endowed with the respective titles that went with their allotted provinces and were left with sufficient power therein to constitute a potential threat to the head of the house and his unitary claim. That threat Elector Frederick wisely banished in defense, in the first instance, of his own interest but also, we may confidently assert, in defense, in his father's despite, of that father's lifework.

THE DEATHROOM WATCH

With the reconciliation with his son a millstone fell from the elector's heart. He was nearing his end. For several years now death had been almost visibly weaving in ever narrowing circles around him, and often his pains became so unbearable that he would implore the skulking visitor to strike. But even though his private anxieties no longer weighed upon his spirit, the public situation, never ceasing to give birth to fresh involvements, closely engaged an attention which, in spite of all but continual physical sufferings, never flagged.

Slowly but infallibly the long French crisis was coming to a head. The Twenty-Year Truce, accepted by emperor and Reich in the hope of arresting it, had proved a deception. Louis's encroachments went on exactly as if he had never pledged himself to renounce them. We have heard of his unfounded claim to the Palatinate and of his subsequent brusque demand that the truce, which still had some eighteen years to run, be forthwith converted into a permanent peace. Nor were these the only evidences of his continued spirit of aggression. By strongly fortifying a number of the Alsatian territories of which the standstill arrangement had given him only the provisional possession, he treated them as permanently his; and he boldly and contrary to treaty threw a bridge across the Rhine at Hüningen which provided him with a convenient line of penetration into southern Germany.

Then in January, 1688, he committed the act that worthily crowned these labors. Under his influence the cathedral chapter of Cologne elected the bishop of Strassburg, a member of the notorious Fürstenberg clan hated throughout the Reich as a nest of traitors, as coadjutor to the archbishop. Under the prevailing practice this was tantamount to securing to Fürstenberg the succession to the archbishopric on the demise of the aged and ailing incumbent. The reaction throughout the Reich was inflamed and instantaneous. To establish an avowed betrayer of his German kin, who moreover as bishop of Strassburg had become a French subject, as ruler of the second ranking electorate of the Reich was equivalent to assigning permanent quarters within the German house to Louis himself; and emperor and princes unanimously voiced their opposition to the unwelcome appointment. When Ambassador Rébenac remonstrated with Frederick William over his taking an attitude so manifestly unfriendly to the French sovereign, he received the spirited reply that it was as illicit for Louis to insinuate himself into a German episcopal election as it would be for the emperor to seek to influence the nomination of the bishop of Rheims or Paris.

With the French intervention at Cologne added to the already terrific European tension it seemed that war might break out at any moment by spontaneous combustion. But it did not break out, at least not at once, because the respective leaders of the opposing sides held back, thinking to profiit by delay. The two leaders still were, as had been the case ever since the French assault upon the Dutch in 1672, Louis XIV and William of Orange. Louis could not help hoping that with his grip on the Reich tightening every day and with the Reich and emperor engaged with all the strength at their command in a struggle with the Ottoman Empire, the hour was approaching when his demand for the making-over of the reunions to him in permanence would no longer be resisted. Could any person in his senses, Louis argued, believe that Leopold and his German following would commit so suicidal an act as to involve themselves in a still more ferocious and exhausting conflict on the Rhine?

While Louis's delay is comprehensible, it was sure that he would terminate it the moment that he became convinced that his opponents were taking more profit from adjournment than he. Reversing his course, he would in that event plunge into war in order to secure the advantage that always accrues to him who delivers the first blow. It was on September 24, 1688, that Louis put an end to a strain become unbearable by a declaration of war against Kaiser and Reich attended by a devastating incursion into the Palatinate. The long-awaited and long-adjourned struggle was at last engaged. But this new phase of Louis's bid for supremacy in Europe lies beyond our view, as the subject of this history had departed this life four months before Louis struck.

The hesitations of William of Orange were even more deep-seated and paralyzing than those of his adversary. William had long ago come to the conclusion that the new and, in his opinion, inevitable war of Europe against France incontestably required for its success the entrance of England into the anti-French coalition. But with the accession to the English throne in 1685 of the fanatic Catholic, James II, the prospect of winning the island kingdom as an ally against Louis had become dim almost to the vanishing point. It was for this reason that Frederick William, in panicky alarm lest James achieve his purpose of bringing the English people back into the Roman fold, had urged William to save the situation by at once crossing the channel with an army on the chance of rousing the Protestant population to rebellion. William had rejected the proposal. As James's son-in-law and heir presumptive to the English crown, he was better acquainted with the English situation than his uncle and was persuaded that, before James could be dislodged, he would first have to discredit himself with his countrymen by open and flagrant attacks on their religious faith and civil liberties. That in his obsessed frame of mind his father-in-law would before long embark on this course William entertained not the least doubt. He adopted, therefore, a waiting policy which, while it seemed the surer way to win the English prize and was confirmed as such by the event, demanded the exercise of a self-restraint hard for him to bear and almost insufferable for his aroused following throughout Europe.

By the winter of 1687–88, after almost three years of rule, the misguided Stuart on the English throne had so thoroughly offended his subjects with a series of attacks on both their faith and their liberties that his position had become sufficiently shaken for William to hold that the moment for action was rapidly approaching. Nonetheless, the opposition to James, although steadily mounting, had not yet become general, and William, determined not to attempt an English landing until the whole country had fallen away from its deluded sovereign, continued to hold himself in leash. In his considered view the time was not ripe, not yet quite ripe; and in faraway Potsdam his Brandenburg relative and ally, letting, as spring approached, no feature of the palpitating English situation escape his intent gaze, accepted his nephew's judgment without murmur or question.

It was destined to be his last, the spring of 1688, advancing from the south as blithely unconcerned with human weal and woe as all its predecessors. He had himself become convinced that his end was close at hand; and it is reasonable to assume that, if in the face of the deepening English crisis on which hung the fate of the impending war he possessed his soul with an unwonted patience, this novel resignation sprang from his Christian submission to a verdict from which there was no escape. All possible preparations for the war that was to remove the French shadow from Germany and Europe had been completed, except the most crucial item of all, the winning of England. That was the task assigned to William of Orange, and it was at least well under way. He, Frederick William, would not live to see the upshot of all these labors, but he had in his time carried his fair share of them and, intrusting the outcome to his God, could go to rest with a good conscience. To this spiritual composure the attitude of his heir, now reconciled and actively participating in the government, made a happy contribution. Although the temperamental gap between himself and his son neither was nor could be bridged, the father had been able to convince himself that his successor saw eye to eye with him in regard to the threatened French hegemony and that he gave the European coalition and its Dutch leader his unqualified devotion. There would be no change in foreign policy with the approaching change of ruler.

In April dropsy set in, adding its curse to the long familiar afflictions of gout, gravel, and asthma. Only rarely and with the greatest effort did he now leave his bed. Still, summoning the iron resolution of which he had given ample proof throughout his forty-eight years of rule, he continued to receive the reports and make the decisions pertaining to his office. On May 7 he summoned the Council to Potsdam and had himself carried into the presence of the men who had been his advisers and collaborators. Both he and they knew that they were holding their last meeting. With moving words he took leave of them, thanking them for the services they had rendered and warmly recommending them to the son and successor at his side. Passing his reign in review, which, in spite of disappointments and failures, had given the country a new and farseen luster, he penetratingly pointed out that the advance was due and solely due to his having, on learning that he lived in an armed world, provided himself with arms. Let his successor look to the army: It was the leading item of his legacy.

His last act as ruler was to issue as the military password for this same day of May 7 the combined salutation: London and Amsterdam. There could be no better evidence of how during his last hours his thoughts hovered around the great issue between William of Orange and his English father-in-law, which he was convinced would decide the future of Europe. The next day, May 8, would for a man of ordinary vigor have been his last. But his enormous vitality continued to resist extinction, and it was not until the morning of May 9 that his tormented body sank into the final monumental composure of death.

Chapter 17

THE GREAT ELECTOR IN HISTORY AND LEGEND

WE CONCLUDE with a résumé and an appreciation.

This history sought to justify itself by declaring at the outset that its subject had founded a state and that this was a distinction sufficiently rare to invite an examination of the founder's career. Having now performed this task, the writer is moved to raise the question with himself and his readers whether his labors have resulted in the portrait of a ruler deserving the asserted founder rank.

To avoid talking at cross-purposes, let us begin by coming to an agreement as to what precisely is meant by the concept "founding a state." Is founding a state a single act performed at a determinable moment and complete in itself? Or is it, rather, in the nature of a continuing process bringing what began as a hopeful prospect by successive measurable additions to an ever ampler and richer expression? The long rolls of history carry the record of innumerable states brought into being in the former manner by masterful individuals with a passion for power and a gift for organization. Most commonly, individuals of this order have figured as leaders of war bands and appear most frequently in the early history of our species. The outstanding and all but invariable characteristic of their purely military creations is that they were short-lived and ended abruptly with the death of their founders.

Founding a state under settled and civilized conditions is an entirely different affair. The human group which in this instance the state embraces is no longer a wandering band of warriors but a society which has progressed sufficiently beyond nomadism to have achieved a permanent residence. With this permanence of place is combined a ceaseless organic transformation, and the attendant social flux necessarily induces a parallel adjustment of political structure. In these circumstances founding a state becomes a continuing action; and it follows that every community that has accumulated a history, in short, every civilized community, boasts a whole roster of men with an adequate, if uneven, claim to the distinction of founder.

It will at once be conceded that the Great Elector takes his place as founder in the civilized category and not among the primitive war-band leaders. An accident of birth made him ruler of a polity which at his accession had already been in existence for five hundred years. If we accept Albrecht the Bear as the first designer of Brandenburg, we cannot but agree that for the mark to have survived along the dangerously exposed eastern frontier of Germany, Albrecht must have been followed by a number of builders in no way inferior to himself; and this was indeed the case. On the extinction of Albrecht's dynasty we encountered two lines of absentee margraves, shameless shirkers of their responsibilities, under whom Brandenburg was threatened with dissolution. But the anarchy which they precipitated was overcome when Emperor Sigismund took pity on the disordered province and enfeoffed Frederick of Hohenzollern with the margraviate. On the strength of his labors of rehabilitation Frederick may fairly be assigned a place as founder at the side of Albrecht. While among the first Hohenzollern's descendants his son, Frederick II, and his great-grandson, Joachim I, invite acceptance as contributory architects of the rising state, we encountered in the first Joachim's successors an unbroken string of feckless rulers until from their painful mediocrity there sprang with the saltatory unexpectedness of nature the man whose policies and actions have engaged our attention in this book and who by every reasonable measuring-scale overtops all his founding predecessors including Albrecht, the initiator of the work.

To the present writer, at least, the towering of Frederick William above the long file of his predecessors does not admit of dispute. These forerunners built, and he inherited from them, a German territorial state which, as an electorate of the Reich, had achieved a certain power and dignity but which in a span of five centuries had not succeeded in reaching a position enabling it in any decisive way to influence German destiny. With Frederick William's arrival on the scene a period of Brandenburg history came to a close which, apart from an animated early chapter of conquest and settlement, presents itself by contrast as, in the main, a kind of harmless vegetating in unenterprising complacency. Although but a twenty-year-old youth at his accession and a fugitive, besides, from Brandenburg, which a foreign state had taken over, he managed, within a few years and in spite of his continued helplessness among the warring powers that were tearing Germany apart, to win sufficient consideration not only to oblige these powers to cease pushing him about at their pleasure but also to play a part out of all proportion to his strength at the Westphalian congress that finally brought peace to the tortured land.

Granted that his success at Westphalia was partly attributable to the small army with which he had succeeded in providing himself, it sprang in far greater measure from a spiritual quality which he had brought into play and which had not failed to make an impression on the armed masters of Europe. They noted and responded with involuntary respect to the unabashed and daring manner in which the young ruler of the war-ruined mark moved among them. While they did not understand at what precisely he was driving or consider it important enough greatly to bother, the ruler himself was visited by no doubts as to his purpose. He was resolved to hold fast to his own, his passionately cherished and imperiled own, consisting of the three groups of inherited territories strung across the broad north German plain. Widely separated from one another, they constituted an almost unsolvable problem of defense and were, in addition, even after the German civil broils had ended, in practically unrelieved jeopardy.

Let us glance at this inheritance as it presented itself to his eyes and begin with the duchy of Prussia, in which he was residing at the time of his accession: It was completely surrounded by the kingdom of Poland, of which, moreover, in terms of feudal law it was a component part. To the west, all the way, indeed, to the utmost German west, lay the Rhinelands of Cleve-Mark; they had been all but alienated from their ruler during the Thirty Years' War and even after the coming of peace looked a good deal like a morsel the nearby Dutch republic was merely awaiting a favorable opportunity to swallow. As for the remaining Hohenzollern possession, Brandenburg, while it had been cleared of the occupying Swedes at the Westphalian turning point, it continued to dwell beneath the mailed fist of these invaders by reason of the devastating decision at the peace settlement which allotted the immediately adjoining territory of western Pomerania to the Scandinavian power.

While the elector's decision firmly and at all costs to maintain his hold on his threatened territories constituted the core of his early policy and while any one of his predecessors, including his distracted, ill-starred father, might be conceived as setting himself in the same circumstances an identical goal, it is unbelievable, in the face of their record, that they would have stuck to their purpose with anything approaching the obstinacy and resourcefulness of their living representative. His pre-eminent endowment was a passionate will to live, and, lustily indulging it, he discovered that it expanded by its own energy into the more massive will to grow. This is the succession observable throughout the domain of nature, whose innumerable organisms push on from survival to expansion, from defense to offense, on the instinctive ground that unremitting increase is their best guaranty against an ever threatening extinction.

In close harmony with this universal pattern, hardly had Frederick William begun the struggle to keep his own when he became convinced that, in order to keep it, he would have to bring it to greater vigor; and the accomplishment of this purpose, through either winning a broader territorial base or achieving a more compact organization of whatever he held or through both of these developments together, became the gist of his labors throughout his long reign. Regarding the territorial program, moreover, a glance at the map sufficed to show him that the logical procedure would be to attempt to bridge the gaps between his three isolated footholds. But overwhelmed with the sheer problem of day-to-day living that never at any time eased its pressure, very early in his reign he had to abandon this objective as outside the realm of practical politics. And when he died the Hohenzollern realm was still, as at his accession, flung in scattered fragments across northern Germany. Nonetheless, he had indicated, if not in quotable passages of his correspondence, by the whole tenor of his striving, that the proper and inescapable concern of a ruler vulnerable, like himself, by reason of the unhappy dispersion and consequent multiplied contacts of his separate units was to draw them together, or at least to begin the work of drawing them together, into an unbroken territorial mass.

So insurmountable were the obstacles piled in the path of a policy of territorial consolidation in Frederick William's time that it would be an error to suggest that he ever regarded it as other than a vague and tantalizing dream. Indeed, for so hardheaded a realist as he it was so entirely impracticable as to have been not even tantalizing. All we can safely say is that the dream came into existence in his day and that it was a direct reflection of his purposeful activity. This activity could not be more aptly set forth figuratively than to picture him as escaping from the quiet provincial waters, among which his predecessors had been content to navigate, in order boldly to steer his small bark out to the open sea. Not only did he by this daring act take on himself the gravest risks, but he made retreat impossible both for himself and for his successors. Willy-nilly they would have to continue to sail the waters on which he had launched them. Even to have made the attempt to retire would have been a humiliating confession of failure. And they did not retire—with results that are written large on the pages of history.

With this conclusion in mind the issue of Frederick William's pre-eminence among the succession of Brandenburg margraves settles itself without further debate. While the unimportant state which he inherited was their work, it was he who gave it a new solidity and set it a new goal. Even his none-too-capable son was able to improve its European status by transforming it into the kingdom of Prussia. Then, under his unusually gifted grandson and great-grandson the forces which he had set in motion vastly expanded their field of operation until through further consistent advances in the nineteenth century a new German empire was brought to birth. In last analysis Frederick William not only created the kingdom of Prussia but was the unconscious projector of a renovated Germany.

FINAL ESTIMATE OF THE MAN AND HIS WORK

The Calvinist element.—If now, before taking leave of Frederick William, we attempt once more to evoke his historical figure with a view to gathering the many elements of personality we have uncovered into an intelligible whole, we may begin with what he regarded as the solid substructure of his existence, his Christian faith. Specifically, he was a communicant of the Reformed church, to which version of Protestantism he showed such fervent attachment that he came to be looked upon in Germany and throughout Europe as one of its staunchest pillars.

Now the Reformed faith presents a moral and spiritual problem that has puzzled observers through the ages. Resting on the gospels and projected by its founder, John Calvin, as a close reproduction of the church of the earliest Fathers, it might be imagined to have attracted into its fold men and women drawn to the ways of humility, resignation, and contempt of this world's goods. Surprisingly, however, the members of this church, regardless of the nation and language to which they belonged, were perhaps less ruled by these renunciatory aspects of Christianity than any other group professing to derive from the Nazarene carpenter. History presents them as fighting Protestants whose fierce religious militancy was unequaled in their day, unless it be by that of their Catholic counterpart and archenemy, the Jesuits. As for material well-being, instead of contemptuously rejecting it, the Calvinists became its leading promoters, scoring in its pursuit such outstanding success that economic historians of the present day stoutly insist that in them are revealed the true fathers of the capitalistic system in its developed modern form.

Of this perplexing upshot of a movement inaugurated as a return to primitive Chirstianity many explanations have been offered. As their consideration with the fulness which the case requires would carry us too far afield, we shall content ourselves with taking up the single sociopsychological factor for the reason that it fell more heavily into the scales than any other. Greeted as the recovery of the lost true faith, Calvinism released in its earliest devotees a burning religious fervor. By turning inward, this warmth of feeling might very well have taken one of the many historical forms of quietism. But it did not turn inward. It turned away from contemplation and toward temporal activity for the sufficient reason that the Calvinist faith became identified, wherever it took hold, with the vigorous merchant class which was at that very moment advancing irresistibly and achieving an ever higher social potential. To these urban leaders the Calvinist demand of a self-governing church opened an escape from the bondage of the Roman clergy and by freeing them from extraneous control released an energy which, applied to the occupations normally engrossing them, explains their amazing forward strides in trade and industry. They were sincere evangelical Christians practicing an exemplary piety at home and abroad. But their piety did not keep them from laboring in shop and counting-house with fiery zeal in the conviction that material success would somehow be credited to them as merit by their God.

The close tie-up between Calvinism and the merchant class does not mean that this sect did not draw converts into its embrace from among the other classes of society. While its peasant following may be agreed to have been unimportant, it gained a notable foothold among the nobility of several countries and even drew a handful of sovereign princes over to its side. Outstanding among these in the second half of the seventeenth century was our Frederick William. Since Calvinism was an activist faith that roused and disciplined the will, it communicated to him, precisely as it did to its merchant followers, an untiring energy in the exercise of the office to which in his view the Lord had called him. Also, as with them, it made him an earnest observer of the prescribed religious duties and prompted him, although not personally engaged in trade, to subscribe to its importance and to court the prosperity that invariably followed in its wake. But let there be no mistake: Far and away the strongest influence flowing from his faith appeared in his readiness to rise alertly each morning from prayer on bended knee in order to labor with unflagging devotion through the day at his allotted post of ruler and statesman.

Agreed that it is reasonable to associate the purposiveness of the Great Elector's statesmanship with his religious faith, let us avoid exaggeration. It may well be that his endowment of will antedated his Calvinism by reason of his having been invested with it at birth. This was and remains so common a phenomenon that it requires no comment. However, even should he have owed his voluntarism in the first place to the dispensing fairies that gathered round his cradle, the contribution to his natural disposition by the faith of his ripe years is undebatable; for, not only must it have greatly fortified his inborn trend, it must, besides, have often fed him as with spiritual manna by giving him an untroubled conscience in the often ruthless exercise of his natural energy.

Steadfastness of purpose and political reliability.—The evidence assembled in this book would seem to put beyond question the elector's endowment with the moral fortitude indispensable for the unwavering pursuit of a chosen line of action. Nonetheless, many contemporaries have recorded their impression of his unsteadiness, and since they were, in the main, foreign diplomats whose business it was closely to scrutinize his actions, they may not be lightly dismissed. Their reports are extant to the effect that the sovereign to whom they were accredited not only shifted his position frequently and without warning but that he did so less on his private initiative than under pressure from this or that other of his councilors. Ambassador Rébenac, who in his day saw the elector more often than any of his colleagues, was particularly explicit regarding these accusations. But numerous other diplomats, some of French, others of Austrian, origin, voiced an identical charge.

In this connection a shortcoming of diplomats at all times, but especially in the dynastic seventeenth century, must be brought into focus. Generally speaking, they saw the sovereign to whom they were accredited only ceremonially and transacted the business with which they were intrusted through one or another of the sovereign's ministers. In these circumstances they were tempted to attribute the position taken by the minister to the minister himself, especially as this spokesman of the ruler would be moved to swell his self-importance by letting it appear that it lay within his power to effect a desirable correction of his sovereign's policy. Quite generally, therefore, the diplomats of that day inclined to believe that the minister counted for more than the master and that it was money well spent to win his favorable consideration with a bribe—a sinister speculation but often enough, alas, only too well founded. Most of the sovereigns of that era, ill educated and morally and physically enfeebled by the early exercise of excessive power, were indubitably dominated by their ministers; and these ministers, always courtiers and frequently base-minded sycophants besides, were ruled by such low moral standards that they were not only open to purchase but greedily invited it.

Frederick William may not be tossed into a heap with his often irresponsible fellow-princes. He followed the practice, and a good practice it surely was, of consulting with many advisers, going the length, at least in the first part of his reign, of inviting free discussion in Council. Also in this same period when, a young man, he had still much to learn, he was admittedly influenced by a succession of fairly outstanding individuals whom he had drawn into his service. Burgsdorf, Blumenthal, Waldeck, Schwerin, played in turn a sort of leading ministerial role. But in spite of what was maliciously rumored at court and confidently reported by the spying foreign agents, not one of them ever achieved a position remotely approaching control. Even in this, his apprentice period, Frederick William shaped his own course. And following the strenuous campaigns in Poland, with which he reached his full political stature, no minister in his employ ever reared his head above his fellows, although the rival French and Austrian ambassadors continued to profess a contrary belief. Indeed, so settled was their conviction that they were willing to back it up with a liberal distribution of "gifts." These the councilors gratefully pocketed with their far-from-hoodwinked master quietly conniving at their action. Knowing that it was he and not they who ruled the state, why should he greatly mind their unclean little game? He would even seem to have been good-naturedly amused over this augmentation of the exiguous stipend with which, owing to his starved treasury, he habitually rewarded them,

Nonetheless, in so far as the judgment of the ambassadors reflected not on his steadiness of purpose and freedom from ministerial management but on an apparent duplicity or double standard in his behavior it rested on more solid ground. He was an impulsive man completely forgetful, when aroused, of the stiff and elaborate diplomatic conventions of his age. We have a Frenchman's word for it that "no other prince uses so little moderation in his official capacity." As a result he might on occasion spray an ambassador with the most startling sincerities. The next day they would be withdrawn with perhaps an apology added, and the overearnest diplomat, who had already reported the explosion to his government, would be obliged to revise himself in a hurried supplementary dispatch. For the experience not to leave a bad aftertaste required a sense of humor for which the diplomatic profession, governed by the master precept of "correctness," has never been particularly famous. Undeniably, therefore, the elector's frequent uncivilized outbursts did himself a disservice. While he unerringly returned to his reasoned course, indeed had departed from it only in words, his unregulated effusions created a suspicion of unreliability in his decorous interlocutors which the occasion did not justify.

Not that there were not occasions, and by no means few and unimportant ones, when the political unreliability of the lord of Brandenburg was real and cried to heaven. An instance that will at once come to mind belonged to the four-year period of the Swedish-Polish War. Frederick William's participation in this conflict was marked by a succession of treaties which register a bewildering assumption and rejection of obligations to one or the other of the two belligerents. But while his shifty conduct substantiates the charge of unreliability, it does not impugn his singleness of purpose. On the contrary, it underscores, if anything, the steadiness with which throughout his zigzag course he pursued as his inalterable goal the sovereignty of Prussia.

Since no one disputes his failure to regard political engagements as heaven-made marriages, for better, for worse, let it suffice to adduce one more instance, this time involving France. When Louis XIV made his highwayman assault on the Dutch in 1672, Frederick William acted on instinct and rushed to the support of the threatened Lowlanders. When the French first stopped and then overwhelmed him with their might, he sued for peace and was granted, all things considered, extremely lenient terms. However, before a year had run its course, he resumed his attack on the French in response to his unchanged sympathy for their Dutch victims. It is certain that Louis XIV looked upon his shiftiness with anger and contempt—close counterpart of the anger and contempt which Charles X of Sweden and Casimir of Poland had registered when at the time of their war they had tried to attach him each to his particular interest and he had brazenly pursued his own.

Admitting, then, that Frederick William may be fairly charged with political opportunism, there remains the question: Is the extraordinary outcry over it made at the time and still echoed in all the history books justified? In the light of the moral law upheld by honorable men since the beginning of civilization (by individual men, let it be observed, and rarely and at best only casually by sovereign entities called states) it certainly is. The Great Elector transgressed the moral law. But if the outcry against him is motivated, openly or secretly, by the purpose to make him out an immoralist among moral paragons or even among rulers practicing a moral code higher than his by as much as a distinguishable shade, it is no better than a hollow noise. An examination of the conduct of Louis XIV, Emperor Leopold I, Charles X of Sweden, Charles II of England, or any other ruler of the age shows exactly the same cunning pursuit of self-interest at all costs. The issue need not be labored, for it does not admit of dispute. There is no higher and lower, morally speaking, among the heads of sovereign states in the seventeenth century for reasons set forth in our survey of the civilization of the age in the third chapter of this book. It was there shown that, in spite of a continued hypocritical profession of both moral and religious checks on the part of states, every organization of this kind had become a law unto itself and regarded the maintenance and increase of its power as its leading and overshadowing end. However, since the faithful observation of a pledge on the part of a government was still assumed as a matter of theory, an act of faithlessness by one party to a treaty never failed to provoke an indignant outcry from the opposed party. The pot boiled over with indignation at the unseemly blackness of the kettle. Frederick William, condemned by the weakness of his state confronted with much stronger polities to a systematically evasive policy, may well in the course of a reign of almost half a century have provoked a larger number of outraged protests than his neighbors; but that there was any difference in principle between his conduct and theirs is a wholly untenable assertion.

Returning to the problem from which we digressed to discuss the elector's political reliability, we are certainly justified in calling attention, as final and conclusive evidence of his planful activity, to his total achievement. Even the most stubborn doubter who will pause to take account of the wide spread between Brandenburg at the elector's accession and Brandenburg at his death will find himself reduced to silence. There is no need again to set forth the immense advance of the electorate in dignity and power not only among its immediate German neighbors but also among the governments of France, England, Austria, Sweden, and the Dutch republic constituting the concert of great powers. Born the half-dispossessed heir apparent to three feeble disconnected territorial groups, he had made his state a minor luminary of the European planetary system—in itself a considerable performance but intrinsically much less important than the domestic reorganization which he had simultaneously brought about. In this respect, too, let us observe measure and not advance the claim that, putting an end to the distinctness of his many dominions, whether inherited or acquired at Westphalia, he had forged them into a single administrative unit. Let us rather declare more modestly that he launched this unitary work, getting so far along with it that his successors were simply unable ever again to let it drop. To view in the perspective of a forty-eight-year rule his achievement in the coordinated foreign and domestic fields is to become directly conscious of the operation of a creative will. The many kinds of labor involved in his arduous double undertaking hang closely together and could not have been made to march abreast had there not been an energy pointed to a goal which was never lost from sight. All debate touching the fact and quality of the elector's resolution comes to an end before his self-erected monument.

And yet—for after all the flow of stout affirmation there is a "yet"—there were occasional lapses of conduct which, as revealing that the Great Elector was not a story-book hero imperturbably moving forward on an unvarying line, may not be overlooked. In history as in life we are constantly stumbling on these disconcerting evidences of the still prevailingly irrational nature of homo sapiens. No sooner have we assured ourselves that the specimen under scrutiny possesses such and such characteristics than to our sorrow or indignation he commits an act completely out of line with what we have agreed to regard as his essential nature. It is the part of wisdom to accept these vagaries as indicating that even in the case of superior intelligences we are at bottom dealing with the average sensual man, who need not have surrendered an animating central purpose because, yielding to his fundamental irrationality, he occasionally indulges in unaccountable singularities of conduct.

In the case of Frederick William there were perhaps fewer of these lapses than with most individuals of equal note but, since they occurred, they must be faced and fitted into the picture of the total actual man. Two such lapses are outstanding. The more important of the two has to do with his testaments and was recounted in the preceding chapter. We there learned that this man of a truly devastating earnestness as the builder of a state was able to persuade himself, no matter whether from affection for his younger sons or from consideration for a loving wife, to impair the solidity of the edifice he had spent a lifetime in erecting. He could not have been blind to the hazardous nature of his proposal to endow his younger sons with independent dominions, even though they were to be small in extent and their sovereignty strictly limited. The only explanation that explains is psychological and referable to a temporarily clouded mind. He was in this testament matter the victim of the contradictory emotions of a father and a ruler. Persuaded that both emotions were right and admirable, he ended by convincing himself that they were not contradictory.

The second departure from his master-line has to do with his candidature for the Polish throne. It was the year 1661. The question of the succession had come to the front in Poland because King Casimir wished to have a successor elected by the feudality during his lifetime. Many candidates entered the race, with a younger member of the house of Bourbon soon far to the front because favored by Casimir's queen, a lady partially of French extraction. Although the appointment of a successor during the life of the incumbent ran contrary to Polish law and custom, many magnates were won over to the plan. Other magnates, however, were violently opposed to it, more particularly to its associated feature of a French successor. One of these dissident notables approached Hoverbeck, the Brandenburg ambassador at Warsaw, with the extraordinary proposal that Frederick William come forward as a rival candidate, and Hoverbeck, though exceedingly cold to the idea, dutifully passed it on to his master.

The communication released what can only be described as a brain storm. Forgetting the incurable political division between his Prussian duchy and the kingdom of Poland, forgetting his character of German prince, forgetting the logic of the twenty-year conduct of his office, he responded enthusiastically to the harebrained scheme and ordered Hoverbeck energetically to support it by offering inducements to the Poles, including, incredible as it sounds, the renunciation of the recently acquired Prussian sovereignty. We have no choice but to believe that the prospect of a royal crown proved so alluring to this ruler of a lower status that it temporarily obliterated in him the knowledge of who he was and of the duty which he owed that knowledge. In these circumstances it was a blessing that he at least sufficiently kept his balance to disclose his mad ambition to only three persons, undoubtedly the friends most mindful of his reputation, the electress Louise Henriette, his brother-in-law of Anhalt, and Otto von Schwerin. They, one and all, like Hoverbeck, rejected it with instinctive aversion. Nonetheless, he clung to it with amazing perversity for several months and did not finally expel it from his system until his Polish partisans made it plain that the indispensable condition of their support was his conversion to Catholicism. The demand brought him face to face with his religious conscience and finis was written to the disturbing episode when he informed the relieved Schwerin that he rejected the crown on these terms since never would he stoop to gain a temporal at the cost of an eternal reward.[1]

Avocations, pastimes.— Frederick William was not so exclusively absorbed all his days with affairs of state that he did not, if only in the instinctive search for relief from pressing cares, at times give himself over to activities enabling him to throw off the galling harness of his calling. As in these avocations he revealed his common humanity, they may under no circumstances be disregarded. Consider, for instance, his patronage of art and learning. Admitted that undoubtedly he was moved to practice it by the view, mandatory in his day, that it belonged to the function of a ruler to further cultural endeavor, it is clear from the freshness of his interest that he did not feel himself an alien in the highlands of the spirit and that he lingered among them with genuine satisfaction. He was

1. "Denn ich das Zeitliche nimmer für das Ewige begehre" (*UA*, IX, 825).

particularly drawn to architecture. The preference was not strange, since it accorded with the passion of his absolutist age to enhance our earthly existence by providing it with as lordly a setting as fancy could devise. Contemporary sculpture and painting were directed to the same end, as will be presently set forth in greater fulness by an examination of that style, the so-called "baroque," which traced the cultural pattern of the period.

With due allowance for his meager resources the Great Elector exercised a generous patronage of all three of the magnifying fine arts, and if the product of his efforts, measured in impressive public buildings and their appropriate sculptural and pictorial adornment, was only mediocre, the fault lay more in the inability of his backward country to supply the necessary collaborators than in his own inadequate taste and judgment. His service was that of an innovator and, as such, he may at least be said to have put an end to the cultural darkness which with the Thirty Years' War had descended on his realm.

With his patronage of the fine arts went hand in hand an eager collecting of both books and antiquities. The former hobby led to his bringing together in the Schloss the considerable library already mentioned, while his passion for antiquities provided the nucleus of not one but a whole series of the notable collections adorning the Berlin of the present day. The later multiplication was made possible by the inclusiveness in seventeenth-century usage of the term "antiquities." Frederick William's collection bearing this name included not only such items as coins, medals, the varied loot of prehistoric graves—veritable antiquities these—but, together with examples of painting and sculpture through the ages, the unsystematic deposits of the recently awakened interest in the sciences of geology and botany. This strange assortment of odds and ends proudly exhibited in the showrooms of the Schloss explains how it came about that half-a-dozen sharply differentiated modern museums are able to trace their origins back to Frederick William's single body of antiquities.

Among pastimes, like the members of the ruling class throughout Europe, he preferably and inescapably cultivated the chase. Everywhere the game was the prerogative of the landowners, and everywhere the smallest infringement of that prerogative by the peasants or others of the nonelect was punished with barbaric cruelty. For the stubborn poacher to be condemned to loss of hand or eyes was by no means rare. Perhaps no other area of social contact more startlingly brings home to the living generation the sharpness of the line drawn in those days between the rulers and the ruled. And than the repressive game laws no section of legislation more convincingly exhibits the ferocious length to which the rulers were prepared to go to perpetuate their privileged position. For both Frederick William and his Junker associates the hunt was the diversion cherished above all others, and so habituated through long custom were they to regard its monopolistic exercise as a right conferred by heaven that they never even in their dreams were moved to question it. While the humane instincts of a democratic age cause us to react with horror to the forest code of the highborn addicts of the chase, we should not forget that its cruel penalties failed to sear their consciences with any sense of guilt.

We may therefore think of Frederick William as never enjoying himself more freely and wholesomely than while hunting in one of the innumerable wooded preserves of his vast private domain. Although he sometimes conducted the sport on a ceremonial scale with a gay cavalcade of gentlemen for whom beaters and packs of hounds rounded up the game, more often, especially in his later years, he was content to take his pleasure modestly attended only by the electress and a few trusty servants. Not infrequently it might happen that he would abandon the court in favor of one of his quiet hunting lodges for days and even weeks at a time. Ambassadors would then complain to their governments that he held himself incommunicado, and even his ministers would grumble over the delay in the dispatch of business. Here, apparently, was an instance where this unusually conscientious ruler put pleasure before duty. But there is another way of looking at his dereliction. He may have thought that, like every dedicated workman, he deserved an occasional respite, and experience may have taught him that a vacation in the woods, far from the madding court, untied the knots of his overburdened spirit like no other remedy and fortified him for a more vigorous resumption of his labors.

Pessimism, misanthropy.—Frederick William, the young prince, enjoyed sound health and a vigorous physique along with a bounding spirit which defied discouragement. Hardly forty years old, he was beset by gout, under the attacks of which his appearance deteriorated so rapidly that by the time he was fifty his face had become heavily wrinkled, his hair had gone gray, and his inflated figure had lost every trace of youthful elasticity. In his last decade he was visited each year with some four or five attacks of his malady increasingly complicated with asthma and gravel, and toward the fag end of his life he must have spent most of his time in bed or in a chair. Inevitably, the recurrent crises with their sharp torments caused such spiritual irritation that he gave himself with less and less restraint to the impulsive and choleric outbreaks that were natural to him. For his wife, his children, his ministers, and even the foreign ambassadors admitted to their rare audiences he became an exemplary manifestation of the testy invalid.

Nor was that all the change that came over him. He fell to brooding, sank into the well of pessimism and misanthropy. The darkened outlook did not become habitual until after the disappointments connected with the second Swedish war and the bitter peace that ended it. At the lowest point of his depression—it was the year 1684—he withdrew from all but the most unavoidable contact with mankind and shut himself up in two small rooms of his Potsdam residence. In these he slept, ate, and met such members of his Council as he saw fit to summon for the dispatch of business. Rébenac wailed to his master, the magnificent Louis, that the rooms were no better than holes (*trous*) and darkly hinted that the lord of Brandenburg was, together with his health, also losing his mind. A man better able to plumb the human spirit would have remembered that pessimism and distrust of men are so regularly the attendant of physical decline that the contrary attitude on the part of the suffering Frederick William would have furnished the more reasonable occasion for comment.

However, it is worth considering whether the impairment, in his last phase, of his natural resilience sprang solely from the painful dissolution of his body. He had a spiritual side which he cultivated with daily prayer and Scripture-reading but of which he took no account in the exercise of his office with its unremitting struggle in behalf of a wider and more untrammeled sway. We picture him, the total man, in our mind's eye, as a being not unrelated to the eternities and yet obliged to occupy himself during all his waking hours with the importunate temporalities that never ceased to press upon him. Beginning with the maturer years that bring reflecton in their wake he must at times have been visited with disgust at this obsessive concern with earthly honors, which to his secret knowledge weighed no more than dust in the scales against the heavenly rewards awaiting him who faithfully followed the ways of the Lord. Unconscious thoughts of this kind rather than definitely conscious ones may very well have increasingly taken hold of him in his declining years. As he was not given to confession and has left behind no introspective reflections, we cannot be sure about his inner conflict and must not press the issue. All that may with some certainty be said about the proved pessimism of his last years is that, while it had its origin in the cruel wasting of his body, it was not unrelated to the quarrel in his breast, which could no longer be kept hid as he neared his end, between the mortal sinner and his immortal soul.

FREDERICK WILLIAM AND THE BAROQUE

Every age has a style of its own. It reveals itself in such relatively unimportant matters as dress and forms of social intercourse, more strikingly and unmistakably in the arts all the way from the handiwork of the joiner and metal-worker to the lofty creations of architecture, sculpture, painting, music, and literature. Scores of influences, political, religious, economic, and aesthetic in their nature, co-operate and fuse to produce a style, which is consequently the ultimate distillation of a particular culture.

The style of the seventeenth-century phase of Western civilization bears the name baroque. Historically viewed, the baroque is the declining aspect of the Renaissance, in substance, a Renaissance modified and colored by the institutions and forces operative in the seventeenth century. As we have already on several occasions taken note of them, we may here confine ourselves to those of their number from whose interaction the baroque may be said more particularly to stem. They are the reinvigorated Catholic church and the absolute monarchy.

It is a curious circumstance that the Catholic church ruled the consciences and lives of its subjects more unquestioningly in the seventeenth century than in the pre-Reformation period when it exercised, territorially, a much wider sway. Its priests and bishops wielded an unchallenged authority in their respective parishes and dioceses and dominated the contracted but still far-flung organization to the single end of bringing it humbly and submissively to the feet of the pope, become, since the Council of Trent, more masterfully than ever before its towering head. The pope of this century was an absolute monarch ruling a community of believers for whom he sat enthroned in more than earthly majesty.

In this arresting situation it was inevitable that the pope should provide for himself in the famous church of St. Peter at Rome a house of worship expressive of his exalted state. True, the foundations of St. Peter's church were laid in the previous, the sixteenth, century; true also, in this same century Michelangelo erected its most noble feature, the soaring, the unrivaled dome. But the great Florentine, in whom we hail the culminating genius of the Renaissance, was also the unconscious herald of the baroque; and the architects, who in the next century succeeded him, completed St. Peter's as the essentially baroque monument that still meets the eye. One may regret that the high-piled façade of Maderna hides the dome from view and regard as far too theatrical for a Christian house of worship the vast entrance court of Bernini with its obelisk and fountains framed by a majestic double colonnade. But the important point from the purely stylistic consideration of St. Peter's is that these and other grandiose features were the appropriate means for bringing to expression the conception which the papacy of the Counter-Reformation entertained of itself. Bernini in particular succeeded in capturing the spirit of seventeenth-century Catholicism and, through the admiration aroused by his creations in sculpture as well as in architecture, more than any other single artist gave the baroque its fashionable vogue.

Now it is undeniable that the baroque which, starting with architecture, cast sculpture, painting, and the handicrafts into a corresponding mold has little or no appeal for the present generation.

To us, drawn by the engineering spirit dominating a mechanical age to simple functional forms, the baroque is extravagant, declamatory, hollow; in short—and that makes our condemnation final—it is unfunctional. Therefore, even when we cannot resist being momentarily impressed by its ample scale and dynamic movement, we unhesitatingly reject it as offensive to the particular style which we have evolved and which is closely expressive of ourselves. While this is exactly as it should be if we are to retain our moral and aesthetic rectitude, still a historian is privileged to point out that there was once another, a seventeenth-century age and that, in reveling in the broken forms and swelling rhythms of the baroque, it was moved by as sincere an impulse to express its genius as is our engineering age in its preference for straight lines and unadorned, unbroken masses.

The other institutional inspirer of the baroque, the absolute monarchy, took over where the Catholic church left off. And since the absolute monarchy was a more pervasive phenomenon than the Catholic church, embracing as it did the Protestant as well as the Catholic areas of Europe, it was the identification of this institution with the baroque that won for it its universal empire. Although the absolute monarchy came into existence throughout Europe in the sixteenth century, it was in its French form that in the course of the succeeding century it forged to the front and gained the pre-eminence of which this book has taken note at every turn. We have dealt at some length with Louis XIV, who not only shone over Europe as the leading luminary of its political sky but who also dictated its fashions, its manners, and its expression in the fine arts. And that expression, succinctly stated, was nothing other than a Gallicly flavored version of the papal baroque. Its culminating wonder was the palace and landscaped gardens of Versailles. The palace was ornamented with sculptures and paintings which proclaimed the unfolding Bourbon grandeur, and the sheer endless suites of rooms were embellished with gilt and plaster decorations, with ornate furniture and embroidered tapestries, which sounded in the more subdued manner suited to their humbler office the identical sublime note. The men and women of the aristocracy that gathered in the vast Hall of Mirrors of the palace to pay court to the king wore costumes of silk, satin, and elaborate lace and were crowned with mountainous coiffures intended to invest them with superhuman dignity, while the grave curtsies and elaborate compliments they exchanged were the indispensable accessories of the colorful masquerade, in terms of which these privileged beings envisaged their earthly sojourn.

While Versailles was taken as a model by the rest of Europe, these lesser states were not guilty of plagiarizing something for which they had no understanding; for, having by their own initiative conformed to the absolute pattern, they were inwardly prepared for the stylistic consequences. That such was the case of the small state of our concern requires no evidence beyond that already adduced. In the course of the reign of Frederick William, Brandenburg became an absolutism by its own energy and the elector an absolute ruler. Certain other elements favorable to the reception of the baroque, such as a dominant nobility, a repressed bourgeoisie, and a wholly submerged peasantry, were also present. In short, Brandenburg was as ripe to express itself in baroque terms as its limited area, slender resources, and general cultural backwardness permitted. And how far did it travel on this road? Neither far nor with startling consequences. It achieved a court which, though from necessary parsimony habitually frugal, burst spasmodically into Lucullian lavishness. Then, too, the head of the court functioned willingly as a patron of the arts and with notable fervor cultivated architecture, everywhere the starting-point of the baroque life-pattern. If the Schloss at Berlin, even after its renovation, remained many levels below Versailles, it served, together with the residences which Frederick William erected at Potsdam, Cöpenick, and Oranienburg, to document his interest in this field. That also is as much as can be truthfully reported of his patronage of sculpture and painting. In so far as Brandenburg may be considered to have expressed itself at all in his day it had recourse to the formulas of the current style.

When all is said, Brandenburg's outstanding baroque exhibit was the Great Elector himself. To begin with, he was endowed by nature with the fine, full-bodied figure that lent itself to the representative purposes so characteristic of the age. When in his middle years his features became weathered and rugged and his body bigger and bulkier, he still acted his sovereign role with unimpaired majesty. The many surviving portraits confirm the written testimony that has reached us. But they also show that this essentially simple man had recourse to all the French devices of personal display, since they exhibit him appareled, though for public purposes only, in satin trousers; lace-enhanced, embroidered coat; silver-buckled shoes; and crowned, for the culminating touch, with the immense, many-locked peruque invented by his court hairdresser to magnify the figure of the *grand monarque.* The baroque called for a sovereign as close as possible an embodiment of an earthly Jove, and no amount of modern contempt for this ideal avails to obscure the fact that Louis XIV and the Great Elector, his smaller German counterpart, came in their periodic official unveilings within reasonable reach of it.

By a happy development in the reign of his successor there has come down to us an impressive witness of the baroque conception of the Great Elector. In that reign Frederick William's efforts to bring the arts to life in his dominions achieved a notable first fruiting, and an eminent native sculptor, Andreas Schlüter, created a bronze equestrian statue of the dead prince which is a baroque masterpiece and conveys a better understanding of the baroque spirit than a volume of reasoned exposition. The statue was completed around the turn of the century and set up on an appropriately adorned pedestal on a bridge across the Spree, where it still stands.

Let us have a look at this horse and rider and begin by reminding ourselves that they are not studied from nature since the settled aim of the baroque was to supersede nature by outdoing it. The artist's single intention was to have the unified horse and rider assert the highest possible measure of power and majesty. In the case of the horse this is achieved by the proudly arched neck and full muscular haunches, more effectively and more subtly still by the turbulent mane and thick undulating mass of the tail. However, what irresistibly draws the eye is the more important rider, who from his battle mount surveys the scene with the look and gesture of a conqueror. He is so far removed from the Frederick William whom we have attended in this book at his grinding labors that we seem to be facing a complete stranger. And so in point of fact he is, for this is not the real Frederick William, the man who daily wrestled for long hours with tough administrative problems and,

By Andreas Schlüter, 1703 (Bettmann Archive)

BRONZE EQUESTRIAN STATUE OF THE GREAT ELECTOR
On a Bridge over the Spree River

on campaign, shared their hardships with his troops. This triumphant rider is the baroque myth of the Great Elector, and every detail is chosen to the one end of making the myth significant. It is so little a portrait statue in the modern manner that the features of the mounted ruler are but vaguely indicated and that all the other elements of which the figure is compounded are selected with the sole view to realize a grandeur beyond human range. The toga-like cloak that floats from the shoulders suggests imperial Rome as does also the vigorously gesturing right arm wielding the commander's truncheon. Against these classical touches the lofty peruque, which duplicates the effect of the horse's mane, and the concentrated dynamism of the tense torso are pure seventeenth century. In sum, the monument interestingly reveals that while the baroque is the expression of the recently achieved absolutism of western Europe, it confesses kinship with the earlier absolutism of long-vanished imperial Rome.

THE LEGENDARY GREAT ELECTOR

Ever since history has come into existence it has quarreled with its forerunner, myth. As the product, or reputed product, of reason, it has made no secret of its disdain of myth, creature of impulse, bias, superstition, in brief, of the associated forces of unreason. But all its contempt has so little discouraged the myth-making fervor native to mankind that myth has flourished uninterruptedly through all the centuries since history has made its entrance on the scene and is at this day as busy as it ever was in recording the past in its own terms.

The long conflict has at last brought the latter-day followers of history round to a more sympathetic view of the method and function of myth. They have come to see that since myth is the child of the emotions, it is concerned less with the facts than with the evaluation of the facts and that, in pursuit of this purpose, it brushes aside as irrelevant the innumerable details that cluster around and to a certain extent obscure a great historical event in order to penetrate to its inmost core, to its final significance. The sum of the significances thus arrived at makes up the version of the past fostered by and handed on by myth, and the importance of this service can hardly be exaggerated. The statement will not be challenged the moment we take note that myth is the only version of the past that ever wins a secure lodgment in the brain and heart of the average man and that from its tenuous materials are constructed the firmest timbers of the social and political faith whereby he lives.

Into this more penetrating view of myth on the part of the present-day historian there has entered also the growing perception that, in spite of the assumption that the particular segment of the past with which he is concerned is fashioned by him in strict accordance with the evidence, he consciously and, more often still, unconsciously diffuses through his presentation a sufficient measure of personal bias to tinge it with something of the character of myth. His predecessors may have deluded themselves into thinking that what they offered under the name of history was a body of objective, mathematically determined fact. Their descendant knows better. He knows that the most detached and single-minded effort of which he is capable will result at best in nothing more permanent than an interpretation appropriate to the generation to which he belongs and that the succeeding generation will unerringly replace his version with one in closer agreement with its altered outlook. His latest wisdom touching the field he cultivates comes to this: Still holding to the view that history is worthily employed in giving the chaos of the past an intelligible shape under the guidance of reason and the available evidence, he is obliged to admit that his predecessors, instead of casting the past into a single, universally acceptable shape, have given it a fairly bewildering variety of forms and that, in the light of this multiplicity, they stand disclosed as themselves no better than myth-makers, although in view of their rational orientation, they may, to do them justice, be differentiated from their older congeners as myth-makers of the intellect.

As with every dominating figure that ever lived, myth busied itself with the Great Elector even while he was alive and has continued to occupy itself with him after his death. In its instinctive way it promptly decided that his master-achievement was the state. With this point settled, it refused to lose itself among the many disturbing contradictions of his character and endowed him with a will tempered like steel and untiringly directed to the subjection of all the residents within the bounds of his dominion to the state's authority. He thus became for the people of Brandenburg and, later, for the people of Prussia and all Germany the embodiment of the law that upholds the state, a stern statuesque Rhadamanthus, happily warmed and humanized by a gleam from the old patriarchal kindliness.

In this mythical character the Great Elector passed into German art and literature and in at least one instance, in a drama by Heinrich von Kleist called *Prinz Friedrich von Homburg,* achieved so elevated a form that no biographer of Frederick William can afford to pass it by. Parenthetically, we may note in this connection that whenever the arts concern themselves with a leading historical figure, they invariably turn to myth rather than to history for their inspiration. When we reflect that myth is itself a form of poetry, any surprise we might feel over this preference promptly vanishes. Now Kleist composed his drama at a moment of the gravest conceivable public crisis. He composed it in the year 1810 when Prussia, the state of his allegiance, lay gagged and bound at the feet of Napoleon. Not only was he, as a patriot, passionately afire with the idea of the early recovery by his country of its liberty, but as a child of the Romantic age—the Romantic movement, let us recall, was just then mounting to its climax—he was persuaded that liberation was the concern not merely of the head of the state but of the whole aroused body of citizens.

Consequently, while Kleist recognized that, in an absolutism such as Prussia had been ever since the time of the Great Elector, the initiative was reserved to the state, he held that the need had now arisen for the hitherto repressed people to come to the support of the state; and he was drawn into an eager debate with himself over the basis on which the collaboration might be effected. He turned the problem over and over until, as an artist of the theater, he relieved himself of its burden by casting it into a drama around a young general of cavalry, Prinz Friedrich von Homburg. The hero was in all his essential qualities a pure invention, although his creator was, of course, aware from his familiarity with his country's history that a man of this name had figured as leader of the horse in the battle around which he makes his play's action turn. This was the battle of Fehrbellin of June 28, 1675, the first completely independent encounter engaged in by the young Brandenburg army and in its issue a brilliant victory. Exclusively intent on his problem of the respective fields of action of the state and the individual, Kleist was as little interested in faithfully reporting the historic battle as he was in portraying the actual Prinz von Homburg. The bare facts, whether of events or persons, he either swept lightly aside or else reshaped to suit the necessities of his invented crisis. This is precipitated when the fictitious Homburg, who, truth to tell, is none other than the romantic Kleist himself, wins the battle by a cavalry charge impulsively delivered contrary to the express order of his sovereign and commander. Crowned victor, he is immediately afterward arrested, tried by military court, and condemned to death.

The cruel knot thus slung had, of course, to be unslung, and it is at this point that the mythical Great Elector steps upon the stage. While it is not possible to follow all the breathless turns taken by the anomalous situation before it is straightened out, it is imperative in the interest of this culmination of the myth to see exactly how the Great Elector is made to function. And while he is presented, as already indicated, as the embodiment of the law, which shall and must prevail if society is to survive, he is so little a fire-breathing deity insistent on the strict observation of his worship that in his mild view the law is nothing other than a compact between ruler and subjects which the latter are as eager to fulfil as the former is to impose. When this curious enforcer of the law is informed that the prince is in a rebellious tumult over the sentence pronounced against him, he offers to cashier it the moment he hears from the prince's own mouth that it is unjust. He takes the proud stand that in his, the law's view, the law owes its authority to the consent of those for whose benefit it is enacted. On the case being in this manner appealed to the offender as to the court of last resort, he is provoked to a re-examination of his disobedience from the general social, instead of from the capriciously personal, point of view and, recovering his moral dignity, resolutely confirms his own death sentence. With the law and its breaker thus reconciled in spirit the transgression cancels itself, and the play ends with all the participants gathered in festive circle around the revered head of the state to celebrate a greater victory than that of Fehrbellin, a victory wherein the law has confirmed its empire over consenting subjects and the subjects have asserted their moral freedom by their voluntary subjection to the law.

Index

PRINTED IN U.S.A.